ADVANCED COLLEGE ESSAY

EXPOSITORY WRITING PROGRAM | NEW YORK UNIVERSITY

Steinhardt School of Culture, Education, and Human Development
The School of Nursing

FOURTH EDITION

Edited by

William M. Morgan and Katherine Berg

Learning Solutions

New York Boston San Francisco
London Toronto Sydney Tokyo Singapore Madrid
Mexico City Munich Paris Cape Town Hong Kong Montreal

Cover Art: Katherine Berg

Pearson Learning Solutions, 501 Boylston Street, Suite 900, Boston, MA 02116
A Pearson Education Company
www.pearsoned.com

Printed in the United States of America

1 2 3 4 5 6 7 8 9 10 V036 15 14 13 12 11 10

000200010270606536

NM/JG

ISBN 10: 0-558-87146-1
ISBN 13: 978-0-558-87146-8

Contents

Course Overview v

Debating Cultural Ideas

How to Tame a Wild Tongue 3
Gloria Anzaldúa

Hiroshima 15
John Berger

The Uses of Doubt 21
Stacey D'Erasmo

Dwelling in Possibilities 31
Mark Edmundson

Welcome to Cancerland 45
Barbara Ehrenreich

The Hidden Teacher 63
Loren Eiseley

Against Meat 73
Jonathan Safran Foer

The Way We Age Now 81
Atul Gawande

Group Think: What Does "Saturday Night Live" Have in Common with German Philosophy? 97
Malcolm Gladwell

A Story About the Body 105
Robert Hass

Politics and the English Language 107
George Orwell

Listen to This 119
Alex Ross

In Praise of Self-Deception 135
David Livingstone Smith

The Blue of Distance 145
Rebecca Solnit

Attack of the Superzeroes 155
Thomas de Zengotita

Reviewing in Contexts

Transgression and Transformation 167
bell hooks

The Melodramatic Moment 173
Daniel Mendelsohn

The Pleasure of Flinching 181
Nicholas Sautin

On Reading a Video Text 189
Robert Scholes

The Track of a Teardrop, a Filmmaker's Path 195
A. O. Scott

The Uncommon Reader 201
George Steiner

Transcending Argument

Argument as Emergence, Rhetoric as Love 219
Jim W. Corder

Sentimental Journeys 235
Joan Didion

Troublemakers: What Pit Bulls Can Teach Us about Profiling 269
Malcolm Gladwell

On the Rights of Molotov Man: Appropriation and the Art of Context 279
Joy Garnett and Susan Meiselas

Letter from Birmingham Jail 293
Martin Luther King, Jr.

A Fist in the Eye of God. 307
Barbara Kingsolver

The Moral Instinct 319
Steven Pinker

Locked Horns 337
Rebecca Solnit

Consider the Lobster 341
David Foster Wallace

A Room of One's Own, Chapter Six 357
Virginia Woolf

Copyright Acknowledgments 371

Course Overview

Advanced College Essay

Advanced College Essay is a second semester writing course designed specifically for students in The Steinhardt School of Culture, Education, and Human Development and The College of Nursing. This course builds upon the foundational reading and writing skills students develop in *Writing the Essay*. It requires students to become more discerning readers and thinkers; to pay attention to essay and argument forms while honing a correct, sophisticated writing style; and to develop their ideas and arguments with diverse and appropriate kinds of evidence. Students compose three essays during the semester, each of which evolves from a series of reading and writing assignments, revisions, and student-teacher conferences. Throughout the semester, students read critically and study the writing of a wide array of professional essayists who write in and across a range of disciplines.

Progressions: The following three progressions provide the framework for the course.

1. **Debating Cultural Ideas:** For this essay, students read deeply from a cluster of rigorous, well-crafted, contemporary essays that contribute to debates about significant ideas in culture, education, and human development. They begin their investigation by choosing two texts to examine carefully and come to understand thoroughly; they must put these essays in meaningful conversation with one another. While locating significant evidence for a shared concern from both texts, students work to describe, analyze, and reflect sufficiently on the views of the idea(s) they encounter. Their writing will ultimately evince a rigorous reading of both essays; that reading will consider the implications of the discovered idea(s), while also drawing on outside texts, cultural or artistic interests, and disciplinary research. The overarching requirement is to deepen the debate and develop their own way of thinking about the discovered idea(s).

Skills Learned:

- Understanding the aims and rhetorical methods of various complex essays that address concerns in culture, education, and human development.
- Identifying, describing, and analyzing evidence from two such essays that offer different understandings of a shared idea.

- Putting these texts into meaningful conversation with one another to arrive at a cohesive, logical, and focused discussion of one's own design.
- Connecting the idea(s) being debated between the texts to relevant contexts in academia and the public world for the purpose of re-examining the texts and re-constituting the discussion on the writer's own terms.
- Developing a convincing and individual account of the debated idea(s) through rigorous reading, careful interpretation, thoughtful research, and subtle reflection.

2. **Reviewing in Contexts:** For this essay, students select a sophisticated film they find so compelling that they can view it over and over as they attempt to figure how it works and what it means. While generating a rich and rigorous reading of their film's formal properties and significant ideas, students also investigate how to use their film as a focal point through which to see and respond to other films, other texts, and the world. Students must ultimately develop a persuasive interpretation of their film's efficacy and significance, assessing it on its own terms while also considering its implications within appropriate, meaningful contexts—history, genre, critical reception, theory, culture, etc.

Skills Learned:

- Developing an understanding of the forms and functions of a thought-provoking review essay.
- Performing a close reading of the formal properties of a complex visual text that is worthy of repeated analysis and interpretation.
- Recognizing and understanding the relationship between selected elements of a complex work of art and the work as a whole.
- Situating a visual text in pertinent cultural, historical, and/or aesthetic contexts as a way of drawing out or rethinking its significance.
- Developing an approach to understanding a complex visual text that is deeply rooted in an astute reading of it but also broadens out beyond it to address a larger idea.

3. **Transcending Argument:** For the third essay, students develop a persuasive account of a contemporary public controversy, studying its rhetoric closely and researching it deeply in order to bring to light and consider an issue of lasting historical and philosophical significance derived from the research.

Skills Learned:

- Identifying a contemporary public controversy worthy of sustained investigation.
- Defining that controversy effectively and identifying and considering various perspectives about it.
- Researching, conceptualizing, and developing an idea about the controversy that goes beyond 'pro' or 'con' responses, that is philosophically informed, and that can be substantiated in the context of history.
- Incorporating a number of written texts into a comprehensive, interesting, and coherent presentation of the controversy, its multiple views and differing rhetorical strategies, while also moving beneath the controversy to consider an idea of significance that is derived from the analysis of the controversy.
- Writing an argumentative essay that reflects curiosity, concession, and elasticity of thought without sacrificing rigorous analysis and a forceful, clear presentation of ideas.

Debating Cultural Ideas

How to Tame a Wild Tongue

Gloria Anzaldúa

"We're going to have to control your tongue," the dentist says, pulling out all the metal from my mouth. Silver bits plop and tinkle into the basin. My mouth is a motherlode.

The dentist is cleaning out my roots. I get a whiff of the stench when I gasp. "I can't cap that tooth yet, you're still draining," he says.

"We're going to have to do something about your tongue," I hear the anger rising in his voice. My tongue keeps pushing out the wads of cotton, pushing back the drills, the long thin needles. "I've never seen anything as strong or as stubborn," he says. And I think, how do you tame a wild tongue, train it to be quiet, how do you bridle and saddle it? How do you make it lie down?

"Who is to say that robbing a people of its language is less violent than war?"
—Ray Gwyn Smith[1]

I remember being caught speaking Spanish at recess—that was good for three licks on the knuckles with a sharp ruler. I remember being sent to the corner of the classroom for "talking back" to the Anglo teacher when all I was trying to do was tell her how to pronounce my name. "If you want to be American, speak 'American.' If you don't like it, go back to Mexico where you belong."

"I want you to speak English. *Pa'hallar buen trabajo tienes que saber hablar el inglés bien. Qué vale toda tu educación si todavía hablas inglés con un* 'accent,'" my mother would say, mortified that I spoke English like a Mexican. At Pan American University, I, and all Chicano students were required to take two speech classes. Their purpose: to get rid of our accents.

Attacks on one's form of expression with the intent to censor are a violation of the First Amendment. *El Anglo con cara de inocente nos arrancó la lengua.* Wild tongues can't be tamed, they can only be cut out.

[1] Ray Gwyn Smith [(b. 1944), Welsh painter and art educator active in the United States], *Moorland Is Cold Country,* unpublished book [Anzaldúa's note].

Overcoming the Tradition of Silence

Ahogadas, escupimos el oscuro.
Peleando con nuestra propia sombra
el silencio nos sepulta.

En boca cerrada no entran moscas. "Flies don't enter a closed mouth" is a saying I kept hearing when I was a child. *Ser habladora* was to be a gossip and a liar, to talk too much. *Muchachitas bien criadas,* well-bred girls don't answer back. *Es una falta de respeto* to talk back to one's mother or father. I remember one of the sins I'd recite to the priest in the confession box the few times I went to confession: talking back to my mother, *hablar pa' 'trás, repelar. Hocicona, repelona, chismosa,* having a big mouth, questioning, carrying tales are all signs of being *mal criada.* In my culture they are all words that are derogatory if applied to women—I've never heard them applied to men.

The first time I heard two women, a Puerto Rican and a Cuban, say the word "*nosotras,*" I was shocked. I had not known the word existed. Chicanas use *nosotros* whether we're male or female. We are robbed of our female being by the masculine plural. Language is a male discourse.

And our tongues have become
dry   the wilderness has
dried out our tongues   and
we have forgotten speech.
—Irena Klepfisz[2]

Even our own people, other Spanish speakers *nos quieren poner candados en la boca.* They would hold us back with their bag of *reglas de academia.*

Oyé como ladra: el lenguaje de la frontera

Quien tiene boca se equivoca.
—Mexican saying

"*Pocho,*[3] cultural traitor, you're speaking the oppressor's language by speaking English, you're ruining the Spanish language," I have been accused by various Latinos and Latinas. Chicano Spanish is considered by the purist and by most Latinos deficient, a mutilation of Spanish.

[2] Irena Klepfisz [(b. 1941), North American critic], "*Di rayze aheym/The Journey Home,*" in *The Tribe of Dina: A Jewish Women's Anthology,* Melanie Kaye/Kantrowitz and Irena Klepfisz, eds. (Montpelier, VT: Sinister Wisdom Books, 1986), 49 [Anzaldúa's note].

[3] An anglicized Mexican or American of Mexican origin who speaks Spanish with an accent characteristic of North Americans and who distorts and reconstructs the language according to the influence of English. Anzaldúa offers a definition later in this selection.

But Chicano Spanish is a border tongue which developed naturally. Change, *evolución, enriquecimiento de palabras nuevas por invención o adopción* have created variants of Chicano Spanish, *un nuevo, lenguaje. Un lenguaje que corresponde a un modo de vivir.* Chicano Spanish is not incorrect, it is a living language.

For a people who are neither Spanish nor live in a country in which Spanish is the first language; for a people who live in a country in which English is the reigning tongue but who are not Anglo; for a people who cannot entirely identify with either standard (formal, Castillian) Spanish nor standard English, what recourse is left to them but to create their own language? A language which they can connect their identity to, one capable of communicating the realities and values true to themselves—a language with terms that are neither *español ni inglés,* but both. We speak a patois, a forked tongue, a variation of two languages.

Chicano Spanish sprang out of the Chicanos' need to identify ourselves as a distinct people. We needed a language with which we could communicate with ourselves, a secret language. For some of us, language is a homeland closer than the Southwest—for many Chicanos today live in the Midwest and the East. And because we are a complex, heterogeneous people, we speak many languages. Some of the languages we speak are:

1. Standard English
2. Working class and slang English
3. Standard Spanish
4. Standard Mexican Spanish
5. North Mexican Spanish dialect
6. Chicano Spanish (Texas, New Mexico, Arizona and California have regional variations)
7. Tex-Mex
8. *Pachuco* (called *caló*)

My "home" tongues are the languages I speak with my sister and brothers, with my friends. They are the last five listed, with 6 and 7 being closest to my heart. From school, the media and job situations, I've picked up standard and working class English. From Mamagrande Locha and from reading Spanish and Mexican literature, I've picked up Standard Spanish and Standard Mexican Spanish. From *los recién llegados,* Mexican immigrants, and *braceros,* I learned the North Mexican dialect. With Mexicans I'll try to speak either Standard Mexican Spanish or the North Mexican dialect. From my parents and Chicanos living in the Valley,[4] I picked up Chicano Texas Spanish,

[4] I.e., of the Rio Grande River in southern Texas, bordering Mexico.

and I speak it with my mom; younger brother (who married a Mexican and who rarely mixes Spanish with English), aunts and older relatives.

With Chicanas from *Nuevo México* or *Arizona* I will speak Chicano Spanish a little, but often they don't understand what I'm saying. With most California Chicanas I speak entirely in English (unless I forget). When I first moved to San Francisco, I'd rattle off something in Spanish, unintentionally embarrassing them. Often it is only with another Chicana *tejana* that I can talk freely.

Words distorted by English are known as anglicisms or *pochismos*. The *pocho* is an anglicized Mexican or American of Mexican origin who speaks Spanish with an accent characteristic of North Americans and who distorts and reconstructs the language according to the influence of English.[5] Tex-Mex, or Spanglish, comes most naturally to me. I may switch back and forth from English to Spanish in the same sentence or in the same word. With my sister and my brother Nune and with Chicano *tejano* contemporaries I speak in Tex-Mex.

From kids and people my own age I picked up *Pachuco*. *Pachuco* (the language of the zoot suiters) is a language of rebellion, both against Standard Spanish and Standard English. It is a secret language. Adults of the culture and outsiders cannot understand it. It is made up of slang words from both English and Spanish. *Ruca* means girl or woman, *vato* means guy or dude, *chale* means no, *simón* means yes, *churo* is sure, talk is *periquiar*, *pigionear* means petting, *que gacho* means how nerdy, *ponte águila* means watch out, death is called *la pelona*. Through lack of practice and not having others who can speak it, I've lost most of the *Pachuco* tongue.

Chicano Spanish

Chicanos, after 250 years of Spanish/Anglo colonization have developed significant differences in the Spanish we speak. We collapse two adjacent vowels into a single syllable and sometimes shift the stress in certain words such as *maíz* / *maiz*, *cohete* / *cuete*. We leave out certain consonants when they appear between vowels: *lado/lao*, *mojado/mojao*. Chicanos from South Texas pronounced *f* as *j* as in *jue* (*fue*). Chicanos use "archaisms," words that are no longer in the Spanish language, words that have been evolved out. We say *semos*, *truje*, *haiga*, *ansina*, and *naiden*. We retain the "archaic" *j*, as in *jalar*, that derives from an earlier *h*, (the French *halar* or the Germanic *halon* which was lost to standard Spanish in the 16th century), but which is still found in several regional dialects such as the one spoken in South Texas. (Due to geography, Chicanos from the Valley of South Texas were cut off linguis-

[5] R. C. Ortega, *Dialectología Del Barrio*, trans. Hortencia S. Alwan (Los Angeles, CA: R. C. Ortega Publisher & Bookseller, 1977), 132 [Anzaldúa's note].

tically from other Spanish speakers. We tend to use words that the Spaniards brought over from Medieval Spain. The majority of the Spanish colonizers in Mexico and the Southwest came from Extremadura—Hernán Cortés was one of them—and Andalucía.[6] Andalucians pronounce *ll* like a *y*, and their *d*'s tend to be absorbed by adjacent vowels: *tirado* becomes *tirao*. They brought *el lenguaje popular, dialectos y regionalismos*.)[7]

Chicanos and other Spanish speakers also shift *ll* to *y* and *z* to *s*.[8] We leave out initial syllables, saying *tar* for *estar*, *toy* for *estoy*; *hora* for *ahora* (*cubanos* and *puertorriqueños* also leave out initial letters of some words.) We also leave out the final syllable such as *pa* for *para*. The intervocalic *y*, the *ll* as in *tortilla, ella, botella*, gets replaced by *tortia* or *tortiya, ea, botea*. We add an additional syllable at the beginning of certain words: *atocar* for *tocar*, *agastar* for *gastar*. Sometimes we'll say *lavaste las vacijas*, other times *lavates* (substituting the *ates* verb endings for the *aste*).

We use anglicisms, words borrowed from English: *bola* from ball, *carpeta* from carpet, *máchina de lavar* (instead of *lavadora*) from washing machine. Tex-Mex argot, created by adding a Spanish sound at the beginning or end of an English word such as *cookiar* for cook, *watchar* for watch, *parkiar* for park, and *rapiar* for rape, is the result of the pressures on Spanish speakers to adapt to English.

We don't use the word *vosotros/as* or its accompanying verb form. We don't say *claro* (to mean yes), *imagínate*, or *me emociona*, unless we picked up Spanish from Latinas, out of a book, or in a classroom. Other Spanish-speaking groups are going through the same, or similar, development in their Spanish.

Linguistic Terrorism

> *Deslenguadas. Somos los del español deficiente.* We are your linguistic nightmare, your linguistic aberration, your linguistic *mestizaje*, the subject of your *burla*. Because we speak with tongues of fire we are culturally crucified. Racially, culturally and linguistically *somos huérfanos*—we speak an orphan tongue.

Chicanas who grew up speaking Chicano Spanish have internalized the belief that we speak poor Spanish. It is illegitimate, a bastard language. And because we internalize how our language has been used against us by the dominant culture, we use our language differences against each other.

[6] Region in southern Spain. Extremadura is a city in central Spain. Cortés (1485–1547), Spanish soldier and explorer active in Mexico.

[7] Eduardo Hernandéz-Chávez, Andrew D. Cohen, and Anthony F. Beltramo, *El Lenguaje de los Chicanos: Regional and Social Characteristics of Language Used by Mexican Americans* (Arlington, VA: Center for Applied Linguistics, 1975), 39 [Anzaldúa's note].

[8] Hernandéz-Chávez, xvii [Anzaldúa's note].

Chicana feminists often skirt around each other with suspicion and hesitation. For the longest time I couldn't figure it out. Then it dawned on me. To be close to another Chicana is like looking into the mirror. We are afraid of what we'll see there. *Pena.* Shame. Low estimation of self. In childhood we are told that our language is wrong. Repeated attacks on our native tongue diminish our sense of self. The attacks continue throughout our lives.

Chicanas feel uncomfortable talking in Spanish to Latinas, afraid of their censure. Their language was not outlawed in their countries. They had a whole lifetime of being immersed in their native tongue; generations, centuries in which Spanish was a first language, taught in school, heard on radio and TV, and read in the newspaper.

If a person, Chicana or Latina, has a low estimation of my native tongue, she also has a low estimation of me. Often with *mexicanas y latinas* we'll speak English as a neutral language. Even among Chicanas we tend to speak English at parties or conferences. Yet, at the same time, we're afraid the other will think we're *agringadas* because we don't speak Chicano Spanish. We oppress each other trying to out-Chicano each other, vying to be the "real" Chicanas, to speak like Chicanos. There is no one Chicano language just as there is no one Chicano experience. A monolingual Chicana whose first language is English or Spanish is just as much a Chicana as one who speaks several variants of Spanish. A Chicana from Michigan or Chicago or Detroit is just as much a Chicana as one from the Southwest. Chicano Spanish is as diverse linguistically as it is regionally.

By the end of this century, Spanish speakers will comprise the biggest minority group in the U.S., a country where students in high schools and colleges are encouraged to take French classes because French is considered more "cultured." But for a language to remain alive it must be used.[9] By the end of this century English, and not Spanish, will be the mother tongue of most Chicanos and Latinos.

So, if you want to really hurt me, talk badly about my language. Ethnic identity is twin skin to linguistic identity—I am my language. Until I can take pride in my language, I cannot take pride in myself. Until I can accept as legitimate Chicano Texas Spanish, Tex-Mex and all the other languages I speak, I cannot accept the legitimacy of myself. Until I am free to write bilingually and to switch codes without having always to translate, while I still have to speak English or Spanish when I would rather speak Spanglish, and as long as I have to accommodate the English speakers rather than having them accommodate me, my tongue will be illegitimate.

[9] Irena Klepfisz, "Secular Jewish Identity: Yidishkayt in America," in *The Tribe of Dina*, Kaye/Kantrowitz, eds., 43 [Anzaldúa's note].

I will no longer be made to feel ashamed of existing. I will have my voice: Indian, Spanish, white. I will have my serpent's tongue—my woman's voice, my sexual voice, my poet's voice. I will overcome the tradition of silence.

My fingers
move sly against your palm
Like women everywhere, we speak in code. . . .
—Melanie Kaye/Kantrowitz[10]

"*Vistas*," *corridos*, *y comida*: My Native Tongue

In the 1960s, I read my first Chicano novel. It was *City of Night* by John Rechy[11] a gay Texan, son of a Scottish father and a Mexican mother. For days I walked around in stunned amazement that a Chicano could write and could get published. When I read *I Am Joaquín*[12] I was surprised to see a bilingual book by a Chicano in print. When I saw poetry written in Tex-Mex for the first time, a feeling of pure joy flashed through me. I felt like we really existed as a people. In 1971, when I started teaching High School English to Chicano students, I tried to supplement the required texts with works by Chicanos, only to be reprimanded and forbidden to do so by the principal. He claimed that I was supposed to teach "American" and English literature. At the risk of being fired, I swore my students to secrecy and slipped in Chicano short stories, poems, a play. In graduate school, while working toward a Ph.D., I had to "argue" with one advisor after the other, semester after semester, before I was allowed to make Chicano literature an area of focus.

Even before I read books by Chicanos or Mexicans, it was the Mexican movies I saw at the drive-in—the Thursday night special of $1.00 a carload—that gave me a sense of belonging. "*Vámonos a las vistas,*" my mother would call out and we'd all—grandmother, brothers, sister and cousins—squeeze into the car. We'd wolf down cheese and bologna white bread sandwiches while watching Pedro Infante in melodramatic tear-jerkers like *Nosotros los pobres,*[13] the first "real" Mexican movie (that was not an imitation of European movies). I remember seeing *Cuando los hijos se van*[14] and surmising that all Mexican movies played up the love a mother has for her children and what

[10] Melanie Kaye/Kantrowitz, "Sign," in *We Speak in Code: Poems and Other Writings* (Pittsburgh, PA: Motheroot Publications, Inc., 1980), 85 [Anzaldúa's note].
[11] American novelist (b. 1934). The book was published in 1963.
[12] Rodolfo Gonzales [(b. 1928), Chicano novelist], *I Am Joaquín/Yo Soy Joaquín* (New York, NY: Bantam Books, 1972). It was first published in 1967 [Anzaldúa's note].
[13] A 1947 film. Infante (1917–1957), Mexican film actor and singer.
[14] A 1941 film.

ungrateful sons and daughters suffer when they are not devoted to their mothers. I remember the singing-type "westerns" of Jorge Negrete and Miguel Aceves Mejía.[15] When watching Mexican movies, I felt a sense of homecoming as well as alienation. People who were to amount to something didn't go to Mexican movies, or *bailes* or tune their radios to *bolero*, *rancherita*, and *corrido* music.

The whole time I was growing up, there was *norteño* music sometimes called North Mexican border music, or Tex-Mex music, or Chicano music, or *cantina* (bar) music. I grew up listening to *conjuntos*, three- or four-piece bands made up of folk musicians playing guitar, *bajo sexto*,[16] drums and button accordion, which Chicanos had borrowed from the German immigrants who had come to Central Texas and Mexico to farm and build breweries. In the Rio Grande Valley, Steve Jordan and Little Joe Hernández were popular, and Flaco Jiménez[17] was the accordion king. The rhythms of Tex-Mex music are those of the polka, also adapted from the Germans, who in turn had borrowed the polka from the Czechs and Bohemians.

I remember the hot, sultry evenings when *corridos*—songs of love and death on the Texas-Mexican borderlands—reverberated out of cheap amplifiers from the local *cantinas* and wafted in through my bedroom window.

Corridos first became widely used along the South Texas/Mexican border during the early conflict between Chicanos and Anglos. The *corridos* are usually about Mexican heroes who do valiant deeds against the Anglo oppressors. Pancho Villa's song, "*La cucaracha*," is the most famous one. *Corridos* of John F. Kennedy[18] and his death are still very popular in the Valley. Older Chicanos remember Lydia Mendoza,[19] one of the great border *corrido* singers who was called *la Gloria de Tejas*. Her "*El tango negro*," sung during the Great Depression, made her a singer of the people. The everpresent *corridos* narrated one hundred years of border history, bringing news of events as well as entertaining. These folk musicians and folk songs are our chief cultural mythmakers, and they made our hard lives seem bearable.

I grew up feeling ambivalent about our music. Country-western and rock-and-roll had more status. In the 50s and 60s, for the slightly educated and

[15] Mexican singer and film actor (b. 1916). Negrete (1911–1953), Mexican singing actor.

[16] Twelve-string guitar tuned one octave lower than normal.

[17] Mexican American musicians. Esteban Jordán (b. 1939). José María De Leon Hérnandez (b. 1940), Leonardo Jiménez (b. 1939).

[18] Thirty-fifth U.S. president (1917–1963), assassinated in Dallas, Texas. Villa (ca. 1877–1923), born Doroteo Arango, Mexican revolutionary leader.

[19] Mexican American singer, songwriter, and musician (b. 1916).

agringado Chicanos, there existed a sense of shame at being caught listening to our music. Yet I couldn't stop my feet from thumping to the music, could not stop humming the words, nor hide from myself the exhilaration I felt when I heard it.

There are more subtle ways that we internalize identification, especially in the forms of images and emotions. For me food and certain smells are tied to my identity, to my homeland. Woodsmoke curling up to an immense blue sky; woodsmoke perfuming my grandmother's clothes, her skin. The stench of cow manure and the yellow patches on the ground; the crack of a .22 rifle and the reek of cordite. Homemade white cheese sizzling in a pan, melting inside a folded *tortilla.* My sister Hilda's hot, spicy *menudo*[20] *chile colorado* making it deep red, pieces of *panza* and hominy floating on top. My brother Carito barbecuing *fajitas* in the backyard. Even now and 3,000 miles away, I can see my mother spicing the ground beef, pork and venison with *chile.* My mouth salivates at the thought of the hot steaming *tamales* I would be eating if I were home.

Si le preguntas a mi mamá, "¿Qué eres?"

> "Identity is the essential core of who
> we are as individuals, the conscious
> experience of the self inside."
>
> —Kaufman[21]

Nosotros los Chicanos straddle the borderlands. On one side of us, we are constantly exposed to the Spanish of the Mexicans, on the other side we hear the Anglos' incessant clamoring so that we forget our language. Among ourselves we don't say *nosotros los americanos, o nosotros los españoles, o nosotros los hispanos.* We say *nosotros los mexicanos* (by *mexicanos* we do not mean citizens of Mexico; we do not mean a national identity, but a racial one). We distinguish between *mexicanos del otro lado* and *mexicanos de este lado.* Deep in our hearts we believe that being Mexican has nothing to do with which country one lives in. Being Mexican is a state of soul—not one of mind, not one of citizenship. Neither eagle nor serpent,[22] but both. And like the ocean, neither animal respects borders.

[20] Mexican soup made of simmered tripe, onion, garlic, chili, and hominy.

[21] Gershen Kaufman [(b. 1943), American psychologist], *Shame: The Power of Caring* (Cambridge: Schenkman Books, Inc. 1980), 68. This book was instrumental in my understanding of shame [from Anzaldúa's note].

[22] Respectively, male and female cultural figurations.

Dime con quien andas y te diré quien eres.
(Tell me who your friends are and I'll tell you who you are.)
—Mexican saying

Si le preguntas a mi mamá, "¿Qué eres?" te dirá, "Soy mexicana." My brothers and sister say the same. I sometimes will answer "*soy mexicana*" and at others will say "*soy Chicana*" *o* "*soy tejana.*" But I identified as "*Raza*" before I ever identified as "*mexicana*" or "Chicana."

As a culture, we call ourselves Spanish when referring to ourselves as a linguistic group and when copping out. It is then that we forget our predominant Indian genes. We are 70 to 80% Indian.[23] We call ourselves Hispanic[24] or Spanish-American or Latin American or Latin when linking ourselves to other Spanish-speaking peoples of the Western hemisphere and when copping out. We call ourselves Mexican-American[25] to signify we are neither Mexican nor American, but more the noun "American" than the adjective "Mexican" (and when copping out).

Chicanos and other people of color suffer economically for not acculturating. This voluntary (yet forced) alienation makes for psychological conflict, a kind of dual identity—we don't identify with the Anglo-American cultural values and we don't totally identify with the Mexican cultural values. We are a synergy of two cultures with various degrees of Mexicanness or Angloness. I have so internalized the borderland conflict that sometimes I feel like one cancels out the other and we are zero, nothing, no one. *A veces no soy nada ni nadie. Pero hasta cuando no lo soy, lo soy.*

When not copping out, when we know we are more than nothing, we call ourselves Mexican, referring to race and ancestry; *mestizo* when affirming both our Indian and Spanish (but we hardly ever own our Black ancestry); Chicano when referring to a politically aware people born and/or raised in the U.S.; *Raza* when referring to Chicanos; *tejanos* when we are Chicanos from Texas.

Chicanos did not know we were a people until 1965 when Cesar Chavez[26] and the farmworkers united and *I Am Joaquín* was published and *la Raza Unida* party[27] was formed in Texas. With that recognition, we became a distinct people. Something momentous happened to the Chicano soul—we

[23] John R. Chávez [(b. 1949), American scholar and educator], *The Lost Land: The Chicano Images of the Southwest* (Albuquerque, NM: University of New Mexico Press. 1984), 88–90 [from Anzaldúa's note].
[24] "Hispanic" is derived from Hispanis (*España*, a name given to the Iberian Peninsula in ancient times when it was a part of the Roman Empire) and is a term designated by the U.S. government to make it easier to handle us on paper [Anzaldúa's note].
[25] The Treaty of Guadalupe Hidalgo created the Mexican-American in 1848 [Anzaldúa's note].
[26] Chicano union organizer (1927–1993).
[27] Known in America as the United Farm Workers; founded in 1962.

became aware of our reality and acquired a name and a language (Chicano Spanish) that reflected that reality. Now that we had a name, some of the fragmented pieces began to fall together—who we were, what we were, how we had evolved. We began to get glimpses of what we might eventually become.

Yet the struggle of identities continues, the struggle of borders is our reality still. One day the inner struggle will cease and a true integration take place. In the meantime, *tenemos que hacerla lucha. ¿Quién está protegiendo los ranchos de mi gente? ¿Quién está tratando de cerrar la fisura entre la india y el blanco en nuestra sangre? El Chicano, sí, el Chicano que anda como un ladrón en su propia casa.*[28]

Los Chicanos, how patient we seem, how very patient. There is the quiet of the Indian about us. We know how to survive. When other races have given up their tongue, we've kept ours. We know what it is to live under the hammer blow of the dominant *norteamericano* culture. But more than we count the blows, we count the days the weeks the years the centuries the eons until the white laws and commerce and customs will rot in the deserts they've created, lie bleached. *Humildes* yet proud, *quietos* yet wild, *nosotros los mexicanos* Chicanos will walk by the crumbling ashes as we go about our business. Stubborn, persevering, impenetrable as stone, yet possessing a malleability that renders us unbreakable, we, the *mestizas* and *mestizos*, will remain.

[28] Anglos, in order to alleviate their guilt for dispossessing the Chicano, stressed the Spanish part of us and perpetrated the myth of the Spanish Southwest. We have accepted the fiction that we are Hispanic, that is Spanish, in order to accommodate ourselves to the dominant culture and its abhorrence of Indians. Chávez, 88–91 [Anzaldúa's note].

Hiroshima

John Berger

The whole incredible problem begins with the need to reinsert those events of 6 August 1945 back into living consciousness.

I was shown a book last year at the Frankfurt Book Fair. The editor asked me some question about what I thought of its format. I glanced at it quickly and gave some reply. Three months ago I was sent a finished copy of the book. It lay on my desk unopened. Occasionally its title and cover picture caught my eye, but I did not respond. I didn't consider the book urgent, for I believed that I already knew about what I would find within it.

Did I not clearly remember the day—I was in the army in Belfast—when we first heard the news of the bomb dropped on Hiroshima? At how many meetings during the first nuclear disarmament movement had I and others not recalled the meaning of that bomb?

And then, one morning last week, I received a letter from America, accompanying an article written by a friend. This friend is a doctor of philosophy and a Marxist. Furthermore, she is a very generous and warm-hearted woman. The article was about the possibilities of a third world war. Vis-à-vis the Soviet Union she took, I was surprised to read, a position very close to Reagan's. She concluded by evoking the likely scale of destruction which would be caused by nuclear weapons, and then welcomed the positive possibilities that this would offer the socialist revolution in the United States.

It was on that morning that I opened and read the book on my desk. It is called *Unforgettable Fire.*[1]

The book consists of drawings and paintings made by people who were in Hiroshima on the day that the bomb was dropped, thirty-six years ago today. Often the pictures are accompanied by a verbal record of what the image represents. None of them is by a professional artist. In 1974, an old man went to the television centre in Hiroshima to show to whomever was interested a picture he had painted, entitled "At about 4 P.M., 6th August 1945, near Yurozuyo bridge."

[1] Edited by Japan Broadcasting Corporation, London, Wildwood House, 1981; New York, Pantheon, 1981.

This prompted an idea of launching a television appeal to other survivors of that day to paint or draw their memories of it. Nearly a thousand pictures were sent in, and these were made into an exhibition. The appeal was worded: "Let us leave for posterity pictures about the atomic bomb, drawn by citizens."

Clearly, my interest in these pictures cannot be an art-critical one. One does not musically analyse screams. But after repeatedly looking at them, what began as an impression became a certainty. These were images of hell.

I am not using the word as hyperbole. Between these paintings by women and men who have never painted anything else since leaving school, and who have surely, for the most part, never travelled outside Japan, between these traced memories which had to be exorcised, and the numerous representations of hell in European medieval art, there is a very close affinity.

This affinity is both stylistic and fundamental. And fundamentally it is to do with the situations depicted. The affinity lies in the degree of the multiplication of pain, in the lack of appeal or aid, in the pitilessness, in the equality of wretchedness, and in the disappearance of time.

> I am 78 years old. I was living at Midorimachi on the day of the A-bomb blast. Around 9 A.M. that morning, when I looked out of my window, I saw several women coming along the street one after another towards the Hiroshima prefectural hospital. I realized for the first time, as it is sometimes said, that when people are very much frightened hair really does stand on end. The women's hair was, in fact, standing straight up and the skin of their arms was peeled off. I suppose they were around 30 years old.

Time and again, the sober eyewitness accounts recall the surprise and horror of Dante's verses about the Inferno. The temperature at the centre of the Hiroshima fireball was 300,000 degrees centigrade. The survivors are called in Japanese *hibakusha*—"those who have seen hell."

> Suddenly, one man who was stark naked came up to me and said in a quavering voice, 'Please help me!' He was burned and swollen all over from the effects of the A-bomb. Since I did not recognize him as my neighbour, I asked who he was. He answered that he was Mr. Sasaki, the son of Mr. Ennosuke Sasaki, who had a lumber shop in Funairi town. That morning he had been doing volunteer labour service, evacuating the houses near the prefectural office in Kato town. He had been burned black all over and had started back to his home in Funairi. He looked miserable—burned and sore, and naked with only pieces of his gaiters trailing behind as he walked. Only the part of his hair covered by his soldier's hat was left, as if he was wearing a bowl. When I touched him, his burned skin slipped off. I did not know what to do, so I asked a passing driver to take him to Eba hospital.

Does not this evocation of hell make it easier to forget that these scenes belonged to life? Is there not something conveniently unreal about hell? The whole history of the twentieth century proves otherwise.

Very systematically in Europe the conditions of hells have been constructed. It is not even necessary to list the sites. It is not even necessary to repeat the calculations of the organizers. We know this, and we choose to forget it.

We find it ridiculous or shocking that most of the pages concerning, for example, Trotsky were torn out of official Soviet history. What has been torn out of our history are the pages concerning the experience of the two atom bombs dropped on Japan.

Of course, the facts are there in the textbooks. It may even be that school children learn the dates. But what these facts mean—and originally their meaning was so clear, so monstrously vivid, that every commentator in the world was shocked, and every politician was obliged to say (whilst planning differently), "Never again"—what these facts mean has now been torn out. It has been a systematic, slow and thorough process of suppression and elimination. This process has been hidden within the reality of politics.

Do not misunderstand me. I am not here using the word "reality" ironically, I am not politically naïve. I have the greatest respect for political reality, and I believe that the innocence of political idealists is often very dangerous. What we are considering is how in this case in the West—not in Japan for obvious reasons and not in the Soviet Union for different reasons—political and military realities have eliminated another reality.

The eliminated reality is both physical—

> Yokogawa bridge above Tenma river, 6th August 1945, 8:30 A.M.
>
> People crying and moaning were running towards the city. I did not know why. Steam engines were burning at Yokogawa station.
>
> Skin of cow tied to wire.
>
> Skin of girl's hip was hanging down.
>
> "My baby is dead, isn't she?"

and moral.

The political and military arguments have concerned such issues as deterrence, defence systems, relative strike parity, tactical nuclear weapons and—pathetically—so-called civil defence. Any movement for nuclear disarmament today has to contend with those considerations and dispute their false interpretation. To lose sight of them is to become as apocalyptic as the Bomb and all utopias. (The construction of hells on earth was accompanied in Europe by plans for heavens on earth.)

What has to be redeemed, reinserted, disclosed and never be allowed to be forgotten, is the other reality. Most of the mass means of communication are closed to what has been suppressed.

These paintings were shown on Japanese television. Is it conceivable that the BBC would show these pictures on Channel One at a peak hour? Without any reference to "political" and "military" realities, under the straight title, *This Is How It Was, 6th August 1945?* I challenge them to do so.

What happened on that day was, of course, neither the beginning nor the end of the act. It began months, years before, with the planning of the action, and the eventual final decision to drop two bombs on Japan. However much the world was shocked and surprised by the bomb dropped on Hiroshima, it has to be emphasized that it was not a miscalculation, an error, or the result (as can happen in war) of a situation deteriorating so rapidly that it gets out of hand. What happened was consciously and precisely planned. Small scenes like this were part of the plan:

> I was walking along the Hihiyama bridge about 3 P.M. on 7th August. A woman, who looked like an expectant mother, was dead. At her side, a girl of about three years of age brought some water in an empty can she had found. She was trying to let her mother drink from it.
>
> As soon as I saw this miserable scene with the pitiful child, I embraced the girl close to me and cried with her, telling her that her mother was dead.

There was a preparation. And there was an aftermath. The latter included long, lingering deaths, radiation sickness, many fatal illnesses which developed later as a result of exposure to the bomb, and tragic genetical effects on generations yet to be born.

I refrain from giving the statistics: how many hundreds of thousands of dead, how many injured, how many deformed children. Just as I refrain from pointing out how comparatively "small" were the atomic bombs dropped on Japan. Such statistics tend to distract. We consider numbers instead of pain. We calculate instead of judging. We relativize instead of refusing.

It is possible today to arouse popular indignation or anger by speaking of the threat and immorality of terrorism. Indeed, this appears to be the central plank of the rhetoric of the new American foreign policy ("Moscow is the world-base of all terrorism") and of British policy towards Ireland. What is able to shock people about terrorist acts is that often their targets are unselected and innocent—a crowd in a railway station, people waiting for a bus to go home after work. The victims are chosen indiscriminately in the hope of producing a shock effect on political decision-making by their government.

The two bombs dropped on Japan were terrorist actions. The calculation was terrorist. The indiscriminacy was terrorist. The small groups of terrorists operating today are, by comparison, humane killers.

Another comparison needs to be made. Today terrorist groups mostly represent small nations or groupings, who are disputing large powers in a position of strength. Whereas Hiroshima was perpetrated by the most powerful alliance in the world against an enemy who was already prepared to negotiate, and was admitting defeat.

To apply the epithet "terrorist" to the acts of bombing Hiroshima and Nagasaki is logically justifiable, and I do so because it may help to re-insert that act into living consciousness today. Yet the word changes nothing in itself.

The first-hand evidence of the victims, the reading of the pages which have been torn out, provokes a sense of outrage. This outrage has two natural faces. One is a sense of horror and pity at what happened; the other face is self-defensive and declares: *this should not happen again (here).* For some the *here* is in brackets, for others it is not.

The face of horror, the reaction which has now been mostly suppressed, forces us to comprehend the reality of what happened. The second reaction, unfortunately, distances us from that reality. Although it begins as a straight declaration, it quickly leads into the labyrinth of defence policies, military arguments and global strategies. Finally it leads to the sordid commercial absurdity of private fall-out shelters.

This split of the sense of outrage into, on one hand, horror, and, on the other hand, expediency occurs because the concept of evil has been abandoned. Every culture, except our own in recent times, has had such a concept.

That its religious or philosophical bases vary is unimportant. The concept of evil implies a force or forces which have to be continually struggled against so that they do not triumph over life and destroy it. One of the very first written texts from Mesopotamia, 1,500 years before Homer, speaks of this struggle, which was the first condition of human life. In public thinking nowadays, the concept of evil has been reduced to a little adjective to support an opinion or hypothesis (abortions, terrorism, ayatollahs).

Nobody can confront the reality of 6th August 1945 without being forced to acknowledge that what happened was evil. It is not a question of opinion or interpretation, but of events.

The memory of these events should be continually before our eyes. This is why the thousand citizens of Hiroshima started to draw on their little scraps of paper. We need to show their drawings everywhere. These terrible images can now release an energy for opposing evil and for the life-long struggle of that opposition.

And from this a very old lesson may be drawn. My friend in the United States is, in a sense, innocent. She looks beyond a nuclear holocaust without considering its reality. This reality includes not only its victims but also its planners and those who support them. Evil from time immemorial has often worn a mask of innocence. One of evil's principal modes of being is *looking beyond* (with indifference) that which is before the eyes.

> August 9th: On the west embankment of a military training field was a young boy four or five years old. He was burned black, lying on his back, with his arms pointing towards heaven.

Only by looking beyond or away can one come to believe that such evil is relative, and therefore under certain conditions justifiable. In reality—the reality to which the survivors and the dead bear witness—it can never be justified.

The Uses of Doubt

Stacey D'Erasmo

A few years ago, I had the pleasure of interviewing Muriel Spark. I was speaking to her over the phone at her house in Italy, and so, in addition to my great admiration for her and the distance between us in years, there was a substantial geographical distance. Knowing that she hadn't published her first novel, *The Comforters*, until she was thirty-nine, I asked if she had ever doubted herself. Her answer came over the wires quite clearly: "I can't say I did," she said without hesitating. "I haven't got a difficult talent. I sit down and write, and I very seldom revise."

Something of a similar nature, perhaps, was expressed by John Cheever who, when asked if megalomania was necessary to writing fiction, replied, "I think writers are inclined to be intensely egocentric. . . . My dear friend Yevtushenko has . . . an ego that can crack crystal at a distance of twenty feet."

Such bravado! Such confidence! These are myths, certainly, and almost definitely lies of one sort or other, but they are powerful ones. In my years as an editor, I knew writers of both fiction and nonfiction who were megalomaniacs, and there was something curiously comforting about their megalomania: it was a known quantity. You could count on it to paper over everything in sight—all lacks, all disappointments, the passage of time, the uncertain status of the written word. Their certainty filled up the space, and, particularly at a newspaper, that was an excellent quality. On the page, too, grandiosity has its pleasures. Think of Norman Mailer, for example, who is never at a loss for words. If he is sometimes foolish, he also radiates a kind of heat, like the sun. All that prose, rolling on and on: this is the product of someone who is a believer, who seems never to doubt that there is a large and willing ear eager to receive as much as he can give.

But the myth of the writer with the crystal-cracking ego, the writer who, as Spark said, "hasn't got a difficult talent," is also alluring because it posits writing as a vast and natural force, like sex, that has only to be unleashed. In an odd way, it casts the writer as an utterly receptive being, ideally, as a kind of full vessel. The writer's task, in this way of thinking, is to remove any impediments—the need to make money, the demands of children, time constraints, guilt, fear, the knowledge that there are other writers in the world—from out of the way of the creative force. Rilke, in *Letters to a Young Poet,* advises his protégé: "Go into yourself. Search for the reason that bids you write; find out whether it is spreading its roots in the deepest places of your heart, acknowledge to yourself whether you would have to die if it were denied you to write. This above all—ask yourself in the stillest hour of the night: *must* I write? Delve into yourself for a deep answer. And if this should be affirmative, if you may meet this earnest question with a strong and simple 'I *must*,' then build your life according to this necessity; your life even into its most indifferent and slightest hour must be a sign of this urge and a testimony to it."

Rilke was writing in 1903, but his poetic vision, and these ideals of vocation and potency, are still very much with us. For instance, they are built into the structure of writing programs, which provide criticism, but which are also generally set up as lengthy retreats from the world, from commerce, and which have hierarchical systems of reward—grants, fellowships, teaching assistantships—that validate the desire to write. In order even to contemplate entering a writing program, you have to have at least a little Rilke in you. You must be willing, for two years, anyway, to "build your life according to this necessity," as he says, and the system of reward enables you, or doesn't, to continue building your life in this way. The perceived winners in this system are those writers who are empowered to build their lives according to this necessity the longest—the ones for whom the program leads to the fellowship, which leads to the big book contract, which leads to the teaching job with the lightest teaching load. A movie deal somewhere along the way, perhaps starring Uma Thurman, is also nice. Doubt, in this fantasy, is scarce.

What I would like to suggest, however, is that doubt, to a writer, is vital. As a writer I exist in a constant state of doubt, and this is not the impediment to my art, it's the precondition of it. Without doubt, I probably would not be writing at all. In one way I mean this very concretely. When I was in my late twenties, I fell apart. I was successful in my work as an editor, I was ambitious, I lived with a woman I thought I loved, and one Monday afternoon I lost my mind. I could not stop crying. I was extremely angry. Everything that I thought I knew, every goal I thought I had, every relationship in which I believed, was thrown into crisis. Everything that had been easy for me became hard. It was as if I had walked off a precipice, and for six months or more I was in a continual state of falling. I was experiencing what might be called, among other things, radical doubt.

Michael Cunningham said to me recently, talking about writing novels, that "there's always that point when the novel falls apart." That day, the book of my life fell apart, and instead of writer's block—I wasn't writing fiction then, anyway—I had life block. I could not write the next sentences of my life from the sentences that had preceded it. There was a break, a gap, a pause, and doubt rushed in. I questioned everything. It was in this condition that I began writing fiction again, though I had given it up some years before, when I was very certain about things. I began writing when I wasn't certain of anything, in fact, when I was as unsure as I have ever been. I continued to write because I continued to doubt my life and the choices I had made. I continued doubting until I had made myself something new. While I was working on my first novel, I kept a little notebook where I would write down my ideas and questions, and on the front of the notebook I wrote that much-quoted line from Kafka, "The book must be the axe for the frozen sea within us." For me, the axe was doubt, and the frozen sea was all that was certain and fixed and seemingly impenetrable.

Doubt teaches many things, and one of them is shame. Doubt is a pedagogy of shame: how can I, what am I thinking, who do I think I am, I'm bad at this, this should not be said, this cannot be said, I am stealing, I am profaning, I am consuming. A female writer friend once said to me, "Do you think we feel so much shame about writing because it's the opposite of martyrdom?" For women in particular, there is a tremendous amount of power bound up in silence and martyrdom, in the vast reaches of the unsaid. Silence is a burden, but it's also regal, like death. It inspires awe. It's unlimited. I think most of us at some point in our lives have known, or have been, one of those great, silent martyrs who inspire shame in other people. Writing, by contrast, is filled with the shame of visibility, of singularity, of the exposure of one's desire for recognition and love and existence. Writing, indeed, is the very sign of desire itself: it asks to be read. It is filled with the desire and the willingness to be known. This can be a very frightening thing, particularly if you are among those people who have traditionally gained power by not saying, not doing, not being seen, not being known. Again, I mean this in a very concrete way: marginalized peoples of all kinds have long been rewarded materially and culturally for maintaining a noble, wounded silence. We love to feel bad for them, to feel how guilty and powerful we are by contrast, and to give them a small percentage of our money and attention—or, these days, a cable channel—as reparation.

Writing throws off this cultural veil, this habit, and in this context I would say that doubt is also our knowledge of history. Doubt knows the stakes of speaking. To repress or deny doubt, or to insist that you never have any, is to say—and this, again, is very tempting for artists, for whom life is already hard enough: *I live outside of history. I am not constrained or marked by any of its material or cultural conditions.* It is also a way of saying: *I am not in defiance of any of the rules, because the rules do not apply to me. I live in heaven, with Rilke.*

But doubt knows different. Doubt marks the gap, the break, in the social contract. Yes, how dare you? Who *do* you think you are? In fact, writing does steal, it does profane, it does consume. Doubt is the prickly awareness that you are seizing the means of production of meaning and that you don't have the right to seize them. But that's exactly the point: you don't have the right. The means of production of meaning do not belong to you. And if you are black, female, queer, peculiar, or whatever, you will be even more aware that you are taking what does not belong to you, and you will probably feel that much more doubt because you have that much more to remember—and because the cultural imperative to forget or not say what you remember is that much more forceful.

I say: remember it. Know your own strength. Doubt is like a divining rod; it begins to tug when it nears something fertile and fluid and underground. For instance, when I was in my early twenties and trying to write fiction, I had a continual sense of doubt about how to represent queerness. I was out, I lived an out life, I had a lover, I was out at my job, I went to about a thousand marches and meetings, but when I sat down to make stories I wasn't sure where to put, or how to do, queerness. This was in the mid-eighties, when minimalism was held in high esteem, so I was doubly vexed. How could I write in the style of Raymond Carver about being queer? If I wrote a Carveresque sentence like "Jane and Elizabeth looked at one another across the table, then looked harder," who would know what the hell I was talking about? I could see the notes in the margins from workshop leaders: "Who are Jane and Elizabeth? Need more information here." Indeed.

Or should I, I wondered, try to write in the high, florid style of Edmund White, have Jane and Elizabeth meet on the piers in New York, troll the meatpacking district for a third, then have Jane fly to Venice the next morning and pick up Francesca on the plane? That had its charm, but it didn't really get at the reality of the Janes and Elizabeths I knew who, among other things, couldn't afford to go to Venice just then. I had a writing teacher during this time, a nice young woman, who said, "You know, we're willing to go with whatever reality you assert. You just have to put them on the page." I tried to take her advice, but I was immediately confronted with doubts and questions. Should I write, "Jane, a lesbian, and Elizabeth, another lesbian, looked at one another across the table. Jane hated Elizabeth for dumping her"? Or, could I go for more subtle markers, like "Jane, who didn't shave, eyed Elizabeth, who had a buzz cut, with weary mistrust"? What could I count on my reader to know? What markers would they understand? This did not seem to me like a problem Raymond Carver had, or even, for that matter, Ed White—the signs and signifiers of gay male life are much more widely known than those of lesbian life. How could I be subtle and literary without dragging in all this clunky expository machinery? A deeper question was, How could I write a story as sophisticated as my emotional reality when I couldn't necessarily count on most readers to know anything about my particular subculture? How could I write from where I stood, without having to teach as well?

This doubt was very troubling and made it difficult for me to write, but it was also right on target and extremely useful. It addressed and invoked the question of invisibility, and it taught me, in a visceral way that no amount of marches or meetings could equal, what I was up against. How could I write, indeed? Who did I think I was? Why would anyone be interested in these lives, especially if they didn't include a trip to Venice? Doubt raised the question of identification and cross-identification: would readers outside my subculture be able or willing to identify with Jane and Elizabeth? What would it mean if they couldn't, or, even more interesting, if they could? Did I, as a writer, have the courage to ask a reader, a real, flesh-and-blood, book-purchasing reader, to cross downward over that cultural power and identity line and become involved with Jane and Elizabeth? Was I willing to expose Jane and Elizabeth to the world?

These questions, these doubts, were not academic, or even particularly personal. They bespoke a long cultural history. And—though I wasn't really thinking about it then—they happened to be exactly the sorts of questions that the marketing people ask editors when a publishing house is thinking about whether or not to buy your book. They do not say, "Is this a good book?" They say, "Who would want to buy this book? Who would care?" They set your advance accordingly.

My response to these doubts, and the knowledge contained in them, was absolutely vital to my being able to continue as a writer. I was either going to have to give up on writing about Jane and Elizabeth, or I was going to have to assert, somehow, that it was possible to write about them. In that latter decision was the beginning of an aesthetic, one that values, for instance, cross-identification, subcultures, exchanges of emotion and power between women, and—not least on the list—is willing to expose a particular subculture to the world and attempt to sell it in the marketplace. These may sound like simple or self-evident things, but it's not hard to see where this aesthetic, which arises from doubt and a corresponding will to survive artistically, was eventually going to lead. I would throw in my lot with the freaks. Surprisingly, I found that over time this doubt drew me more toward realism. I became less interested in wordplay and intertextuality, more compelled by that initial doubt, that problem: how do I get Jane and Elizabeth, as they are—eating breakfast, fighting, making love, walking down the street—on the page? How do I make them visible? I slowed down to accommodate that discovery, that simply seeing Jane and Elizabeth whole and present, not in Venice but in Brooklyn, this morning, arguing or whatever, is shocking. It's even necessary. In this way, doubt led me to a very rich place, and it built a writerly muscle that I needed. I don't know what I would have written about if I hadn't paid attention to it. Without it, I think my writing would have become very strained and abstract, or disappeared altogether.

Doubt—that "black, forbidding doubt," as James Jones once called it, the kind that swoops down on you at your desk and flattens out your soul—is also very valuable in terms of commitment to one's art. The desire that often follows it—the wish, as he also said, to know that you have "the spark of genius"—is the desire to be reassured, but also to be swept away. It's like wanting to get drunk in Vegas and wake up married instead of having to go through that whole tedious "do I love her, is this the right thing to do, what about my family, who's paying for the wedding" thing. Doubt reminds you of all that can go wrong, of how foolish you are, how daunting your task, how much greater are the writers who went before you. (Woolf, of course, is the great figure of doubt, exquisitely poised between the devil and the deep blue sea; many have followed her lyricism, but not so many her abiding knowledge of the abyss.)

Doubt is right. There is a lot that can go wrong, you are foolish, the task is daunting, and greater writers have gone before you. You can add to this: the world isn't fair, terrible untalented people get everything, Uma Thurman probably won't option your book, and one bar of a single pop song will probably stay in most people's minds longer than any beautifully crafted novel you ever write. Doubt wakes up in bed next to you on the morning after and looks you in the eye.

However, if you can stand it, doubt is very useful in that it asks for a conscious commitment to art. This is no small task. It's infinitely preferable to feel swept up, to feel required in some way, to feel that you know you are The One. But art, arguably, is better when it doesn't know, and I think the artist is better as well in a conscious state of not-knowing. Art is not, by definition, a sure thing. Buying real estate in certain neighborhoods is a sure thing. Being a certain kind of lawyer is a sure thing. Making art is making a conscious commitment to uncertainty, to risk, to unpredictability. Doubt tells you that this is so, and it is. Doubt requires the writer to say, "I do this because I wish to." Not because I must, or because I am certain of a reward, or because I know it will be a work of genius. Simply, because I desire it.

I think that this is a very radical act. Especially these days, when greed has approached the status of a civic virtue, I think it is quite an amazing thing for anyone to say, "I am going to embark on an uncertain, unguaranteed, wayward task that will not necessarily produce a profit of either love or money, and I am going to do this because I desire it." Doubt requires you to own your desire and to value it to a foolish degree.

Because, compared to the doings of the world, it is foolish. I know a woman, a photographer, who worked for years in commercial photography. For several years running, Cartier hired her every Christmas to go up in a cherry picker at dawn and take a picture of the Cartier building with a red ribbon wrapped around it, just as the sun was coming up. They'd light up every single one of the many floors with special lights, and she usually had to do the shot three or four dawns in a row to get the right one. I think it's safe to assume that this particular promotional shot for Cartier cost a fair amount of money and that a great deal of time and attention went into its planning and that they paid my friend a fair amount of money to do it. But she had a persistent doubt, a somewhat inchoate, intensely private desire to make a very different kind of image. After a while, she turned Cartier down and began working on several very beautiful series of photographs that she hasn't tried to show or sell and that each take five years or more to produce. When I go to see her and she shows me her work, I am reminded of the radical privacy that's necessary for art, and the way that privacy doesn't cohere to a schedule or to what's "reasonable."

I am also reminded that for my friend, as it did for me, doubt called up the beginnings of an aesthetic—in this case, an aesthetic that is willing to set aside the blazing Cartier building with a red ribbon wrapped around it, that is willing to assert in the face of this blinding display that a wayward, uncertain, unguaranteed desire of dubious value in the eyes of the world is, nevertheless, worthwhile and that an adult life can be built from that desire. Moreover, that you are willing to put your body on the line for it. I first learned this lesson from coming out, which I did not think of at the time as an aesthetic. But later, I came to believe that without some sort of aesthetic like this, the writer, like the lover, is very, very fragile. Sheer ego may crack crystal, but it's a bit too crystalline itself for this multiple-image-drenched world. The Cartier shot, after all, is only one of literally millions of promotional shots, videos, advertisements, headlines, websites, celebrities, and all the other costly, often brilliant, collectively produced cultural products that surround us. I think even genius might doubt itself in the face of a Gap ad, or what they'd pay you to make one.

Last, there is, of course, much useful doubt in the process of writing itself. The way in which, as Michael Cunningham said, "there's always that point when the novel falls apart." He was speaking practically, but the point he's describing could also be called "the entire twentieth century," since the novel has been falling apart at least since that century began, if the novel was ever whole to begin with, which we know it wasn't—think of earlier works such as Laurence Sterne's *Tristram Shandy*, or *Don Quixote*, or even Henry James, all of whose novels are in a constant state of breakdown, of collapse—his loose, baggy monsters. And, of course, think of Woolf and Proust and Joyce, all the modernist form-breakers. The novel has been broken into interesting pieces for a long, long time, and it continues to be broken, sometimes by philosophy, or, most recently, by technology: e-books, hypertext, cybernovels, etc.

So, one way to think about what Cunningham said is to translate it as "There always comes that point when you remember that the novel has long since fallen apart and you doubt your narrative methods not to mention the power of the word itself, which you now know to be an empty signifier and, besides, the author has been dead since at least 1968 so why are you bothering to attempt to traffic in the thereness of that category at all?" This can be a moment of some anxiety and profound doubt. This is the moment at which I gained thirty-five pounds when I was in graduate school in English lit.

I said before that I've become increasingly interested in realism, but all realism at this point in literary history is a kind of hyper-realism: we know that it is only one lens, and this, to me, renders it immediately poignant and fragile and curious. You know that you're working with very permeable and transient material that is always on the point of dissolving—to my eye, the more realistic something is, the more it seems on the cusp of disappearing, and I find that very beautiful right now. Think, for instance, of any number of photorealistic paintings in which the almost photographic precision of the image somehow makes it incredibly weightless, like something projected on a screen. So, in this way, doubt about the validity of writing realistic novels, or any novels at all, is a powerful and useful shadow to my project. It's part of what I see when I look at the world, and at the world I'm attempting to construct. Without this particular doubt, I don't know how interesting realism would be to me. It needs its shadow, at least in my mind, to be relevant.

But the pragmatic side of Cunningham's observation—"there's always that point when the novel falls apart"—is, for the novelist's purposes, more important and mysterious than the literary historical one. In my experience, there does always come that moment, somewhere about half or a third of the way through, when the novel falls apart. You've set out in your little novelistic boat, sails full, you have your vision, your characters are in play, the pages are scrolling by, and suddenly, say, on a Wednesday morning, you realize it has a fatal flaw. This happened to me about a year ago with the new novel I'd been working on for some time already. I realized that I had something all wrong—I'd been working with several characters in first-person, and all at once I saw that this was not going to work, it was too arch in this context, it was limiting, and strangely distancing. The characters sounded like dead people, somehow, speaking from beyond the grave, which was exactly the opposite of the effect I wanted. I saw that I had made a mistake, and I was filled with doubt. Where there had been busy-ness and talk, there was now a gap, a pause. The novel fell out of my hands and broke.

I knew that the problem went to the core of the book. I had a different narrative voice to construct, with different obligations and completely different effects. The entire gravity of my novel was changed. Instead of creating the illusion that these characters were speaking through me, I was going to have to find a narrative vantage point that simultaneously knew it was outside of the characters but that also brought them closer. Somehow, the book was going to have to *be* more real by *seeming* less real. How was I going to do that? It was exhausting even to think about it. I turned the computer off, and the screen went black, and it stayed that way for some time.

After a while, I began the novel again, making what was essentially a quarter-turn in perspective, and, somehow, the entire thing began to move in a way it hadn't done before. Was it the effect of the turn, or the gap that had preceded it? I don't know. I only know that, in writing novels, as well as in life, there is often a crisis somewhere along the way, a necessary breaking. That moment of doubt—which can last an afternoon, or a month, or fifteen years, or a lifetime—is the moment at which the writer realizes that things cannot continue as planned. It's the moment when the novel escapes. I'm not Muriel Spark—I do have a difficult talent, and it gets away from me, and that's the great pleasure of it. I think it's tremendously undervalued, that moment when the novel falls apart, the commitment to art falls apart, the life falls apart. I say: let it fall.

Dwelling in Possibilities

Mark Edmundson

Our students' spectacular hunger for life makes them radically vulnerable.

At the beginning of school last fall, I ran into a student on the University of Virginia Lawn, not far from the famous statue of Homer instructing an admiring pupil. Homer's student is in a toga. Mine was wearing wraparound sunglasses like Bono's, black jeans, and a red T-shirt emblazoned with Chinese characters in white. Over his shoulder he carried his laptop.

We asked each other the usual question: What did you do over the summer? What he did, as I recall, was a brief internship at a well-regarded Internet publication, a six-country swing though Europe, then back to enjoy his family and home, reconnect with high-school friends, and work on recording a rock CD. What had I done? I had written five drafts of a chapter for a book on the last two years of Sigmund Freud's life. I had traveled to Crozet, a few miles away, to get pizza. I'd sojourned overnight in Virginia Beach, the day after I woke up distressed because I couldn't figure out how to begin my chapter. I'd driven to the beach, figured it out (I thought), and then I'd come home. My young friend looked at me with a mixture of awe and compassion. I felt a little like one of those aged men of the earth who populate Wordsworth's poetry. One of them, the Old Cumberland Beggar, goes so slowly that you never actually see him move, but if you return to the spot where you first encountered him two hours past, lo, he has gone a little way down the road. The footprints are there to prove it.

I headed back to my office for draft No. 6, or something comparably glamorous. Where was my student going? He was no doubt heading into a more turbocharged version of his summer, a life of supreme intensity created in collaboration with the laptop slung over his shoulder. For his student generation is a singular one, at least in my experience of 30 or so years teaching: Its members have a spectacular hunger for life and more life. They want to study, travel, make friends, make more friends, read everything (superfast), take in all the movies, listen to every hot band, keep up with everyone they've ever known. And there's something else, too, that distinguishes them: They live to multiply possibilities. They're enemies of closure. For as much as they want to do and actually manage to do, they always strive to keep their options open, never to shut possibilities down before they have to.

This hunger for life has a number of consequences, for now and for the future. It's part of what makes this student generation appealing, highly promising—and also radically vulnerable. These students may go on to do great and good things, but they also present dangers to themselves and to the common future. They seem almost to have been created, as the poet says, "half to rise and half to fall." As a teacher of theirs (and fellow citizen), I'm more than a little concerned about which it's going to be.

Internet technology was on hand for my current students from about the time they were eight years old; it was in 1995 that the Netscape browser made the Internet accessible to everyone. And the Internet seems to me to have shaped their generation as much as the multichannel TV, with that critical device, the remote control, shaped the students who registered for my classes a decade ago. What is the Internet to current students?

Consider first what it is not. A friend of mine, who has assiduously kept a journal for 40 years, calls the journal, which now runs to about 40 volumes, a "life thickener." His quotations and pictures and clips and drawings and paintings give density and meaning to the blind onrush that life can be. He looks back through the volumes and sees that there was a life and that to him it meant something. To my students, I suspect, my friend would look like a medieval monk, laboring over his manuscripts, someone with a radically pre-postmodern feel for time, someone who did not, in fact, understand what time actually is.

An Internet-linked laptop, one may safely say, is not a life thickener. At the fingertips of my students, the laptop is a multiplier of the possible. "I dwell in possibility," says Emily Dickinson, "a fairer house than prose." Well, my students want to dwell there with her and, it seems, to leave me in the weed-grown bungalow, prose.

My university recently passed an edict: No one, damn it (insofar as edicts can say damn it), is going to triple major. Everyone now who is worth his tuition money double majors: The students in my classes are engineering/English; politics/English; chemistry/English. An urban legend in my leaf-fringed 'hood is that someone got around this inane dictum about triple majors by majoring in four subjects—there was, it seems, no rule against that. The top students at my university, the ones who set the standard for the rest, even if they drive the rest a little crazy, want to take eight classes a term, major promiscuously, have a semester abroad at three different colleges, connect with every likely person who has a page on Facebook, have 30 pages on Facebook, be checked in with and check in at every living moment.

One day I tried an experiment in a class I was teaching on English and American Romanticism. We had been studying Thoreau and talking about his reflections (sour) on the uses of technology for communication. ("We are in great haste," he famously said, "to construct a magnetic telegraph from Maine to Texas; but Maine and Texas, it may be, have nothing important to communicate.") I asked the group, "How many places were you simultaneously yesterday—at the most?" Suppose you were chatting on your cellphone, partially watching a movie in one corner of the computer screen, instant messaging with three people (a modest number), and glancing occasionally at the text for some other course than ours—grazing, maybe, in Samuelson's Economics rather than diving deep into Thoreau's "Economy"—and then, also, tossing the occasional word to your roommate? Well, that would be seven, seven places at once. Some students—with a little high-spirited hyperbole thrown in, no doubt—got into double digits. Of course it wouldn't take the Dalai Lama or Thoreau to assure them that anyone who is in seven places at once is not anywhere in particular—not present, not here now. Be everywhere now—that's what the current technology invites, and that's what my students aspire to do.

Internet-linked computers are of course desiring machines—machines for the stimulation of desire. But so is a TV, so in a certain sense is a movie screen. What makes the Internet singular is its power to expand desire, expand possibility beyond the confines of prior media. (My students are possibility junkies.) You can multiply the number of possible clothing purchases near to infinity and do it with stunning speed. You can make all the pleated skirts in the world appear almost all at once, for you to choose from. As we talked about this in class—with Thoreau's disapproving specter looking on (sometimes it appears that Thoreau disapproves of everything, except the drinking of cold water)—something surprising came out. The moment of maximum Internet pleasure was not the moment of closure, where you sealed the deal; it was the moment when the choices had been multiplied to the highest sum. It was the moment of maximum promise, when you touched the lip of the possible: of four majors and eight courses per term and a gazillion hits on your Facebook page, and being everyplace (almost) at once, and gazing upon all the pleated skirts that the world doth hold.

This is what Immanuel Kant, were he around to see it, might have called the computer sublime (he called something like it mathematical sublimity). The moment when you make the purchase, close the deal, pick a girlfriend, set a date: All those things, the students around the Thoreau table concurred, were a letdown, consummations not really to be wished for. The students were a little surprised by the conclusions they came to about themselves. "It's when I can see it all in front of me," one young woman said, "that's when I'm the happiest."

Ask an American college student what he's doing on Friday night. Ask him at 5:30 Friday afternoon. "I don't know" will likely be the first response. But then will come a list of possibilities to make the average Chinese menu look sullenly costive: the concert, the play, the movie, the party, the stay-at-home, chilling (or chillaxing), the monitoring of SportsCenter, the reading (fast, fast) of an assignment or two. University students now are virtual Hamlets of the virtual world, pondering possibility, faces pressed up against the sweet-shop window of their all-purpose desiring machines. To ticket or not to ticket, buy or not to, party or no: Or perhaps to simply stay in and to multiply options in numberless numbers, never to be closed down.

And once you do get somewhere, wherever it might be, you'll find that, as Gertrude Stein has it, there's "no there there." At a student party, about a fourth of the people have their cellphones locked to their ears. What are they doing? "They're talking to their friends." About? "About another party they might conceivably go to." And naturally the simulation party is better than the one that they're now at (and not at), though of course there will be people at that party on their cellphones, talking about other simulacrum gatherings, spiraling on into M.C. Escher infinity.

It's possible that recent events in the world have added intensity to students' quest for more possibilities, more and more life. The events of September 11, which current college students experienced in their early teens, were an undoubted horror. But they had the effect, I think, of waking America's young people up from a pseudo-nihilistic doze. Before New York, Pennsylvania, and Virginia, the middle-class American teenager's world had been a pleasure dome, full of rare delights. It was the reign of television: the oracle that knows everything and can take you anywhere. Television brought images of bliss, and its ads showed you the products that you needed to buy in order to achieve it. The well-known Jeep ad that depicted hip kids tossing Frisbees and laughing like rock stars had nothing to do with the properties of a Jeep. It was a persona ad that advertised the sort of person you'd be when you acquired the product. The ad was an emblem of the consumer moment: Buy in order to be.

Students wanted to be cool. They wanted to be beyond reproach. There was a sense abroad that if you simply did what you were supposed to do, kept low to the ground and stayed on the conveyor belt, the future that TV promised would be yours. Everything was a mode of entertainment, or could be transformed into one, after it had been submitted to Letterman-like or Leno-like ridicule. The president was a genial boy from Arkansas who awoke one day and found himself in office. But that had not slaked his boyishness at all. He still wanted a version of what everyone did: all-nighters, pizza, and his pals. The president was a dog who couldn't stay on the porch. My students—the guys in particular—often found him the perfect image of success: You need never grow up; need never abandon college-boy mode. The couch where you sat, hours a day, in lordly condescension, monitoring the box, would in time morph into an airship to swoosh you into your dreams.

But then there came the day of near apocalypse in America, September 11, 2001. The prospect of hanging, Doctor Johnson observed, does wonders to concentrate the mind. Well, the mind of America has been concentrated. No one believes that the whole edifice is likely to come down around us soon. But everyone now lives charged with the knowledge that today, tomorrow, next week, we can suffer an event that will change everything drastically. A dirty bomb in the middle of a great city, poison wafting in soft clouds through a subway system, a water supply subtly tainted: Such things would not only derange the lives of those they touch directly, they'd discompose and remake America in ways that would be, to say the least, none too sweet. Tomorrow the deck may be shuffled and recut by the devil's hand. So what shall we do now?

The answer that comes from current students would seem to be this: Live, live. Before the bombs go off in San Francisco or the water goes vile in New York, and the new Mahdi appears on a billion screens at once to pronounce another turn in the holy war that, for him, has been going on since the first crusader scraped an armored foot on the soil of the Holy Land. On that bad day there will be, at the very least, the start of a comprehensive closing down. There will be no more free travel, no more easy money, and much less loose talk. Life will become a confinement, a prison, a pound. So now, as James's Strether instructs Little Bilham, you must "live all you can; it's a mistake not to." There's a humane hunger to my students' hustle for more life—but I think it's possible that down below bubbles a fear. Do it now, for later may be too late.

It's clearly a new university world that I'm living in, though it took me some time to see it. My revelation occurred a few months ago. Up to that point, I was always happy to see students bringing their laptops into class. The sight of them conjured up visions of upbeat newsmagazine covers: Kids in ordered rows behind their computers, tapping in the new millennium. And the students who brought their laptops seemed to be the most engaged: They'd be skittering fast across the keys, alert and alive, and glancing up from time to time to toss a few sentences into the conversation. These were the plugged-in kids, the committed ones. But then one day I made a rare trip to the blackboard and on the way glanced over a laptopper's shoulder. There was what appeared to be YouTube in one corner (Shakira? The Hips Don't Lie video?) and e-mail front and center—but nothing much to do with the ostensible subject of the class. How could I have missed it? This sort of thing is now the way of the classroom world.

Three thousand first-year students entered my university last year, and 2,906 of them brought laptops with them; 90 brought desktops. Four students—the incoming James Deans and Marlon Brandos?—showed up computerless. (Ten years ago, half of our first-year students came to school without computers.) At Virginia, as at just about every other university, almost all buildings are now equipped with wireless routers. This began to happen about four years ago, and many of us professors barely noticed it, in part because we generally travel only from office to classroom. But our students are nomads, on the move all day. Wherever they sit, they set up Internet Command Central. Now students in almost any classroom can get directly onto the Internet and, given the shieldlike screens on their laptops, they can call up what they like. Especially in the big lecture classes now, everyone's flitting from Web site to Web site, checking e-mail, and instant messaging. Do they pay any attention to the class? My students tell me that they're experts in paying attention to many things at once: It's no problem at all.

A Romantic, says Nietzsche, is someone who always wants to be elsewhere. If that's so, then the children of the Internet are Romantics, for they perpetually wish to be someplace else, and the laptop reliably helps take them there—if only in imagination. The e-mailer, the instant messenger, the Web browser are all dispersing their energies and interests outward, away from the present, the here and now. The Internet user is constantly connecting with people and institutions far away, creating surrogate communities that displace the potential community at hand.

Then too, booking by computer has made travel easier and, by eliminating a certain number of middlemen, kept it reasonably cheap. So there's an inducement to take off physically as well. The Internet is perhaps the most centrifugal technology ever devised. The classroom, where you sit down in one space at one time and ponder a text or an issue in slow motion, is coming to feel ever more antiquated. What's at a premium now is movement, making connections, getting all the circuitry fizzing and popping.

For students now, life is elsewhere. Classes matter to them, but classes are just part of an ever-enlarging web of activities and diversions. Students now seek to master their work—not to be taken over by it and consumed. They want to dispatch it, do it well and quickly, then get on to the many other things that interest them. For my students live in the future and not the present; they live with their prospects for success and pleasure. They dwell in possibility.

"By their drugs shall ye know them," it says somewhere in the Scriptures, no doubt. The answer to the question, "What drugs are college students taking now?" is, as it has been for some time, "All of the above." But the drugs that have most recently entered the scene and had an impact are the ones designed to combat attention-deficit disorder: Adderall, Ritalin, Concerta, and Daytrana, which delivers the meds through a patch. These are all pharmaceuticals, obtained by prescription, though often the people taking them have never gotten diagnosed. The ADD drugs seem to be omnipresent; they're on sale in every dorm at prices that rise exponentially as the week of final exams approaches. "Twenty dollars for a hit," one student told me, "on the night before an exam in the intro econ class." Their effect is, pretty subtly, but pretty surely, to speed the taker up. They kick him forward, give him fresh juice to keep exploring possibilities, buying and doing and buying and doing.

The idea is to keep moving, never to stop. It's now become so commonplace as to be beneath notice, but there was a time that every city block contiguous to a university did not contain a shop dispensing a speed-you-up drug and inviting people to sit down and enjoy it along with wireless computer access. Laptops seem to go with coffee and other stimulants, in much the way that blood-and-gold sunsets went with LSD and Oreo cookies with weed. (It's possible, I sometimes think, that fully half of the urban Starbucks in America are located in rental properties that, in an earlier incarnation, were head shops.) Nor were there always energy drinks: vile-tasting concoctions coming in cans costumed like superheroes, designed to make you run as fast and steady as your computer, your car, and—this is Darwinian capitalism after all—your colleagues. You've got to keep going. Almost all of my students have one book—an old book—that they've read and treasured, and read again. It's the American epic of free movement, On the Road, a half-century old last year, but to them one of the few things in the culture of my generation that's still youthful.

The sports that this generation has put its stamp on—X-games sorts of things, like snowboarding, surfing, and skateboarding—are all about velocity, motion, skimming. They're about speeding flawlessly through space, without being diverted, slowed down, or captured by mere gravity. (Gravity, in all senses, is what my students are out to avoid.) Like the drugs, the sports help to keep the kids moving elsewhere.

How about their music? It's a little hard to say. Students no longer turn their speakers out the dorm window and blast the quad with Poco's "Deliverin'." Music now comes personal, a whisper in the ear, through the iPod, so that everyone can walk around with the soundtrack to his own movie purring. This constant music plug-in is another mode of being elsewhere, about right for the current dispensation. As to the sort of music, well, the kind of stuff that runs through iPods is varied. Many of my students delight in listening to bands that absolutely no one but themselves seems to have heard of. When I ask them in class to tell me their favorite tunes, I'm reminded of the days when my friends and I would show each other our baseball cards. As you flipped yours over, the other guy responded with "Got it. Got it. Don't got it. Got it." "Don't got it" came with a wince. The coolest kid in the room now is clearly the one whose favorite bands are the ones the others wince most over—the ones they don't got.

But the students have a collective musical taste, too. When they're together at a party, when they've unplugged their iPods and put their cellphones, temporarily, on vibrate, what they generally want is rap. Whatever the content of rap, its form is propulsive forward motion—the beat, the energy pulse, is what it's about. It drives you forward, runs gas through the motor. Rap is part of the constant stimulation that students seem unable to live without.

When a seminar is over now, the students reach their hands into their pockets and draw—it looks a little like Gunfight at the O.K. Corral. But what they're reaching for, after discussing Thoreau, say, on the pleasures of solitude, are their cellphones. They've been unwired, off the drug, for more than an hour, and they need a fix. The cellphoning comes as a relief: The students have been (give or take) in one place, at one time, pondering a few passages from Walden. Now they need to disperse themselves again, get away from the immediate, dissolve the present away.

But I teach at a university known for high-powered students who are also sometimes high-octane partiers. Is what I'm saying true for all universities? Well, I do some traveling and talking to colleagues at other places, and from what I can tell, the more high-prestige the institution, the more frenetic and centrifugal the pace. At Harvard and Yale, I'd now expect to find kids who've hit a white incandescence or maybe who've fused completely with the Internet, living within it, like characters out of Neuromancer, finding in their merger with the machine a kind of high that can take the place of happiness.

Skate fast over the surfaces of life and cover all the extended space you can, says the new ethos. Perhaps the greatest of all surface skimmers, the poet laureate of the way we live now at college, was William Wordsworth's arch-antagonist, George Gordon, Lord Byron. The poetry of Wordsworth, the explorer of inner space, is deliberate, slow, ponderous, like those old men of the woods he loves to depict, and that I perhaps resemble to my fast-skimming students. The complaint against Wordsworth is that he is tiresome—he has no time for sex or violence, just muted natural beauty and a mystical sublime. Byron—rich, beautiful, glamorous, with startlingly white skin, black hair, and swanlike neck—doesn't celebrate violence. Sex is his game. In Don Juan, the hero skims and skips from one encounter to the next. His desires are mobile: He can play the woman's part as well as the man's. Desire doesn't provoke complex ambivalence in Byron, just the need to move from one beckoning satisfaction to the next. Byron's poetry has all the velocity of this ever-moving, ever-changing desire: His rhymes are shrewd, arch, unexpected, and seem to be turned with a flick of his wrist. Thus Byron on Wordsworth's good friend Samuel Taylor Coleridge, who has just published his Biographia Literaria, a book Byron dislikes because it is dense and difficult, something you must read at least twice: "And Coleridge, too, has lately taken wing, / But like a hawk encumbered with his hood,—/ Explaining metaphysics to the nation—/ I wish he would explain his Explanation."

Byron claimed to compose best on horseback and to be able to concoct dozens of lines in an outing. Wordsworth shouted his lines aloud as he trudged through the Lake District, his dog browsing ahead of him to bark if strangers, who might hear his bellowing and think him mad, appeared on the trail. Byron disliked Wordsworth for one reason above all the rest: boring. The poet of "rocks and stones and trees" was boring. Byron wished never to be bored. So he kept moving, kept accelerating from one point to the next, not in hopes of being satisfied—that he took to be an illusion—but so as not to be overcome by the noontide demon, ennui. In 1825, the year after Byron died, the first passenger locomotive appeared, and maybe, says Camille Paglia, Byron's aristocratic spirit flew by metempsychosis into the machine. Well, perhaps Byron's restless daemon has migrated again, this time from locomotive to laptop.

Students now are Romantics—of a Byronic sort. He would have adored their world of fast travel, fast communication—and fast relationships. There is no more Byronic form of erotic life than the hookup. When after the publication of Childe Harold Byron became a celebrity—"I awoke and found myself famous," he said—he was beset with erotic opportunities. Women sent him notes begging for liaisons; they followed his carriage through the streets; they smuggled themselves into his rooms. And frequently Byron, who was probably more often seduced than seducing, was pleased to comply. In his superspeed erotic life, Byron is said to have hooked up hundreds of times.

What exactly does it mean to hook up? It means managing to have good sex without activating all the strong feelings that sex usually brings. Hooking up is a fantasy of frictionless sex—sex free of deep emotion. It's sex that lets you keep on sliding over surfaces, moving from partner to partner as smoothly as you move from site to site on the laptop. In fact, the Internet-linked computer is an erotic bazaar, a hookup machine. All of those personal pages on MySpace and Facebook are, among other things, personal ads. (Byron would love shopping there—and, more, being shopped for.) Here students can find objects more alluring and numerous than pleated skirts. They can find sexual possibilities without end.

Hooking up, of course, is a kind of myth. Sex usually does provoke strong feelings, even when people swear to each other that—this time, this time—it won't. Not everyone is wired like Lord Byron. Students often find that they need continuity and comfort in what can be a harsh college world. Many of them hold faithfully to boyfriends and girlfriends through all four years of school (albeit sometimes with special spring-break dispensations). And a few of those students busting out of my class, grabbing for their cellphones, are calling not the alluring near stranger who just IM-ed them, but their parents. In every class I teach, there are at least two or three students who call home every day.

For the way that my students live now is dangerous—some of them know it, some learn in time. "In skating over thin ice," Emerson says, "our safety is in our speed." But sometimes, like it or not, we're slowed down or stopped, and then trouble begins. Last term a young woman, an art-history and commerce major in one of my classes, stopped by my office. She's a marvelous student; I've never taught anyone who could read poetry with much more subtlety and feeling. She was pale, sleepless; her teeth were chattering softly. I invited her to sit down and then asked some questions. "How many courses are you taking?" Five, no six, seven. "Audits?" Yes, one. "A thesis?" Almost done: She planned to knock out 40 pages over the weekend, but now her father, whom she clearly adored, was sick, and she'd have to go home and then how could she. . . .

"It's too much," I said. "What?" She hadn't heard me exactly. "What you're doing? It's too much." And then came—as it almost always does when I say these words, or something like them—a feeling of great relief. Someone with a claim to authority has said that it's OK to be tired, OK to ease up. OK to rest. When my students crash on their own, they crash like helicopters dropping straight out of the sky. They're often unaware that they're on the verge of trouble. They're doing what they are supposed to do, what their parents want, with all those courses and the multiple majors, and they haven't got much of any resources to look inside and to see that matters are out of joint—no one has thought to help them acquire those. Did Byron ever fall apart, victim of his own hunger for speed and space? If so, he told us little about it.

I wonder, thinking back to that fall day on the Lawn, was it something like an encounter I had had—to take the reincarnation trope a step further—with Lord Byron? He was all for glamour and motion. I was all for—well, what was I for? Was it the magic of the fifth draft on a project about a thinker, Freud, about whom—let us be generous—not everyone seems to care a great deal? I admit that I love that line of Yeats's about how writing is ceaseless stitching and unstitching, but "if it does not seem a moment's thought / Our stitching and unstitching has been naught." The stitching-unstitching business fascinates me. Yet my student had been to six countries, six!—and that was only part of his summer's story. If you asked returning students now for that old composition standard, What I Did This Summer, they'd have to hit you with three-decker novels.

And what do I have to offer the speedsters, I, a slow person from the generation of one kind of Coke, three TV stations, one mom and one dad? How exactly do we professors teach this kind of student? What does she need to know?

Many of my colleagues have a ready answer, and its essence is this: If you can't lick 'em, join 'em. In effect, they've made the courses an extension of the Internet. Their classes are laser-and-light shows, fast-moving productions that mime the colors and sound and above all the velocity of the laptop. There are movie screens, sound systems, Internet tie-ins. And, these colleagues say, it works. One professor I know of equips his students with hand-held wireless input devices that have 12 buttons and look a lot like TV remotes. Every five minutes or so, he stops teaching and polls the kids to see how well they're doing. I admire the resourcefulness that's on display here—and I admire the skill and energy that many of my fellow teachers have deployed to meet students halfway. And yet. . . .

Not long ago, a younger colleague came by my office to chat and at a certain point informed me that her son, who was 4 years old, had a favorite dinosaur and that it was called the Edmontosaurus. ("Edmundosaurus" is what I could have sworn she said.) She remarked, with what seemed untainted good will, that this may be the very oldest of the dinosaurs. A few weeks later she came by again—was she wheeling a TV in front of her, taking it to class?—and ended up telling me about this "Edmundosaurus" one more time. Well, the kind of schooling I endorse goes back at least as far as Socrates and maybe further, though not quite full-throttle to the thunder lizards.

If Socrates looked out on the current dispensation, what would he see? He'd see the velocity and the hunger for more life, faster, faster—sure. But given his interests, he'd notice something else, too. He'd see that by the time students get to college, they have been told who they are and what the world is many times over. Parents and friends, teachers, counselors, priests and rabbis, ministers and imams have had their say. They've let each student know how they size him up, and they've let him know what they think he should value. Every student has been submitted to what Socrates liked to call doxa, common sense, general belief.

And a student may be all the things the people who raised her say she is; she may want the things they have shown her are worth wanting. She may genuinely be her father and mother's daughter. But then again, she may not.

The primary reason to study Blake and Dickinson and Freud and Dickens is not to become more cultivated, or more articulate, or to be someone who at a cocktail party is never embarrassed (but can embarrass others). The ultimate reason to read them is to see if they may know you better than you know yourself. They may help you to cut through established opinion—doxa—about who you are and what the world is. They may give you new ways of seeing and saying things, and those ways may be truer for you than the ones that you grew up with. Genuine education is a process that gives students a second chance. They've been socialized once by their parents and teachers; now it's time for a second, maybe a better, shot. It's time—to be a little idealizing about it—for Socrates to have a turn.

For a student to be educated, she has to face brilliant antagonists. She has to encounter thinkers who see the world in different terms than she does. Does she come to college as a fundamentalist guardian of crude faith? Then two necessary books for her are Freud's Future of an Illusion and Nietzsche's The Anti-Christ. Once she's weathered the surface insults, she may find herself in an intellectual version of paradise, where she can defend her beliefs or change them, and where what's on hand is not a chance conversation, as Socrates liked to say, but a dialogue about how to live. Is the student a scion of high-minded liberals who think that religion is the OxyContin—the redneck heroin—of Redneck Nation? Then on might come William James and The Varieties of Religious Experience or Schopenhauer's essays on faith. It's this kind of dialogue, deliberate, gradual, thoughtful, that immersion in the manic culture of the Internet and Adderall conditions students not to have. The first step for the professor now is to slow his classroom down. The common phrase for what he wants to do is telling: We "stop and think." Stop. Our students rarely get a chance to stop. They're always in motion, always spitting out what comes first to mind, never challenging, checking, revising.

Not long ago a young man came to my office, plopped down, and looked at me with tired urgency. "Give me 10 minutes on Freud," he said. "Convince me that he really has something important to tell me." Despite appearances, this was a good moment. It was a chance to try to persuade him to slow it down. Get one of Freud's books—Civilization and Its Discontents is usually the best place to start—read it once and again, then let's talk.

When you have that kind of conversation, one on one, you begin, however modestly, to create a university. Why does the encounter need to take place face to face? The student and teacher need to create a bond of good feeling, where they are free to speak openly with each other. They need to connect not just through cold print, but through gestures, intonations, jokes. The student needs to discover what the teacher knows, and what she exemplifies about how to live. The teacher needs contact with the student's energy and hopes. That kind of connection happens best in person; perhaps it can happen only that way.

It's not a luxury, this Socratic education whose goal is self-knowledge. Constantly I see my students leaving the university, determined to do not what they want and need to do, but what their parents and their friends believe that they ought to do. And in this they can in some measure succeed. Society has a great span of resources to assist someone in doing what he's not cut out for yet still must be done. Alcohol, drugs, divorce, and buying, buying, buying what you don't need will all help you jam your round peg of a self into this or that square-holed profession.

But those students who, through whatever form of struggle, really have come to an independent sense of who they are and what they want genuinely seem to thrive in the world. Thoreau says that if you advance in the direction of your dreams, you'll find uncommon success, and teaching a few generations of students has persuaded me that he is right. The ones who do what they love without a lot of regard for conventional success tend to turn out happy and strong. As to those willing to advance in the direction of other people's dreams—well, prime the credit cards, crank the porn channel!

We teachers need to remind ourselves from time to time that our primary job is not to help our students to acquire skills, marketable skills, bankables. And we don't pre-eminently teach communication and computation and instill habits of punctuality and thoroughness. We're not here to help our students make their minds resemble their laptops, fast and feverish. We didn't get into teaching to make trains of thought run on time.

As to our students, all honor to them: They may have much to teach the five-drafter. By their hunger for more life they convey hope that the world is still in some measure a splendid place, worth seeing and appreciating. Into spontaneity they can liberate us. But life is more than spontaneity and whim. To live well, we must sometimes stop and think, and then try to remake the work in progress that we currently are. There's no better place for that than a college classroom where, together, we can slow it down and live deliberately, if only for a while.

And to that end—Edmundosaurus, take the mike!—starting this year, no more laptops in my classroom. You can leave them at home. You can check 'em at the door.

Welcome to Cancerland

A Mammogram Leads to a Cult of Pink Kitsch

Barbara Ehrenreich

I was thinking of it as one of those drive-by mammograms, one stop in a series of mundane missions including post office, supermarket, and gym, but I began to lose my nerve in the changing room, and not only because of the kinky necessity of baring my breasts and affixing tiny X-ray opaque stars to the tip of each nipple. I had been in this place only four months earlier, but that visit was just part of the routine cancer surveillance all good citizens of HMOs or health plans are expected to submit to once they reach the age of fifty, and I hadn't really been paying attention then. The results of that earlier session had aroused some "concern" on the part of the radiologist and her confederate, the gynecologist, so I am back now in the role of a suspect, eager to clear my name, alert to medical missteps and unfair allegations. But the changing room, really just a closet off the stark windowless space that houses the mammogram machine, contains something far worse, I notice for the first time now—an assumption about who I am, where I am going, and what I will need when I get there. Almost all of the eye-level space has been filled with photocopied bits of cuteness and sentimentality: pink ribbons, a cartoon about a woman with iatrogenically flattened breasts, an "Ode to a Mammogram," a list of the "Top Ten Things Only Women Understand" ("Fat Clothes" and "Eyelash Curlers" among them), and, inescapably, right next to the door, the poem "I Said a Prayer for You Today," illustrated with pink roses.

It goes on and on, this mother of all mammograms, cutting into gym time, dinnertime, and lifetime generally. Sometimes the machine doesn't work, and I get squished into position to no purpose at all. More often, the X ray is successful but apparently alarming to the invisible radiologist, off in some remote office, who calls the shots and never has the courtesy to show her face with an apology or an explanation. I try pleading with the technician: I have no known risk factors, no breast cancer in the family, had my babies relatively young and nursed them both. I eat right, drink sparingly, work out, and doesn't that count for something? But she just gets this tight little professional smile on her face, either out of guilt for the torture she's inflicting or because she already knows something that I am going to be sorry to find out for myself. For an hour and a half the procedure is repeated: the squishing, the snapshot, the technician bustling off to consult the radiologist and returning with a demand for new angles and more definitive images. In the intervals while she's off with the doctor I read the *New York Times* right down to the personally irrelevant sections like theater and real estate, eschewing the stack of women's magazines provided for me, much as I ordinarily enjoy a quick read about sweat-proof eyeliners and "fabulous sex tonight," because I have picked up this warning vibe in the changing room, which, in my increasingly anxious state, translates into: femininity is death. Finally there is nothing left to read but one of the free local weekly newspapers, where I find, buried deep in the classifieds, something even more unsettling than the growing prospect of major disease—a classified ad for a "breast cancer teddy bear" with a pink ribbon stitched to its chest.

Yes, atheists pray in their foxholes—in this case, with a yearning new to me and sharp as lust, for a clean and honorable death by shark bite, lightning strike, sniper fire, car crash. Let me be hacked to death by a madman, is my silent supplication—anything but suffocation by the pink sticky sentiment embodied in that bear and oozing from the walls of the changing room.

My official induction into breast cancer comes about ten days later with the biopsy, which, for reasons I cannot ferret out of the surgeon, has to be a surgical one, performed on an outpatient basis but under general anesthesia, from which I awake to find him standing perpendicular to me, at the far end of the gurney, down near my feet, stating gravely. "Unfortunately, there is a cancer." It takes me all the rest of that drug-addled day to decide that the most heinous thing about that sentence is not the presence of cancer but the absence of me—for I, Barbara, do not enter into it even as a location, a geographical reference point. Where I once was—not a commanding presence perhaps but nonetheless a standard assemblage of flesh and words and gesture—"there is a cancer." I have been replaced by it, is the surgeon's implication. This is what I am now, medically speaking.

In my last act of dignified self-assertion, I request to see the pathology slides myself. This is not difficult to arrange in our small-town hospital, where the pathologist turns out to be a friend of a friend, and my rusty Ph.D. in cell biology (Rockefeller University, 1968) probably helps. He's a jolly fellow, the pathologist, who calls me "hon" and sits me down at one end of the dual-head microscope while he mans the other and moves a pointer through the field. These are the cancer cells, he says, showing up blue because of their overactive DNA. Most of them are arranged in staid semicircular arrays, like suburban houses squeezed into a cul-de-sac, but I also see what I know enough to know I do not want to see: the characteristic "Indian files" of cells on the march. The "enemy," I am supposed to think—an image to save up for future exercises in "visualization" of their violent deaths at the hands of the body's killer cells, the lymphocytes and macrophages. But I am impressed, against all rational self-interest, by the energy of these cellular conga lines, their determination to move on out from the backwater of the breast to colonize lymph nodes, bone marrow, lungs, and brain. These are, after all, the fanatics of Barbaraness, the rebel cells that have realized that the genome they carry, the genetic essence of me, has no further chance of normal reproduction in the postmenopausal body we share, so why not just start multiplying like bunnies and hope for a chance to break out?

It has happened, after all; some genomes have achieved immortality through cancer. When I was a graduate student, I once asked about the strain of tissue-culture cells labeled "HeLa" in the heavy-doored room maintained at body temperature. "HeLa," it turns out, refers to one Henrietta Lacks, whose tumor was the progenitor of all HeLa cells. She died; they live, and will go on living until someone gets tired of them or forgets to change their tissue-culture medium and leaves them to starve. Maybe this is what my rebel cells have in mind, and I try beaming them a solemn warning: The chances of your surviving me in tissue culture are nil. Keep up this selfish rampage and you go down, every last one of you, along with the entire Barbara enterprise. But what kind of a role model am I, or are multicellular human organisms generally, for putting the common good above mad anarchistic individual ambition? There is a reason, it occurs to me, why cancer is our metaphor for so many runaway social processes, like corruption and "moral decay": we are no less out of control ourselves.

After the visit to the pathologist, my biological curiosity drops to a lifetime nadir. I know women who followed up their diagnoses with weeks or months of self-study, mastering their options, interviewing doctor after doctor, assessing the damage to be expected from the available treatments. But I can tell from a few hours of investigation that the career of a breast-cancer patient has been pretty well mapped out in advance for me: You may get to negotiate the choice between lumpectomy and mastectomy, but lumpectomy is commonly followed by weeks of radiation, and in either case if the lymph nodes turn out, upon dissection, to be invaded—or "involved," as it's less threateningly put—you're doomed to chemotherapy, meaning baldness, nausea, mouth sores, immunosuppression, and possible anemia. These interventions do not constitute a "cure" or anything close, which is why the death rate from breast cancer has changed very little since the 1930s, when mastectomy was the only treatment available. Chemotherapy, which became a routine part of breast-cancer treatment in the eighties, does not confer anywhere near as decisive an advantage as patients are often led to believe, especially in postmenopausal women like myself—a two or three percentage point difference in ten-year survival rates,[1] according to America's best-known breast-cancer surgeon, Dr. Susan Love.

I know these bleak facts, or sort of know them, but in the fog of anesthesia that hangs over those first few weeks, I seem to lose my capacity for self-defense. The pressure is on, from doctors and loved ones, to do something right away—kill it, get it out now. The endless exams, the bone scan to check for metastases, the high-tech heart test to see if I'm strong enough to withstand chemotherapy—all these blur the line between selfhood and thing-hood anyway, organic and inorganic, me and it. As my cancer career unfolds, I will, the helpful pamphlets explain, become a composite of the living and the dead—an implant to replace the breast, a wig to replace the hair. And then what will I mean when I use the word "I"? I fall into a state of unreasoning passive aggressivity: They diagnosed this, so it's their baby. They found it, let them fix it.

I could take my chances with "alternative" treatments, of course, like punk novelist Kathy Acker, who succumbed to breast cancer in 1997 after a course of alternative therapies in Mexico, or actress and ThighMaster promoter Suzanne Somers, who made tabloid headlines last spring by injecting herself with mistletoe brew. Or I could choose to do nothing at all beyond mentally exhorting my immune system to exterminate the traitorous cellular faction. But I have never admired the "natural" or believed in the "wisdom of the body." Death is as "natural" as anything gets, and the body has always seemed to me like a retarded Siamese twin dragging along behind me, an hysteric really, dangerously overreacting, in my case, to everyday allergens and minute ingestions of sugar. I will put my faith in science, even if this means that the dumb old body is about to be transmogrified into an evil clown—puking, trembling, swelling, surrendering significant parts, and oozing post-surgical fluids. The surgeon—a more genial and forthcoming one this time—can fit me in; the oncologist will see me. Welcome to Cancerland.

Fortunately, no one has to go through this alone. Thirty years ago, before Betty Ford, Rose Kushner, Betty Rollin, and other pioneer patients spoke out, breast cancer was a dread secret, endured in silence and euphemized in obituaries as a "long illness." Something about the conjuncture of "breast,"

[1] In the United States, one in eight women will be diagnosed with breast cancer at some point. The chances of her surviving for five years are 86.8 percent. For a black woman this falls to 72 percent; and for a woman of any race whose cancer has spread to the lymph nodes, to 77.7 percent.

signifying sexuality and nurturance, and that other word, suggesting the claws of a devouring crustacean, spooked almost everyone. Today however, it's the biggest disease on the cultural map, bigger than AIDS, cystic fibrosis, or spinal injury, bigger even than those more prolific killers of women—heart disease, lung cancer, and stroke. There are roughly hundreds of websites devoted to it, not to mention newsletters, support groups, a whole genre of first-person breast-cancer books; even a glossy, upper-middle-brow, monthly magazine, *Mamm*. There are four major national breast-cancer organizations, of which the mightiest, in financial terms, is The Susan G. Komen Foundation, headed by breast-cancer veteran and Bush's nominee for ambassador to Hungary Nancy Brinker. Komen organizes the annual Race for the Cure©, which attracts about a million people—mostly survivors, friends, and family members. Its website provides a microcosm of the new breast-cancer culture, offering news of the races, message boards for accounts of individuals' struggles with the disease, and a "marketplace" of breast-cancer-related products to buy.

More so than in the case of any other disease, breast-cancer organizations and events feed on a generous flow of corporate support. Nancy Brinker relates how her early attempts to attract corporate interest in promoting breast cancer "awareness" were met with rebuff. A bra manufacturer, importuned to affix a mammogram-reminder tag to his product, more or less wrinkled his nose. Now breast cancer has blossomed from wallflower to the most popular girl at the corporate charity prom. While AIDS goes begging and low-rent diseases like tuberculosis have no friends at all, breast cancer has been able to count on Revlon, Avon, Ford, Tiffany, Pier 1, Estée Lauder, Ralph Lauren, Lee Jeans, Saks Fifth Avenue, JC Penney, Boston Market, Wilson athletic gear—and I apologize to those I've omitted. You can "shop for the cure" during the week when Saks donates 2 percent of sales to a breast-cancer fund; "wear denim for the cure" during Lee National Denim Day, when for a $5 donation you get to wear blue jeans to work. You can even "invest for the cure," in the Kinetics Assets Management's new no-load Medical Fund, which specializes entirely in businesses involved in cancer research.

If you can't run, bike, or climb a mountain for the cure—all of which endeavors are routine beneficiaries of corporate sponsorship—you can always purchase one of the many products with a breast-cancer theme. There are 2.2 million American women in various stages of their breast-cancer careers, who, along with anxious relatives, make up a significant market for all things breast-cancer-related. Bears, for example: I have identified four distinct lines, or species, of these creatures, including "Carol," the Remembrance Bear; "Hope," the Breast Cancer Research Bear, which wears a pink turban as if to conceal chemotherapy-induced baldness; the "Susan Bear," named for Nancy Brinker's deceased sister, Susan; and the new Nick & Nora Wish

Upon a Star Bear, available, along with the Susan Bear, at the Komen Foundation website's "marketplace."

And bears are only the tip, so to speak, of the cornucopia of pink-ribbon-themed breast-cancer products. You can dress in pink-beribboned sweatshirts, denim shirts, pajamas, lingerie, aprons, loungewear, shoelaces, and socks; accessorize with pink rhinestone brooches, angel pins, scarves, caps, earrings, and bracelets; brighten up your home with breast-cancer candles, stained-glass pink-ribbon candleholders, coffee mugs, pendants, wind chimes, and night-lights; pay your bills with special BreastChecks or a separate line of Checks for the Cure. "Awareness" beats secrecy and stigma of course, but I can't help noticing that the existential space in which a friend has earnestly advised me to "confront [my] mortality" bears a striking resemblance to the mall.

This is not, I should point out, a case of cynical merchants exploiting the sick. Some of the breast-cancer tchotchkes and accessories are made by breast-cancer survivors themselves, such as "Janice," creator of the "Daisy Awareness Necklace," among other things, and in most cases a portion of the sales goes to breast-cancer research. Virginia Davis of Aurora, Colorado, was inspired to create the "Remembrance Bear" by a friend's double mastectomy and sees her work as more of a "crusade" than a business. This year she expects to ship 10,000 of these teddies, which are manufactured in China, and send part of the money to the Race for the Cure. If the bears are infantilizing—as I try ever so tactfully to suggest is how they may, in rare cases, be perceived—so far no one has complained. "I just get love letters," she tells me, "from people who say, 'God bless you for thinking of us.' "

The ultrafeminine theme of the breast-cancer "marketplace"—the prominence, for example, of cosmetics and jewelry—could be understood as a response to the treatments' disastrous effects on one's looks. But the infantilizing trope is a little harder to account for, and teddy bears are not its only manifestation. A tote bag distributed to breast cancer patients by the Libby Ross Foundation (through places such as the Columbia Presbyterian Medical Center) contains, among other items, a tube of Estée Lauder Perfumed Body Crème, a hot-pink satin pillowcase, an audiotape "Meditation to Help You with Chemotherapy," a small tin of peppermint pastilles, a set of three small inexpensive rhinestone bracelets, a pink-striped "journal and sketch book," and—somewhat jarringly—a small box of crayons. Marla Willner, one of the founders of the Libby Ross Foundation, told me that the crayons "go with the journal—for people to express different moods, different thoughts . . ." though she admitted she has never tried to write with crayons herself. Possibly the idea is that regression to a state of childlike dependency puts one in the best frame of mind with which to endure the prolonged and toxic treatments. Or it may be that, in some versions of the prevailing gender ideology, femininity is by its nature incompatible with full adulthood—a state of arrested development. Certainly men diagnosed with prostate cancer do not receive gifts of Matchbox cars.

But I, no less than the bear huggers, need whatever help I can get, and start wading out into the Web in search of practical tips on hair loss, lumpectomy versus mastectomy, how to select a chemotherapy regimen, what to wear after surgery and eat when the scent of food sucks. There is, I soon find, far more than I can usefully absorb, for thousands of the afflicted have posted their stories, beginning with the lump or bad mammogram, proceeding through the agony of the treatments; pausing to mention the sustaining forces of family, humor, and religion; and ending, in almost all cases, with warm words of encouragement for the neophyte. Some of these are no more than a paragraph long—brief waves from sister sufferers; others offer almost hour-by-hour logs of breast-deprived, chemotherapized lives:

> Tuesday, August 15, 2000: Well, I survived my 4th chemo. Very, very dizzy today. Very nauseated, but no barfing! It's a first. . . . I break out in a cold sweat and my heart pounds if I stay up longer than 5 minutes.
>
> Friday, August 18, 2000: . . . By dinner time, I was full out nauseated. I took some meds and ate a rice and vegetable bowl from Trader Joe's. It smelled and tasted awful to me, but I ate it anyway. . . . Rick brought home some Kern's nectars and I'm drinking that. Seems to have settled my stomach a little bit.

I can't seem to get enough of these tales, reading on with panicky fascination about everything that can go wrong—septicemia, ruptured implants, startling recurrences a few years after the completion of treatments, "mets" (metastases) to vital organs, and—what scares me most in the short term—"chemo-brain," or the cognitive deterioration that sometimes accompanies chemotherapy. I compare myself with everyone, selfishly impatient with those whose conditions are less menacing, shivering over those who have reached Stage IV ("There is no Stage V," as the main character in *Wit,* who has ovarian cancer, explains), constantly assessing my chances.

Feminism helped make the spreading breast-cancer sisterhood possible, and this realization gives me a faint feeling of belonging. Thirty years ago, when the disease went hidden behind euphemism and prostheses, medicine was a solid patriarchy, women's bodies its passive objects of labor. The Women's Health Movement, in which I was an activist in the seventies and eighties, legitimized self-help and mutual support and encouraged women to network directly, sharing their stories, questioning the doctors, banding together. It is hard now to recall how revolutionary these activities once seemed, and probably few participants in breast-cancer chat rooms and message boards realize that when post-mastectomy patients first proposed meeting in support groups in the mid-1970s, the American Cancer Society responded with a firm and fatherly "no." Now no one leaves the hospital without a brochure directing her to local support groups and, at least in my case, a follow-up call from a social worker to see whether I am safely ensconced in one. This cheers me briefly, until I realize that if support groups have won the stamp of medical approval this may be because they are no longer perceived as seditious.

In fact, aside from the dilute sisterhood of the cyber (and actual) support groups, there is nothing very feminist—in an ideological or activist sense—about the mainstream of breast-cancer culture today. Let me pause to qualify: You can, if you look hard enough, find plenty of genuine, self-identified feminists within the vast pink sea of the breast-cancer crusade, women who are militantly determined to "beat the epidemic" and insistent on more user-friendly approaches to treatment. It was feminist health activists who led the campaign, in the seventies and eighties, against the most savage form of breast-cancer surgery—the Halsted radical mastectomy, which removed chest muscle and lymph nodes as well as breast tissue and left women permanently disabled. It was the Women's Health Movement that put a halt to the surgical practice, common in the seventies, of proceeding directly from biopsy to mastectomy without ever rousing the patient from anesthesia. More recently, feminist advocacy groups such as the San Francisco–based Breast Cancer Action and the Cambridge-based Women's Community Cancer Project helped blow the whistle on "high-dose chemotherapy," in which the bone marrow was removed prior to otherwise lethal doses of chemotherapy and later replaced—to no good effect, as it turned out.

Like everyone else in the breast-cancer world, the feminists want a cure, but they even more ardently demand to know the cause or causes of the disease without which we will never have any means of prevention. "Bad" genes of the inherited variety are thought to account for fewer than 10 percent of breast cancers, and only 30 percent of women diagnosed with breast cancer have any known risk factor (such as delaying childbearing or the late onset of menopause) at all. Bad lifestyle choices like a fatty diet have, after brief popularity with the medical profession, been largely ruled out. Hence suspicion should focus on environmental carcinogens, the feminists argue, such as plastics, pesticides (DDT and PCBs, for example, though banned in this country, are still used in many Third World sources of the produce we eat), and the industrial runoff in our ground water. No carcinogen has been linked definitely to human breast cancer yet, but many have been found to cause the disease in mice, and the inexorable increase of the disease in industrialized nations—about one percent a year between the 1950s and the 1990s—further hints at environmental factors, as does the fact that women migrants to industrialized countries quickly develop the same breast-cancer rates as those who are native born. Their emphasis on possible ecological factors, which is not shared by groups such as Komen and the American Cancer

Society, puts the feminist breast-cancer activists in league with other, frequently rambunctious, social movements—environmental and anticorporate.

But today theirs are discordant voices in a general chorus of sentimentality and good cheer; after all, breast cancer would hardly be the darling of corporate America if its complexion changed from pink to green. It is the very blandness of breast cancer, at least in mainstream perceptions, that makes it an attractive object of corporate charity and a way for companies to brand themselves friends of the middle-aged female market. With breast cancer, "there was no concern that you might actually turn off your audience because of the life style or sexual connotations that AIDS has," Amy Langer, director of the National Alliance of Breast Cancer Organizations, told the *New York Times* in 1996. "That gives corporations a certain freedom and a certain relief in supporting the cause." Or as Cindy Pearson, director of the National Women's Health Network, the organizational progeny of the Women's Health Movement, puts it more caustically: "Breast cancer provides a way of doing something for women, without being feminist."

In the mainstream of breast-cancer culture, one finds very little anger, no mention of possible environmental causes, few complaints about the fact that, in all but the more advanced, metastasized cases, it is the "treatments," not the disease, that cause illness and pain. The stance toward existing treatments is occasionally critical—in *Mamm*, for example—but more commonly grateful; the overall tone, almost universally upbeat. The Breast Friends website, for example, features a series of inspirational quotes: "Don't Cry Over Anything that Can't Cry Over You," "I Can't Stop the Birds of Sorrow from Circling my Head, But I Can Stop Them from Building a Nest in My Hair," "When Life Hands Out Lemons, Squeeze Out a Smile," "Don't wait for your ship to come in . . . Swim out to meet it," and much more of that ilk. Even in the relatively sophisticated *Mamm*, a columnist bemoans not cancer or chemotherapy but the end of chemotherapy, and humorously proposes to deal with her separation anxiety by pitching a tent outside her oncologist's office. So pervasive is the perkiness of the breast-cancer world that unhappiness requires a kind of apology, as when "Lucy," whose "long term prognosis is not good," starts her personal narrative on breastcancertalk.org by telling us that her story "is not the usual one, full of sweetness and hope, but true nevertheless."

There is, I discover, no single noun to describe a woman with breast cancer. As in the AIDS movement, upon which breast-cancer activism is partly modeled, the words "patient" and "victim," with their aura of self-pity and passivity, have been ruled un-P.C. Instead, we get verbs: Those who are in the midst of their treatments are described as "battling" or "fighting," sometimes intensified with "bravely" or "fiercely"—language suggestive of Katharine Hepburn with her face to the wind. Once the treatments are over, one achieves the status of "survivor," which is how the women in my local support group identify themselves, A.A.-style, as we convene to share war stories and rejoice in our "survivorhood": "Hi, I'm Kathy and I'm a three-year survivor." For those who cease to be survivors and join the more than 40,000 American women who succumb to breast cancer each year—again, no noun applies. They are said to have "lost their battle" and may be memorialized by photographs carried at races for the cure—our lost, brave sisters, our fallen soldiers. But in the overwhelmingly Darwinian culture that has grown up around breast cancer, martyrs count for little; it is the "survivors" who merit constant honor and acclaim. They, after all, offer living proof that expensive and painful treatments may in some cases actually work.

Scared and medically weakened women can hardly be expected to transform their support groups into bands of activists and rush out into the streets, but the equanimity of breast-cancer culture goes beyond mere absence of anger to what looks, all too often, like a positive embrace of the disease. As "Mary" reports, on the Bosom Buds message board:

> I really believe I am a much more sensitive and thoughtful person now. It might sound funny but I was a real worrier before. Now I don't want to waste my energy on worrying. I enjoy life so much more now and in a lot of aspects I am much happier now.

Or this from "Andee":

> This was the hardest year of my life but also in many ways the most rewarding. I got rid of the baggage, made peace with my family, met many amazing people, learned to take very good care of my body so it will take care of me, and reprioritized my life.

Cindy Cherry, quoted in the *Washington Post,* goes further:

> If I had to do it over, would I want breast cancer? Absolutely. I'm not the same person I was, and I'm glad I'm not. Money doesn't matter anymore. I've met the most phenomenal people in my life through this. Your friends and family are what matter now.

The First Year of the Rest of Your Life, a collection of brief narratives with a foreword by Nancy Brinker and a share of the royalties going to the Komen Foundation, is filled with such testimonies to the redemptive powers of the disease: "I can honestly say I am happier now than I have ever been in my life—even before the breast cancer." "For me, breast cancer has provided a good kick in the rear to get me started rethinking my life. . . ." "I have come out stronger, with a new sense of priorities . . ." Never a complaint about lost time, shattered sexual confidence, or the long-term weakening of the arms caused by lymph-node dissection and radiation. What does not destroy you, to paraphrase Nietzsche, makes you a spunkier, more evolved, sort of person.

The effect of this relentless brightsiding is to transform breast cancer into a rite of passage—not an injustice or a tragedy to rail against, but a normal marker in the life cycle, like menopause or graying hair. Everything in mainstream breast-cancer culture serves, no doubt inadvertently, to tame and normalize the disease: the diagnosis may be disastrous, but there are those cunning pink rhinestone angel pins to buy and races to train for. Even the heavy traffic in personal narratives and practical tips, which I found so useful, bears an implicit acceptance of the disease and the current barbarous approaches to its treatment: you can get so busy comparing attractive head scarves that you forget to question a form of treatment that temporarily renders you both bald and immuno-incompetent. Understood as a rite of passage, breast cancer resembles the initiation rites so exhaustively studied by Mircea Eliade: First there is the selection of the initiates—by age in the tribal situation, by mammogram or palpation here. Then come the requisite ordeals—scarification or circumcision within traditional cultures, surgery and chemotherapy for the cancer patient. Finally, the initiate emerges into a new and higher status—an adult and a warrior—or in the case of breast cancer, a "survivor."

And in our implacably optimistic breast-cancer culture, the disease offers more than the intangible benefits of spiritual upward mobility. You can defy the inevitable disfigurements and come out, on the survivor side, actually prettier, sexier, more femme. In the lore of the disease—shared with me by oncology nurses as well as by survivors—chemotherapy smoothes and tightens the skin, helps you lose weight; and, when your hair comes back, it will be fuller, softer, easier to control, and perhaps a surprising new color. These may be myths, but for those willing to get with the prevailing program, opportunities for self-improvement abound. The American Cancer Society offers the "Look Good . . . Feel Better" program, "dedicated to teaching women cancer patients beauty techniques to help restore their appearance and self-image during cancer treatment." Thirty thousand women participate a year, each copping a free makeover and bag of makeup donated by the Cosmetic, Toiletry, and Fragrance Association, the trade association of the cosmetics industry. As for that lost breast: after reconstruction, why not bring the other one up to speed? Of the more than 50,000 mastectomy patients who opt for reconstruction each year, 17 percent go on, often at the urging of their plastic surgeons, to get additional surgery so that the remaining breast will "match" the more erect and perhaps larger new structure on the other side.

Not everyone goes for cosmetic deceptions, and the question of wigs versus baldness, reconstruction versus undisguised scar, defines one of the few real disagreements in breast-cancer culture. On the more avant-garde, upper-middleclass side, *Mamm* magazine—which features literary critic Eve Kosofsky Sedgwick as a columnist—tends to favor the "natural" look. Here, mastectomy scars can be "sexy" and baldness something to celebrate. The January 2001 cover story features women who "looked upon their baldness not just as a loss, but also as an opportunity: to indulge their playful sides . . . to come in contact, in new ways, with their truest selves." One decorates her scalp with temporary tattoos of peace signs, panthers, and frogs; another expresses herself with a shocking purple wig; a third reports that unadorned baldness makes her feel "sensual, powerful, able to recreate myself with every new day." But no hard feelings toward those who choose to hide their condition under wigs or scarves; it's just a matter, *Mamm* tells us, of "different aesthetics." Some go for pink ribbons; others will prefer the Ralph Lauren Pink Pony breast-cancer motif. But everyone agrees that breast cancer is a chance for creative self-transformation—a makeover opportunity, in fact.

Now, cheerfulness, up to and including delusion and false hope, has a recognized place in medicine. There is plenty of evidence that depressed and socially isolated people are more prone to succumb to diseases, cancer included, and a diagnosis of cancer is probably capable of precipitating serious depression all by itself. To be told by authoritative figures that you have a deadly disease, for which no real cure exists, is to enter a liminal state fraught with perils that go well beyond the disease itself. Consider the phenomenon of "voodoo death"—described by ethnographers among, for example, Australian aborigines—in which a person who has been condemned by a suitably potent curse obligingly shuts down and dies within a day or two. Cancer diagnoses could, and in some cases probably do, have the same kind of fatally dispiriting effect. So, it could be argued, the collectively pumped-up optimism of breast-cancer culture may be just what the doctor ordered. Shop for the Cure, dress in pink-ribbon regalia, organize a run or hike—whatever gets you through the night.

But in the seamless world of breast-cancer culture, where one website links to another—from personal narratives and grassroots endeavors to the glitzy level of corporate sponsors and celebrity spokespeople—cheerfulness is more or less mandatory, dissent a kind of treason. Within this tightly knit world, attitudes are subtly adjusted, doubters gently brought back to the fold. In *The First Year of the Rest of Your Life,* for example, each personal narrative is followed by a study question or tip designed to counter the slightest hint of negativity—and they are very slight hints indeed, since the collection includes no harridans, whiners, or feminist militants:

> Have you given yourself permission to acknowledge you have some anxiety or "blues" and to ask for help for your emotional well-being?

> Is there an area in your life of unresolved internal conflict? Is there an area where you think you might want to do some "healthy mourning"?
>
> Try keeping a list of the things you find "good about today."

As an experiment, I post a statement on the Komen.org message board, under the subject line "angry," briefly listing my own heartfelt complaints about debilitating treatments, recalcitrant insurance companies, environmental carcinogens, and, most daringly, "sappy pink ribbons." I receive a few words of encouragement in my fight with the insurance company, which has taken the position that my biopsy was a kind of optional indulgence, but mostly a chorus of rebukes. "Suzy" writes to say, "I really dislike saying you have a bad attitude towards all of this, but you do, and it's not going to help you in the least." "Mary" is a bit more tolerant, writing, "Barb, at this time in your life, it's so important to put all your energies toward a peaceful, if not happy, existence. Cancer is a rotten thing to have happen and there are no answers for any of us as to why. But to live your life, whether you have one more year or 51, in anger and bitterness is such a waste . . . I hope you can find some peace. You deserve it. We all do. God bless you and keep you in His loving care. Your sister, Mary."

"Kitty," however, thinks I've gone around the bend: "You need to run, not walk, to some counseling. . . . Please, get yourself some help and I ask everyone on this site to pray for you so you can enjoy life to the fullest."

I do get some reinforcement from "Gerri," who has been through all the treatments and now finds herself in terminal condition: "I am also angry. All the money that is raised, all the smiling faces of survivors who make it sound like it is o.k. to have breast cancer. IT IS NOT O.K.!" But Gerri's message, like the others on the message board, is posted under the mocking heading "What does it mean to be a breast-cancer survivor?"

"Culture" is too weak a word to describe all this. What has grown up around breast cancer in just the last fifteen years more nearly resembles a cult—or, given that it numbers more than two million women, their families, and friends—perhaps we should say a full-fledged religion. The products—teddy bears, pink-ribbon brooches, and so forth—serve as amulets and talismans, comforting the sufferer and providing visible evidence of faith. The personal narratives serve as testimonials and follow the same general arc as the confessional autobiographies required of seventeenth-century Puritans: first there is a crisis, often involving a sudden apprehension of mortality (the diagnosis or, in the old Puritan case, a stern word from on high); then comes a prolonged ordeal (the treatment or, in the religious case, internal struggle with the Devil); and finally, the blessed certainty of salvation, or its breast-cancer equivalent, survivorhood. And like most recognized religions, breast cancer has its great epideictic events, its pilgrimages and mass gatherings where the faithful convene and draw strength from their numbers. These are the annual races for a cure, attracting a total of about a million people at more than eighty sites—70,000 of them at the largest event, in Washington, D.C., which in recent years has been attended by Dan and Marilyn Quayle and Al and Tipper Gore. Everything comes together at the races: celebrities and corporate sponsors are showcased; products are hawked; talents, like those of the "Swinging, Singing Survivors" from Syracuse, New York, are displayed. It is at the races, too, that the elect confirm their special status. As one participant wrote in the *Washington Post:*

> I have taken my "battle scarred" breasts to the Mall, donned the pink shirt, visor, pink shoelaces, etc. and walked proudly among my fellow veterans of the breast cancer war. In 1995, at the age of 44, I was diagnosed and treated for Stage II breast cancer. The experience continues to redefine my life.

Feminist breast-cancer activists, who in the early nineties were organizing their own mass outdoor events—demonstrations, not races—to demand increased federal funding for research, tend to keep their distance from these huge, corporate-sponsored, pink gatherings. Ellen Leopold, for example—a member of the Women's Community Cancer Project in Cambridge and author of *A Darker Ribbon: Breast Cancer, Women, and Their Doctors in the Twentieth Century*—has criticized the races as an inefficient way of raising money. She points out that the Avon Breast Cancer Crusade, which sponsors three-day, sixty-mile walks, spends more than a third of the money raised on overhead and advertising, and Komen may similarly fritter away up to 25 percent of its gross. At least one corporate-charity insider agrees. "It would be much easier and more productive," says Rob Wilson, an organizer of charitable races for corporate clients, "if people, instead of running or riding, would write out a check to the charity."

To true believers, such criticisms miss the point, which is always, ultimately, "awareness." Whatever you do to publicize the disease—wear a pink ribbon, buy a teddy, attend a race—reminds other women to come forward for their mammograms. Hence, too, they would argue, the cult of the "survivor": If women neglect their annual screenings, it must be because they are afraid that a diagnosis amounts to a death sentence. Beaming survivors, proudly displaying their athletic prowess, are the best possible advertisement for routine screening mammograms, early detection, and the ensuing round of treatments. Yes, miscellaneous businesses—from tiny distributors of breast-cancer wind chimes and note cards to major corporations seeking a woman-friendly image—benefit in the process, not to mention the breast-cancer industry itself, the estimated $12–16 billion-a-year business in surgery, "breast health centers," chemotherapy "infusion suites," radiation treatment centers, mammograms, and drugs ranging from anti-emetics (to help you survive the nausea of chemotherapy) to tamoxifen (the hormonal treatment for women with estrogen-sensitive tumors). But what's to complain about? Seen through pink-tinted lenses, the entire breast-cancer enterprise—from grass-roots support groups and websites to the corporate providers of therapies and sponsors of races—looks like a beautiful example of synergy at work: cult activities, paraphernalia, and testimonies encourage women to undergo the diagnostic procedures, and since a fraction of these diagnoses will be positive, this means more members for the cult as well as more customers for the corporations, both those that provide medical products and services and those that offer charitable sponsorships.

But this view of a life-giving synergy is only as sound as the science of current detection and treatment modalities, and, tragically, that science is fraught with doubt, dissension, and what sometimes looks very much like denial. Routine screening mammograms, for example, are the major goal of "awareness," as when Rosie O'Donnell exhorts us to go out and "get squished." But not all breast-cancer experts are as enthusiastic. At best the evidence for the salutary effects of routine mammograms—as opposed to breast self-examination—is equivocal, with many respectable large-scale studies showing a vanishingly small impact on overall breast-cancer mortality. For one thing, there are an estimated two to four false positives for every cancer detected, leading thousands of healthy women to go through unnecessary biopsies and anxiety. And even if mammograms were 100 percent accurate, the admirable goal of "early" detection is more elusive than the current breast-cancer dogma admits. A small tumor, detectable only by mammogram, is not necessarily young and innocuous; if it has not spread to the lymph nodes, which is the only form of spreading detected in the common surgical procedure of lymph-node dissection, it may have already moved on to colonize other organs via the bloodstream. David Plotkin, director of the Memorial Cancer Research Foundation of Southern California, concludes that the benefits of routine mammography "are not well established; if they do exist, they are not as great as many women hope." Alan Spievack, a surgeon recently retired from the Harvard Medical School, goes further, concluding from his analysis of dozens of studies that routine screening mammography is, in the words of famous British surgeon Dr. Michael Baum, "one of the greatest deceptions perpetrated on the women of the Western world."

Even if foolproof methods for early detection existed,[2] they would, at the present time, serve only as portals to treatments offering dubious protection and considerable collateral damage. Some women diagnosed with breast cancer will live long enough to die of something else, and some of these lucky ones

[2] Some improved prognostic tools, involving measuring a tumor's growth rate and the extent to which it is supplied with blood vessels, are being developed but are not yet in use.

will indeed owe their longevity to a combination of surgery, chemotherapy, radiation, and/or anti-estrogen drugs such as tamoxifen. Others, though, would have lived untreated or with surgical excision alone, either because their cancers were slow-growing or because their bodies' own defenses were successful. Still others will die of the disease no matter what heroic, cell-destroying therapies are applied. The trouble is, we do not have the means to distinguish between these three groups. So for many of the thousands of women who are diagnosed each year, Plotkin notes, "the sole effect of early detection has been to stretch out the time in which the woman bears the knowledge of her condition." These women do not live longer than they might have without any medical intervention, but more of the time they do live is overshadowed with the threat of death and wasted in debilitating treatments.

To the extent that current methods of detection and treatment fail or fall short, America's breast-cancer cult can be judged as an outbreak of mass delusion, celebrating survivorhood by downplaying mortality and promoting obedience to medical protocols known to have limited efficacy. And although we may imagine ourselves to be well past the era of patriarchal medicine, obedience is the message behind the infantilizing theme in breast-cancer culture, as represented by the teddy bears, the crayons, and the prevailing pinkness. You are encouraged to regress to a little-girl state, to suspend critical judgment, and to accept whatever measures the doctors, as parent surrogates, choose to impose.

Worse, by ignoring or underemphasizing the vexing issue of environmental causes, the breast-cancer cult turns women into dupes of what could be called the Cancer Industrial Complex: the multinational corporate enterprise that with the one hand doles out carcinogens and disease and, with the other, offers expensive, semi-toxic pharmaceutical treatments. Breast Cancer Awareness Month, for example, is sponsored by AstraZeneca (the manufacturer of tamoxifen), which, until a corporate reorganization in 2000, was a leading producer of pesticides, including acetochlor, classified by the EPA as a "probable human carcinogen." This particularly nasty conjuncture of interests led the environmentally oriented Cancer Prevention Coalition (CPC) to condemn Breast Cancer Awareness Month as "a public relations invention by a major polluter which puts women in the position of being unwitting allies of the very people who make them sick." Although AstraZeneca no longer manufactures pesticides, CPC has continued to criticize the breast-cancer crusade—and the American Cancer Society—for its unquestioning faith in screening mammograms and careful avoidance of environmental issues. In a June 12, 2001, press release, CPC chairman Samuel S. Epstein, M.D., and the well-known physician activist Quentin Young castigated the American Cancer Society for its "longstanding track record of indifference and even hostility to cancer prevention. . . . Recent examples include issuing a joint statement with the Chlorine Institute justifying the continued global use of persistent organochlorine pesticides, and also supporting the industry in trivializing dietary pesticide residues as avoidable risks of childhood cancer. ACS policies are further exemplified by allocating under 0.1 percent of its $700 million annual budget to environmental and occupational causes of cancer."

In the harshest judgment, the breast-cancer cult serves as an accomplice in global poisoning—normalizing cancer, prettying it up, even presenting it, perversely, as a positive and enviable experience.

When, my three months of chemotherapy completed, the oncology nurse calls to congratulate me on my "excellent blood work results," I modestly demur. I didn't do anything, I tell her, anything but endure—marking the days off on the calendar, living on Protein Revolution canned vanilla health shakes, escaping into novels and work. Courtesy restrains me from mentioning the fact that the tumor markers she's tested for have little prognostic value, that there's no way to know how many rebel cells survived chemotherapy and may be carving out new colonies right now. She insists I should be proud; I'm a survivor now and entitled to recognition at the Relay for Life being held that very evening in town.

So I show up at the middle-school track where the relay's going on just in time for the Survivors' March: about 100 people, including a few men, since the funds raised will go to cancer research in general, are marching around the track eight to twelve abreast while a loudspeaker announces their names and survival times and a thin line of observers, mostly people staffing the raffle and food booths, applauds. It could be almost any kind of festivity, except for the distinctive stacks of cellophane-wrapped pink Hope Bears for sale in some of the booths. I cannot help but like the funky small-town Gemütlichkeit of the event, especially when the audio system strikes up that universal anthem of solidarity, "We Are Family," and a few people of various ages start twisting to the music on the gerry-rigged stage. But the money raised is going far away, to the American Cancer Society, which will not be asking us for our advice on how to spend it.

I approach a woman I know from other settings, one of our local intellectuals, as it happens, decked out here in a pink-and-yellow survivor T-shirt and with an American Cancer Society "survivor medal" suspended on a purple ribbon around her neck. "When do you date your survivorship from?" I ask her, since the announced time, five and a half years, seems longer than I recall. "From diagnosis or the completion of your treatments?" The question seems to annoy or confuse her, so I do not press on to what I really want to ask: At what point, in a downwardly sloping breast-cancer career, does one put aside one's survivor regalia and admit to being in fact a die-er? For the dead are with us even here, though in much diminished form. A series of paper bags, each about the right size for a junior burger and fries, lines the track. On them are the names of the dead, and inside each is a candle that will be lit later, after dark, when the actual relay race begins.

My friend introduces me to a knot of other women in survivor gear, breast-cancer victims all, I learn, though of course I would not use the V-word here. "Does anyone else have trouble with the term 'survivor'?" I ask, and, surprisingly, two or three speak up. It could be "unlucky," one tells me; it "tempts fate," says another, shuddering slightly. After all, the cancer can recur at any time, either in the breast or in some more strategic site. No one brings up my own objection to the term, though: that the mindless triumphalism of "survivorhood" denigrates the dead and the dying. Did we who live "fight" harder than those who've died? Can we claim to be "braver," better, people than the dead? And why is there no room in this cult for some gracious acceptance of death, when the time comes, which it surely will, through cancer or some other misfortune?

No, this is not my sisterhood. For me at least, breast cancer will never be a source of identity or pride. As my dying correspondent Gerri wrote: "IT IS NOT O.K.!" What it is, along with cancer generally or any slow and painful way of dying, is an abomination, and, to the extent that it's man-made, also a crime. This is the one great truth that I bring out of the breast-cancer experience, which did not, I can now report, make me prettier or stronger, more feminine or spiritual—only more deeply angry. What sustained me through the "treatments" is a purifying rage, a resolve, framed in the sleepless nights of chemotherapy, to see the last polluter, along with, say, the last smug health-insurance operative, strangled with the last pink ribbon. Cancer or no cancer, I will not live that long of course. But I know this much right now for sure: I will not go into that last good night with a teddy bear tucked under my arm.

The Hidden Teacher

Loren Eiseley

> Sometimes the best teacher teaches only once to a single child or to a grownup past hope.
>
> —Anonymous

I

The putting of formidable riddles did not arise with today's philosophers. In fact, there is a sense in which the experimental method of science might be said merely to have widened the area of man's homelessness. Over two thousand years ago, a man named Job, crouching in the Judean desert, was moved to challenge what he felt to be the injustice of his God. The voice in the whirlwind, in turn, volleyed pitiless questions upon the supplicant—questions that have, in truth, precisely the ring of modern science. For the Lord asked of Job by whose wisdom the hawk soars, and who had fathered the rain, or entered the storehouses of the snow.

A youth standing by, one Elihu, also played a role in this drama, for he ventured diffidently to his protesting elder that it was not true that God failed to manifest Himself. He may speak in one way or another, though men do not perceive it. In consequence of this remark perhaps it would be well, whatever our individual beliefs, to consider what may be called the hidden teacher, lest we become too much concerned with the formalities of only one aspect of the education by which we learn.

We think we learn from teachers, and we sometimes do. But the teachers are not always to be found in school or in great laboratories. Sometimes what we learn depends upon our own powers of insight. Moreover, our teachers may be hidden, even the greatest teacher. And it was the young man Elihu who observed that if the old are not always wise, neither can the teacher's way be ordered by the young whom he would teach.

For example, I once received an unexpected lesson from a spider.

It happened far away on a rainy morning in the West. I had come up a long gulch looking for fossils, and there, just at eye level, lurked a huge yellow-and-black orb spider, whose web was moored to the tall spears of buffalo grass at the edge of the arroyo. It was her universe, and her senses did not extend beyond the lines and spokes of the great wheel she inhabited. Her extended claws could feel every vibration throughout that delicate structure. She knew the tug of wind, the fall of a raindrop, the flutter of a trapped moth's wing. Down one spoke of the web ran a stout ribbon of gossamer on which she could hurry out to investigate her prey.

Curious, I took a pencil from my pocket and touched a strand of the web. Immediately there was a response. The web, plucked by its menacing occupant, began to vibrate until it was a blur. Anything that had brushed claw or wing against that amazing snare would be thoroughly entrapped. As the vibrations slowed, I could see the owner fingering her guidelines for signs of struggle. A pencil point was an intrusion into this universe for which no precedent existed. Spider was circumscribed by spider ideas; its universe was spider universe. All outside was irrational, extraneous, at best raw material for spider. As I proceeded on my way along the gully, like a vast impossible shadow, I realized that in the world of spider I did not exist.

Moreover, I considered, as I tramped along, that to the phagocytes, the white blood cells, clambering even now with some kind of elementary intelligence amid the thin pipes and tubing of my body—creatures without whose ministrations I could not exist—the conscious "I" of which I was aware had no significance to these amoeboid beings. I was, instead, a kind of chemical web that brought meaningful messages to them, a natural environment seemingly immortal if they could have thought about it, since generations of them had lived and perished, and would continue to so live and die, in that odd fabric which contained my intelligence—a misty light that was beginning to seem floating and tenuous even to me.

I began to see that, among the many universes in which the world of living creatures existed, some were large, some small, but that all, including man's were in some way limited or finite. We were creatures of many different dimensions passing through each other's lives like ghosts through doors.

In the years since, my mind has many times returned to that far moment of my encounter with the orb spider. A message has arisen only now from the misty shreds of that webbed universe. What was it that had so troubled me about the incident? Was it that spidery indifference to the human triumph?

If so, that triumph was very real and could not be denied. I saw, had many times seen, both mentally and in the seams of exposed strata, the long backward stretch of time whose recovery is one of the great feats of modern science. I saw the drifting cells of the early seas from which all life, including our own, has arisen. The salt of those ancient seas is in our blood, its lime is in our bones. Every time we walk along a beach some ancient urge disturbs us so that we find ourselves shedding shoes and garments or scavenging among seaweed and whitened timbers like the homesick refugees of a long war.

And war it has been indeed—the long war of life against its inhospitable environment, a war that has lasted for perhaps three billion years. It began with strange chemicals seething under a sky lacking in oxygen; it was waged through long ages until the first green plants learned to harness the light of the nearest star, our sun. The human brain, so frail, so perishable, so full of inexhaustible dreams and hungers, burns by the power of the leaf.

The hurrying blood cells charged with oxygen carry more of that element to the human brain than to any other part of the body. A few moments' loss of vital air and the phenomenon we know as consciousness goes down into the black night of inorganic things. The human body is a magical vessel, but its life is linked with an element it cannot produce. Only the green plant knows the secret of transforming the light that comes to us across the far reaches of space. There is no better illustration of the intricacy of man's relationship with other living things.

The student of fossil life would be forced to tell us that if we take the past into consideration the vast majority of earth's creatures—perhaps over 90 percent—have vanished. Forms that flourished for a far longer time than man has existed upon earth have become either extinct or so transformed that their descendants are scarcely recognizable. The specialized perish with the environment that created them, the tooth of the tiger fails at last, the lances of men strike down the last mammoth.

In three billion years of slow change and groping effort only one living creature has succeeded in escaping the trap of specialization that has led in time to so much death and wasted endeavor. It is man, but the word should be uttered softly, for his story is not yet done.

With the rise of the human brain, with the appearance of a creature whose upright body enabled two limbs to be freed for the exploration and manipulation of his environment, there had at last emerged a creature with a specialization—the brain—that, paradoxically, offered escape from specialization. Many animals driven into the nooks and crannies of nature have achieved momentary survival only at the cost of later extinction.

Was it this that troubled me and brought my mind back to a tiny universe among the grass blades, a spider's universe concerned with spider thought?

Perhaps.

The mind that once visualized animals on a cave wall is now engaged in a vast ramification of itself through time and space. Man has broken through the boundaries that control all other life. I saw, at last, the reason for my recollection of that great spider on the arroyo's rim, fingering its universe against the sky.

The spider was a symbol of man in miniature. The wheel of the web brought the analogy home clearly. Man, too, lies at the heart of a web, a web extending through the starry reaches of sidereal space, as well as backward into the dark realm of prehistory. His great eye upon Mount Palomar looks into a distance of millions of light-years, his radio ear hears the whisper of even more remote galaxies, he peers through the electron microscope upon the minute particles of his own being. It is a web no creature of earth has ever spun before. Like the orb spider, man lies at the heart of it, listening. Knowledge has given him the memory of earth's history beyond the time of his emergence. Like the spider's claw, a part of him touches a world he will never enter in the flesh. Even now, one can see him reaching forward into time with new machines, computing, analyzing, until elements of the shadowy future will also compose part of the invisible web he fingers.

Yet still my spider lingers in memory against the sunset sky. Spider thoughts in a spider universe—sensitive to raindrop and moth flutter, nothing beyond, nothing allowed for the unexpected, the inserted pencil from the world outside.

Is man at heart any different from the spider, I wonder: man thoughts, as limited as spider thoughts, contemplating now the nearest star with the threat of bringing with him the fungus rot from earth, wars, violence, the burden of a population he refuses to control, cherishing again his dream of the Adamic Eden he had pursued and lost in the green forests of America. Now it beckons again like a mirage from beyond the moon. Let man spin his web, I thought further; it is his nature. But I considered also the work of the phagocytes swarming in the rivers of my body, the unresting cells in their mortal universe. What is it we are a part of that we do not see, as the spider was not gifted to discern my face, or my little probe into her world?

We are too content with our sensory extensions, with the fulfillment of that Ice Age mind that began its journey amidst the cold of vast tundras and that pauses only briefly before its leap into space. It is no longer enough to see as a man see—even to the ends of the universe. It is not enough to hold nuclear energy in one's hand like a spear, as a man would hold it, or to see the lightning, or times past, or time to come, as a man would see it. If we continue to do this, the great brain—the human brain—will be only a new version of the old trap, and nature is full of traps for the beast that cannot learn.

It is not sufficient any longer to listen at the end of a wire to the rustlings of galaxies; it is not enough even to examine the great coil of DNA in which is coded the very alphabet of life. These are our extended perceptions. But beyond lies the great darkness of the ultimate Dreamer, who dreamed the light and the galaxies. Before act was, or substance existed, imagination grew in the dark. Man partakes of that ultimate wonder and creativeness. As we turn from the galaxies to the swarming cells of our own being, which toil for something, some entity beyond their grasp, let us remember man, the self-fabricator who came across an ice age to look into the mirrors and the magic of science. Surely he did not come to see himself or his wild visage only. He came because he is at heart a listener and a searcher for some transcendent realm beyond himself. This he has worshiped by many names, even in the dismal caves of his beginning. Man, the self-fabricator, is so by reason of gifts he had no part in devising—and so he searches as the single living cell in the beginning must have sought the ghostly creature it was to serve.

II

The young man Elihu, Job's counselor and critic, spoke simply of the "Teacher," and it is of this teacher I speak when I refer to gifts man had no part in devising. Perhaps—though it is purely a matter of emotional reactions to words—it is easier for us today to speak of this teacher as "nature," that omnipresent all which contained both the spider and my invisible intrusion into her carefully planned universe. But nature does not simply represent reality. In the shapes of life, it prepares the future; it offers alternatives. Nature teaches, though what it teaches is often hidden and obscure, just as the voice from the spinning dust cloud belittled Job's thought but gave back no answers to its own formidable interrogation.

A few months ago I encountered an amazing little creature on a windy corner of my local shopping center. It seemed, at first glance, some long-limbed, feathery spider teetering rapidly down the edge of a store front. Then it swung into the air and, as hesitantly as a spider on a thread, blew away into the parking lot. It returned in a moment on a gust of wind and ran toward me once more on its spindly legs with amazing rapidity.

With great difficulty I discovered the creature was actually a filamentous seed, seeking a hiding place and scurrying about with the uncanny surety of a conscious animal. In fact, it *did* escape me before I could secure it. Its flexible limbs were stiffer than milkweed down, and, propelled by the wind, it ran rapidly and evasively over the pavement. It was like a gnome scampering somewhere with a hidden packet—for all that I could tell, a totally new one: one of the jumbled alphabets of life.

A new one? So stable seem the years and all green leaves, a botanist might smile at my imaginings. Yet bear with me a moment. I would like to tell a tale, a genuine tale of childhood. Moreover, I was just old enough to know the average of my kind and to marvel at what I saw. And what I saw was straight from the hidden Teacher, whatever be his name.

It is told in the Orient of the Hindu god Krishna that his mother, wiping his mouth when he was a child, inadvertently peered in and beheld the universe, though the sight was mercifully and immediately veiled from her. In a sense, this is what happened to me. One day there arrived at our school a newcomer, who entered the grade above me. After some days this lad, whose look of sleepy-eyed arrogance is still before me as I write, was led into my mathematics classroom by the principal. Our class was informed severely that we should learn to work harder.

With this preliminary exhortation, great rows of figures were chalked upon the blackboard, such difficult mathematical problems as could be devised by adults. The class watched in helpless wonder. When the preparations had been completed, the young pupil sauntered forward and, with a glance of infinite boredom that swept from us to his fawning teachers, wrote the answers, as instantaneously as a modern computer, in their proper place upon the board. Then he strolled out with a carelessly exaggerated yawn.

Like some heavy-browed child at the wood's edge, clutching the last stone hand ax, I was witnessing the birth of a new type of humanity—one so beyond its teachers that it was being used for mean purposes while the intangible web of the universe in all its shimmering mathematical perfection glistened untaught in the mind of a chance little boy. The boy, by then grown self-centered and contemptuous, was being dragged from room to room to encourage us, the paleanthropes, to duplicate what, in reality, our teachers could not duplicate. He was too precious an object to be released upon the playground among us, and with reason. In a few months his parents took him away.

Long after, looking back from maturity, I realized that I had been exposed on that occasion, not to human teaching, but to the Teacher, toying with some sixteen billion nerve cells interlocked in ways past understanding. Or, if we do not like the anthropomorphism implied in the word teacher, then nature, the old voice from the whirlwind fumbling for the light. At all events, I had been the fortunate witness to life's unbounded creativity—a creativity seemingly still as unbalanced and chance-filled as in that far era when a black-scaled creature had broken from an egg and the age of the giant reptiles, the creatures of the prime, had tentatively begun.

Because form cannot be long sustained in the living, we collapse inward with age. We die. Our bodies, which were the product of a kind of hidden teaching by an alphabet we are only beginning dimly to discern, are dismissed into their elements. What is carried onward, assuming we have descendants, is the little capsule of instructions such as I encountered hastening by me in the shape of a running seed. We have learned the first biological lesson: that in each generation life passes through the eye of a needle. It exists for a time molecularly and in no recognizable semblance to its adult condition. It *instructs* its way again into man or reptile. As the ages pass, so do variants of the code. Occasionally, a species vanishes on a wind as unreturning as that which took the pterodactyls.

Or the code changes by subtle degrees through the statistical altering of individuals; until I, as the fading Neanderthals must once have done, have looked with still-living eyes upon the creature whose genotype was quite possibly to replace me. The genetic alphabets, like genuine languages, ramify and evolve along unreturning pathways.

If nature's instructions are carried through the eye of a needle, through the molecular darkness of a minute world below the field of human vision and of time's decay, the same, it might be said, is true of those monumental structures known as civilizations. They are transmitted from one generation to another in invisible puffs of air known as words—words that can also be symbolically incised on clay. As the delicate printing on the mud at the water's edge retraces a visit of autumn birds long since departed, so the little scrabbled tablets in perished cities carry the seeds of human thought across the deserts of millennia. In this instance the teacher is the social brain, but it, too, must be compressed into minute hieroglyphs, and the minds that wrought the miracle efface themselves amidst the jostling torrent of messages, which, like the genetic code, are shuffled and reshuffled as they hurry through eternity. Like a mutation, an idea may be recorded in the wrong time, to lie latent like a recessive gene and spring once more to life in an auspicious era.

Occasionally, in the moments when an archaeologist lifts the slab over a tomb that houses a great secret, a few men gain a unique glimpse through that dark portal out of which all men living have emerged, and through which messages again must pass. Here the Mexican archaeologist Ruz Lhuillier speaks of his first penetration of the great tomb hidden beneath dripping stalactites at the pyramid of Palenque: "Out of the dark shadows, rose a fairy-tale vision, a weird ethereal spectacle from another world. It was like a magician's cave carved out of ice, with walls glittering and sparkling like snow crystals." After shining his torch over hieroglyphs and sculptured figures, the explorer remarked wonderingly: "We were the first people for more than a thousand years to look at it."

Or again, one may read the tale of an unknown pharaoh who had secretly arranged that a beloved woman of his household should be buried in the tomb of the god-king—an act of compassion carrying a personal message across the millennia in defiance of all precedent.

Up to this point we have been talking of the single hidden teacher, the taunting voice out of that old Biblical whirlwind which symbolizes nature. We have seen incredible organic remembrance passed through the needle's eye of a microcosmic world hidden completely beneath the observational powers of creatures preoccupied and ensorcelled by dissolution and decay. We have seen the human mind unconsciously seize upon the principles of that very code to pass its own societal memory forward into time. The individual, the momentary living cell of the society, vanishes, but the institutional structures stand, or if they change, do so in an invisible flux not too dissimilar from that persisting in the stream of genetic continuity.

Upon this world, life is still young, not truly old as stars are measured. Therefore it comes about that we minimize the role of the synapsid reptiles, our remote forerunners, and correspondingly exalt our own intellectual achievements. We refuse to consider that in the old eye of the hurricane we may be, and doubtless are, in aggregate, a slightly more diffuse and dangerous dragon of the primal morning that still enfolds us.

Note that I say "in aggregate." For it is just here, among men, that the role of messages, and, therefore, the role of the individual teacher—or, I should say now, the hidden teachers—begin to be more plainly apparent and their instructions become more diverse. The dead pharaoh, though unintentionally, by a revealing act, had succeeded in conveying an impression of human tenderness that has outlasted the trappings of a vanished religion.

Like most modern educators I have listened to student demands to grade their teachers. I have heard the words repeated until they have become a slogan, that no man over thirty can teach the young of this generation. How would one grade a dead pharaoh, millennia gone, I wonder, one who did not intend to teach, but who, to a few perceptive minds, succeeded by the simple nobility of an act.

Many years ago, a student who was destined to become an internationally known anthropologist sat in a course in linguistics and heard his instructor, a man of no inconsiderable wisdom, describe some linguistic peculiarities of Hebrew words. At the time, the young student, at the urging of his family, was contemplating a career in theology. As the teacher warmed to his subject, the student, in the back row, ventured excitedly, "I believe I can understand that, sir. It is very similar to what exists in Mohegan."

The linguist paused and adjusted his glasses. "Young man," he said, "Mohegan is a dead language. Nothing has been recorded of it since the eighteenth century. Don't bluff."

"But sir," the young student countered hopefully, "It can't be dead so long as an old woman I know still speaks it. She is Pequot-Mohegan. I learned a bit of vocabulary from her and could speak with her myself. She took care of me when I was a child."

"Young man," said the austere, old-fashioned scholar, "be at my house for dinner at six this evening. You and I are going to look into this matter."

A few months later, under careful guidance, the young student published a paper upon Mohegan linguistics, the first of a long series of studies upon the forgotten languages and ethnology of the Indians of the northeastern forests. He had changed his vocation and turned to anthropology because of the attraction of a hidden teacher. But just who was the teacher? The young man himself, his instructor, or that solitary speaker of a dying tongue who had so yearned to hear her people's voice that she had softly babbled it to a child?

Later, this man was to become one of my professors. I absorbed much from him, though I hasten to make the reluctant confession that he was considerably beyond thirty. Most of what I learned was gathered over cups of coffee in a dingy campus restaurant. What we talked about were things some centuries older than either of us. Our common interest lay in snakes, scapulimancy, and other forgotten rites of benighted forest hunters.

I have always regarded this man as an extraordinary individual, in fact, a hidden teacher. But alas, it is all now so old-fashioned. We never protested the impracticality of his quaint subjects. We were all too ready to participate in them. He was an excellent canoeman, but he took me to places where I fully expected to drown before securing my degree. To this day, fragments of his unused wisdom remain stuffed in some back attic of my mind. Much of it I have never found the opportunity to employ, yet it has somehow colored my whole adult existence. I belong to that elderly professor in somewhat the same way that he, in turn, had become the wood child of a hidden forest mother.

There are, however, other teachers. For example, among the hunting peoples there were the animal counselors who appeared in prophetic dreams. Or, among the Greeks, the daemonic supernaturals who stood at the headboard while a man lay stark and listened—sometimes to dreadful things. "You are asleep," the messengers proclaimed over and over again, as though the man lay in a spell to hear his doom pronounced. "You, Achilles, you, son of Atreus. You are asleep, asleep," the hidden ones pronounced and vanished.

We of this modern time know other things of dreams, but we know also that they can be interior teachers and healers as well as the anticipators of disaster. It has been said that great art is the night thought of man. It may emerge without warning from the soundless depths of the unconscious, just as supernovas may blaze up suddenly in the farther reaches of void space. The critics, like astronomers, can afterward triangulate such worlds but not account for them.

A writer friend of mine with bitter memories of his youth, and estranged from his family, who, in the interim, had died, gave me this account of the matter in his middle years. He had been working, with an unusual degree of reluctance, upon a novel that contained certain autobiographical episodes. One night he dreamed; it was a very vivid and stunning dream in its detailed reality.

He found himself hurrying over creaking snow through the blackness of a winter night. He was ascending a familiar path through a long-vanished orchard. The path led to his childhood home. The house, as he drew near, appeared dark and uninhabited, but, impelled by the power of the dream, he stepped upon the porch and tried to peer through a dark window into his own old room.

"Suddenly," he told me, "I was drawn by a strange mixture of repulsion and desire to press my face against the glass. I knew intuitively they were all there waiting for me within, if I could but see them. My mother and my father. Those I had loved and those I hated. But the window was black to my gaze. I hesitated a moment and struck a match. For an instant in that freezing silence I saw my father's face glimmer wan and remote behind the glass. My mother's face was there, with the hard, distorted lines that marked her later years.

"A surge of fury overcame my cowardice. I cupped the match before me and stepped closer, closer toward that dreadful confrontation. As the match guttered down, my face was pressed almost to the glass. In some quick transformation, such as only a dream can effect, I saw that it was my own face into which I stared, just as it was reflected in the black glass. My father's haunted face was but my own. The hard lines upon my mother's aging countenance were slowly reshaping themselves upon my living face. The light burned out. I awoke sweating from the terrible psychological tension of that nightmare. I was in a far port in a distant land. It was dawn. I could hear the waves breaking on the reef."

"And how do you interpret the dream?" I asked, concealing a sympathetic shudder and sinking deeper into my chair.

"It taught me something," he said slowly, and with equal slowness a kind of beautiful transfiguration passed over his features. All the tired lines I had known so well seemed faintly to be subsiding.

"Did you ever dream it again?" I asked out of a comparable experience of my own.

"No, never," he said, and hesitated. "You see, I had learned it was just I, but more, much more, I had learned that I was they. It makes a difference. And at the last, late—much too late—it was all right. I understood. My line was dying, but I understood. I hope they understood, too." His voice trailed into silence.

"It is a thing to learn," I said. "You were seeking something and it came." He nodded, wordless. "Out of a tomb," he added after a silent moment, "my kind of tomb—the mind."

On the dark street, walking homeward, I considered my friend's experience. Man, I concluded, may have come to the end of that wild being who had mastered the fire and the lightning. He can create the web but not hold it together, not save himself except by transcending his own image. For at last, before the ultimate mystery, it is himself he shapes. Perhaps it is for this that the listening web lies open: that by knowledge we may grow beyond our past, our follies, and ever closer to what the Dreamer in the dark intended before the dust arose and walked. In the pages of an old book it has been written that we are in the hands of a Teacher, nor does it yet appear what man shall be.

Against Meat

Jonathan Safran Foer

The Fruits of Family Trees

When I was young, I would often spend the weekend at my grandmother's house. On my way in, Friday night, she would lift me from the ground in one of her fire-smothering hugs. And on the way out, Sunday afternoon, I was again taken into the air. It wasn't until years later that I realized she was weighing me.

My grandmother survived World War II barefoot, scavenging Eastern Europe for other people's inedibles: rotting potatoes, discarded scraps of meat, skins and the bits that clung to bones and pits. So she never cared if I colored outside the lines, as long as I cut coupons along the dashes. I remember hotel buffets: while the rest of us erected Golden Calves of breakfast, she would make sandwich upon sandwich to swaddle in napkins and stash in her bag for lunch. It was my grandmother who taught me that one tea bag makes as many cups of tea as you're serving, and that every part of the apple is edible.

Her obsession with food wasn't an obsession with money. (Many of those coupons I clipped were for foods she would never buy.)

Her obsession wasn't with health. (She would beg me to drink Coke.)

My grandmother never set a place for herself at family dinners. Even when there was nothing more to be done—no soup bowls to be topped off, no pots to be stirred or ovens checked—she stayed in the kitchen, like a vigilant guard (or prisoner) in a tower. As far as I could tell, the sustenance she got from the food she made didn't require her to eat it.

We thought she was the greatest chef who ever lived. My brothers and I would tell her as much several times a meal. And yet we were worldly enough kids to know that the greatest chef who ever lived would probably have more than one recipe (chicken with carrots), and that most great recipes involved more than two ingredients.

And why didn't we question her when she told us that dark food is inherently more healthful than light food, or that the bulk of the nutrients are found in the peel or crust? (The sandwiches of those weekend stays were made with the saved ends of pumpernickel loaves.) She taught us that animals that are bigger than you are very good for you, animals that are smaller than you are good for you, fish (which aren't animals) are fine for you, then tuna (which aren't fish), then vegetables, fruits, cakes, cookies and sodas. No foods are bad for you. Sugars are great. Fats are tremendous. The fatter a child is, the fitter it is—especially if it's a boy. Lunch is not one meal, but three, to be eaten at 11, 12:30 and 3. You are always starving.

In fact, her chicken with carrots probably was the most delicious thing I've ever eaten. But that had little to do with how it was prepared, or even how it tasted. Her food was delicious because we believed it was delicious. We believed in our grandmother's cooking more fervently than we believed in God.

More stories could be told about my grandmother than about anyone else I've ever met—her otherworldly childhood, the hairline margin of her survival, the totality of her loss, her immigration and further loss, the triumph and tragedy of her assimilation—and while I will one day try to tell them to my children, we almost never told them to one another. Nor did we call her by any of the obvious and earned titles. We called her the Greatest Chef.

The story of her relationship to food holds all of the other stories that could be told about her. Food, for her, is not food. It is terror, dignity, gratitude, vengeance, joy, humiliation, religion, history and, of course, love. It was as if the fruits she always offered us were picked from the destroyed branches of our family tree.

Possible Again

When I was 2, the heroes of all my bedtime books were animals. The first thing I can remember learning in school was how to pet a guinea pig without accidentally killing it. One summer my family fostered a cousin's dog. I kicked it. My father told me we don't kick animals. When I was 7, I mourned the death of a goldfish I'd won the previous weekend. I discovered that my father had flushed it down the toilet. I told my father—using other, less familial language—we don't flush animals down the toilet. When I was 9, I had a baby sitter who didn't want to hurt anything. She put it just like that when I asked her why she wasn't having chicken with my older brother and me.

"Hurt anything?" I asked.

"You know that chicken is chicken, right?"

Frank shot me a look: Mom and Dad entrusted this stupid woman with their precious babies?

Her intention might or might not have been to convert us, but being a kid herself, she lacked whatever restraint it is that so often prevents a full telling of this particular story. Without drama or rhetoric, skipping over or euphemizing, she shared what she knew.

My brother and I looked at each other, our mouths full of hurt chickens, and had simultaneous how-in-the-world-could-I-have-never-thought-of-that-before-and-why-on-earth-didn't-someone-tell-me? moments. I put down my fork. Frank finished the meal and is probably eating a chicken as I type these words.

What our baby sitter said made sense to me, not only because it seemed so self-evidently true, but also because it was the extension to food of everything my parents had taught me. We don't hurt family members. We don't hurt friends or strangers. We don't even hurt upholstered furniture. My not having thought to include farmed animals in that list didn't make them the exceptions to it. It just made me a child, ignorant of the world's workings. Until I wasn't. At which point I had to change my life.

Until I didn't. My vegetarianism, so bombastic and unyielding in the beginning, lasted a few years, sputtered and quietly died. I never thought of a response to our baby sitter's code but found ways to smudge, diminish and ignore it. Generally speaking, I didn't cause hurt. Generally speaking, I strove to do the right thing. Generally speaking, my conscience was clear enough. Pass the chicken, I'm starving.

Mark Twain said that quitting smoking is among the easiest things you can do; he did it all the time. I would add vegetarianism to the list of easy things. In high school I became vegetarian more times than I can now remember, most often as an effort to claim a bit of identity in a world of people whose identities seemed to come effortlessly. I wanted a slogan to distinguish my mom's Volvo's bumper, a bake-sale cause to fill the self-conscious half-hour of school break, an occasion to get closer to the breasts of activist women. (And I continued to think it was wrong to hurt animals.) Which isn't to say that I refrained from eating meat. Only that I refrained in public. Many dinners of those years began with my father asking, "Any dietary restrictions I need to know about tonight?"

When I went to college, I started eating meat more earnestly. Not "believing in it"—whatever that would mean—but willfully pushing the questions out of my mind. It might well have been the prevalence of vegetarianism on campus that discouraged my own—I find myself less likely to give money to a street musician whose case is overflowing with bills.

But when, at the end of my sophomore year, I became a philosophy major and started doing my first seriously pretentious thinking, I became a vegetarian again. The kind of active forgetting that I was sure meat eating required felt too paradoxical to the intellectual life I was trying to shape. I didn't know the details of factory farming, but like most everyone, I knew the gist: it is miserable for animals, the environment, farmers, public health, biodiversity, rural communities, global poverty and so on. I thought life could, should and must conform to the mold of reason, period. You can imagine how annoying this made me.

When I graduated, I ate meat—lots of every kind of meat—for about two years. Why? Because it tasted good. And because more important than reason in shaping habits are the stories we tell ourselves and one another. And I told a forgiving story about myself to myself: I was only human.

Then I was set up on a blind date with the woman who would become my wife. And only a few weeks later we found ourselves talking about two surprising topics: marriage and vegetarianism.

Her history with meat was remarkably similar to mine: there were things she believed while lying in bed at night, and there were choices made at the breakfast table the next morning. There was a gnawing (if only occasional and short-lived) dread that she was participating in something deeply wrong, and there was the acceptance of complexity and fallibility. Like me, she had intuitions that were very strong, but apparently not strong enough.

People marry for many different reasons, but one that animated our decision to take that step was the prospect of explicitly marking a new beginning. Jewish ritual and symbolism strongly encourage this notion of demarcating a sharp division with what came before—the most well-known example being the smashing of the glass at the end of the wedding ceremony. Things were as they were, but they will be different now. Things will be better. We will be better.

Sounds and feels great, but better how? I could think of endless ways to make myself better (I could learn foreign languages, be more patient, work harder), but I'd already made too many such vows to trust them anymore. I could also think of ways to make "us" better, but the meaningful things we can agree on and change in a relationship are few.

Eating animals, a concern we'd both had and had both forgotten, seemed like a place to start. So much intersects there, and so much could flow from it. In the same week, we became engaged and vegetarian.

Of course our wedding wasn't vegetarian, because we persuaded ourselves that it was only fair to offer animal protein to our guests, some of whom traveled from great distances to share our joy. (Find that logic hard to follow?) And we ate fish on our honeymoon, but we were in Japan, and when in Japan. . . . And back in our new home, we did occasionally eat burgers and chicken soup and smoked salmon and tuna steaks. But only whenever we felt like it.

And that, I thought, was that. And I thought that was just fine. I assumed we'd maintain a diet of conscientious inconsistency. Why should eating be different from any of the other ethical realms of our lives? We were honest people who occasionally told lies, careful friends who sometimes acted clumsily. We were vegetarians who from time to time ate meat.

But then we decided to have a child, and that was a different story that would necessitate a different story.

About half an hour after my son was born, I went into the waiting room to tell the gathered family the good news.

"You said 'he'! So it's a boy?"

"What's his name?"

"Who does he look like?"

"Tell us everything!"

I answered their questions as quickly as I could, then went to the corner and turned on my cellphone.

"Grandma," I said. "We have a baby."

Her only phone is in the kitchen. She picked up halfway into the first ring. It was just after midnight. Had she been clipping coupons? Preparing chicken with carrots to freeze for someone else to eat at some future meal? I'd never once seen or heard her cry, but tears pushed through her words as she asked, "How much does it weigh?"

A few days after we came home from the hospital, I sent a letter to a friend, including a photo of my son and some first impressions of fatherhood. He responded, simply, "Everything is possible again." It was the perfect thing to write, because that was exactly how it felt. The world itself had another chance.

Eating Animals

Seconds after being born, my son was breast-feeding. I watched him with an awe that had no precedent in my life. Without explanation or experience, he knew what to do. Millions of years of evolution had wound the knowledge into him, as it had encoded beating into his tiny heart and expansion and contraction into his newly dry lungs.

Almost four years later, he is a big brother and a remarkably sophisticated little conversationalist. Increasingly the food he eats is digested together with stories we tell. Feeding my children is not like feeding myself: it matters more. It matters because food matters (their physical health matters, the pleasure they take in eating matters), and because the stories that are served with food matter.

Some of my happiest childhood memories are of sushi "lunch dates" with my mom, and eating my dad's turkey burgers with mustard and grilled onions at backyard celebrations, and of course my grandmother's chicken with carrots. Those occasions simply wouldn't have been the same without those foods—and that is important. To give up the taste of sushi, turkey or chicken is a loss that extends beyond giving up a pleasurable eating experience. Changing what we eat and letting tastes fade from memory create a kind of cultural loss, a forgetting. But perhaps this kind of forgetfulness is worth accepting—even worth cultivating (forgetting, too, can be cultivated). To remember my values, I need to lose certain tastes and find other handles for the memories that they once helped me carry.

My wife and I have chosen to bring up our children as vegetarians. In another time or place, we might have made a different decision. But the realities of our present moment compelled us to make that choice. According to an analysis of U.S.D.A. data by the advocacy group Farm Forward, factory farms now produce more than 99 percent of the animals eaten in this country. And despite labels that suggest otherwise, genuine alternatives—which do exist, and make many of the ethical questions about meat moot—are very difficult for even an educated eater to find. I don't have the ability to do so with regularity and confidence. ("Free range," "cage free," "natural" and "organic" are nearly meaningless when it comes to animal welfare.)

According to reports by the Food and Agriculture Organization of the U.N. and others, factory farming has made animal agriculture the No. 1 contributor to global warming (it is significantly more destructive than transportation alone), and one of the Top 2 or 3 causes of all of the most serious environmental problems, both global and local: air and water pollution, deforestation, loss of biodiversity. . . . Eating factory-farmed animals—which is to say virtually every piece of meat sold in supermarkets and prepared in restaurants—is almost certainly the single worst thing that humans do to the environment.

Every factory-farmed animal is, as a practice, treated in ways that would be illegal if it were a dog or a cat. Turkeys have been so genetically modified they are incapable of natural reproduction. To acknowledge that these things matter is not sentimental. It is a confrontation with the facts about animals and ourselves. We know these things matter.

Meat and seafood are in no way necessary for my family—unlike some in the world, we have easy access to a wide variety of other foods. And we are healthier without it. So our choices aren't constrained.

While the cultural uses of meat can be replaced—my mother and I now eat Italian, my father grills veggie burgers, my grandmother invented her own "vegetarian chopped liver"—there is still the question of pleasure. A vegetarian diet can be rich and fully enjoyable, but I couldn't honestly argue, as many vegetarians try to, that it is as rich as a diet that includes meat. (Those who eat chimpanzee look at the Western diet as sadly deficient of a great pleasure.) I love calamari, I love roasted chicken, I love a good steak. But I don't love them without limit.

This isn't animal experimentation, where you can imagine some proportionate good at the other end of the suffering. This is what we feel like eating. Yet taste, the crudest of our senses, has been exempted from the ethical rules that govern our other senses. Why? Why doesn't a horny person have as strong a claim to raping an animal as a hungry one does to confining, killing and eating it? It's easy to dismiss that question but hard to respond to it. Try to imagine any end other than taste for which it would be justifiable to do what we do to farmed animals.

Children confront us with our paradoxes and dishonesty, and we are exposed. You need to find an answer for every why—Why do we do this? Why don't we do that?—and often there isn't a good one. So you say, simply, because. Or you tell a story that you know isn't true. And whether or not your face reddens, you blush. The shame of parenthood—which is a good shame—is that we want our children to be more whole than we are, to have satisfactory answers. My children not only inspired me to reconsider what kind of eating animal I would be, but also shamed me into reconsideration.

And then, one day, they will choose for themselves. I don't know what my reaction will be if they decide to eat meat. (I don't know what my reaction will be if they decide to renounce their Judaism, root for the Red Sox or register Republican.) I'm not as worried about what they will choose as much as my ability to make them conscious of the choices before them. I won't measure my success as a parent by whether my children share my values, but by whether they act according to their own.

In the meantime, my choice on their behalf means they will never eat their great-grandmother's singular dish. They will never receive that unique and most direct expression of her love, will perhaps never think of her as the greatest chef who ever lived. Her primal story, our family's primal story, will have to change.

Or will it? It wasn't until I became a parent that I understood my grandmother's cooking. The greatest chef who ever lived wasn't preparing food, but humans. I'm thinking of those Saturday afternoons at her kitchen table, just the two of us—black bread in the glowing toaster, a humming refrigerator that couldn't be seen through its veil of family photographs. Over pumpernickel ends and Coke, she would tell me about her escape from Europe, the foods she had to eat and those she wouldn't. It was the story of her life—"Listen to me," she would plead—and I knew a vital lesson was being transmitted, even if I didn't know, as a child, what that lesson was. I know, now, what it was.

Listen to Me

"We weren't rich, but we always had enough. Thursday we baked bread, and challah and rolls, and they lasted the whole week. Friday we had pancakes. Shabbat we always had a chicken, and soup with noodles. You would go to the butcher and ask for a little more fat. The fattiest piece was the best piece. It wasn't like now. We didn't have refrigerators, but we had milk and cheese.

We didn't have every kind of vegetable, but we had enough. The things that you have here and take for granted. . . . But we were happy. We didn't know any better. And we took what we had for granted, too.

"Then it all changed. During the war it was hell on earth, and I had nothing. I left my family, you know. I was always running, day and night, because the Germans were always right behind me. If you stopped, you died. There was never enough food. I became sicker and sicker from not eating, and I'm not just talking about being skin and bones. I had sores all over my body. It became difficult to move. I wasn't too good to eat from a garbage can. I ate the parts others wouldn't eat. If you helped yourself, you could survive. I took whatever I could find. I ate things I wouldn't tell you about.

"Even at the worst times, there were good people, too. Someone taught me to tie the ends of my pants so I could fill the legs with any potatoes I was able to steal. I walked miles and miles like that, because you never knew when you would be lucky again. Someone gave me a little rice, once, and I traveled two days to a market and traded it for some soap, and then traveled to another market and traded the soap for some beans. You had to have luck and intuition.

"The worst it got was near the end. A lot of people died right at the end, and I didn't know if I could make it another day. A farmer, a Russian, God bless him, he saw my condition, and he went into his house and came out with a piece of meat for me."

"He saved your life."

"I didn't eat it."

"You didn't eat it?"

"It was pork. I wouldn't eat pork."

"Why?"

"What do you mean why?"

"What, because it wasn't kosher?"

"Of course."

"But not even to save your life?"

"If nothing matters, there's nothing to save."

The Way We Age Now

Atul Gawande

The hardest substance in the human body is the white enamel of the teeth. With age, it wears away nonetheless, allowing the softer, darker layers underneath to show through. Meanwhile, the blood supply to the pulp and the roots of the teeth atrophies, and the flow of saliva diminishes; the gums tend to become inflamed and pull away from the teeth, exposing the base, making them unstable and elongating their appearance, especially the lower ones. Experts say they can gauge a person's age to within five years from the examination of a single tooth—if the person has any teeth left to examine.

Scrupulous dental care can help avert tooth loss, but growing old gets in the way. Arthritis, tremors, and small strokes, for example, make it difficult to brush and floss, and, because nerves become less sensitive with age, people may not realize that they have cavity and gum problems until it's too late. In the course of a normal lifetime, the muscles of the jaw lose about forty per cent of their mass and the bones of the mandible lose about twenty per cent, becoming porous and weak. The ability to chew declines, and people shift to softer foods, which are generally higher in fermentable carbohydrates and more likely to cause cavities. By the age of sixty, Americans have lost, on average, a third of their teeth. After eighty-five, almost forty per cent have no teeth at all.

Even as our bones and teeth soften, the rest of our body hardens. Blood vessels, joints, the muscle and valves of the heart, and even the lungs pick up substantial deposits of calcium and turn stiff. Under a microscope, the vessels and soft tissues display the same form of calcium that you find in bone. When you reach inside an elderly patient during surgery, the aorta and other major vessels often feel crunchy under your fingers. A recent study has found that loss of bone density may be an even better predictor of death from atherosclerotic disease than cholesterol levels. As we age, it's as if the calcium flows out of our skeletons and into our tissues.

To maintain the same volume of blood flow through narrowed and stiffened blood vessels, the heart has to generate increased pressure. As a result, more than half of us develop hypertension by the age of sixty-five. The heart becomes thicker-walled from having to pump against the pressure, and less able to respond to the demands of exertion. The peak output of the heart decreases steadily from the age of thirty. People become gradually less able to run as far or as fast as they used to, or to climb a flight of stairs without becoming short of breath.

Why we age is the subject of vigorous debate. The classical view is that aging happens because of random wear and tear. A newer view holds that aging is more orderly and genetically driven. Proponents of this view point out that animals of similar species and exposure to wear and tear have markedly different life spans. The Canada goose has a longevity of 23.5 years; the emperor goose only 6.3 years. Perhaps animals are like plants, with lives that are, to a large extent, internally governed. Certain species of bamboo, for instance, form a dense stand that grows and flourishes for a hundred years, flowers all at once, and then dies.

The idea that living things shut down and not just wear down has received substantial support in the past decade. Researchers working with the now famous worm *C. elegans* (two of the last five Nobel Prizes in medicine went to scientists doing work on the little nematode) were able to produce worms that live more than twice as long and age more slowly by altering a single gene. Scientists have since come up with single-gene alterations that increase the life spans of *Drosophila* fruit flies, mice, and yeast.

These findings notwithstanding, scientists do not believe that our life spans are actually programmed into us. After all, for most of our hundred-thousand-year existence—all but the past couple of hundred years—the average life span of human beings has been thirty years or less. (Research suggests that subjects of the Roman Empire had an average life expectancy of twenty-eight years.) Today, the average life span in developed countries is almost eighty years. If human life spans depend on our genetics, then medicine has got the upper hand. We are, in a way, freaks living well beyond our appointed time. So when we study aging what we are trying to understand is not so much a natural process as an unnatural one. Inheritance has surprisingly little influence on longevity. James Vaupel, of the Max Planck Institute for Demographic Research, in Rostock, Germany, notes that only six per cent of how long you'll live, compared with the average, is explained by your parents' longevity; by contrast, up to ninety per cent of how tall you are, compared with the average, is explained by your parents' height. Even genetically identical twins vary widely in life span: the typical gap is more than fifteen years.

If our genes explain less than we imagined, the wear-and-tear model may explain more than we knew. Leonid Gavrilov, a researcher at the University of Chicago, argues that human beings fail the way all complex systems fail: randomly and gradually. As engineers have long recognized, many simple devices do not age. They function reliably until a critical component fails, and the whole thing dies instantly. A windup toy works smoothly until a gear rusts or a spring breaks, and then it doesn't work at all. But complex systems—power plants, say—have to survive and function despite having thousands of critical components. Engineers therefore design these machines with multiple layers of redundancy: with backup systems, and backup systems for the backup systems. The backups may not be as efficient as the first-line components, but they allow the machine to keep going even as damage accumulates. Gavrilov argues that, within the parameters established by our genes, that's exactly how human beings appear to work. We have an extra kidney, an extra lung, an extra gonad, extra teeth. The DNA in our cells is frequently damaged under routine conditions, but our cells have a number of DNA repair systems. If a key gene is permanently damaged, there are usually extra copies of the gene nearby. And, if the entire cell dies, other cells can fill in.

Nonetheless, as the defects in a complex system increase, the time comes when just one more defect is enough to impair the whole, resulting in the condition known as frailty. It happens to power plants, cars, and large organizations. And it happens to us: eventually, one too many joints are damaged, one too many arteries calcify. There are no more backups. We wear down until we can't wear down anymore.

It happens in a bewildering array of ways. Hair grows gray, for instance, simply because we run out of the pigment cells that give hair its color. The natural life cycle of the scalp's pigment cells is just a few years. We rely on stem cells under the surface to migrate in and replace them. Gradually, however, the stem-cell reservoir is used up. By the age of fifty, as a result, half of the average person's hairs have gone gray.

Inside skin cells, the mechanisms that clear out waste products slowly break down and the muck coalesces into a clot of gooey yellow-brown pigment known as lipofuscin. These are the age spots we see in skin. When lipofuscin accumulates in sweat glands, the sweat glands cannot function, which helps explain why we become so susceptible to heat stroke and heat exhaustion in old age.

The eyes go for different reasons. The lens is made of crystallin proteins that are tremendously durable, but they change chemically in ways that diminish their elasticity over time—hence the farsightedness that most people develop beginning in their fourth decade. The process also gradually yellows the lens.

Even without cataracts (the whitish clouding of the lens caused by excessive ultraviolet exposure, high cholesterol, diabetes, cigarette smoking, and other unhelpful conditions), the amount of light reaching the retina of a healthy sixty-year-old is one-third that of a twenty-year-old.

I spoke to Felix Silverstone, who for twenty-four years was the senior geriatrician at the Parker Jewish Institute, in New York, and has published more than a hundred studies on aging. There is, he said, "no single, common cellular mechanism to the aging process." Our bodies accumulate lipofuscin and oxygen free-radical damage and random DNA mutations and numerous other microcellular problems. The process is gradual and unrelenting. "We just fall apart," he said.

This is not an appealing prospect, and people naturally prefer to avoid the subject of their decrepitude. There have been dozens of best-selling books on aging, but they tend to have titles like "Younger Next Year," "The Fountain of Age," "Ageless," "The Sexy Years." Still, there are costs to averting our eyes from the realities. For one thing, we put off changes that we need to make as a society. For another, we deprive ourselves of opportunities to change the individual experience of aging for the better.

For nearly all of human existence, people died young. Life expectancy improved as we overcame early death—in particular, deaths from childbirth, infection, and traumatic injury. By the nineteen-seventies, just four out of every hundred people born in industrialized countries died before the age of thirty. It was an extraordinary achievement, but one that seemed to leave little room for further gain; even *eliminating* deaths before thirty would not raise over-all life expectancy significantly. Efforts shifted, therefore, to reducing deaths during middle and old age, and, in the decades since, the average life span has continued upward. Improvements in the treatment and prevention of heart disease, respiratory illness, stroke, cancer, and the like mean that the average sixty-five-year-old can expect to live another nineteen years—almost four years longer than was the case in 1970. (By contrast, from the nineteenth century to 1970, sixty-five-year-olds gained just three years of life expectancy.)

The result has been called the "rectangularization" of survival. Throughout most of human history, a society's population formed a sort of pyramid: young children represented the largest portion—the base—and each successively older cohort represented a smaller and smaller group. In 1950, children under the age of five were eleven per cent of the U.S. population, adults aged forty-five to forty-nine were six per cent, and those over eighty were one per cent. Today, we have as many fifty-year-olds as five-year-olds. In thirty years, there will be as many people over eighty as there are under five.

Americans haven't come to grips with the new demography. We cling to the notion of retirement at sixty-five—a reasonable notion when those over sixty-five were a tiny percentage of the population, but completely untenable as they approach twenty per cent. People are putting aside less in savings for old age now than they have in any decade since the Great Depression. More than half of the very old now live without a spouse, and we have fewer children than ever before—yet we give virtually no thought to how we will live out our later years alone.

Equally worrying, and far less recognized, medicine has been slow to confront the very changes that it has been responsible for—or to apply the knowledge we already have about how to make old age better. Despite a rapidly growing elderly population, the number of certified geriatricians fell by a third between 1998 and 2004. Applications to training programs in adult primary-care medicine are plummeting, while fields like plastic surgery and radiology receive applications in record numbers. Partly, this has to do with money—incomes in geriatrics and adult primary care are among the lowest in medicine. And partly, whether we admit it or not, most doctors don't like taking care of the elderly.

"Mainstream doctors are turned off by geriatrics, and that's because they do not have the faculties to cope with the Old Crock," Felix Silverstone, the geriatrician, explained to me. "The Old Crock is deaf. The Old Crock has poor vision. The Old Crock's memory might be somewhat impaired. With the Old Crock, you have to slow down, because he asks you to repeat what you are saying or asking. And the Old Crock doesn't just have a chief complaint—the Old Crock has fifteen chief complaints. How in the world are you going to cope with all of them? You're overwhelmed. Besides, he's had a number of these things for fifty years or so. You're not going to cure something he's had for fifty years. He has high blood pressure. He has diabetes. He has arthritis. There's nothing glamorous about taking care of any of those things."

There is, however, a skill to it, a developed body of professional expertise. And until I visited my hospital's geriatrics clinic and saw the work that geriatricians do, I did not fully grasp the nature of that expertise, or how important it could be for all of us.

The geriatrics clinic—or, as my hospital calls it, the Center for Older Adult Health—is only one floor below my surgery clinic. I pass by it almost every day, and I can't remember ever giving it a moment's thought. One morning, however, I wandered downstairs and, with the permission of the patients, sat in on a few visits with Juergen Bludau, the chief geriatrician.

"What brings you here today?" the doctor asked Jean Gavrilles, his first patient of the morning. She was eighty-five years old, with short, frizzy white hair, oval glasses, a lavender knit shirt, and a sweet, ready smile. Small but sturdy in appearance, she had come in walking steadily, her purse and coat clutched under one arm, her daughter trailing behind her, no support required beyond her mauve orthopedic shoes. She said that her internist had recommended that she come.

About anything in particular? the doctor asked.

The answer, it seemed, was yes and no. The first thing she mentioned was a lower-back pain that she'd had for months, which shot down her leg and sometimes made it difficult to get out of bed or up from a chair. She also had bad arthritis, and she showed us her fingers, which were swollen at the knuckles and bent out to the sides with what's called a swan-neck deformity. She'd had both knees replaced a decade earlier. She had high blood pressure "from stress," she said, and handed him her list of medications. She had glaucoma and needed to have eye exams every four months. She never used to have "bathroom problems," but lately, she admitted, she'd started wearing a pad. She'd also had surgery for colon cancer and, by the way, now had a lung nodule that the radiology report said could be a metastasis—a biopsy was recommended.

Bludau asked her to tell him about her life. She said that she lived alone, except for her Yorkshire terrier, in a single-family house in the West Roxbury section of Boston. Her husband died of lung cancer twenty-three years ago. She did not drive. She had a son living in the area who did her shopping once a week and checked on her each day—"just to see if I'm still alive," she joked. Another son and two daughters lived farther away, but they helped as well. Otherwise, she took care of herself quite capably. She did her own cooking and cleaning. She managed her medicines and her bills. "I have a system," she said. She had a high-school education, and during the war she'd worked as a riveter at the Charlestown Navy Yard. She also worked for a time at the Jordan Marsh department store in downtown Boston. But that was a long time ago. She stuck to home now, with her yard and her terrier and her family when they visited.

The doctor asked her about her day in great detail. She usually woke around five or six o'clock, she said—she didn't seem to need much sleep anymore. She would get out of bed as the back pain allowed, take a shower, and get dressed. Downstairs, she'd take her medicines, feed the dog, and eat breakfast. Bludau asked what she had for breakfast. Cereal and a banana. She hated bananas, she said, but she'd heard they were good for her potassium, so she was afraid to stop. After breakfast, she'd take her dog for a little walk in the yard. She did chores—laundry, cleaning, and the like. In the late morning, she took a break to watch "The Price Is Right." At lunchtime, she had a sandwich and orange juice. If the weather was nice, she'd sit out in the yard afterward. She'd loved working in her garden, but she couldn't do that anymore. The afternoons were slow. She might do some more chores. She might nap or talk on the phone. Eventually, she would make dinner—a salad and maybe a baked potato or a scrambled egg. At night, she watched the Red Sox or the Patriots or college basketball—she loved sports. She usually went to bed at about midnight.

Bludau asked her to sit on the examining table. As she struggled to climb up, her balance teetering on the step, the doctor held her arm. He checked her blood pressure, which was normal. He examined her eyes and ears and had her open her mouth. He listened to her heart and lungs briskly, through his stethoscope. He began to slow down only when he looked at her hands. The nails were neatly trimmed.

"Who cuts your nails?" he asked.

"I do," Gavrilles replied.

I tried to think what could be accomplished in this visit. She was in good condition for her age, but she faced everything from advancing arthritis and incontinence to what might be metastatic colon cancer. It seemed to me that, with just a forty-minute visit, Bludau needed to triage by zeroing in on either the most potentially life-threatening problem (the possible metastasis) or the problem that bothered her the most (the back pain). But this was evidently not what he thought. He asked almost nothing about either issue. Instead, he spent much of the exam looking at her feet.

"Is that really necessary?" she asked, when he instructed her to take off her shoes and socks.

"Yes," he said. After she'd left, he told me, "You must always examine the feet." He described a bow-tied gentleman who seemed dapper and fit, until his feet revealed the truth: he couldn't bend down to reach them, and they turned out not to have been cleaned in weeks, suggesting neglect and real danger.

Gavrilles had difficulty taking her shoes off, and, after watching her struggle a bit, Bludau leaned in to help. When he got her socks off, he took her feet in his hands, one at a time. He inspected them inch by inch—the soles, the toes, the web spaces. Then he helped her get her socks and shoes back on and gave her and her daughter his assessment.

She was doing impressively well, he said. She was mentally sharp and physically strong. The danger for her was losing what she had. The single most serious threat she faced was not the lung nodule or the back pain. It was falling. Each year, about three hundred and fifty thousand Americans fall and break a hip. Of those, forty per cent end up in a nursing home, and twenty per cent are never able to walk again. The three primary risk factors for falling are poor balance, taking more than four prescription medications, and muscle weakness. Elderly people without these risk factors have a twelve-per-cent chance of falling in a year. Those with all three risk factors have almost a hundred-per-cent chance. Jean Gavrilles had at least two. Her balance was poor. Though she didn't need a walker, he had noticed her splay-footed gait as she came in. Her feet were swollen. The toenails were unclipped. There were sores between the toes. And the balls of her feet had thick, rounded calluses.

She was also on five medications. Each was undoubtedly useful, but, together, the usual side effects would include dizziness. In addition, one of the blood-pressure medications was a diuretic, and she seemed to drink few liquids, risking dehydration and a worsening of the dizziness. Her tongue was bone dry when Bludau examined it.

She did not have significant muscle weakness, and that was good. When she got out of her chair, he said, he noted that she had not used her arms to push herself up. She simply stood up—a sign of well-preserved muscle strength. From the details of the day she described, however, she did not seem to be eating nearly enough calories to maintain that strength. Bludau asked her whether her weight had changed recently. She admitted that she had lost about seven pounds in the previous six months.

The job of any doctor, Bludau later told me, is to support quality of life, by which he meant two things: as much freedom from the ravages of disease as possible, and the retention of enough function for active engagement in the world. Most doctors treat disease, and figure that the rest will take care of itself. And if it doesn't—if a patient is becoming infirm and heading toward a nursing home—well, that isn't really a *medical* problem, is it?

To a geriatrician, though, it *is* a medical problem. People can't stop the aging of their bodies and minds, but there are ways to make it more manageable, and to avert at least some of the worst effects. So Bludau referred Gavrilles to a podiatrist, whom he wanted her to visit once every four weeks, for better care of her feet. He didn't see medications that he could eliminate, but he switched her diuretic to a blood-pressure medicine that wouldn't cause dehydration. He recommended that she eat a snack during the day, get all the low-calorie and low-cholesterol food out of the house, and see whether family or friends could join her for more meals. "Eating alone is not very stimulating," he said. And he asked her to see him again in three months, so that he could make sure the plan was working.

Nine months later, I checked in with Gavrilles and her daughter. She turned eighty-six this past November. She is eating better, and has even gained a pound or two. She still lives comfortably and independently in her own home. And she has not had a single fall.

In the story of Jean Gavrilles and her geriatrician, there's a lesson about frailty. Decline remains our fate; death will come. But, until that last backup system inside each of us fails, decline can occur in two ways. One is early and precipitately, with an old age of enfeeblement and dependence, sustained primarily by nursing homes and hospitals. The other way is more gradual, preserving, for as long as possible, your ability to control your own life.

Good medical care can influence which direction a person's old age will take. Most of us in medicine, however, don't know how to think about decline. We're good at addressing specific, individual problems: colon cancer, high blood pressure, arthritic knees. Give us a disease, and we can do something about it. But give us an elderly woman with colon cancer, high blood pressure, arthritic knees, and various other ailments besides—an elderly woman at risk of losing the life she enjoys—and we are not sure what to do.

Several years ago, researchers in St. Paul, Minnesota, identified five hundred and sixty-eight men and women over the age of seventy who were living independently but were at high risk of becoming disabled because of chronic health problems, recent illness, or cognitive changes. With their permission, the researchers randomly assigned half of them to see a team of geriatric specialists. The others were asked to see their usual physician, who was notified of their high-risk status. Within eighteen months, ten per cent of the patients in both groups had died. But the patients who had seen a geriatrics team were a third less likely to become disabled and half as likely to develop depression. They were forty per cent less likely to require home health services.

Little of what the geriatricians had done was high-tech medicine: they didn't do lung biopsies or back surgery or PET scans. Instead, they simplified medications. They saw that arthritis was controlled. They made sure toenails were trimmed and meals were square. They looked for worrisome signs of isolation and had a social worker check that the patient's home was safe.

How do we reward this kind of work? Chad Boult, who was the lead investigator of the St. Paul study and a geriatrician at the University of Minnesota, can tell you. A few months after he published his study, demonstrating how much better people's lives were with specialized geriatric care, the university closed the division of geriatrics.

"The university said that it simply could not sustain the financial losses," Boult said from Baltimore, where he is now a professor at the Johns Hopkins Bloomberg School of Public Health. On average, in Boult's study, the geriatric services cost the hospital $1,350 more per person than the savings they produced, and Medicare, the insurer for the elderly, does not cover that cost. It's a strange double standard. No one insists that a twenty-five-thousand-dollar pacemaker or a coronary-artery stent save money for insurers. It just has to *maybe* do people some good. Meanwhile, the twenty-plus members of the proven geriatrics team at the University of Minnesota had to find new jobs. Scores of medical centers across the country have shrunk or closed their geriatrics units. Several of Boult's colleagues no longer advertise their geriatric training for fear that they'll get too many elderly patients. "Economically, it has become too difficult," Boult said.

But the finances are only a symptom of a deeper reality: people have not insisted on a change in priorities. We all like new medical gizmos and demand that policymakers make sure they are paid for. They feed our hope that the troubles of the body can be fixed for good. But geriatricians? Who clamors for geriatricians? What geriatricians do—bolster our resilience in old age, our capacity to weather what comes—is both difficult and unappealingly limited. It requires attention to the body and its alterations. It requires vigilance over nutrition, medications, and living situations. And it requires each of us to contemplate the course of our decline, in order to make the small changes that can reshape it. When the prevailing fantasy is that we can be ageless, the geriatrician's uncomfortable demand is that we accept we are not.

For Felix Silverstone, understanding human aging has been the work of a lifetime. He was a national leader in geriatrics for five decades. But he is now himself eighty-seven years old. He can feel his own mind and body wearing down, and much of what he spent his career studying is no longer abstract to him.

Felix has been fortunate. He didn't have to stop working, even after he suffered a heart attack in his sixties which cost him half his heart function; nor was he stopped by a near-cardiac arrest at the age of seventy-nine. "One evening, sitting at home, I suddenly became aware of palpitations," he told me. "I was just reading, and a few minutes later I became short of breath. A little bit after that, I began to feel heavy in the chest. I took my pulse, and it was over two hundred." He is the sort of person who, in the midst of chest pain, would take the opportunity to examine his own pulse. "My wife and I had a little discussion about whether or not to call an ambulance. We decided to call."

When Felix got to the hospital, the doctors had to shock him to bring his heart back. He'd had ventricular fibrillation, and an automatic defibrillator had to be installed in his chest. Within a few weeks, though, he felt well again, and his doctor cleared him to return to work full time. He stayed in medical practice after the attack, multiple hernia repairs, gallbladder surgery, arthritis that ended his avid piano playing, compression fractures of his aging spine that stole three full inches of his once five-foot-seven-inch height, and hearing loss. "I switched to an electronic stethoscope," he said. "They're a nuisance, but they're very good."

Finally, at eighty-two, he had to retire. The problem wasn't his health; it was that of his wife, Bella. They'd been married for more than sixty years. Felix had met Bella when he was an intern and she was a dietitian at Kings County Hospital, in Brooklyn. They brought up two sons in Flatbush. When the boys left home, Bella got her teaching certification and began working with children who had learning disabilities. In her seventies, however, retinal disease diminished her vision, and she had to stop working. A decade later, she became almost completely blind. Felix no longer felt safe leaving her at home alone, and in 2001 he gave up his practice. They moved to Orchard Cove, a retirement community in Canton, Massachusetts, outside Boston, where they could be closer to their sons.

"I didn't think I would survive the change," Felix said. He'd observed in his patients how difficult the transitions of age could be. Examining his last patient, packing up his home, he felt that he was about to die. "I was taking apart my life as well as the house," he recalled. "It was terrible."

We were sitting in a library off Orchard Cove's main lobby. There was light streaming through a picture window, tasteful art on the walls, white-upholstered Federal-style armchairs. It was like a nice hotel, only with no one under seventy-five walking around. Felix and Bella have a two-bedroom apartment with forest views and plenty of space. In the living room, he has his grand piano and, at his desk, piles of medical journals that he still subscribes to—"for my soul," he said. Theirs is an independent-living unit. It comes with housekeeping, linen changes, and dinner each evening. When they need to, they can upgrade to assisted living, which provides three prepared meals and up to an hour with a personal-care assistant each day.

This was not the average retirement community, but even in an average one rent runs thirty-two thousand dollars a year. Entry fees are typically sixty thousand to a hundred and twenty thousand dollars on top of that. Meanwhile, the median income of people eighty and older is only about fifteen thousand dollars. More than half of the elderly who live in long-term-care facilities go through their entire savings and have to go on Medicaid—welfare—in order to afford it. And, ultimately, the average American spends a year or more of his old age disabled and living in a nursing home (at twice the cost), which is a destination Felix desperately hopes to avoid.

He tries to note the changes he's experiencing objectively, like a good geriatrician. He notices that his skin has dried out. His sense of smell has diminished. His night vision has become poor. He tires easily. He has begun to lose teeth. He takes measures where he can. He uses lotion to avoid skin cracks; he protects himself from the heat; he gets on an exercise bike three times a week; he sees a dentist twice a year.

He's most concerned about the changes in his brain. "I can't think as clearly as I used to," he said. "I used to be able to read the *Times* in half an hour. Now it takes me an hour and a half." Even then, he's not sure that he has understood as much as he did before, and his memory gives him trouble. "If I go back and look at what I've read, I recognize that I went through it, but sometimes I don't really remember it," he said. "It's a matter of short-term registration. It's hard to get the signal in and have it stay put."

He makes use of methods that he once taught his patients. "I try to deliberately focus on what I'm doing, rather than do it automatically," he told me. "I haven't lost the automaticity of action, but I can't rely on it the way I used to. For example, I can't think about something else and get dressed and be sure I've gotten all the way dressed." He recognizes that the strategy doesn't always work. He sometimes told me the same story twice in a conversation. The lines of thought in his mind would fall into well-worn grooves and, however hard he tried to put them onto a new path, sometimes they resisted. Felix's knowledge as a geriatrician has forced him to recognize his own decline, but that hasn't made it easier to accept.

"I get blue occasionally," he said. "I think I have recurring episodes of depression. They are not enough to disable me, but they are . . ." He paused to find the right word. "They are uncomfortable."

What buoys him, despite his limitations, is having a purpose. It's the same purpose, he says, that sustained him in medicine: to be of service, in some way, to those around him. He had been in Orchard Cove for only a few months before he was helping to steer a committee to improve the health-care services there. He tried to form a journal-reading club for retired physicians. He even guided a young geriatrician through her first independent-research study—a survey of the residents' attitudes toward Do Not Resuscitate orders.

More important is the responsibility that he feels for his children and grandchildren—and, most of all, for Bella. Her blindness and recent memory troubles have made her deeply dependent. Without him, I suspect, she would probably be in a nursing home. He helps her dress. He administers her medicines. He makes her breakfast and lunch. He takes her on walks and to doctors' appointments. "She is my purpose now," he said. Bella doesn't always like his way of doing things. "We argue constantly—we're at each other about a lot of things," Felix said. "But we're also very forgiving."

He does not feel this responsibility to be a burden. With the narrowing of his own life, his ability to look after Bella has become his main source of self-worth. "I am exclusively her caregiver," he said. "I am glad to be." And this role has heightened his sense that he must be attentive to the changes in his own capabilities; he is no good to her if he isn't honest with himself about what he can and can't do.

One evening, Felix invited me to dinner. The formal dining hall was restaurant-like, with reserved seating, table service, and jackets required. I was wearing my white hospital coat and had to borrow a navy blazer from the maitre d'. Felix, in a brown suit and a stone-colored oxford shirt, gave his arm to Bella, who wore a blue-flowered knee-length dress that he'd picked out for her, and guided her to the table. She was amiable and chatty and had youthful-seeming eyes. But, once she'd been seated, she couldn't find the plate in front of her, let alone the menu. Felix ordered for her: wild-rice soup, an omelette, mashed potatoes, and mashed cauliflower. "No salt," he instructed the waiter; she had high blood pressure. He ordered salmon and mashed potatoes for himself. I had the soup and a London broil.

When the food arrived, Felix told Bella where she could find the different items on her plate by the hands of a clock. He put a fork in her hand. Then he turned to his own meal.

Both made a point of chewing slowly. She was the first to choke. It was the omelette. Her eyes watered. She began to cough. Felix guided her water glass to her mouth. She took a drink and managed to get the omelette down.

"As you get older, the lordosis of your spine tips your head forward," he said to me. "So when you look straight ahead it's like looking up at the ceiling for anyone else. Try to swallow while looking up: you'll choke once in a while. The problem is common in the elderly. Listen." I realized that I could hear someone in the dining room choking on his food every minute or so. Felix turned to Bella. "You have to eat looking down, sweetie," he said.

A couple of bites later, though, he himself was choking. It was the salmon. He began coughing. He turned red. Finally, he was able to cough up the bite. It took a minute for him to catch his breath. "Didn't follow my own advice," he said.

Felix Silverstone is, without question, up against the debilities of his years. Once, it would have been remarkable simply to have lived to see eighty-seven. Now what's remarkable is that he has the control over his life that he does. When he started in geriatric practice, it was almost inconceivable that an eighty-seven-year-old with his history of health problems could live independently, care for his disabled wife, and continue to contribute to research. Even today, most people his age cannot live as he does.

Partly, he has been lucky. His memory, for example, has not deteriorated significantly. But he has also managed his old age well. His goal has been modest: to have as decent a life as medical knowledge and the limits of his body will allow. So he saved and did not retire early, and therefore is not in financial straits. He kept his social contacts, and avoided isolation. He monitored his bones and teeth and weight. And he has made sure to find a doctor who had the geriatric skills to help him hold on to an independent life.

I asked Chad Boult, the geriatrics professor now at Johns Hopkins, what can be done to insure that there are enough geriatricians for our country's surging elderly population. "Nothing," he said. "It's too late." Creating geriatricians takes years, and we already have far too few. This year, just three hundred doctors will complete geriatrics training, not nearly enough to replace the geriatricians going into retirement, let alone meet the needs of the next decade.

Yet Boult believes that we still have time for another strategy: he would direct geriatricians toward training all primary-care doctors in caring for the very old, instead of providing the care themselves. Even this is a tall order—ninety-seven per cent of medical students take no course in geriatrics, and the strategy requires that the nation pay geriatricians to teach rather than to provide patient care. But, if the will is there, Boult estimates that it would be possible to establish courses in every medical school and internal-medicine training program within a decade. "We've got to do something," he said. "Life for older people can be better than it is today."

Boult and his colleagues have yet another strategy, just in case—a strategy that they have called Guided Care, and that doesn't depend on doctors at all. They're recruiting local nurses for a highly compressed, three-week course in how to recognize specific problems in the elderly, such as depression, malnutrition, isolation, and danger of falling; how to formulate a plan to remedy those problems; and how to work with patients, families, and doctors to follow through on the plan. In a test of the strategy, the researchers are putting the nurses to work in primary-care practices around Baltimore and Washington, D.C., and studying the results. It is a meagre solution for a huge problem, but it is cheap, which insurers demand, and, if it provides even a fraction of the benefit geriatricians have, it could nudge medical care in the right direction.

"I can still drive, you know," Felix Silverstone said to me. "I'm a very good driver."

After our dinner together, he had to go on an errand to refill Bella's prescriptions in Stoughton, a few miles away, and I asked if I could go along. He had a gold 1998 Toyota Camry with automatic transmission and thirty-nine thousand miles on the odometer. It was pristine, inside and out. He backed out of a narrow parking space and zipped out of the garage. His hands did not shake. Taking the streets of Canton at dusk on a new-moon night, he brought the car to an even stop at the red lights, signalled when he was supposed to, took turns without a hitch.

I was, I admit, braced for disaster. The risk of a fatal car crash with a driver who's eighty-five or older is more than three times higher than it is with a driver between sixteen and twenty. The very old are the highest-risk drivers on the road. This past fall, in Los Angeles, George Weller was convicted of manslaughter after he confused the accelerator with the brake pedal and plowed his Buick into a crowd of shoppers at the Santa Monica Farmers' Market. Ten people were killed, and more than sixty were injured. He was eighty-six.

But Felix showed no difficulties. At one point during our drive, poorly marked road construction at an intersection channelled our line of cars almost directly into oncoming traffic. Felix corrected course swiftly, pulling over into the proper lane. There is no saying how much longer he will be able to count on his driving ability. The day may well come when he will have to give up his keys.

At the moment, though, he wasn't concerned; he was glad simply to be on the road. The evening traffic was thin as he turned onto Route 138. He brought the Camry to a tick over the forty-five-mile-per-hour speed limit. He had his window rolled down and his elbow on the sash. The air was clear and cool, and we listened to the sound of the wheels on the pavement.

"The night is lovely, isn't it?" he said.

Group Think

What Does "Saturday Night Live" Have in Common with German Philosophy?

Malcolm Gladwell

Lorne Michaels, the creator of "Saturday Night Live," was married to one of the show's writers, Rosie Shuster. One day when the show was still young, an assistant named Paula Davis went to Shuster's apartment in New York and found Dan Aykroyd getting out of her bed—which was puzzling, not just because Shuster was married to Michaels but because Aykroyd was supposedly seeing another member of the original "S.N.L." cast, Laraine Newman. Aykroyd and Gilda Radner had also been an item, back when the two of them worked for the Second City comedy troupe in Toronto, although by the time they got to New York they were just friends, in the way that everyone was friends with Radner. Second City was also where Aykroyd met John Belushi, because Belushi, who was a product of the Second City troupe in Chicago, came to Toronto to recruit for the "National Lampoon Radio Hour," which he starred in along with Radner and Bill Murray (who were also an item for a while). The writer Michael O'Donoghue (who famously voiced his aversion to the appearance of the Muppets on "S.N.L." by saying, "I don't write for felt") also came from *The National Lampoon*, as did another of the original writers, Anne Beatts (who was, in the impeccably ingrown logic of "S.N.L.," living with O'Donoghue). Chevy Chase came from a *National Lampoon* spinoff called "Lemmings," which also starred Belushi, doing his legendary Joe Cocker impersonation. Lorne Michaels hired Belushi after Radner, among others, insisted on it, and he hired Newman because he had worked with her on a Lily Tomlin special, and he hired Aykroyd because Michaels was also from Canada and knew him from the comedy scene there. When Aykroyd got the word, he came down from Toronto on his Harley.

In the early days of "S.N.L.," as Tom Shales and James Andrew Miller tell us in "Live from New York" (Little, Brown; $25.95), everyone knew everyone and everyone was always in everyone else's business, and that fact goes a long way toward explaining the extraordinary chemistry among the show's cast. Belushi would stay overnight at people's apartments, and he was notorious for getting hungry in the middle of the night and leaving spaghetti-sauce imprints all over the kitchen, or setting fires by falling asleep with a lit joint. Radner would go to Jane Curtin's house and sit and watch Curtin and her husband, as if they were some strange species of mammal, and say things like "Oh, now you are going to turn the TV on together. How will you decide what to watch?" Newman would hang out at Radner's house, and Radner would be eating a gallon of ice cream and Newman would be snorting heroin. Then Radner would go to the bathroom to make herself vomit, and say, "I'm so full, I can't hear." And they would laugh. "There we were," Newman recalls, "practicing our illnesses together."

The place where they all really lived, though, was the "S.N.L." office, on the seventeenth floor of NBC headquarters, at Rockefeller Center. The staff turned it into a giant dormitory, installing bunk beds and fooling around in the dressing rooms and staying up all night. Monday night was the first meeting, where ideas were pitched. On Tuesday, the writing started after dinner and continued straight through the night. The first read-through took place on Wednesday at three in the afternoon. And then came blocking and rehearsals and revisions. "It was emotional," the writer Alan Zweibel tells Shales and Miller. "We were a colony. I don't mean this in a bad way, but we were Guyana on the seventeenth floor. We didn't go out. We stayed there. It was a stalag of some sort." Rosie Shuster remembers waking up at the office and then going outside with Aykroyd, to "walk each other like dogs around 30 Rock just to get a little fresh air." On Saturdays, after the taping was finished, the cast would head downtown to a storefront that Belushi and Aykroyd had rented and dubbed the Blues Bar. It was a cheerless dive, with rats and crumbling walls and peeling paint and the filthiest toilets in all of New York. But did anyone care? "It was the end of the week and, well, you were psyched," Shuster recalls. "It was like you were buzzing, you'd get turbocharged from the intense effort of it, and then there's like adrenal burnout later. I remember sleeping at the Blues Bar, you know, as the light broke." Sometimes it went even later. "I remember rolling down the armor at the Blues Bar and closing the building at eleven o'clock Sunday morning—you know, when it was at its height—and saying good morning to the cops and firemen," Aykroyd said. "S.N.L." was a television show, but it was also an adult fraternity house, united by bonds of drugs and sex and long hours and emotion and affection that went back years. "The only entrée to that boys club was basically by fucking somebody in the club," Anne Beatts tells Shales and Miller. "Which wasn't the reason you were fucking them necessarily. I mean, you didn't go 'Oh, I want to get into this, I think I'll have to have sex with this person.' It was just that if you were drawn to funny people who were doing interesting things, then the only real way to get to do those things yourself was to make that connection."

We are inclined to think that genuine innovators are loners, that they do not need the social reinforcement the rest of us crave. But that's not how it works, whether it's television comedy or, for that matter, the more exalted realms of art and politics and ideas. In his book "The Sociology of Philosophies," Randall Collins finds in all of known history only three major thinkers who appeared on the scene by themselves: the first-century Taoist metaphysician Wang Ch'ung, the fourteenth-century Zen mystic Bassui Tokusho, and the fourteenth-century Arabic philosopher Ibn Khaldun. Everyone else who mattered was part of a movement, a school, a band of followers and disciples and mentors and rivals and friends who saw each other all the time and had long arguments over coffee and slept with one another's spouses. Freud may have been the founder of psychoanalysis, but it really began to take shape in 1902, when Alfred Adler, Wilhelm Stekel, Max Kahane, and Rudolf Reitler would gather in Freud's waiting room on Wednesdays, to eat strudel and talk about the unconscious. The neo-Confucian movement of the Sung dynasty in China revolved around the brothers Ch'eng Hao and Ch'eng I, their teacher Chou Tun-i, their father's cousin Chang Tsai, and, of course, their neighbor Shao Yung. Pissarro and Degas enrolled in the École des Beaux-Arts at the same time, then Pissarro met Monet and, later, Cézanne at the Académie Suisse, Manet met Degas at the Louvre, Monet befriended Renoir at Charles Gleyre's studio, and Renoir, in turn, met Pissarro and Cézanne and soon enough everyone was hanging out at the Café Guerbois on the Rue des Batignolles. Collins's point is not that innovation attracts groups but that innovation is found in groups: that it tends to arise out of social interaction—conversation, validation, the intimacy of proximity, and the look in your listener's eye that tells you you're onto something. German Idealism, he notes, centered on Fichte, Schelling, and Hegel. Why? Because they all lived together in the same house. "Fichte takes the early lead," Collins writes,

> inspiring the others on a visit while they are young students at Tübingen in the 1790s, then turning Jena into a center for the philosophical movement to which a stream of the soon-to-be-eminent congregate; then on to Dresden in the heady years 1799–1800 to live with the Romantic circle of the Schlegel brothers (where August Schlegel's wife, Caroline, has an affair with Schelling, followed later by a scandalous divorce and remarriage). Fichte moves on to Berlin, allying with Schleiermacher (also of the Romantic circle) and with Humboldt to establish the new-style university; here Hegel eventually comes and founds his school, and Schopenhauer lectures fruitlessly in competition.

There is a wonderful illustration of this social dimension of innovation in Jenny Uglow's new book, "The Lunar Men" (Farrar, Straus & Giroux; $30), which is the story of a remarkable group of friends in Birmingham in the mid-eighteenth century. Their leader was Erasmus Darwin, a physician, inventor, and scientist, who began thinking about evolution a full fifty years before his grandson Charles. Darwin met, through his medical practice, an industrialist named Mathew Boulton and, later, his partner James Watt, the steam-engine pioneer. They, in turn, got to know Josiah Wedgwood, he of the famous pottery, and Joseph Priestley, the preacher who isolated oxygen and became known as one of history's great chemists, and the industrialist Samuel Galton (whose son married Darwin's daughter and produced the legendary nineteenth-century polymath Francis Galton), and the innovative glass-and-chemicals entrepreneur James Keir, and on and on. They called themselves the Lunar Society because they arranged to meet at each full moon, when they would get together in the early afternoon to eat, piling the table high, Uglow tells us, with wine and "fish and capons, Cheddar and Stilton, pies and syllabubs." Their children played underfoot. Their wives chatted in the other room, and the Lunar men talked well into the night, clearing the table to make room for their models and plans and instruments. "They developed their own cryptic, playful language and Darwin, in particular, liked to phrase things as puzzles—like the charades and poetic word games people used to play," Uglow writes. "Even though they were down-to-earth champions of reason, a part of the delight was to feel they were unlocking esoteric secrets, exploring transmutations like alchemists of old."

When they were not meeting, they were writing to each other with words of encouragement or advice or excitement. This was truly—in a phrase that is invariably and unthinkingly used in the pejorative—a mutual-admiration society. "Their inquiries ranged over the whole spectrum, from astronomy and optics to fossils and ferns," Uglow tells us, and she goes on:

> One person's passion—be it carriages, steam, minerals, chemistry, clocks—fired all the others. There was no neat separation of subjects. Letters between [William] Small and Watt were a kaleidoscope of invention and ideas, touching on steam-engines and cylinders; cobalt as a semi-metal; how to boil down copal, the resin of tropical trees, for varnish; lenses and clocks and colours for enamels; alkali and canals; acids and vapours—as well as the boil on Watt's nose.

What were they doing? Darwin, in a lovely phrase, called it "philosophical laughing," which was his way of saying that those who depart from cultural or intellectual consensus need people to walk beside them and laugh with them to give them confidence. But there's more to it than that. One of the peculiar features of group dynamics is that clusters of people will come to decisions that are far more extreme than any individual member would have come to on his own. People compete with each other and egg each other on, showboat and grandstand; and along the way they often lose sight of what they truly believed when the meeting began. Typically, this is considered a bad thing, because it means that groups formed explicitly to find middle ground often end up someplace far away. But at times this quality turns out to be tremendously productive, because, after all, losing sight of what you truly believed when the meeting began is one way of defining innovation.

Uglow tells us, for instance, that the Lunar men were active in the campaign against slavery. Wedgwood, Watt, and Darwin pushed for the building of canals, to improve transportation. Priestley came up with soda water and the rubber eraser, and James Keir was the man who figured out how to mass-produce soap, eventually building a twenty-acre soapworks in Tipton that produced a million pounds of soap a year. Here, surely, are all the hallmarks of group distortion. Somebody comes up with an ambitious plan for canals, and someone else tries to top that by building a really big soap factory, and in that feverish atmosphere someone else decides to top them all with the idea that what they should really be doing is fighting slavery.

Uglow's book reveals how simplistic our view of groups really is. We divide them into cults and clubs, and dismiss the former for their insularity and the latter for their banality. The cult is the place where, cut off from your peers, you become crazy. The club is the place where, surrounded by your peers, you become boring. Yet if you can combine the best of those two states—the right kind of insularity with the right kind of homogeneity—you create an environment both safe enough and stimulating enough to make great thoughts possible. You get Fichte, Schelling, and Hegel, and a revolution in Western philosophy. You get Darwin, Watt, Wedgwood, and Priestley, and the beginnings of the Industrial Revolution. And sometimes, on a more modest level, you get a bunch of people goofing around and bringing a new kind of comedy to network television.

One of "S.N.L." 's forerunners was a comedy troupe based in San Francisco called the Committee. The Committee's heyday was in the nineteen-sixties, and its humor had the distinctive political bite of that period. In one of the group's memorable sketches, the actor Larry Hankin played a condemned prisoner being led to the electric chair by a warden, a priest, and a prison guard. Hankin was strapped in and the switch was thrown—and nothing happened. Hankin started to become abusive, and the three men huddled briefly together. Then, as Tony Hendra recounts, in "Going Too Far," his history of "boomer humor":

> They confer and throw the switch again. Still nothing. Hankin starts cackling with glee, doubly abusive. They throw it yet again. Nothing yet again.

> Hankin then demands to be set free—he can't be executed more than once, they're a bunch of assholes, double jeopardy, nyah-nyah, etc., etc. Totally desperate, the three confer once more, check that they're alone in the cell, and kick Hankin to death.

Is that sketch funny? Some people thought so. When the Committee performed it at a benefit at the Vacaville prison, in California, the inmates laughed so hard they rioted. But others didn't, and even today it's clear that this humor is funny only to those who can appreciate the particular social and political sensibility of the Committee. We call new cultural or intellectual movements "circles" for a reason: the circle is a closed loop. You are either inside or outside. In "Live from New York," Lorne Michaels describes going to the White House to tape President Ford saying, "Live from New York, it's Saturday Night," the "S.N.L." intro: "We'd done two or three takes, and to relax him, I said to him—my sense of humor at the time—'Mr. President, if this works out, who knows where it will lead?' Which was completely lost on him." In another comic era, the fact that Ford did not laugh would be evidence of the joke's failure. But when Michaels says the joke "was completely lost on him" it isn't a disclaimer—it's the punch line. He said what he said because he knew Ford would not get it. As the writers of "Saturday Night Live" worked on sketches deep into the night, they were sustained by something like what sustained the Lunar men and the idealists in Tübingen—the feeling that they all spoke a private language.

To those on the inside, of course, nothing is funnier than an inside joke. But the real significance of inside jokes is what they mean for those who aren't on the inside. Laughing at a joke creates an incentive to join the joke-teller. But not laughing—not getting the joke—creates an even greater incentive. We all want to know what we're missing, and this is one of the ways that revolutions spread from the small groups that spawn them.

"One of Michaels's rules was, no groveling to the audience either in the studio or at home," Shales and Miller write. "The collective approach of the show's creators could be seen as a kind of arrogance, a stance of defiance that said in effect, 'We think this is funny, and if you don't, you're wrong.' . . . To viewers raised on TV that was forever cajoling, importuning, and talking down to them, the blunt and gutsy approach was refreshing, a virtual reinvention of the medium."

The successful inside joke, however, can never last. In "A Great Silly Grin" (Public Affairs; $27.50), a history of nineteen-sixties British satire, Humphrey Carpenter relates a routine done at the comedy club the Establishment early in the decade. The sketch was about the rebuilt Coventry Cathedral, which had been destroyed in the war, and the speaker was supposed to be the Cathedral's architect, Sir Basil Spence:

> First of all, of course, we owe an enormous debt of gratitude to the German people for making this whole project possible in the first place. Second, we owe a debt of gratitude to the people of Coventry itself, who when asked to choose between having a cathedral and having hospitals, schools and houses, plumped immediately (I'm glad to say) for the cathedral, recognizing, I think, the need of any community to have a place where the whole community can gather together and pray for such things as hospitals, schools and houses.

When that bit was first performed, many Englishmen would have found it offensive. Now, of course, hardly anyone would. Mocking British establishment pieties is no longer an act of rebellion. It is the norm. Successful revolutions contain the seeds of their demise: they attract so many followers, eager to be in on the joke as well, that the circle breaks down. The inside becomes indistinguishable from the outside. The allure of exclusivity is gone.

At the same time, the special bonds that created the circle cannot last forever. Sooner or later, the people who slept together in every combination start to pair off. Those doing drugs together sober up (or die). Everyone starts going to bed at eleven o'clock, and bit by bit the intimacy that fuels innovation slips away. "I was involved with Gilda, yeah. I was in love with her," Aykroyd tells Shales and Miller. "We were friends, lovers, then friends again," and in a way that's the simplest and best explanation for the genius of the original "S.N.L." Today's cast is not less talented. It is simply more professional. "I think some people in the cast have fun crushes on other people, but nothing serious," Cheri Oteri, a cast member from the late nineteen-nineties, tells Shales and Miller, in what might well serve as the show's creative epitaph. "I guess we're kind of boring—no romances, no drugs. I had an audition once with somebody who used to work here. He's very, very big in the business now. And as soon as I went in for the audition, he went, 'Hey, you guys still doing coke over at SNL?' Because back when he was here, they were doing it. What *are* we doing, for crying out loud? Oh yeah. Thinking up characters."

A Story About the Body

Robert Hass

The young composer, working that summer at an artist's colony, had watched her for a week. She was Japanese, a painter, almost sixty, and he thought he was in love with her. He loved her work, and her work was like the way she moved her body, used her hands, looked at him directly when she made amused and considered answers to his questions. One night, walking back from a concert, they came to her door and she turned to him and said, "I think you would like to have me. I would like that too, but I must tell you that I have had a double mastectomy," and when he didn't understand, "I've lost both my breasts." The radiance that he had carried around in his belly and chest cavity—like music—withered very quickly, and he made himself look at her when he said, "I'm sorry. I don't think I could." He walked back to his own cabin through the pines, and in the morning he found a small blue bowl on the porch outside his door. It looked to be full of rose petals, but he found when he picked it up that the rose petals were on top; the rest of the bowl—she must have swept them from the corners of her studio—was full of dead bees.

Politics and the English Language

George Orwell

Most people who bother with the matter at all would admit that the English language is in a bad way, but it is generally assumed that we cannot by conscious action do anything about it. Our civilization is decadent and our languages—so the argument runs—must inevitably share in the general collapse. It follows that any struggle against the abuse of language is a sentimental archaism, like preferring candles to electric light or hansom cabs to aeroplanes. Underneath this lies the half-conscious belief that language is a natural growth and not an instrument which we shape for our own purposes.

Now, it is clear that the decline of a language must ultimately have political and economic causes: it is not due simply to the bad influence of this or that individual writer. But an effect can become a cause, reinforcing the original cause and producing the same effect in an intensified form, and so on indefinitely. A man may take to drink because he feels himself to be a failure, and then fail all the more completely because he drinks. It is rather the same thing that is happening to the English language. It becomes ugly and inaccurate because our thoughts are foolish, but the slovenliness of our language makes it easier for us to have foolish thoughts. The point is that the process is reversible. Modern English, especially written English, is full of bad habits which spread by imitation and which can be avoided if one is willing to take the necessary trouble. If one gets rid of these habits one can think more clearly, and to think clearly is a necessary first step towards political regeneration: so that the fight against bad English is not frivolous and is not the exclusive concern of professional writers. I will come back to this presently, and I hope that by that time the meaning of what I have said here will have become clearer. Meanwhile, here are five specimens of the English language as it is now habitually written.

These five passages have not been picked out because they are especially bad—I could have quoted far worse if I had chosen—but because they illustrate various of the mental vices from which we now suffer. They are a little below the average, but are fairly representative samples. I number them so that I can refer back to them when necessary:

> "(1) I am not, indeed, sure whether it is not true to say that the Milton who once seemed not unlike a seventeenth-century Shelley had not become, out of an experience ever more bitter in each year, more alien [*sic*] to the founder of that Jesuit sect which nothing could induce him to tolerate."
>
> Professor Harold Laski (Essay in *Freedom of Expression*)

> "(2) Above all, we cannot play ducks and drakes with a native battery of idioms which prescribes such egregious collocations of vocables as the Basic *put up with* for *tolerate* or *put at a loss for bewilder.*"
>
> Professor Lancelot Hogben (Interglossa)

> "(3) On the one side we have the free personality: by definition it is not neurotic, for it has neither conflict nor dream. Its desires, such as they are, are transparent, for they are just what institutional approval keeps in the forefront of consciousness; another institutional pattern would alter their number and intensity; there is little in them that is natural, irreducible, or culturally dangerous. But *on the other side,* the social bond itself is nothing but the mutual reflection of these self-secure integrities. Recall the definition of love. Is not this the very picture of a small academic? Where is there a place in this hall of mirrors for either personality or fraternity?"
>
> Essay on psychology in Politics (New York)

> "(4) All the 'best people' from the gentlemen's clubs, and all the frantic fascist captains, united in common hatred of Socialism and bestial horror of the rising tide of the mass revolutionary movement, have turned to acts of provocation, to foul incendiarism, to medieval legends of poisoned wells, to legalize their own destruction of proletarian organizations, and rouse the agitated petty-bourgeoisie to chauvinistic fervour on behalf of the fight against the revolutionary way out of the crisis."
>
> Communist Pamphlet

> "(5) If a new spirit *is* to be refused into this old country, there is one thorny and contentious reform which must be tackled, and that is the humanization and galvanization of the B.B.C. Timidity here will bespeak cancer and atrophy of the soul. The heart of Britain may be sound and of strong beat, for instance, but the British lion's roar at present is like that of Bottom in Shakespeare's *Midsummer Night's Dream*—as gentle as any sucking dove. A virile new Britain cannot continue indefinitely to be traduced in the eyes or rather ears, of the world by the effete languors of Langham Place, brazenly masquerading as 'standard English'. When the Voice of Britain is heard at

nine o'clock, better far and infinitely less ludicrous to hear aitches honestly dropped than the present priggish, inflated, inhibited, school-ma'amish arch braying of blameless bashful mewing maidens!"

Letter in *Tribune*

Each of these passages has faults of its own, but, quite apart from avoidable ugliness, two qualities are common to all of them. The first is staleness of imagery: the other is lack of precision. The writer either has a meaning and cannot express it, or he inadvertently says something else, or he is almost indifferent as to whether his words mean anything or not. This mixture of vagueness and sheer incompetence is the most marked characteristic of modern English prose, and especially of any kind of political writing. As soon as certain topics are raised, the concrete melts into the abstract and no one seems able to think of turns of speech that are not hackneyed: prose consists less and less of *words* chosen for the sake of their meaning, and more and more of *phrases* tacked together like the sections of a prefabricated henhouse. I list below, with notes and examples, various of the tricks by means of which the work of prose-construction is habitually dodged:

Dying Metaphors

A newly invented metaphor assists thought by evoking a visual image, while on the other hand a metaphor which is technically "dead" (e.g. *iron resolution*) has in effect reverted to being an ordinary word and can generally be used without loss of vividness. But in between these two classes there is a huge dump of worn-out metaphors which have lost all evocative power and are merely used because they save people the trouble of inventing phrases for themselves. Examples are: *Ring the changes on, take up the cudgels for, to the line, ride roughshod over, stand shoulder to shoulder with, play into the hands of, no axe to grind, grist to the mill, fishing in troubled waters, on the order of the day, Achilles heel, swan song, hotbed.* Many of these are used without knowledge of their meaning (what is a "rift," for instance?), and incompatible metaphors are frequently mixed, a sure sign that the writer is not interested in what he is saying. Some metaphors now current have been twisted out of their original meaning without those who use them even being aware of the fact. For example, *toe the line* is sometimes written *tow the line.* Another example is *the hammer and the anvil,* now always used with the implication that the anvil gets the worst of it. In real life it is always the anvil that breaks the hammer, never the other way about: a writer who stopped to think what he was saying would be aware of this, and would avoid perverting the original phrase.

Operators or Verbal False Limbs

These save the trouble of picking out appropriate verbs and nouns, and at the same time pad each sentence with extra syllables which give it an appearance of symmetry. Characteristic phrases are: *render inoperative, militate against, make contact with, be subjected to, give rise to, give grounds for, have the effect of, play a leading part (role) in, make itself felt, take effect, exhibit a tendency to, serve the purpose of, etc., etc.* The keynote is the elimination of simple verbs. Instead of being a single word, such as *break, stop, spoil, mend, kill,* a verb becomes a *phrase,* made up of a noun or adjective tacked on to some general-purposes verb such as *prove, serve, form, play, render.* In addition, the passive voice is wherever possible used in preference to the active, and noun constructions are used instead of gerunds *(by examination of* instead of *by examining).* The range of verbs is further cut down by means of the *-ize* and *de-* formation, and the banal statements are given an appearance of profundity by means of the *not un-* formation. Simple conjunctions and prepositions are replaced by such phrases as *with respect to, having regard to, the fact that, by dint of, in view of, in the interest of, on the hypothesis that;* and the ends of sentences are saved from anticlimax by such resounding commonplaces as *greatly to be desired, cannot be left out of account, a development to be expected in the near future, deserving of serious consideration, brought to a satisfactory conclusion,* and so on and so forth.

Pretentious Diction

Words like *phenomenon, element, individual* (as noun), *objective, categorical, effective, virtual, basic, primary, promote, constitute, exhibit, exploit, utilize, eliminate, liquidate,* are used to dress up simple statements and give an air of scientific impartiality to biased judgments. Adjectives like *epoch-making, epic, historic, unforgettable, triumphant, age-old, inevitable, inexorable, veritable,* are used to dignify the sordid processes of international politics, while writing that aims at glorifying war usually takes on an archaic colour, its characteristic words being: *realm, throne, chariot, mailed fist, trident, sword, shield, buckler, banner, jackboot, clarion.* Foreign words and expressions such as *cul de sac, ancien régime, deus ex machina, mutatis mutandis, status quo, Gleichschaltung, Weltanschauung,* are used to give an air of culture and elegance. Except for the useful abbreviations *i.e., e.g.,* and *etc.*, there is no real need for any of the hundreds of foreign phrases now current in English. Bad writers, and especially scientific, political and sociological writers, are nearly aways haunted by the notion that Latin or Greek words are grander than Saxon ones, and unnecessary words like *expedite, ameliorate, predict, extraneous, deracinated, clandestine, subaqueous* and hundreds of others constantly gain ground from their Anglo-Saxon opposite numbers.[1] The jargon peculiar to Marxist writing (*hyena, hangman, cannibal, petty bourgeois, these gentry, lacquey, flunkey, mad dog, White Guard,* etc.,) consists largely of words and phrases translated from Russian, German or French; but the normal way of coining a new word is to use a Latin or Greek root with the appropriate affix and, where necessary, the *-ize* formation. It is often easier to make up words of this kind *(deregionalize, impermissible, extramarital, nonfragmentatory* and so forth) than to think up the English words that will cover one's meaning. The result, in general, is an increase in slovenliness and vagueness.

Meaningless Words

In certain kinds of writing, particularly in art criticism and literary criticism, it is normal to come across long passages which are almost completely lacking in meaning.[2] Words like *romantic, plastic, values, human, dead, sentimental, natural, vitality,* as used in art criticism, are strictly meaningless in the sense that they not only do not point to any discoverable object, but are hardly ever expected to do so by the reader. When one critic writes, "The outstanding feature of Mr. X's work is its living quality," while another writes, "The immediately striking thing about Mr. X's work is its peculiar deadness," the reader accepts this as a simple difference of opinion. If words like *black* and *white* were involved instead of the jargon words *dead* and *living,* he would see at once that language was being used in an improper way. Many political words are similarly abused. The word *Fascism* has now no meaning except in so far as it signifies "something not desirable." The words *democracy, socialism, freedom, patriotic, realistic, justice,* have each of them several different meanings which cannot be reconciled with one another. In the case of a word like *democracy,* not only is there no agreed definition, but the attempt to make one is resisted from all sides. It is almost universally felt that when we call a country democratic we are praising it: consequently the defenders of every kind of régime claim that it is a democracy, and fear that they might have to stop using the word if it were tied down to any one meaning. Words of this

[1] An interesting illustration of this is the way in which the English flower names which were in use till very recently are being ousted by Greek ones, *snapdragon* becoming *antirrhinum, forget-me-not* becoming *myosotis,* etc. It is hard to see any practical reason for this change of fashion: it is probably due to an instinctive turning-away from the more homely word and a vague feeling that the Greek word is scientific [Orwell's note].

[2] Example: "Comfort's catholicity of perception and image, strangely Whitmanesque in range, almost the exact opposite in aesthetic compulsion, continues to evoke that trembling atmospheric accumulative hinting at a cruel, an inexorably serene timelessness. . . . Wrey Gardiner scores by aiming at simple bull's-eyes with precision. Only they are not so simple, and through this contented sadness runs more than the surface bittersweet of resignation" (*Poetry Quarterly*) [Orwell's note].

kind are often used in a consciously dishonest way. That is, the person who uses them has his own private definition, but allows his hearer to think he means something quite different. Statements like *Marshal Pétain was a true patriot, The Soviet Press is the freest in the world, The Catholic Church is opposed to persecution,* are almost always made with intent to deceive. Other words used in variable meanings, in most cases more or less dishonestly, are: *class, totalitarian, science, progressive, reactionary, bourgeois, equality.*

Now that I have made this catalogue of swindles and perversions, let me give another example of the kind of writing that they lead to. This time it must of its nature be an imaginary one. I am going to translate a passage of good English into modern English of the worst sort. Here is a well-known verse from *Ecclesiastes*:

> "I returned and saw under the sun, that the race is not to the swift, nor the battle to the strong, neither yet bread to the wise, nor yet riches to men of understanding, nor yet favour to men of skill; but time and chance happeneth to them all."

Here it is in modern English:

> "Objective consideration of contemporary phenomena compels the conclusion that success or failure in competitive activities exhibits no tendency to be commensurate with innate capacity, but that a considerable element of the unpredictable must invariably be taken into account."

This is a parody, but not a very gross one. Exhibit (3), above, for instance, contains several patches of the same kind of English. It will be seen that I have not made a full translation. The beginning and ending of the sentence follow the original meaning fairly closely, but in the middle the concrete illustrations—race, battle, bread—dissolve into the vague phrase "success or failure in competitive activities." This had to be so, because no modern writer of the kind I am discussing—no one capable of using phrases like "objective consideration of contemporary phenomena"—would ever tabulate his thoughts in that precise and detailed way. The whole tendency of modern prose is away from concreteness. Now analyse these two sentences a little more closely. The first contains forty-nine words but only sixty syllables, and all its words are those of everyday life. The second contains thirty-eight words of ninety syllables: eighteen of its words are from Latin roots, and one from Greek. The first sentence contains six vivid images, and only one phrase ("time and chance") that could be called vague. The second contains not a single arresting phrase, and in spite of its ninety syllables it gives only a shortened version of the meaning contained in the first. Yet without a doubt it is the second kind of sentence that is gaining ground in modern English. I do not want to exaggerate. This kind of writing is not yet universal, and outcrops of simplicity will occur here and there in the worst-written page. Still, if you or I were told to write a few lines on the uncertainty of human fortunes, we should probably come much nearer to my imaginary sentence than to the one from *Ecclesiastes.*

As I have tried to show, modern writing at its worst does not consist in picking out words for the sake of their meaning and inventing images in order to make the meaning clearer. It consists in gumming together long strips of words which have already been set in order by someone else, and making the results presentable by sheer humbug. The attraction of this way of writing is that it is easy. It is easier—even quicker, once you to have the habit—to say *In my opinion it is a not unjustifiable assumption that* than to say *I think.* If you use ready-made phrases, you not only don't have to hunt about for words; you also don't have to bother with the rhythms of your sentences, since these phrases are generally so arranged as to be more or less euphonious. When you are composing in a hurry—when you are dictating to a stenographer, for instance, or making a public speech—it is natural to fall into a pretentious, Latinized style. Tags like *a consideration which we should do well to bear in mind* or *a conclusion to which all of us would readily assent* will save many a sentence from coming down with a bump. By using stale metaphors, similes and idioms, you save much mental effort, at the cost of leaving your meaning vague, not only for your reader but for yourself. This is the significance of mixed metaphors. The sole aim of a metaphor is to call up a visual image. When these images clash—as in *The Fascist octopus has sung its swan song, the jackboot is thrown into the melting pot*—it can be taken as certain that the writer is not seeing a mental image of the objects he is naming; in other words he is not really thinking. Look again at the examples I gave at the beginning of this essay. Professor Laski (1) uses five negatives in fifty-three words. One of these is superfluous, making nonsense of the whole passage, and in addition there is the slip *alien* for akin, making further nonsense, and several avoidable pieces of clumsiness which increase the general vagueness. Professor Hogben (2) plays ducks and drakes with a battery which is able to write prescriptions, and, while disapproving of the everyday phrase *put up with,* is unwilling to look *egregious* up in the dictionary and see what it means. (3), if one takes an uncharitable attitude towards it, is simply meaningless: probably one could work out its intended meaning by reading the whole of the article in which it occurs. In (4), the writer knows more or less what he wants to say, but an accumulation of stale phrases chokes him like tea leaves blocking a sink. In (5), words and meaning have almost parted company. People who write in this manner usually have a general emotional meaning—they dislike one thing and want to express solidarity with another—but they are not interested in the detail of what they are saying. A scrupulous writer, in every sentence that he writes, will ask himself at least four questions, thus: What am I trying to say? What words will express it? What image or idiom will make it clearer? Is this image fresh enough to have an effect? And he will probably ask himself two more: Could I put it more shortly? Have I said anything that is avoidably ugly? But you are not obliged to go to all this trouble. You can shirk it by simply throwing your mind open and letting the ready-made phrases come crowding in. They will construct your sentences for you—even think your thoughts for you, to a certain extent—and at need they will perform the important service of partially concealing your meaning even from yourself. It is at this point that the special connection between politics and the debasement of language becomes clear.

In our time it is broadly true that political writing is bad writing. Where it is not true, it will generally be found that the writer is some kind of rebel, expressing his private opinions and not a "party line." Orthodoxy, of whatever colour, seems to demand a lifeless, imitative style. The political dialects to be found in pamphlets, leading articles, manifestos, White Papers and the speeches of under-secretaries do, of course, vary from party to party, but they are all alike in that one almost never finds in them a fresh, vivid, home-made turn of speech. When one watches some tired hack on the platform mechanically repeating the familiar phrases—*bestial atrocities, iron heel, blood-stained tyranny, free peoples of the world, stand shoulder to shoulder*—one often has a curious feeling that one is not watching a live human being but some kind of dummy: a feeling which suddenly becomes stronger at moments when the light catches the speaker's spectacles and turns them into blank discs which seem to have no eyes behind them. And this is not altogether fanciful. A speaker who uses that kind of phraseology has gone some distance towards turning himself into a machine. The appropriate noises are coming out of his larynx, but his brain is not involved as it would be if he were choosing his words for himself. If the speech he is making is one that he is accustomed to make over and over again, he may be almost unconscious of what he is saying, as one is when one utters the responses in church. And this reduced state of consciousness, if not indispensable, is at any rate favourable to political conformity.

In our time, political speech and writing are largely the defence of the indefensible. Things like the continuance of British rule in India, the Russian purges and deportations, the dropping of the atom bombs on Japan, can indeed be defended, but only by arguments which are too brutal for most people to face, and which do not square with the professed aims of political parties. Thus political language has to consist largely of euphemism, question-begging and sheer cloudy vagueness. Defenceless villages are bombarded from the air, the inhabitants driven out into the countryside, the cattle machine-gunned, the huts set on fire with incendiary bullets: this is called *pacification.* Millions of peasants are robbed of their farms and sent trudging along the roads with no more than they can carry: this is called *transfer of population* or *rectification of frontiers.* People are imprisoned for years without trial, or shot in the back of the neck or sent to die of scurvy in Arctic lumber camps: this is called *elimination of unreliable elements.* Such phraseology is needed if one wants to name things without calling up mental pictures of them. Consider for instance some comfortable English professor defending Russian totalitarianism. He cannot say outright, "I believe in killing off your opponents when you can get good results by doing so." Probably, therefore, he will say something like this:

"While freely conceding that the Soviet régime exhibits certain features which the humanitarian may be inclined to deplore, we must, I think, agree that a certain curtailment of the right to political opposition is an unavoidable concomitant of transitional periods, and that the rigors which the Russian people have been called upon to undergo have been amply justified in the sphere of concrete achievement."

The inflated style is itself a kind of euphemism. A mass of Latin words falls upon the facts like soft snow, blurring the outlines and covering up all the details. The great enemy of clear language is insincerity. When there is a gap between one's real and one's declared aims, one turns as it were instinctively to long words and exhausted idioms, like a cuttlefish squirting out ink. In our age there is no such thing as "keeping out of politics." All issues are political issues, and politics itself is a mass of lies, evasions, folly, hatred and schizophrenia. When the general atmosphere is bad, language must suffer. I should expect to find—this is a guess which I have not sufficient knowledge to verify—that the German, Russian and Italian languages have all deteriorated in the last ten or fifteen years, as a result of dictatorship.

But if thought corrupts language, language can also corrupt thought. A bad usage can spread by tradition and imitation, even among people who should and do know better. The debased language that I have been discussing is in some ways very convenient. Phrases like *a not unjustifiable assumption, leaves much to be desired, would serve no good purpose, a consideration which we should do well to bear in mind,* are a continuous temptation, a packet of aspirins always at one's elbow. Look back through this essay, and for certain you will find that I have again and again committed the very faults I am protesting against. By this morning's post I have received a pamphlet dealing with conditions in Germany. The author tells me that he "felt impelled" to write it. I open it at random, and here is almost the first sentence that I see: "(The Allies) have an opportunity not only of achieving a radical transformation of Germany's social and political structure in such a way as to avoid a nationalistic reaction in Germany itself, but at the same time of laying the foundations of a co-operative and unified Europe." You see, he "feels impelled" to write—feels, presumably, that he has something new to say—and yet his words, like cavalry horses answering the bugle, group themselves automatically into the familiar dreary pattern. This invasion of one's mind by ready-made phrases *(lay the foundations, achieve a radical transformation)* can only be prevented if one is constantly on guard against them, and every such phrase anaesthetizes a portion of one's brain.

I said earlier that the decadence of our language is probably curable. Those who deny this would argue, if they produced an argument at all, that language merely reflects existing social conditions, and that we cannot influence its development by any direct tinkering with words and constructions. So far as the general tone or spirit of a language goes, this may be true, but it is not true in detail. Silly words and expressions have often disappeared, not through any evolutionary process but owing to the conscious action of a minority. Two recent examples were *explore every avenue* and *leave no stone unturned,* which were killed by the jeers of a few journalists. There is a long list of fly-blown metaphors which could similarly be got rid of if enough people would interest themselves in the job; and it should also be possible to laugh the *not un-* formation out of existence,[3] to reduce the amount of Latin and Greek in the average sentence, to drive out foreign phrases and strayed scientific words, and, in general, to make pretentiousness unfashionable. But all these are minor points. The defence of the English language implies more than this, and perhaps it is best to start by saying what it does *not* imply.

To begin with it has nothing to do with archaism, with the salvaging of obsolete words and turns of speech, or with the setting up of a "standard English" which must never be departed from. On the contrary, it is especially concerned with the scrapping of every word or idiom which has outworn its usefulness. It has nothing to do with correct grammar and syntax, which are of no importance so long as one makes one's meaning clear, or with the avoidance of Americanisms, or with having what is called a "good prose style." On the other hand it is not concerned with fake simplicity and the attempt to make written English colloquial. Nor does it even imply in every case preferring the Saxon word to the Latin one, though it does imply using the fewest and shortest words that will cover one's meaning. What is above all needed is to let the meaning choose the word, and not the other way about. In prose, the worst thing one can do with words is to surrender to them. When you think of a concrete object, you think wordlessly, and then, if you want to describe the thing you have been visualizing you probably hunt about

[3] One can cure oneself of the *not un-*formation by memorizing this sentence: *A not unblack dog was chasing a not unsmall rabbit across a not ungreen field* [Orwell's note].

till you find the exact words that seem to fit. When you think of something abstract you are more inclined to use words from the start, and unless you make a conscious effort to prevent it, the existing dialect will come rushing in and do the job for you, at the expense of blurring or even changing your meaning. Probably it is better to put off using words as long as possible and get one's meaning as clear as one can through pictures or sensations. Afterwards one can choose—not simply *accept*—the phrases that will best cover the meaning, and then switch round and decide what impression one's words are likely to make on another person. This last effort of the mind cuts out all stale or mixed images, all prefabricated phrases, needless repetitions, and humbug and vagueness generally. But one can often be in doubt about the effect of a word or a phrase, and one needs rules that one can rely on when instinct fails. I think the following rules will cover most cases:

(i) Never use a metaphor, simile or other figure of speech which you are used to seeing in print.

(ii) Never use a long word where a short one will do.

(iii) If it is possible to cut a word out, always cut it out.

(iv) Never use the passive where you can use the active.

(v) Never use a foreign phrase, a scientific word or a jargon word if you can think of an everyday English equivalent;

(vi) Break any of these rules sooner than say anything outright barbarous.

These rules sound elementary, and so they are, but they demand a deep change of attitude in anyone who has grown used to writing in the style now fashionable. One could keep all of them and still write bad English, but one could not write the kind of stuff that I quoted in those five specimens at the beginning of this article.

I have not here been considering the literary use of language, but merely language as an instrument for expressing and not for concealing or preventing thought. Stuart Chase and others have come near to claiming that all abstract words are meaningless, and have used this as a pretext for advocating a kind of political quietism. Since you don't know what Fascism is, how can you struggle against Fascism? One need not swallow such absurdities as this, but one ought to recognize that the present political chaos is connected with the decay of language, and that one can probably bring about some improvement by starting at the verbal end. If you simplify your English, you are freed from the worst follies of orthodoxy. You cannot speak any of the necessary dialects, and when you make a stupid remark its stupidity will be obvious, even to yourself. Political language—and with variations this is true of all political parties, from Conservatives to Anarchists—is designed to make lies sound truthful and murder respectable, and to give an appearance of solidity to pure wind. One cannot change this all in a moment, but one can at least change one's own habits, and from time to time one can even, if one jeers loudly enough, send some worn-out and useless phrase—some *jackboot, Achilles' heel, hotbed, melting pot, acid test, veritable inferno* or other lump of verbal refuse—into the dustbin where it belongs.

Listen to This

Alex Ross

I hate "classical music": not the thing but the name. It traps a tenaciously living art in a theme park of the past. It cancels out the possibility that music in the spirit of Beethoven could still be created today. It banishes into limbo the work of thousands of active composers who have to explain to otherwise well-informed people what it is they do for a living. The phrase is a masterpiece of negative publicity, a tour de force of anti-hype. I wish there were another name. I envy jazz people who speak simply of "the music." Some jazz aficionados also call their art "America's classical music," and I propose a trade: they can have "classical," I'll take "the music."

For at least a century, the music has been captive to a cult of mediocre élitism that tries to manufacture self-esteem by clutching at empty formulas of intellectual superiority. Consider some of the rival names in circulation: "art" music, "serious" music, "great" music, "good" music. Yes, the music can be great and serious; but greatness and seriousness are not its defining characteristics. It can also be stupid, vulgar, and insane. Music is too personal a medium to support an absolute hierarchy of values. The best music is music that persuades us that there is no other music in the world. This morning, for me, it was Sibelius's Fifth; late last night, Dylan's "Sad-Eyed Lady of the Lowlands"; tomorrow, it may be something entirely new. I can't rank my favorite music any more than I can rank my memories. Yet some discerning souls believe that the music should be marketed as a luxury good, one that supplants an inferior popular product. They say, in effect, "The music you love is trash. Listen instead to our great, arty music." They gesture toward the heavens, but they speak the language of high-end real estate. They are making little headway with the unconverted because they have forgotten to define the music as something worth loving. If it is worth loving, it must be great; no more need be said.

When people hear "classical," they think "dead." The music is described in terms of its distance from the present, its resistance to the mass—what it is not. You see magazines with listings for Popular Music in one section and for Classical Music in another, so that the latter becomes, by implication,

Unpopular Music. No wonder that stories of its imminent demise are so commonplace. The Web site ArtsJournal features a media file with the deliberately ridiculous name Death of Classical Music Archive, whose articles recycle a familiar litany of problems: record companies are curtailing their classical divisions; orchestras are facing deficits; the music is barely taught in public schools, almost invisible on television, ignored or mocked by Hollywood. But the same story could have been written ten years ago or twenty. If this be death, the record is skipping. A complete version of the Death of Classical Music Archive would go back to the fourteenth century, when the sensuous melodies of *ars nova* were thought to signal the end of civilization.

The classical audience is assumed to be a moribund crowd of the old, the white, the rich, and the bored. Statistics provided by the National Endowment for the Arts suggest that the situation is not quite so dire. Yes, the audience is older than that for any other art—the median age is forty-nine—but it is not the wealthiest. Musicals, plays, ballet, and museums all get larger slices of the $50,000-or-more income pie (as does the ESPN channel, for that matter). If you want to see an in-your-face, Swiss-bank-account display of wealth, go look at the millionaires sitting in the skyboxes at a Billy Joel show, if security lets you. Nor is the classical audience aging any faster than the rest of America. The music may not be a juggernaut, but it is a major world. American orchestras sell around thirty million tickets each year. Brilliant new talents are thronging the scene; the musicians of the august Berlin Philharmonic are, on average, a generation younger than the Rolling Stones.

The music is always dying, ever-ending. It is an ageless diva on a nonstop farewell tour, coming around for one absolutely final appearance. It is hard to name because it never really existed to begin with—not in the sense that it stemmed from a single time or place. It has no genealogy, no ethnicity: leading composers of today hail from China, Estonia, Argentina, Queens. The music is simply whatever composers create—a long string of written-down works to which various performing traditions have become attached. It encompasses the high, the low, empire, underground, dance, prayer, silence, noise. Composers are genius parasites; they feed voraciously on the song matter of their time in order to engender something new. They have gone through a rough stretch in the past hundred years, facing external obstacles (Hitler and Stalin were amateur music critics) as well as problems of their own invention ("Why doesn't anyone like our beautiful twelve-tone music?"). But they may be on the verge of an improbable renaissance, and the music may take a form that no one today would recognize. For now, it is like the "sunken cathedral" that Debussy depicts in one of his Preludes—a city that chants beneath the waves.

The critic Greg Sandow recently wrote in his online journal that we partisans of the classical need to speak more from the heart about what the music means. He admits that it's easier to analyze his ardor than to express it. The music does not lend itself to the same generational storytelling as, say, "Sgt. Pepper." There may be kids out there who lost their virginity during Brahms's D-Minor Piano Concerto, but they don't want to tell the story and you don't want to hear it. The music attracts the reticent fraction of the population. It is an art of grand gestures and vast dimensions that plays to mobs of the quiet and the shy. It is a paradise for passive-aggressives, sublimation addicts, and other relics of the Freudian world. Which may explain why it has a hard time expressing itself in the time of Dr. Phil.

I am a thirty-six-year-old white American male who first started listening to popular music at the age of twenty. In retrospect, this seems strange; perhaps "freakish" is not too strong a word. Yet it seemed natural at the time. I feel as though I grew up not during the seventies and eighties but during the thirties and forties, the decades of my parents' youth. They came of age in the great American middlebrow era, when the music had a much different place in the culture than it does today. In those years, in what now seems like a surreal dream world, millions listened as Toscanini conducted the NBC Symphony on national radio. Walter Damrosch explained the classics to schoolchildren, singing ditties to help them remember the themes. (My mother remembers one of them: "This is / The sympho-nee / That Schubert wrote but never fi-nished . . .") NBC would broadcast Ohio State vs. Indiana one afternoon, a recital by Lotte Lehmann the next. In my house, it was the Boston Symphony broadcast followed by the Redskins game. I was unaware of a yawning gap between the two.

Early on, I reached for my parents' record collection, which was well stocked with artifacts of the Golden Age. I listened to Toscanini's Brahms, Koussevitzky's Sibelius, the Budapest Quartet. The look and feel of the records were inseparable from the sound they made. They said so much to me that for a long time I had no curiosity about other music. There was Otto Klemperer's Zeppelin-like, slow-motion account of "The St. Matthew Passion," with nightmare-spawning art by the Master of Delft. Toscanini's fierce recordings were decorated with Robert Hupka's snapshots of the Maestro in motion, his face registering every emotion between ecstasy and disgust. Mozart's Divertimento in E-Flat featured the famous portrait in which the composer looks down at the world in sorrow, like a general surveying a hopeless battle. While listening, I read along in the liner notes, which were generally written in the over-the-top everyman-orator style that Orson Welles parodied brilliantly in "Citizen Kane." Tchaikovsky's Violin Concerto, for example, was said to be "melancholy, sometimes progressing to abysmal depths." None of this made sense at the time; I had no acquaintance with melancholy, let alone abysmal depths. What mattered was the exaggerated swoop of the thought, which roughly matched the pattern of the sound.

The first music that I loved to the point of distraction was Beethoven's "Eroica" Symphony. My parents had a disk of Leonard Bernstein conducting the New York Philharmonic—one of a series of Music-Appreciation Records put out by the Book-of-the-Month Club. A companion record provided Bernstein's analysis of the symphony, a road map to its forty-five-minute sprawl. I now had names for the shapes that I perceived. (The conductor's "Joy of Music" and "Infinite Variety of Music" remain the best introductory books of their kind.) Bernstein drew attention to something that happens about ten seconds in—a C-sharp that unexpectedly sounds against the plain E-flat-major harmony. "There has been a stab of intrusive otherness," he said, cryptically but seductively, in his nicotine baritone. Over and over, I listened to this note of otherness. I bought a score and deciphered the notation. I learned some time-beating gestures from Max Rudolf's conducting manual. I held my family hostage in the living room as I led the record player in a searingly intense performance of the "Eroica."

Did Lenny get a little carried away when he called that soft C-sharp in the cellos a "shock," a "wrench," a "stab"? If you were to play the "Eroica" for a fourteen-year-old hip-hop scholar versed in the works of Eminem and 50 Cent, he might find it shockingly boring at best. No one is slicing up his wife or getting shot nine times. But I would submit to my young gangsta interlocutor that those artists are relatively shocking—relative to the social norms of their day. Although the "Eroica" ceased to be controversial in the these-crazy-kids-today sense around 1830, within the "classical" frame it has continued to deliver its surprises right on cue. Seven bars of E-flat major, then the C-sharp that hovers for a moment before disappearing: it is like a speaker stepping up to a microphone, launching into the first words of a grand oration, and then faltering, as if he had just remembered something from childhood or seen a sinister face in the crowd.

I don't identify with the listener who responds to the "Eroica" by saying, "Ah, civilization." That wasn't what Beethoven wanted: his intention was to shake the European mind. I don't listen to music to be civilized; sometimes, I listen precisely to escape the ordered world. What I love about the "Eroica" is the way it manages to have it all, uniting Romanticism and Enlightenment, civilization and revolution, brain and body, order and chaos. It knows which way you think the music is going and veers triumphantly in the wrong direction. The Danish composer Carl Nielsen once wrote a monologue for the spirit of Music, in which he or she or it says, "I love the vast surface of silence; and it is my chief delight to break it."

Around the time I got stabbed by Beethoven's C-sharp, I began trying to write music myself. My career as a composer lasted from the age of eight to the age of twenty. I lacked both genius and talent. My spiral-bound manuscript book includes an ambitious program of future compositions: thirty piano sonatas, twelve violin sonatas, various symphonies, concertos, fantasias, and funeral marches, most of them in the key of D minor. Scattered ideas for these works appear in the following pages, but they don't go anywhere, which was the story of my life as a composer. Still, I treasure the observation of one of my college teachers, who wrote on the final page of my end-of-term submission that I had created a "most interesting and slightly peculiar sonatina." I put down my pen and withdrew into silence, like Sibelius in Järvenpää.

My inability to finish anything, much less anything good, left me with a profound respect for this impossible mode of making a living. Composition at its most intense is a rebellion against reality. No one except the very young demands new music, and even when we are young the gates of inattention crash down quickly. Composers manufacture a product that is universally deemed superfluous—at least until their music enters public consciousness, at which point people begin to say that they could not live without it. For more than a century, the repertory has consisted largely of music by dead composers. Yet half of those on the American Symphony Orchestra League's top-ten most-performed list—Mahler, Strauss, Ravel, Shostakovich, Prokofiev—hadn't been born when the first draft of the repertory got written.

Throughout my teens, I took piano lessons from a man named Denning Barnes. He also taught me composition, music history, and the art of listening. He was a wiry man with tangled hair, whose tweed jackets emitted an odd smell that was neither pleasant nor unpleasant, just odd. He was intimate with Beethoven, Schubert, and Chopin, and he also loved twentieth-century music. Scriabin, Bartók, and Berg were three favorites. He opened another door for me, in a wall that I never knew existed. His own music, as far as I can remember, was rambunctious, jazzy, a little nuts. One day he pounded out one of the variations in Beethoven's final piano sonata and said that it was an anticipation of boogie-woogie. I had no idea what boogie-woogie was, but I was excited by the idea that Beethoven had anticipated it. The marble-bust Beethoven of my childhood suddenly became an eagle-eyed sentinel on the ramparts of sound, spying nameless entities on the horizon. "Boogie-woogie" was a creature out of Bernstein's serious-fun world, and Mr. Barnes was my private Bernstein. There was not a snobbish bone in his body; he was a skeleton of enthusiasm, a fifteen-dollar-an-hour guerrilla fighter for the music he loved. He died of a brain tumor in 1989. The last time I saw him, we played a hair-raising version of Schubert's Fantasia in F Minor for four hands. It was full of wrong notes, most of them at my end of the keyboard, but it felt great and made a mighty noise, and to this day I have never been able to tolerate any other performance of the work, not even Britten and Richter's.

By high school, a terrible truth had dawned: I was the only person my age who liked this stuff. Actually, there were other classical nerds at my school, but we were too diffident to form a posse. Several "normal" friends dragged me to a showing of "Pink Floyd—The Wall," after which I conceded that one passage sounded Mahlerian. Only in college did my musical fortress finally crumble. I spent most of my days and nights at the campus radio station, where I had a show and helped organize the classical contingent. I fanatically patrolled the boundaries of the classical broadcasting day, refusing to surrender even fifteen minutes of "Chamber Music Masterworks" and the like. At 10 p.m., the schedule switched from classical to punk, and only punk of the most recondite kind. Once a record sold more than a few hundred copies, it was kicked off the playlist. The d.j.s liked to start their sets with the shrillest, crudest songs in order to scandalize the classical crowd. I tried to one-up them by ending my show with squalls of Xenakis. They hit back with Sinatra singing "Only the Lonely." Once, they followed up my heartfelt tribute to Herbert von Karajan with Skrewdriver's rousing neo-Nazi anthem "Prisoner of Peace": "Free Rudolf Hess / How long can they keep him there? We can only guess." Touché.

The thing about these cerebral punk rockers is that they were easily the most interesting people I'd ever met. Between painstakingly researched tributes to Mission of Burma and the Butthole Surfers, they composed undergraduate theses on fourth-century Roman fortifications and the liberal thought of Lionel Trilling. I began hanging around in the studio after my show was over, suppressing an instinctive fear of their sticker-covered leather jackets and multicolored hair. I informed them, as Mr. Barnes would have done, that Schoenberg had anticipated all of this. And I began listening to new things. The first two rock records I bought were Pere Ubu's "Terminal Tower" compilation and Sonic Youth's "Daydream Nation." I crept from underground rock to alternative rock and finally to the full-out commercial kind. Soon I was astounding my friends with pronouncements like " 'Highway 61 Revisited' is a pretty good album," or "The White Album is a masterpiece." I abandoned the notion of classical superiority, which led to a crisis of faith: if the music wasn't great and serious and high and mighty, what was it?

For a little while, living in Northern California after college, I thought of giving up on the music altogether. I sold off a lot of my CDs, including all my copies of the symphonies of Arnold Bax, in order to pay for more Pere Ubu and Sonic Youth. I cut my hair short, wore angry T-shirts, and started hanging out at the Berkeley punk club 924 Gilman Street. I became a fan of a band called Blatz, which was about as far from Bax as I could get. (Their big hit was "Fuk Shit Up.") Fortunately, no one needed to point out to my face that I was in the wrong place. It is a strange American dream, this notion that music can give you a new personality, a new class, even a new race. The out-of-body experience is thrilling as long as it lasts, but most people are eventually deposited back at the point where they started, and they may begin to hate the music for lying to them. When I went back to the classical ghetto, I chose to accept its limitations. I realized that, despite the outward decrepitude of the culture, there was still a bright flame within. It occurred to me that if I could somehow get from Brahms to Blatz, others could go the same route in the opposite direction. I have always wanted to talk about classical music as if it were popular music and popular music as if it were classical.

For many, popular music is the soundtrack of raging adolescence, while the other kind chimes in during the long twilight of maturity. For me, it's the reverse. Listening to the "Eroica" reconnects me with a kind of childlike energy, a happy ferocity about the world. Since I came to pop music late, I invest it with more adult feeling. To me, it's penetrating, knowing, full of microscopic shades of truth about the way things really are. Dylan's "Blood on the Tracks" anatomizes a doomed relationship with a saturnine clarity that a canonical work such as "Die Schöne Müllerin" can't match. (Listening recently to Ian Bostridge sing the Schubert cycle, I had the thought that the protagonist might never have spoken to the miller girl for whose sake he drowns himself. How classical of him.) If I were in a perverse mood, I'd say that the "Eroica" is the raw, thuggish thing—a blast of ego and id—whereas a song like Radiohead's "Everything in Its Right Place" is all cool adult irony. The idea that life is flowing along with unsettling smoothness, the dark C-sharpness of the world sensed but not confirmed, is a resigned sort of sentiment that Beethoven probably never even felt, much less communicated. What I refuse to accept is that one kind of music soothes the mind and another kind soothes the soul. Depends on whose mind, whose soul.

On my iPod I've been listening to the new Missy Elliott song "Wake Up." It's an austere hip-hop track with a political edge. Something about the music sets off my classical radar. There are, effectively, only three notes, free-floating and ambiguous. The song begins with a clip of a voice shouting "Wake up!" The voice rises up a tritone, and that interval determines the notes. The idea of generating music from the singsong of speech is ancient, but "Wake Up" reminds me in particular of two minimalist pieces by Steve Reich, "It's Gonna Rain" and "Come Out." Both use tapes of impassioned black voices to create seething electronic soundscapes. Whether Elliott and her producer, Timbaland, have listened to Reich is beside the point. (If you say, "Of course they haven't," ask yourself what makes you so certain.) The song works much like Reich's compositions, building a world from a sliver of sound. It's almost manic and obsessive enough to be classical music.

The fatal phrase came into circulation late in the game. From Monteverdi to Beethoven, modern music was the only music, bartered about in a marketplace that resembled modern pop culture. Concerts were eclectic hootenannies in which opera arias collided with chunks of sonatas. Barrel-organ grinders carried the best-known arias out into the streets, where they were blended with folk tunes. Concerts in pre-classical America were a stylistic free-for-all, a mirror of the country's mixed-up nature. Walt Whitman mobilized grand opera as a metaphor for democracy; the voices of his favorite singers were integral to the swelling sound of his "barbaric yawp."

In Europe, the past began to overwhelm the present just after 1800. Johann Nikolaus Forkel's 1802 biography of Bach, one of the first major books devoted to a dead composer, may be the founding document of the classical mentality. All the earmarks are there: the longing for lost worlds, the adulation of a single godlike entity, the horror of the present. Bach was "the first classic that ever was, or perhaps ever will be," Forkel proclaimed. "If the art is to remain an art and not to be degraded into a mere idle amusement, more use must be made of classical works than has been done for some time." By "idle amusement" Forkel had in mind the prattling of Italian opera; his biography is addressed to "patriotic admirers of true musical art," namely the German. The notion that the music of Forkel's time was teetering toward extinction is, of course, amusing in retrospect; in the summer of 1802, Beethoven began work on the "Eroica." Scholars eventually defined the Classical Era as Viennese music of the late eighteenth century, especially Mozart and Haydn, who, in their day, had been racy, modern figures. The word was nonsense from the outset.

The rise of "classical music" mirrored the rise of the commercial middle class, which employed Beethoven as an escalator to the social heights. Concert halls grew quiet and reserved, habits and attire formal. Improvisation was phased out; the score became sacred. Audiences were discouraged from applauding while the music was going on—it had been the custom to clap after a good tune or a dazzling solo—or between movements. Patrons of the Wagner festival in Bayreuth proved notoriously militant in the suppression of applause. At an early performance of "Parsifal," listeners hissed an unmusical vulgarian who yelled out "Bravo!" after the Flower Maidens scene. The troublemaker had reason to feel embarrassed; he had written the opera. The Wagnerians were taking Wagner more seriously than he took himself—an alarming development.

Composers liked the fact that listeners were quieting down; the subtle shock of a C-sharp wouldn't register if the crowd were chattering away. Even so, the emergence of a self-styled élite audience had limited appeal for the likes of Beethoven and Verdi, who did not come from that world. The nineteenth-century masters were, most of them, monstrous egomaniacs, but they were not snobs. Verdi wrote for the masses, and he scandalously proclaimed the box office the only barometer of success. Wagner, surrounded by luxury, royalty, and extreme pretension, nonetheless railed against the emergence of a "classical" repertory, for which he blamed the Jews. His nauseating anti-Semitism went hand in hand with a sometimes deeply charming populism.

In a letter to Liszt, he raged against the "monumental character" of the music of his time, the "clinging and sticking to the past." Another letter demanded, "*Kinder! macht Neues! Neues!, und abermals Neues!*" Ezra Pound condensed this thought as "Make it new."

Unfortunately, the European bourgeoisie, having made a demigod of Beethoven, began losing interest in even the most vital living composers. In 1859, a critic wrote, "New works do not succeed in Leipzig. Again at the fourteenth Gewandhaus concert a composition was borne to its grave." The crazy modern music in question was Brahms's First Piano Concerto. By 1870, seventy-five per cent of works in the Gewandhaus repertory were by dead composers. The fetishizing of the past had a degrading effect on composers' morale. They began to doubt their ability to please this implacable audience, which seemed prepared to reject their wares no matter what style they wrote in. If no one cares, composers reasoned, we might as well write for connoisseurs—or for each other. This was the mentality that gave birth to the phenomenon of Arnold Schoenberg. The relationship between composer and public became a vicious circle; the more the composer asserted independence, the more the public clung to the past. A critic who attended the première of the "Eroica" saw the impasse coming: "Music could quickly come to such a point, that everyone who is not precisely familiar with the rules and difficulties of the art would find absolutely no enjoyment in it."

The American middle class carried the worship of the classics to a necrophiliac extreme. Lawrence Levine, in his book "Highbrow/Lowbrow," gives a devastating portrait of the country's musical culture at the turn of the twentieth century. It was a world that abhorred virtuosity, extravagance, anything that smacked of entertainment. Orchestras dedicated themselves to "the great works of the great composers greatly performed, the best and profoundest art, these and these alone," in the redundant words of the conductor Theodore Thomas, who was the founder of the modern American orchestra. Early in his career, Thomas tried to attract the masses, conducting in parks and beer gardens. Later, he decided that the working classes could never appreciate greatly great great music like Beethoven's. He was a marvellous conductor, by all accounts, but his infatuation with "cultivated persons" set a bad precedent.

Within a decade or two, American symphonic culture was so ossified that progressive spirits were calling for change. "America is saddled, hag-ridden, with culture," the critic-composer Arthur Farwell wrote in 1911. "There is a conventionalism, a cynicism, a self-consciousness, in symphony concert, recital, and opera." Daniel Gregory Mason, a maverick Columbia professor, similarly attacked the "prestige-hypnotized" plutocrats who ran the New York Philharmonic. He found more excitement at open-air concerts at Lewisohn Stadium, in Harlem, where the audience freely expressed its enthusiasm. Mason delightedly quoted a notice that read, "We would respectfully request that the audience refrain from throwing mats." His sentiment still rings true—concerts would be better if there were more throwing of mats.

In the nineteen-thirties, Farwell's populist philosophy took root. A generation of composers, conductors, and broadcasters embraced the idea of "music for all." The storied middlebrow age began. David Sarnoff, the head of NBC, had a vision of Toscanini conducting for a vast public, and the public duly materialized. The first broadcast day of CBS featured an American opera: "The King's Henchman," by Deems Taylor. Hollywood studios hired composers such as Korngold, Copland, and Herrmann and pursued the modernist giants Schoenberg and Stravinsky (both of whom asked for too much money). F.D.R. funded a Federal Music Project that in two and a half years entertained ninety-five million people; there were concerts in delinquent-boys' homes and rural Oklahoma towns. A Boston reporter pictured one Federal opera performance as a storming of the Bastille: "Drivers, chauffeurs, and footmen were occupying the seats of the master and the madame at 83 cents a chair."

Perhaps the boldest forward leap was the invention of a hybrid music combining European tradition and new popular forms. Duke Ellington wrote symphonic jazz for Carnegie Hall; his "Black, Brown, and Beige" was heard there in 1943. Morton Gould and Leonard Bernstein wrote for orchestra, jazz ensemble, and Broadway without worrying about the ranking of each. The ultimate phenomenon was George Gershwin, who rose through Tin Pan Alley and then through the orchestral world, transforming America's idea of what a composer was. For all his Jazz Age glamour, some part of Gershwin remained a lonely classical kid—the hard-practicing pianist who had filled scrapbooks with concert programs from Cooper Union and Wanamaker's Auditorium. In Vienna, in 1928, Gershwin met his idol, Alban Berg, who had the Kolisch Quartet play him the "Lyric Suite." Gershwin then sat down at the piano, but hesitated, wondering aloud whether he was worthy of the occasion. "Mr. Gershwin," Berg said sternly, "music is music."

The middlebrow utopia sputtered out quickly, and for a variety of reasons. Federally funded arts projects fell victim to a classic American culture war—the Republicans versus the New Deal—for which fanatics on both the left and the right were to blame. Orchestras that had flourished on radio foundered on television. (No one wants to get that close to oboists.) But the real problem was with the competition. Jazz was satisfying a hunger for popular art that in previous eras only classical composers had been able to satisfy. Ellington and Mingus were pulling off the same synthetic feat that Mozart and Verdi had accomplished before them; they were picking up pieces of every form of available music—African-American, Latin, Gypsy, Debussy, operetta—and transforming them through the force of their personalities.

Lately, I have been reading the young intellectuals who embraced jazz in the twenties, and I recognize their urge to join the party. Carl Van Vechten, the notorious author of "Nigger Heaven," started out as a music critic for the *Times;* he witnessed "The Rite of Spring" and embraced Stravinsky as a savior. Then his attention began to wander. He found more life and truth in ragtime, Tin Pan Alley, and, eventually, blues and jazz. In a 1917 article for *Vanity Fair,* he predicted that Tin Pan Alley songwriters were likely to be considered "the true grandfathers of the Great American Composer of the year 2001." For young African-American music mavens, the disenchantment was more bitter and more personal. Some were children of a middle class that had taken to heart Dvořák's 1893 prophecy of a great age of Negro music. The likes of James Weldon Johnson awaited the black Beethoven who would write the music of God's trombones. Soon enough, these aspiring violinists, pianists, and composers came up against a wall of racism. Only in popular music could they make a living. Many—Fletcher Henderson, for example—turned to jazz.

The twenties saw a huge change in music's social function. Classical music had given the middle class aristocratic airs; now popular music helped the middle class to feel down and dirty. There is American musical history in one brutally simplistic sentence. I recently watched a silly 1934 movie entitled "Murder at the Vanities," which seemed to sum up the genre wars of the era. It is set behind the scenes of a Ziegfeld-style variety show, one of whose numbers features a performer, dressed vaguely as Franz Liszt, who plays the Second Hungarian Rhapsody. Duke Ellington and his band keep popping up behind the scenes, throwing in insolent riffs. Eventually, they drive away the effete classical musicians and play a takeoff called "Ebony Rhapsody": "It's got those licks, it's got those tricks / That Mr. Liszt would never recognize." Liszt comes back with a submachine gun and mows down the band. The metaphor wasn't so far off the mark. Although many in the classical world were fulsome in their praise of jazz—Ernest Ansermet lobbed the word "genius" at Sidney Bechet—others fired verbal machine guns in an effort to slay the upstart. Daniel Gregory Mason, the man who wanted more throwing of mats, was one of the worst offenders, calling jazz a "sick moment in the progress of the human soul."

The contempt flowed both ways. The culture of jazz, at least in its white precincts, was much affected by that inverse snobbery which endlessly congratulates itself on escaping the élite. (The singer in "Murder at the Vanities" brags of finding a rhythm that Liszt, of all people, could never comprehend: what a snob.) Classical music became a foil against which popular musicians could assert their earthy cool. Composers, in turn, were irritated by the suggestion that they constituted some sort of moneyed behemoth. They were the ones who were feeling bulldozed by the power of cash. Such was the complaint made by Lawrence Gilman, of the *Tribune,* after Paul Whiteman and his Palais Royal Orchestra played "Rhapsody in Blue" at Aeolian Hall. Gilman didn't like the "Rhapsody," but what really incensed him was

Whiteman's suggestion that jazz was an underdog fighting against symphony snobs. "It is the Palais Royalists who represent the conservative, reactionary, respectable elements in the music of today," Gilman wrote. "They are the aristocrats, the Top Dogs, of contemporary music. They are the Shining Ones, the commanders of huge salaries, the friends of Royalty." The facts back Gilman up. By the late twenties, Gershwin was making at least a hundred thousand dollars a year. In 1938, Copland, the best-regarded composer of American concert music, had $6.93 in his checking account.

All music becomes classical music in the end. Reading the histories of other genres, I often get a warm sense of déjà vu. The story of jazz, for example, seems to recapitulate classical history at high speed. First, the youth-rebellion period: Satchmo and the Duke and Bix and Jelly Roll teach a generation to lose itself in the music. Second, the era of bourgeois grandeur: the high-class swing band parallels the Romantic orchestra. Stage 3: artists rebel against the bourgeois image, echoing the classical modernist revolution, sometimes by direct citation (Charlie Parker works the opening notes of "The Rite of Spring" into "Salt Peanuts"). Stage 4: free jazz marks the point at which the vanguard loses touch with the mass and becomes a self-contained avant-garde. Stage 5: a period of retrenchment. Wynton Marsalis's attempt to launch a traditionalist jazz revival parallels the neo-Romantic music of many late-twentieth-century composers. But this effort comes too late to restore the art to the popular mainstream. Jazz recordings sell about the same as classical recordings, three per cent of the market.

The same progression worms its way through rock and roll. What were my hyper-educated punk-rock friends but Stage 3 high modernists, rebelling against the bloated Romanticism of Stage 2 stadium rock? Right now, there seems to be a lot of Stage 5 classicism going on in what remains of rock and roll. The Strokes, the Hives, the Vines, the Stills, the Thrills, and so on hark back to some lost pure moment of the sixties or seventies. Their names are all variations on the Kinks. Many of them use old instruments, old amplifiers, old soundboards. One rocker was recently quoted as saying, "I intentionally won't use something I haven't heard before." *Macht Neues*, kids! So far, hip-hop has proved resistant to this kind of classicizing cycle, but you never know. It is just a short step from old school to the Second Viennese School.

The original classical is left in an interesting limbo. It has a chance to be liberated from the social clichés that currently pin it down. It is no longer the one form carrying the burden of the past. Moreover, it has the advantage of being able to sustain constant reinterpretation, to renew itself with each repetition. The best kind of classical performance is never a retreat into the past but rather an intensification of the present. When you hear a great orchestra perform Beethoven's "Eroica," it isn't like a rock band trying to mimic the Beatles—it is like the Beatles re-incarnated. The mistake that apostles of the classical have always made is to have joined their love of the past to a dislike of the present. The music has other ideas: it hates the past and wants to escape.

I have seen the future, and it is called Shuffle—the setting on the iPod that skips randomly from one track to another. I've transferred about a thousand songs, works, and sonic events from my CD collection to my computer and on to the MP3 player. There is something thrilling about setting the player on Shuffle and letting it decide what to play next. Sometimes its choices are a touch delirious—I had to veto an attempt to forge a link between György Kurtág and Oasis—but the little machine often goes crashing through barriers of style in ways that change how I listen. For example, it recently made a segue from the furious crescendo of "The Dance of the Earth," ending Part I of "The Rite of Spring," right into the hot jam of Louis Armstrong's "West End Blues." The first became a gigantic upbeat to the other. For a second, I felt that I was at some madly fashionable party at Carl Van Vechten's. On the iPod, music is freed from all fatuous self-definitions and delusions of significance. There are no record jackets depicting bombastic Alpine scenes or celebrity conductors with a family resemblance to Rudolf Hess. Instead, music is music.

It seems to me that a lot of younger listeners think the way the iPod thinks. They are no longer so invested in a single genre, one that promises to mold their being or save the world. This gives the life-style disaster called "classical music" more of a chance. Although the music is far from attaining any sort of countercultural cachet, it is no longer a plausible target for teen rebellion, given that all the parents listen to the Eagles. (A colleague pointed out to me that the movie "School of Rock" pictures a private school where classical music is forced down students' throats. The closing credits don't specify which alternate universe this is set in.) Committed rock fans are likely to know a fair amount about twentieth-century composition, especially the avant-garde. Mavens of electronic dance music list among their heroes Stockhausen, Terry Riley, and, especially, Steve Reich, who avoids the temptation to sue his less inventive admirers. Mark Prendergast's book "The Ambient Century," a history of the new electronic genres, begins, startlingly enough, with Gustav Mahler.

The new buzzword in progressive circles is "post-classical." The phrase was coined by the writer Joseph Horowitz, and it neatly expresses exasperation with the C word without jettisoning it. It also hints that life will go on even if monuments of the old classical empire falter. The scholar Robert Fink is even predicting a Richard Strauss-style "death and transfiguration." Post-classical composers are writing music heavily influenced by minimalism and its electronic spawn, but they are still immersed in the complexity of composition. They just don't need to advertise an entire course of study on the surface of a work. Likewise, new generations of musicians are dropping the mask of Olympian detachment (silent, stone-faced musician walks onstage and begins to play). They've started mothballing the tuxedo, explaining the music from the stage, using lighting and backdrops to produce a mildly theatrical experience. They are finding allies in the "popular" world, some of whom care less about record sales than the average star violinist. The London Sinfonietta, for example, will be playing a program next month of Aphex Twin, Jamie Lidell, and other sonic scientists from the Warp Records label, pairing their work with the constructions of Reich and Cage. The borders between "popular" and "classical" are becoming creatively blurred, and only the Johann Forkels in each camp see a problem.

The strange thing about the music in America today is that large numbers of people seem aware of it, curious about it, even mildly knowledgeable about it, but they do not go to concerts. The people who try to market orchestras have a name for these annoying phantoms: they are "culturally aware non-attenders," to quote a recent article in the magazine *Symphony.* I know the type; most of my friends are case studies. They know the principal names and periods of musical history: they know what Nietzsche said about Wagner, they can pick Schoenberg and Stravinsky out of a lineup, they own Glenn Gould's "Goldberg Variations" and some Mahler and perhaps a CD of Arvo Pärt. They follow all the other arts—they go to gallery shows, read new novels, see art films. Yet they have never paid money for a classical concert. They almost make a point of their ignorance. "I don't know a thing about Beethoven," they say, which is not what they would say if the subject were Henry James or Stanley Kubrick. This is one area where even sophisticates wrap themselves in the all-American anti-intellectual flag. It's not all their fault: centuries of classical intolerance have gone into the creation of the culturally aware non-attender. When I tell people what I do for a living, I see the same look again and again—a flinching sideways glance, as if they were about to be reprimanded for not knowing about C-sharps. After this comes the serene declaration of ignorance. The old culture war is fought and lost before I say a word.

I'm imagining myself on the other side—as a thirty-six-year-old pop fan who wants to try something different. On a lark, I buy a record of Otto Klemperer conducting the "Eroica," picking this one because Klemperer is the father of Colonel Klink, on "Hogan's Heroes." I hear two impressive loud chords, then something that the liner notes allege is a "truly heroic" theme. It sounds kind of feeble, lopsided, waltz-like. My mind drifts. A few days later, I try again. This time, I hear some attractive adolescent grandeur, barbaric yawps here and there. The rest is mechanical, remote. But each time I go back I map out a little more of the imaginary world. I invent stories for each thing as it happens. Big chords, hero standing backstage, a troubling thought, hero orating over loudspeakers, some ideas for songs that don't catch on, a man or woman pleading, hero shouts back, tension, anger, conspiracies—assassination attempt? The nervous splendor of it all gets under my skin. I go to a bookstore and look at the classical shelf, which seems to have more books for Idiots and Dummies than any other section. I read Bernstein's essay in "The Infinite Variety of Music," coordinate some of the examples with the music, read fun stories of the composer screaming about Napoleon, and go back and listen again. Sometime after the tenth listen, the music becomes my own; I know what's around almost every corner and I exult in knowing. It's as if I could predict the news.

I am now enough of a fan that I buy a twenty-five-dollar ticket to hear a famous orchestra play the "Eroica" live. It is not a very heroic experience. I feel dispirited from the moment I walk in the hall. My black jeans draw disapproving glances from men who seem to be modelling the Johnny Carson collection. I look around dubiously at the twenty shades of beige in which the hall is decorated. The music starts, but I find it hard to think of Beethoven's detestation of all tyranny over the human mind when the man next to me is a dead ringer for my dentist. The assassination sequence in the first movement is less exciting when the musicians have no emotion on their faces. I cough; a thin man, reading a dog-eared score, glares at me. When the movement is about a minute from ending, an ancient woman creeps slowly up the aisle, a look of enormous dissatisfaction on her face, followed at a few paces by a blank-faced husband. Finally, three grand chords to finish, which the composer obviously intended to set off a roar of applause. I start to clap, but the man with the score glares again. One does not applaud in the midst of greatly great great music, even if the composer wants one to! Coughing, squirming, whispering, the crowd visibly suppresses its urge to express pleasure. It's like mass anal retention. The slow tread of the Funeral March, or *Marcia funebre,* as everyone insists on calling it, begins. I start to feel that my newfound respect for the music is dragging along behind the hearse.

But I stay with it. For the duration of the Marcia, I try to disregard the audience and concentrate on the music. It strikes me that what I'm hearing is an entirely natural phenomenon, nothing more than the vibrations of creaky old instruments reverberating around a boxlike hall. Each scrape of a bow translates into a strand of sound; what I see is what I hear. So when the cellos and basses make the floor tremble with their big deep note in the middle of the march (what Bernstein calls the "*wham!*") the force of the moment is purely physical. Amplifiers are for sissies, I'm starting to think. The orchestra isn't playing with the same cowed intensity as Klemperer's heroes, but the tone is warmer and deeper and rounder than on the CD. I make my peace with the stiffness of the scene by thinking of it as a cool frame for a hot event. Perhaps this is how it has to be: Beethoven needs a passive audience as a foil.

To my left, a sleeping dentist; to my right, an angry aesthete; and, in front of me, the funeral march that rises to a fugal fury, and breaks down into softly sobbing memories of themes, and then gives way to an entirely new mood—hard-driving, laughing, lurching, a little drunk.

Two centuries ago, Beethoven bent over the manuscript of the "Eroica" and struck out Napoleon's name. It is often said that he made himself the protagonist of the work instead. Indeed, he engendered an archetype—the rebel artist hero—that modern artists are still recycling. I wonder, though, if Beethoven's gesture meant what people think it did. Perhaps he was freeing his music from a too specific interpretation, from his own preoccupations. He was setting his symphony adrift, as a message in a bottle. He could hardly have imagined it travelling two hundred years, through the dark heart of the twentieth century and into the pulverizing electronic age. But he knew it would go far, and he did not weigh it down. There was now a torn, blank space on the title page. The symphony became a fragmentary, unfinished thing, and unfinished it remains. It becomes whole again only in the mind and soul of someone listening for the first time, and listening again. The hero is you.

In Praise of Self-Deception

David Livingstone Smith

Where shall I stand, when the text of my life deconstructs itself at every turn of the page?

—Bas van Fraassen

'Know thyself' is one of the most successful slogans in history. Thales of Miletus—a philosopher, who flourished in the 6th century before Christ, is credited with having coined the phrase, and Plato tells us that it was inscribed at the entrance to the temple of Apollo at Delphi, and it is still popular today, over 2500 years later. 'Know thyself' sounds terrific in theory, but how feasible—or desirable—is it in practice? According to the Roman writer Diogenes Laertius, who wrote a popular, gossipy book six centuries later called *Lives of the Eminent Philosophers*, Thales described knowing oneself as 'the most difficult thing in life'.[1] Thales was not alone in this. Even the great Enlightenment philosopher Immanuel Kant also spoke grimly of the 'hard descent into the Hell of self-knowledge' and claimed that self-observation leads to 'the gloomiest melancholia', while his younger countryman, the German polymath Wolfgang von Goethe kicked the condemnation up a notch when he stated that 'know thyself' is a 'deception . . . to confuse humanity with impossible demands.' 'Know thyself?' he wrote, 'If I knew myself I would

[1] Plato discusses 'know thyself' in *Charmides* (164d–165b). For Diogenes Laertus' remarks on Thales, see Laertus, D. *Lives of the Philosophers* (Washington: Regnery, 1969).

run away.'[2] Mark Twain, whose insightful writings were relished by the likes of Charles Darwin, William James and Sigmund Freud hinted *why* knowing oneself might be so trying: 'Man, "Know thyself—& then thou wilt despise thyself, to a dead moral certainty." '[3]

On the face of it, there is something puzzling about the idea that self-knowledge is difficult to attain. After all, we are more intimately related to ourselves than we are to anything else in the universe, aren't we? We have to live with ourselves day in and day out, so shouldn't it follow that we *know* ourselves better than we know anything else?

To come to grips with the idea of self-knowledge, we need to understand what 'knowledge' is—what it means to *know* something. The English verb 'to know' has two meanings that are often confused. In some languages, each of these two meanings has a word all its own (in German, these are '*kennen*' and '*wissen*', and in French '*connaître*' and '*savoir*'). The British philosopher Bertrand Russell was the first person to address the ambiguity of the English 'know', and tried to rectify the problem by drawing a distinction between 'knowledge by acquaintance' and 'knowledge by description' (nowadays shortened to 'acquaintance' and 'knowledge').[4] To be acquainted with something means that you have come into contact with it (this, by the way,

[2] Kant's remarks are in Ak 25: 252 and Ak 25:863, cf.. 25:477–478, 865 in *Kant's gesammelte Schriften.* (Berlin: Georg Reimer, 1900ce).

Goethe, J.W. von 'Significant help given by an ingenious turn of phrase.' In *Scientific Studies.* Trans. D. Miller (New York: Suhrkamp, 1988) p. 39 and 'Sprichwörtlich' In *Münchner Ausgabe: Sämtliche Werke nach Epochen seines Schaffens, Vol. 9.* (München: C. Hanser, 1985), p. 144. For research studies on depression, self-deception and mental health that support Kant's claims see Lane, R. D., Merikangas, K. R., Schwartz, G. E., et al. 'Inverse relationship between defensiveness and lifetime prevalence of psychiatric disorder', *American Journal of Psychiatry*, 147 [1990]: 573–578. Sackheim, H. A. and Gur, R. C. 'Self deception, other deception, and self-reported psychopathology'. *Journal of Consulting Clinical Psychology*, 47 [1979]: 213–215. Sackheim, H. A. and Wegner, A. Z. 'Attributional patterns in depression and euthymia.' *Archives of General Psychiatry*, 43 [1986]: 553–560. Taylor, S. E. and Brown, J. D. 'Illusion and well-being: a social psychological perspective on mental health', *Psychological Bulletin*, 103 [1988]: 193–210; Lewinsohn, P. M *et. al.* 'Social competence and depression: the role of illusionary self-perceptions', *Journal of Abnormal Psychology*, 89 [1980]: 203–212. Alloy, L. B. and Abramson, L.Y. 'Depression and pessimism for the future: biased use of statistically relevant information in predictions of self versus others.' *Journal of Personality and Social Psychology*, 41 [1987]: 1129–1140; Alloy, L. B. and Abramson, L.Y. 'Judgement of contingency in depressed and nondepressed students: sadder but wiser?' *Journal of Experimental Psychology: General*, 108(4) [1979]: 441–485. Alloy, L. B. and Abramson, L.Y. 'Learned helplessness, depression and the illusion of control', *Journal of Personality and Social Psychology*, 42 [1982]: 1114–1126.

[3] For Darwin and Twain see Twain, M. 'Our guest'. In *Collected Tales, Sketches, Speeches and Essays, 1891–1910.* (New York: Library of America, 1992). For Freud and Twain see Gay, P. *Freud: A Life for Our Time.* (New York: W.W. Norton & Co., 1998). For James and Twain see Horn, J.G. *Mark Twain and William James: Crafting a Free Self.* (Columbia, MO: University of Missouri Press, 1996). The quotation is from a letter to W. D. Howells, 8/31/1884 in Paine, A.B. *Mark Twain's Letters.* (New York: Classic Books, 2000).

[4] Russell, B. *The Problems of Philosophy* (Oxford: Oxford University Press, 2001).

is the basis of the *Biblical* 'know' as a synonym for sexual intercourse). Knowledge, on the other hand, concerns what is true of things. When we are acquainted with a thing we 'know' it, but when we have knowledge of it—in the strict Russellian sense—we know *about* it. I am certainly not *acquainted* with Julius Caesar. I've never met the man, and, unless there turns out to be an Afterlife, or someone invents a time machine, I never will be acquainted with him. But I know that Julius Caesar's mother was named Aurelia, that his wife was named Cornelia, that he led expeditions to Gaul and Britain, and so on. Russell's clarification proved to be amazingly useful, because it cut through a whole thicket of confusions with one swift, clean stroke.

Let's think about self-knowledge in light of Russell's distinction. Obviously, we are all acquainted with ourselves, given that we are identical to ourselves and have to live with ourselves 24/7. The same cannot be said about knowing about ourselves. Sure, I know that I was born in Brooklyn, that I am six feet four inches tall, that I live in Maine, and so on. I know quite a lot about myself, but these pedestrian facts are not the kinds of things that most people are concerned with when they talk about self-knowledge. The discourse of self-knowledge is about the true driving forces of one's life—one's core desires, beliefs and fears—the things that 'make you tick' as opposed to superficial appearances. So the idea of self-knowledge presupposes a differentiating grade in the psyche, a metaphorical distinction between surface and depth, the peripheral and the central. Self-knowledge, in the interesting sense, means knowing about the wellsprings of our own behavior and it is precisely this that Thales, Kant, Goethe and Twain—not to mention Nietzsche and Freud—regarded as excruciatingly difficult.

If self-knowledge seems straightforward to you, and you just don't get what all the fuss is about, you may be one of a surprisingly large number of people who are trapped in the gravely misconceived view of the mind formalized by René Descartes in the 17th century. The Cartesian vision of the mind consists of three interlocking components. First, Descartes held that the mind is something distinct from the body. The body is an 'extended substance.' In philosophical lingo a 'substance' is, roughly, a 'thing', and an 'extended substance' is a material object that takes up space. Descartes thought that the mind is an unextended 'thinking substance' that is not composed of matter, and does not occupy space. This segues into the second component. The mind, is a *simple* substance: it is unitary, indivisible and without parts. Finally, the mind is 'transparent' to itself, automatically and incorrigibly aware of its own contents. It is important to understand that both the second and third pair of characteristics spin-off from the first one. A mind that does not occupy space is by definition indivisible and an indivisible mind—a mind without parts—a mind without parts must be aware of *all* of its inner states if it is aware of *any* of them. There is just no conceptual elbow-room for a Cartesian mind to hide anything from itself.

Today we know that Descartes was wrong. There is every reason to believe that the mind is the brain, an organ that is extended in space and composed of parts—lots of them. The chunk of meat between your ears consists of just under one hundred billion nerve cells, each of which is connected to up to ten thousand others. Living brains sizzle with activity, as each member of this enormous population sends and receives electrical signals to and from its neighbors, generating constantly changing patterns of activation.

Normal human beings have an extraordinarily wide range of abilities: they can count, comprehend language, discriminate between colors, flirt, enjoy music, understand a joke, be embarrassed, empathize with the feelings of others, find their way home, get a joke, catch a ball, etc., etc. This versatility is very impressive. How can it be explained? One option is to suppose that the brain is an immensely elastic all-purpose organ—a sort of polymath or 'Renaissance man' excelling in a great many talents simultaneously. However, over the last two decades, many cognitive scientists have found it useful to regard our hugely complex brains as composed of hundreds or even thousands of miniature 'brains'—stable, functional systems—that they call 'mental modules'. Each of these modules is a hidebound specialist that is brilliant at performing tasks that fall within its domain, but utterly incapable of handling anything outside it. The brain resembles a committee of *idiots savants* more than it does a single genius.

Descartes also erred in claiming that the mind is transparent to itself. We now know that most mental activity is unconscious. The cognitive processes that enable you to type a sentence, whack a tennis ball over the net, remember a loved one's birthday, or perform virtually any other mental or physical act lie beyond the reach of self-awareness. They are as alien to your conscious mind, as inaccessible to introspection, as the workings of your pancreas. Most mental processes are unconscious in consequence of the functional architecture of the brain: we aware of the sorts of mental contents that it is useful for us to be aware of, and not others. Driving a brain is like driving a car: for the most part, all that matters is that it gets you where you want to go. However, the boundary between conscious and unconscious is not always so rigidly fixed: some mental contents can in principle become conscious, but are prevented from doing so. The act of excluding mental contents from awareness is called self-deception, a phenomenon acknowledged to be central to the human condition at least since the time of the ancient Greeks. 'Were a portrait of man to be drawn . . . in which there would be highlighted whatever is most human,' wrote philosopher Herbert Fingarette on the first page of a classic study of self-deception, '. . . we should surely place well in the foreground man's enormous capacity for self-deception'. Throngs of philosophers, playwrights, and novelists have agreed. The Dark Continent of self-deception has even found a place on the map of contemporary psychology. As one review of the now extensive scientific research literature summed up 'In general, people's self-views hold only a tenuous to modest relationship with their actual behavior and performance. . . . Indeed, at times, other people's predictions of a person's outcomes prove more accurate than a person's self-predictions.'[5] For example, surgical residents overestimate their skills compared to objective measures on medical board exams. College students who do a good job estimating how long their roommates' romantic relationships will last fail miserably at predicting the length of their own. Lawyers are unrealistically sanguine about their prospects for victory in court, investors make unwarranted assumptions about the potential of their investments, and most of us think that we are better than average at assessing ourselves.[6]

On the face of it, the very idea of self-deception seems incoherent. How can one and the same person be both the perpetrator and dupe of their own deception? Isn't that as impossibly circular as pulling yourself up by your own bootstraps? Not really. The seeming impossibility of self-deception is an artifact of a wrong-headed conception of the mind—a variant on Descartes' mistake of thinking of the mind as a simple substance. Most of us share a broadly similar and largely unarticulated assumption about our conscious mental processes, which seems so obviously true that it is difficult to question. The assumption is that thinking is an intrinsically conscious process, and that we are aware of our thoughts at the very moment that we think them. However, as Freud pointed out just over a century ago, it may be more accurate to regard *all* cognition as occurring unconsciously, and consciousness as a kind of afterthought. Freud thought that we are never aware of our thoughts while we are thinking them: we only become conscious of them after the fact. Consciousness, on this view, is merely a passive medium of representation. All of the cognitive action is unconscious.

We cannot directly observe the neurochemical activities that go on between our ears. But even if we could—say, by some new technological marvel—we

[5] Dunning, D., Heath, C. & Suls, J.M. 'Flawed self-assessment: implications for health, education and the workplace.' *Psychological Science in the Public Interest*, 5(3): 69–106. p. 69.

[6] For surgeons see Risucci, D.A., Torolani, A.J. & Ward, R.A. 'Ratings of surgical residents by self, supervisors and peers.' *Surgical Gynecology and Obstetrics*, 169 [1989]: 519–526. For college students' love affairs see MacDonald, T.K. & Ross, M. 'Assessing the accuracy of predictions about dating relationships. How and why do lovers' predictions differ from those of observers?' *Personality and Social Psychology Bulletin*, 25 [1999]: 1417–1429. For lawyers, see Loftus, E.F. & Wagenaar, W.A. 'Lawyers' predictions of success.' *Jurimetrics Journal*, 29 [1988]: 437–453. For doctors see Odean, T. 'Volume, volatility, price and profit when all traders are above average.' *Journal of Finance*, 8 [1998]: 1887–1934. For unbiased self-assessment see Friedrich, J. 'On seeing oneself as less self-serving than others: the ultimate self-serving bias?' *Teaching of Psychology*, 23 [1996]: 107–109 and Pronin, E., Linn, D.Y. & Ross, I. 'The bias blind spot: perceptions of bias in self versus others.' *Personality and Social Psychology Bulletin*, 28 [2002]: 369–381.

would not understand what these brain processes *mean.* If someone were to show you a detailed snapshot of the processes going on in your brain at precisely 11:13:06 EST on February 16, 2005, you would be none the wiser about your mental state at that time. This does not mean that thinking involves some mysterious extra ingredient that transcends the neurological domain. It simply means that neural messages are not accessible to us as such. Freud reasoned that there must be a mechanism that *translates* unconscious neural activation vectors into a medium that we can understand. He thought that our brains translate the 'language' of neural activation vectors into linguistic symbols, representing electrochemical signals leaping across synapses as the silent monologue that we call conscious thought.

If this general picture is right, it suggests that self-deception occurs when the translating mechanism fails. The translation is garbled, inaccurate or otherwise misleading and the text of our conscious thought—which is, after all the only *ostensibly* direct means of accessing our inner workings—is censored by an invisible hand. Imagine that the processes described in Freud's theory are unfolding in your brain right now. As you sit, a stream of thoughts is generated in the unconscious depths of your brain. These enter your consciousness as a sequence of unspoken sentences. Now, imagine what would happen if the system that translates neural information into unspoken sentences malfunctioned, so that the monologue flowing through your consciousness no longer veraciously expressed your thoughts. If this happened, *you would no longer be aware of what you are really thinking.* And worse, you would be none the wiser because there would be no way for to compare your real thoughts, which are unconscious, with the thoughts that you falsely *believe* yourself to be thinking. Freud may or may not have gotten the details right, but his theory shows that re-jigging one's model of the mind can make self-deception seem a lot less preposterous.[7] By modifying our conception of how the mind works, and especially our conception of the role of consciousness, it becomes easy to understand how self-deception is possible.

There is a further puzzle posed by self-deception, this time a biological one. If self-deception is a piece of human nature, found everywhere and in all historical epochs, the odds are that it was a product of evolution. Evolution is driven by selection. Mother Nature chooses which traits to retain and which

[7] For the details of Freud's theory see Smith, D. L. *Freud's Philosophy of the Unconscious. Studies in Cognitive Systems, Vol. 23.* (Dordrecht, NL: Kluwer, 1999) and Smith, D. L. ' "Some unimaginable substratum": a contemporary introduction to Freud's philosophy of mind'. In Chung, M. C. & Feltham, C. (Eds.) *Psychoanalytic Knowledge and the Nature of Mind.* New York: Palgrave [2003]. There is a substantial scientific literature supporting Freud's hypothesis that consciousness is mediated by inner speech. For an excellent review see Morin, A. 'Possible links between self-awareness and inner speech: theoretical background, underlying mechanisms and empirical evidence.' *Journal of Consciousness Studies,* 12(4–5)[2005]: 115–134.

to discard, and she only favors those traits that are adaptive—traits that benefit an organism's genes, either by increasing its breeding opportunities or by boosting its survival prospects. If self-deception is an adaptive trait, there must be some sense in which a person can benefit by depriving themselves of information. Of course, this conjecture flies in the face of the commonsense assumption that information is good, and the more of it we have, the more successfully we can negotiate hazards and exploit the opportunities presented by the world around us. But commonsense is a good servant but a bad master. Scientific understanding typically involves getting under the skin of reality, and moving from the merely obvious to the genuinely veridical.

To understand self-deception, we first have to consider why we deceive others. As is often the case with fundamental questions about the human condition, Plato covered the basics. In *The Republic*, he describes a conversation that unfolded at an informal get-together at the home of a wealthy merchant in the port of Piraeus, just outside of Athens. Eventually, the discussion turned to the nature of justice and Thrasymachus, who comes across as a bit of a bully, argued that fair play is for simpleminded fools and that astute people are ruthlessly self-serving. Eventually Plato's brother Adeimantus remarks, in support of Thrasymachus, that:

> If I am unjust, but have gained a reputation for justice, then I am promised a wonderful life. Therefore since 'Appearance,' as the wise men have pointed out to me, 'overpowers truth' and controls happiness, I must turn all my attention to that. I must draw an exact likeness of goodness around myself, as a front and a façade. . . . 'The trouble with that,' someone will say, 'is that it is hard to be evil and get away with it for ever.' 'Well,' we shall say, 'nothing great was ever easy.' But if we are going to be happy, we must follow where the trail of our argument leads us.[8]

Adeimantus was right. Appearance trumps reality because appearance is all we ever have to go by. We are condemned to judge books by their covers, so if a person appears to be good, reliable, virtuous, and so on, we conclude that they really *are* good, reliable, virtuous, and so on. Obviously, then, it pays to cultivate appearances and—as Adeimantus pointed out to Socrates—exploiting others is a rewarding pastime. Wheelers and dealers have access to wealth, status and sexual opportunities that are denied to their more conscientious brethren. But cheating is also a gamble, promising profits but threatening losses. A person caught red-handed defrauding other community members is likely to be punished. At best, he will be treated with suspicion and at worst he may be killed. The obvious way to maximize benefits while keeping losses to a bare minimum is to deceive others. This way,

[8] Plato *The Republic*. Trans. Griffith, T. (Cambridge: Cambridge University Press, 2000) p. 46.

the successful cheater can savor the best of both worlds: reaping the rewards of an unblemished reputation while at the same time getting extra benefits on the side.

What does this say about the evolution of human nature? Nature selects for what *works.* So, if dishonesty works, we should expect to find deception pervading the biosphere. And this is precisely what we find. Nature is a tapestry of guile, of organisms that use every manipulative trick in the book to help them survive and reproduce. The scientific literature overflows with examples. Some are masters of camouflage and seamlessly merge with their environments; others imitate toxic or disgusting objects to avoid being eaten, or disguise themselves as members of the opposite sex to avoid costly sexual competition or to finagle expensive courtship gifts.[9] *Homo sapiens* is also a deceptive species, and our use of tactics infinitely more devious than the techniques available to nonhuman organisms. Furthermore, our background awareness that social life is a complex game of manipulation and counter-manipulation makes us naturally wary of one another. Think of a time that you told a serious lie, and how you felt when you were telling it. Your heart was probably pounding in your chest, your breathing was rapid and shallow, and you had a sinking feeling in the pit of your stomach. The sensation of warmth spreading across your cheeks warned you of an impending blush and there seemed no way to stem the rising tide of anxiety. And worst of all, your *awareness* of all this made you even *more* anxious and maladroit. Could this be a situation where it pays not to know what you are up to? Mark Twain seems to have been the first person to think of this. 'When a person cannot deceive himself,' he wrote, 'the chances are against his being able to deceive other people.'[10] Too much self-awareness can be a hindrance when trying to deceive others.

This idea was rediscovered and elaborated by evolutionary biologist Robert Trivers in the 1970s. Trivers suggested that the capacity for self-deception may have been selected for because it helps us deceive others more effectively.

> Biologists propose that the overriding function of self-deception is the more fluid deception of *others.* That is, hiding aspects of reality from the conscious mind also hides these aspects more deeply from others. An *unconscious* deceiver is not expected to show signs of the stress associated with consciously trying to perpetrate deception.[11]

---

[9] Chapter 2 of my book *Why We Lie: The Evolutionary Roots of Deception and the Unconscious Mind* (New York: St. Martins Press, 2004) details many examples of non-human deception.

[10] Twain, M. (1924) *Mark Twain's Autobiography.* (New York: Harper & Brothers, 1924).

[11] Trivers, R. L. 'Introduction.' In J. S. Lockhard & D. L Paulhus (Eds.) *Self-Deception: An Adaptive Mechanism?* (Englewood Cliffs, NJ: Prentice Hall, 1988) vii.

A liar that believes his or her own lies is far more convincing than one who doesn't, because there is no reason to be awkward and self-conscious. He who lies best lies least consciously, and the accomplished self-deceiver can manage to deliver self-serving falsehoods without even breaking a sweat.[12] Human beings invest a great deal in 'impression management.' In the developed world, we spend vast amounts of money on cosmetics, cosmetic surgery, hair dye, hairpieces, fashionable clothing, perfumes and assorted bling-bling, all for the purpose of creating a desirable impression on others. We are also masters of 'spin', posturing, strategic omission and outright lying to seduce others into seeing us in precisely the ways that we want to be seen. For this to work, we have to keep ourselves in the dark about what we are doing. A woman applying blush and lipstick, who dyes her hair to eliminate those telltale strands of gray, cannot afford to be fully aware that she is counterfeiting signs of fertility to create a false impression of her reproductive value. A statesman proclaiming his desire to serve his nation cannot afford to realise that his heartfelt altruism is in the service of a quest for power and status—ultimately to maximize his sexual prospects. And you and I cannot afford to see through the innumerable deceptions that we unwittingly perpetrate in our daily lives. Our lives are awash with deceit, but becoming aware of it would be to sip from a poisoned chalice, because it would undermine the foundations on which our lives are built. Self-deception is not a pathological state, a deviation from the norm of truthfulness. It is normal, 'healthy' and adaptive. It helps get us through the night, oils the machinery of social intercourse and blunts the jagged edges of our relationships with one another. In this sense, there is arguably something nihilistic about urging others to seek self-knowledge, and something self-destructive about pursuing it.

[12] Trivers, R.L. 'Self-deception in service of deceit.' In *Natural Selection and Social Theory: Selected Papers of Robert Trivers.* (Oxford: Oxford University Press, 2002).

The Blue of Distance

Rebecca Solnit

In 1527 the Spaniard Álvar Núñez Cabeza de Vaca refused his commander's orders to take the ships of their expedition to a safe port while the commander and most of the men marched inland to explore. Narváez, the commander, asked why, and Cabeza de Vaca, the expedition's second in command, answered "that I felt certain he would never find the ships again, or they him, as anyone could predict from the woefully inadequate preparation; that I would rather hazard the danger that lay ahead in the interior than give any occasion for questioning my honor by remaining safely aboard." So the incompetent Narváez, Cabeza de Vaca, and three hundred men traveled north for fifteen days among the dwarf fan palms of an uninhabited expanse of what Juan Ponce de León had named Florida fourteen years before. They had met natives who told them that to the north was "a province called Apalachen, where was much gold and plenty of everything we wanted." Honor and greed would be the two gates through which Cabeza de Vaca entered the realm of the utter unknown.

The Apalachen they found was a village of forty thatched houses with ripe corn in the fields, dry corn in storage, deerskins, and "small, poor quality shawls" as all its treasure. The gold seekers marched onward, wading through lakes, tramping for days, skirmishing with natives, eating their horses, building barges to head toward Mexico and the Spanish settlements there, not knowing how far away they were, dying of armor-piercing arrows, of disease, of hunger, of drowning. No one will ever be lost like those early conquistadors again, wandering a continent about which they knew nothing, not its topography, its climate, encountering inhabitants with whom there was no common language, plunging into a place for which they had no words for places, for plants, for the animals—skunks, alligators, bison—so unlike those of their own continent.

Eduardo Galeano notes that America was conquered, but not discovered, that the men who arrived with a religion to impose and dreams of gold never really knew where they were, and that this discovery is still taking place in our time. This suggests that most European-Americans remained lost over the centuries, lost not in practical terms but in the more profound sense of apprehending where they truly were, of caring what the history of the place was and its nature. Instead, they named it after the places they had left and tried to reconstruct those places through imported plants, animals, and practices, though pumpkin, maple, and other staples would enter their diet as words like Connecticut and Dakota and raccoon would enter their vocabularies. But Cabeza de Vaca and his companions would be conquered by this land and its people, and he at least seems to have found out where he was. All but four of the six hundred men who set out on the expedition died in this place they did not know, either quickly, of violence, illness, or hunger, or slowly, as slaves or adopted members of tribes, and their stories are mostly lost to history.

At the Mississippi Delta, Narváez put the strongest and healthiest men on his barge and rowed ahead, abandoning the two other barges. Days passed. One barge was lost in a storm. Cabeza de Vaca commanded the other, whose men had all "fallen over on one another, close to death. Few were any longer conscious. Not five could stand. When night fell, only the navigator and I remained able to tend the barge. Two hours after dark, he told me I must take over; he believed he was going to die that night." After midnight, Cabeza de Vaca recalls, "I would have welcomed death rather than see so many around me in such a condition." At dawn, he heard breakers; at daylight, they found the land that was probably Galveston Island in Texas; and the men "began to recover their senses, their locomotion, and their hope." Natives fed them fish and roots; they embarked again but the barge capsized near shore; and "the survivors escaped as naked as they were born, with the loss of everything we had." They fell upon the mercy of the natives again. Winter had come, the Spaniards commenced to starve, the natives began to die of the dysentery that came with them, and the sixteen survivors of the ninety or so shipwrecked named the place the Island of Doom.

Cabeza de Vaca became a slave to this tribe, leading an "unbearable" life of hard work, including digging roots out of water and out of canebrakes. He was pared back to nothing, no language, no clothes, no weapons, no power, but he escaped and established a career as a trader of seashells, red ocher, and mesquite beans in the region. He seems to have had remarkable physical stamina and an ability to reinvent himself again and again. He walked for days and weeks on one austere meal a day. He became a slave again. He met up with some fellow survivors and with them escaped this new captivity. They arrived in the territory of another indigenous nation where they were welcomed as healers and stayed until spring. And what is remarkable about this point in his narrative is that he reports that he got lost looking for mesquite bean pods. He had so adapted to this new life he had fallen into that he no longer considered himself lost until he lost track of the route and his companions in the pathless region of the mesquites. He traveled for five days, carrying burning brands so he could keep himself warm with fires at night, and on the fifth he caught up with his fellow survivors from the Narváez expedition and with the Indians, who fed him prickly pears.

Because they went naked in the scorching sun, he reports, he and his companions "shed our skins twice a year like snakes" and suffered sores from sun, wind, and chafing labor (though one of them, Estevanico or Esteban, "the negro," was from Africa and must have fared better when it came to burning). And again "we became physicians, of whom I was the boldest and most venturous in trying to cure anything. Confidence in our ministrations as infallible extended to a belief that none could die while we were among them." Months passed among various tribes, years had passed since the disasters in Florida. They continued to travel west. Somewhere along the way they seem to have become sacred beings, these naked, relentless survivors whose journey had became a triumphal procession accompanied by three or four thousand locals. Each new village greeted them as miracle workers, holding dances in their honor. They received copper rattles, coral beads, turquoises, five green arrowheads whose malachite Cabeza de Vaca took for emerald, and an offering of six hundred deer hearts. They had been wandering for nine years by the time they arrived in what he called the Village of Hearts.

Soon after, they found evidence and heard news of conquistadors: they had arrived in what is now New Mexico, a "vast territory, which we found vacant, the inhabitants having fled to the mountains in fear of Christians." Assuring the natives that they were going to "order them to stop killing, enslaving, and dispossessing the Indians," Cabeza de Vaca and his three companions pressed on. In the report he would write afterward, Cabeza de Vaca advised that only kindness would win these people to Spanish subjection and to Christianity. One day he set out with his black-skinned companion and eleven natives, walking more than thirty miles. The following morning they caught up with slave-hunting Spaniards on horseback, who were stunned by this naked figure at ease among the people and places of this other continent. Although he had been striving for nearly a decade to return to his own people, the initial meeting was not easy. The Spaniards they met wanted to enslave Cabeza de Vaca's entourage, and he and his fellow survivors "became so angry that we went off forgetting the many Turkish-shaped bows, the many pouches, and the five emerald arrowheads, etc., which we thus lost." The Indians among whom they retreated refused to believe they were of the same tribe as the conquistadors, because "we came from the sunrise; they from the sunset; we healed the sick, they killed the sound; we came naked and barefoot, they clothed, horsed, and lanced; we coveted nothing but gave whatever we were given, while they robbed whomever they found and bestowed nothing on anyone." These men who came from the sunset were what he had been when he landed in Florida.

It took some time after he arrived in a Spanish town in Mexico before he could stand to wear clothes or sleep anywhere but on the floor. He had gone about naked, shed his skin like a snake, had lost his greed, his fear, been stripped of almost everything a human being could lose and live, but he had learned several languages, he had become a healer, he had come to admire and identify with the Native nations among whom he lived; he was not who he had been. The language of his report to the king is terse, impersonal; his declarative sentences describe only the tangibles of places, foods, encounters, and even these are given in the starkest terms, with little description, little detail. The terms in which to describe the extraordinary metamorphosis of his soul did not exist, at least for him. He was among the first, and the first to come back and tell the tale, of Europeans lost in the Americas, and like many of them he ceased to be lost not by returning but by turning into something else.

Cabeza de Vaca and his companions plunged into the American landscape, but in the centuries afterward many entered it involuntarily, as captives. Some of those who returned wrote or dictated accounts of their experiences, and these became a distinctly American genre of literature, the captivity narrative. Of course the stories of those who did not return remained unrecorded; their journeys were out of writing, out of English, into another terrain of story.

Often, initially, these strays and captives felt that they were far from home, distant from their desires, and then at some point, in a stunning reversal, they came to be at home and what they had longed for became remote, alien, unwanted. For some, perhaps there was a moment when they realized that the old longings had become little more than habit and that they were not yearning to go home but had been home for some time; for others the dreams of home must have faded by stages among the increasingly familiar details of their surroundings. They must have learned their surroundings like a language and one day woken up fluent in them. Somehow, for these castaways the far became near and the near far. They did not reject the unfamiliar but embraced it, in the course of which it became familiar. By the end of his decade of wandering, Cabeza de Vaca was no longer in harmony with his own culture, but he had kept it as a destination, a goal, that kept him purposeful and moving, even though arrival was another trauma. Many others refused to return.

In the midst of winter, in the frontier town of Deerfield, Massachusetts, 1704, Eunice Williams, age seven, was captured by a party of French and Indian raiders, along with all the other members of her family and many of their neighbors, 112 in all. They were given moccasins to wear and marched from northern Massachusetts to near Montreal through New Hampshire, in the snow. Some of the captors were wounded and dying, and some of the captives who could not keep up—notably infants, women who had recently given birth, including Williams's mother—were killed, their bodies left in the snow along the route. Many children were carried some or all of the way. Some of these child captives were not just prisoners but potential adoptees; Eunice's older brother Stephen Williams was taken by the Abenaki and then by a Pennacook chief, though he was "redeemed" as the religiously loaded term went, or ransomed, in the spring of 1705. Eunice was kept by the Mohawk Iroquois near Montreal, and she never returned.

The Iroquois practiced a ceremonious form of adoption in which a captive could replace a family member who had died, and sometimes captives were explicit replacements for those killed in battle. The captive was given a new name and treated as a member of the family. Sometimes the given name belonged to some one who had died, and the newly named person inherited something of the affections and identity of the deceased. Ceremoniously, officially, Eunice Williams became someone else. Within a few years, all her surviving family members had returned to their Puritan communities, but the people among whom she lived said they would "as soon part with their hearts" as with her. She remained, soon forgot how to speak English, had a new name, then a Catholic baptismal name (becoming Catholic was almost more shocking to her Puritan preacher father than becoming Indian), eventually a second Iroquois name.

In 1713 in her late teens she married a member of the community named François Xavier Arosen with whom she remained until his death fifty-two years later. Her brother Stephen would write in his diary in 1722 that he had seen a man come from Canada. "He brings bad news thence. My poor sister lives with her Indian husband; has had two children, one is living, the other not." The Williams family never ceased to mourn her loss and to regard her as spiritually lost as well. But Eunice Williams had ceased to be a captive long ago. She finally met with Stephen and her other brothers in 1740, traveled with them to their home, and even attended "publick worship" with them. "Yet this might be as a pledge yt she may return to the house and ordinances of God from wch she has been so long Sepratd," though according to tradition she refused to "put off her Indian blankets" and camped out in a meadow with her husband rather than residing in a relative's home. She was negotiating her emotional and cultural distance carefully, on her terms rather than theirs. On a few further occasions, she revisited her birth family, but she never left the community that had captured her, and in it she died at age ninety-five.

Her family always spoke as though she had crossed over into another world beyond reach, but what is striking is that even in the eighteenth century the boundaries were blurred. The Mohawks among whom she lived had close ties to the Jesuits of Montreal, and there was considerable movement between the various French, English, and Native communities. But it was different enough.

She no longer spoke the language of her blood relatives, did not see them for more than three decades, and had settled among a people whose every belief and practice was profoundly different from the Puritans'. John Demos, in his book on Williams, *The Unredeemed Captive*, suggests that the Iroquois were kinder to children, and perhaps the thing hardest for whites to accept or, often, even to imagine is that some captives preferred native culture. Looking back, the cultures of Cabeza de Vaca's Spaniards and Eunice Williams's family look more forbidding, if no less remote, than the indigenous cultures among which they came to live. There is something obdurate, obsessive, inflexible about them, as hard and angular as conquistadors' armor, as dreary as Puritan theology.

Some of this is evident in Stephen Williams's refusal to regard her as anything other than a tragedy, a captive, a person waiting to return, to understand that she had become someone else. The word *lost* in this context has many shades. The captive is at first literally lost, taken into terra incognita. And unless that captive is redeemed, he or more frequently she remains lost to the people who were left behind, and thus the language of lostness is often used to describe the person as lost the way that a possession is lost—a lost umbrella, lost keys—without recognizing that he or more commonly she may well have ceased either to be a captive or to be lost. But the word *lost* has spiritual implications, as in the line of the penitent slave trader's hymn "I once was lost but now am found"; the person taken among the heathen was commonly imagined to be spiritually lost, estranged from Christianity and civilization. Thus, whatever the condition of the former captives, they were forever imagined as lost. But they did not always imagine themselves that way, and it seems that the captives had in a sense to lose their past to join the present, and this abandonment of memory, of old ties, is the steep cost of adaptation.

Mary Jemison, who was captured with her family in Pennsylvania in 1758, told her story to a scribe, and so her voice survives as Williams's does not. There was a raid on her parents' frontier farm when she was about fifteen. An Indian followed them with a lash, forcing the children to maintain the pace. They were marched, kept without food and water for days, and then taken to "the border of a dark and dismal swamp." There she and a little boy were given moccasins, signs that their journey would continue, while the other captives, including her parents and siblings, were killed "and mangled in the most shocking manner." Like Eunice Williams, she was adopted. She was to replace a brother who had died, and the two Seneca women—"kind good natured women; peaceable and mild in their dispositions"—to whom she was given she referred to as sisters ever after. The trauma of captivity, of the murder of family members, and a sudden new life among another culture and another language must have been considerable, but adapting to it all was a matter of survival, and these child captives survived and then flourished in their new lives. The rupture must have been as sudden and violent as birth.

More than a year later, the Senecas among whom she lived brought her along on a visit to Fort Pitt (the future Pittsburgh), where the whites took such an interest in her that her sisters "hurried me into their canoe and recrossed the river" and rowed the long journey home without stopping. "The sight of white people who could speak English inspired me with an unspeakable anxiety to go home with them, and share in the blessings of civilization. My sudden departure and escape from them, seemed like a second captivity, and for a long time I brooded the thought of my miserable situation with almost as much sorrow and dejection as I had done those of my first sufferings. Time, the destroyer of every affection, wore away my unpleasant feelings, and I became as contented as before. We tended our cornfields through the summer. . . ." She married, she bore a child, she lost a husband, and by that time she was at home among the Seneca.

Once again the possibility of returning to the white community appeared when a Dutchman began stalking her in hope of capturing her and turning her in for a bounty. Jemison chose not to be captured again and ran "with all the speed I was mistress of" to a hiding place. Inspired by the Dutchman, a Seneca leader thought of turning her in for the bounty himself, and she went and hid again in the weeds with her young son. She was desperate to remain where she had once yearned to leave. She remarried, bore six more children, and came to own a vast expanse of land, "by virtue of a deed from the Chiefs of the Six Nations," on which she lived the rest of her long life. That life she called, in her autobiography filtered through the pen of a scribe, "a tragical medley that I hope will never be repeated." But it was the deaths and discord of her children of which she spoke; her troubles had all become personal, and the land she lived on was itself a meeting ground between the two cultures, for she leased out land to white farmers.

For these eastern captives, the boundaries between cultures began to blur as the geographies overlapped. For Cynthia Ann Parker, there was no such blurring. In 1836, when she was nine, she and her family were captured by Comanches on the Texas plains where they had recently settled (or invaded). The rest of her family was massacred. She alone survived, married a prominent member of her new community, Peta Nocona, and bore two sons and a daughter. A quarter century later there was another battle, this time initiated by white men, and she was captured on horseback with her youngest child in arms. She was led to believe that her husband had died in the battle, but it appears that this was a mistake. Even so she never saw her husband or sons again. An uncle in Fort Worth claimed her and kept her captive, locked up at night lest she flee with her daughter. She never relearned English properly during the decade she lived among the culture that had once been and was no longer hers. A man who met her recollected that she "had a wild expression and would look down when people looked at her. She could use an ax equal to a man and disliked a lazy person. She was an expert in tanning hides with the hair on them, or plaiting or knitting either ropes or whips. She thought her two boys were lost on the prairie. This dissatisfied her very much." The whites always regarded her as having been rescued, but she seems to have regarded herself as having been imprisoned. The daughter died and ten years after her capture, Parker, who had starved herself into weakness, died of the flu. She never saw her sons again, though one came to claim her remains forty years after her death and rebury her in his world.

There are less dire stories, such as that of Thomas Jefferson Mayfield, whose family moved from Texas to California in the 1840s. They settled in the San Joaquin Valley, where their indigenous neighbors kept them stocked with fish, game, and acorn bread. When his mother died, his father, feeling unable to care for the boy while keeping up his roving business, allowed him to go off with the Choinumne Yokuts. After all the captivity narratives in which contact begins as masculine battle and after Cabeza de Vaca's violent plunge into the unknown, it's the mildness of Mayfield's transition from one culture to another that's startling. The Yokuts were maternal substitutes, though no single woman adopted him: they all looked after him, and he seems to have run in a pack of children. For a decade, his home was with them, and for periods of as long as three years he didn't see his father. Eventually, as the Civil War broke out and the Yokuts were increasingly hemmed in by white settlers, he shifted back to the culture he was born in. His memoir in some ways marks the end of the captivity narrative (though there would be other captives later in the nineteenth century), because the indigenous nations were ceasing to be free in their own land; they themselves were becoming captives within the spreading dominant culture, and few found as amiable a reception as these children did. It was no longer individuals but whole cultures being brought up abruptly into collision with difference, traversing that distance between the near and the far.

Reading these stories, it's tempting to think that the arts to be learned are those of tracking, hunting, navigating, skills of survival and escape. Even in the everyday world of the present, an anxiety to survive manifests itself in cars and clothes for far more rugged occasions than those at hand, as though to express some sense of the toughness of things and of readiness to face them. But the real difficulties, the real arts of survival, seem to lie in more subtle realms. There, what's called for is a kind of resilience of the psyche, a readiness to deal with what comes next. These captives lay out in a stark and dramatic way what goes on in every life: the transitions whereby you cease to be who you were. Seldom is it as dramatic, but nevertheless, something of this journey between the near and the far goes on in every life. Sometimes an old photograph, an old friend, an old letter will remind you that you are not who you once were, for the person who dwelt among them, valued this, chose that, wrote thus, no longer exists. Without noticing it you have traversed a great distance; the strange has become familiar and the familiar if not strange at least awkward or uncomfortable, an outgrown garment. And some people travel far more than others. There are those who receive as birthright an adequate or at least unquestioned sense of self and those who set out to reinvent themselves, for survival or for satisfaction, and travel far. Some people inherit values and practices as a house they inhabit; some of us have to burn down that house, find our own ground, build from scratch, even as a psychological metamorphosis. As a cultural metamorphosis the transition is far more dramatic.

The people thrown into other cultures go through something of the anguish of the butterfly, whose body must disintegrate and reform more than once in its life cycle. In her novel *Regeneration*, Pat Barker writes of a doctor who "knew only too well how often the early stages of change or cure may mimic deterioration. Cut a chrysalis open, and you will find a rotting caterpillar. What you will never find is that mythical creature, half caterpillar, half butterfly, a fit emblem of the human soul, for those whose cast of mind leads them to seek such emblems. No, the process of transformation consists almost entirely of decay." But the butterfly is so fit an emblem of the human soul that its name in Greek is psyche, the word for soul. We have not much language to appreciate this phase of decay, this withdrawal, this era of ending that must precede beginning. Nor of the violence of the metamorphosis, which is often spoken of as though it were as graceful as a flower blooming.

I write this and then one day, with a free hour in between a conversation and an obligation, go to the old Conservatory of Flowers near my home, recently restored and reopened. I had not been there in nine years, since it was ravaged by a great winter storm. I thought I would look at the gleaming dark leaves large as maps, at the vines and mosses and orchids, and breathe that humid air, the steamy glories I remembered. But the west wing of the great greenhouse with its milky windowpanes had become a butterfly garden and in the middle of that chamber was a butterfly hatchery, a window a few inches in front of a wooden plank, or rather shallow series of shelves, to which were pinned platoons of future butterflies, sorted by species. The chrysalises had taken on the shape of the butterflies inside, and some rocked as though stirred by a faint breeze, though the adjacent chrysalises were still. Four butterflies emerged while I watched, and seven more when I returned another day.

They came out with their wings packed down like furled parachutes, like crumpled letters. Even as they emerged it seemed incredible that their wide wings had once fit in so slender a space. As they emerged, their bodies were visible as they would never quite be again, once the wings expanded and came to dominate the creature, and during those moments they looked like bugs, like insects, instead of what they would be when they were all brilliantly colored wing like some sentient cousin of flowers. Their bodies were still plump with the fluid they had to pump into those wings in the first minutes of their emergence to make them the straight sheets with which they flew. Each clung to its chrysalis while its wings unfolded by almost imperceptible stages. Some did not get quite free, and their wings never fully straightened. One butterfly sat still with an orange wing curled into the chrysalis. One seemed permanently stuck halfway out, its yellow-and-black wings like buds that would not flower. One flailed frantically, trying to drag itself out by crawling onto adjacent unopened chrysalises until they too began to thrash, a contagious panic. That one finally dropped free, though it may have been too late for its wings to straighten. The process of transformation consists mostly of decay and then of this crisis when emergence from what came before must be total and abrupt.

But the changes in a butterfly's life are not always so dramatic. The strange resonant word *instar* describes the stage between two successive molts, for as it grows, a caterpillar, like a snake, like Cabeza de Vaca walking across the Southwest, splits its skin again and again, each stage an instar. It remains a caterpillar as it goes through these molts, but no longer one in the same skin. There are rituals marking such splits, graduations, indoctrinations, ceremonies of change, though most changes proceed without such clear and encouraging recognition. *Instar* implies something both celestial and ingrown, something heavenly and disastrous, and perhaps change is commonly like that, a buried star, oscillating between near and far.

Attack of the Superzeroes

Why Washington, Einstein, and Madonna Can't Compete with You

Thomas de Zengotita

Twilight of the Heroes

A headmaster of my acquaintance once sent me an article lamenting the loss of the heroes for today's youth. The article concluded, as all such articles must, with a solution-to-the-problem: a strategy for presenting George Washington, of all people, in a way guaranteed to secure admiration. I barely glanced at it. There is no such strategy. Just talking about "how to present" is already hopeless capitulation.

At about the same time, the *New York Times* ran a story that showed exactly why. It was about a new team of curators at Mount Vernon, where attendance had been dismal lately, especially compared with the numbers Monticello was racking up. What with a couple of bios on the stands, scientific and architectural projects on display, a Nick Nolte movie, and the hi-tech DNA sex scandal over Sally Hemings—well, there was buzz out there for Tom. The folks at Mount Vernon were determined to liven up the stodgy image of their founding father, show evidence of cool hobbies, make those wooden teeth a plus, and generally put their hero back on top of the charts.

The centerpiece of their plan was a tour of the grounds and mansion, culminating in a "Death and Funeral Procession Tour" complete with black armbands for visitors to the "death scene."

"Death scene" meant the room where the real George Washington really died, furnished with the things that were really there at the time. But the folks (re)creating this death chamber understood that real wasn't real enough. More was required. They planned to pipe the appropriate smells into the room. They didn't follow through with this idea, but linger over the implications of the fact that they even had thought of it. Presumably sane and sincere people were driven to overreach so ludicrously because, in their hearts, they understood that the real George Washington could never compete with the likes of Oprah or Harry Potter. They had to grab visitors by the lapels and shout, "This is real! It really happened! Right here! Goddamit, smell it if you don't believe me!"

Real isn't real enough. That's what tells us that we've crossed a threshold, a point beyond which no real person can be a public hero anymore.

This phenomenon is universal. Lamenting the absence of heroes is endemic. It cuts across all the cultural categories. NOW, GLAAD, and the NAACP worry about it as much as defenders of the canon. Everyone agrees that we need heroes; they just don't agree on *which* heroes should be resurrected or discovered—that is, represented.

Here's a thought experiment to show why they can't succeed: Say you wanted to ensure that the Holocaust would never be forgotten, the full horror of it, the reality. The only way to do it, at this point, would be to ban all representations. No photographs or documentaries, no depictions of skeletal survivors being rescued, no ovens, no piles of shoes and bones. And no memoirs, no Anne Frank, no museums, no memorials, no movies—no *Shoah,* certainly no *Schindler's List* or *Sophie's Choice,* definitely no *Life Is Beautiful.* A taboo, in other words.

But all the representations would still exist, preserved in a single archive, and the educational requirement would be this: at a certain age, every child in the land spends a week in that archive. And that's it. They would never forget, believe me.

But, you might protest, it would traumatize those kids, it would scar them for life. Exactly. That's why they would never forget. But look, we want them to remember and understand the full horror, the reality, but we don't want trauma.

Ah, well then—you're stuck. The reality of the Holocaust *can't* be grasped without causing psychic damage. So we'll have to find some form of never-forgetting that won't be *too* burdensome but, at the same time, one hopes, not too trivializing either.

Which is just to say that we'll end up with—just what we've got.

The real-heroes issue is more complex but shaped by the same pressures. Having a real hero means devoting yourself, subordinating yourself, and that's asking a bit too much of people these days. Devotion isn't trauma, but it does seem a bit severe, a bit medieval. Cult wackos come to mind. Devoted followers are anachronistic in a world made for devoted fans.

Some people thought that the absence of national crisis in recent decades might explain the hero vacuum, but that one lost its purchase after 9/11. Nobody would call Bush or Blair heroes in the old-fashioned sense, though they tried gamely to fill the position. They just couldn't. Forget the politics, it was deeper than that. They were just too *small.* Even Rudy Giuliani—more lionized than anyone since, I don't know, Alexander the Great?—even he had sense enough not to make a speech at the Ground Zero services. He knew he wasn't big enough for that.

On the flip side, we had all the hyperbole during the Iraq invasion—when not just Jessica Lynch but every G.I. in the world got christened "hero." Runaway inflation devalued that ancient concept almost overnight.

But the favored explanation says that real heroes have been replaced by sports and entertainment stars. And that's right, as far as it goes, but it would be better to phrase it this way: in today's environment, real heroes must become stars if they are to exist in public culture. That is, they must perform. But as soon as they do, they can't compete with real stars—who *are* performers. How neat is that?

The essence of real heroes in the good old days—Newton and Napoleon and Goethe—was that they were essentially *un*real. They were not known as people. They *were* their works and deeds, their myths. They were fictional constructs, even in their own lifetimes, invented by the people who idolized them, on the basis of a few stories and images—so very few. The whole dynamic is a function of representational quantity and quality.

Real heroes of the past were represented with a frugality almost impossible to credit today: some texts committed to memory; some images known to everyone; places he stood, things he touched; most important of all, a store of anecdotes, circulating informally, the way elephant jokes used to.

Anthropologists know the special power of such stories. They come alive with each retelling because they are subject to constant variation. Unlike printed accounts, they are undetectably adaptable. There is no official version. Unadulterated perfection and immediate relevance are guaranteed. Paucity of representation allows the imagination of followers to supply their hero with just the attributes they need to see in him.

At the same time, these inventions were anchored to flesh. People knew that, unlike Paul Bunyan, their heroes were real. They were perfect *and* real—perhaps someone you knew personally, your uncle or your brother, was there on that glorious day and saw, with his own eyes, Napoleon take his stand upon the bridge at Lodi, and he has been telling the story with irresistible fervor and pathos ever since.

As recently as Einstein and Lindbergh, the essential representational conditions held. Just think how utterly impossible it would be now for a president to be paralyzed from the waist down, as Franklin Roosevelt was—and the public in ignorance of it. Take that as a measure. Think also of the way special-effects movies about outer space made coverage of real space adventures boring for most people. The pathetic production values and shapeless plot, flickering videos of people you can barely identify doing lame things with vials and tubes? Please.

In the same way, as soon as real heroes are represented publicly, repeatedly, they are doomed. In effect, virtual heroes—the real performers—present themselves so fabulously and consistently across decades they make it impossible for hero-candidates from reality to succeed. We don't have real heroes anymore because they are too *real*; representations of them are too rich and detailed. There is no room for us to supply them with mythic life.

Method Acting

If you are of a certain age you remember where you were when you heard that JFK had been assassinated. You probably have a story about your experience.

Where I was when JFK was assassinated was in the dance studio of an acting school in Manhattan. About thirty would-be actors and actresses were milling around the room in leotards, stretching, contemplating their mirror images, leaning against the walls, musing, chatting, waiting for our instructor to come in.

The studio door opened and, instead of the instructor, there was the assistant to the school's director. She looked around, groping for words, and finally said, "President Kennedy has been shot. We don't yet know how serious it is." And then she left. There was some stirring and murmuring for a minute or so, a couple of people followed her out, and then someone said, "It's an improv."

Well. Ever hang out with really serious acting students? This was irresistible. We turned as one to consult our repertoire of methods, methods for accessing analogous memories, for identifying specific intentions, for reacting rather than acting. We were determined to "be in the moment," which was what one learned to do in those days, studying under Strasberg or Meisner or Adler, mentors to Brando and Dean, heirs to the prophet Stanislavsky, who had scorned the postures of "acting" and made inner truth—being real—the holy grail of his art. That was the point of all the strenuous psychological techniques known collectively as The Method, and we were devoted to them. So when, some minutes later, the assistant returned to announce, her voice breaking, that the president was dead, well, at *that* point, the party really got started.

Acting students fall into two basic categories: the ones who love to do anger and the ones who love to do tears. I was the anger type, thank heaven, so there wasn't much emoting for me to do. The situation didn't suit my talents; this was a moment for the impresarios of tears. And how they went at it. Within minutes, maybe half the people in the room were crying. Some were into silent weeping, sitting in a corner, face uptilted, the gaze averting now and then to rest at random on some stretch of ceiling where the pattern of the peeling paint signified the meaninglessness of it all. A couple of girls were crumpled to their knees, doing the helpless palms-turned-upward thing, keening like Electra over the corpse of Agamemnon. Still others linked up for hugs and consolation and testimonials to Camelot. And so on.

Eventually one of the people who had left the room after the first announcement came back and began to set us straight. The president was in fact dead. This was not an improvisation. Someone turned on a transistor radio. Reality was re-established.

I got out of there immediately. What I saw in those newly stricken faces, already looking as stricken as faces can look, was more than I cared to see. The embarrassment was excruciating, unique in my experience, before or since. It wasn't that we were exposed as phonies in the usual sense. Affectation and sincerity were not ultimately the issue. This went much deeper. It was the realization that there was nothing left, no level or nuance of feeling that hadn't become a resource for our enterprise of Method acting. It was the spiritual equivalent of the last step in the dark, the one that isn't there when you put your foot down.

Of course that's a special case—extreme, condensed, taut with ironic perfection. But it stayed with me over the years, stimulated by more complicated cases that seemed to echo the original. It was as if the mourning actors had established a pure standard to which messier manifestations of reflexivity could only aspire. If you happen to be philosophically inclined, you might say they exemplified a phenomenological essence.

I was reminded of them, for example, years later, watching other mourners, assembled in their millions on the streets of London. Di's mourners, so obviously exhibiting their grief, not even pretending that they weren't exhibiting it, understanding that this was their role in the Global Show that their very presence was producing—a show about them "being in the moment" in what amounted to a worldwide improv. Celebrities all, celebrities at last.

There is no direct parallel between the JFK improv and Di's funeral, but there's that common element, and I detect its traces, more elusively embedded, whenever I watch the bereaved on TV. I always wonder, as I watch them in the glow—some for a passing moment, others, turning grief into a worthy cause, taking up residence, launching a second life—I always wonder: what is this *doing* to you?

And it isn't just displays of grief that get enacted in this way. Take how athletes now celebrate themselves after nearly every play. And by extension, the way fans celebrate not just the team or the victory but themselves. There's that same element, that same quality, to be found in the way those exhilarated men position themselves, beefy faces alight with a peculiar blend of exultation and hostility, tendons bulging in their necks, fists pounding the air, bodies thrust forward as if to bulldoze past all compromise, apparently frenzied, apparently berserk, bellowing in tones suggestive of profound vindication, bellowing "Yeaauh! Yeaauh! Yeaauh!" And each "Yeaauh" lifts above the preceding one, as if to reinforce it but also to comment on it, even to parody it, and suddenly you realize that this is also a performance, and a contest, a folk art—and oh-so-self-conscious after all.

And, by further extension, all the high-fiving and hissed-yes-pointing and thumbs-upping in the culture as a whole, in commercials, in our lives, in the continuous play of expressions and gestures that signify degrees of—what shall we call it?—triumphal intensity. The alchemy at work across this spectrum is, at bottom, the same. It precipitates a fusion of the real and represented, a culture of performance that ultimately constitutes a quality of being, a type of person—the mediated person. And, as we shall see, this type of person doesn't have heroes.

The Flattery or Representation

So whence this folk genre, the "where I was when The Event took place" story? Why, for example, didn't members of the greatest generation craft fables of their personal experience of the Attack on America in 1941?

Because they weren't there, that's why.

Be assured that people who were physically at Pearl Harbor *did* have stories of their personal experience, and told them again and again as the years went by. Stories like that are anthropologically grounded. But people who just heard about Pearl Harbor on the radio and read about it in the papers didn't tell such stories, because it didn't feel as if it had happened to them, personally, at all. It's that simple.

One of the most popular public-service-type TV shows of the 1950s was called *You Are There*. The name sounds hokey now, but that was the original miracle of television: everyone became a participant/eyewitness to events on the world stage. And that's why people spontaneously told their stories about the Kennedy assassination, no matter where they were physically. They saw and heard it all unfold. Not just on TV, of course—all the media were contributing—but it was TV that made you feel as if you were there. Reams of coverage, endless coverage, amazing coverage—in a way *more* compelling than if you had been there physically, because virtually you were there from so many different perspectives. You weren't in one spot, the way you would have been if you had been physically there, squashed behind a fat lady, looking in your purse for your sunglasses when the shots went off, thinking they were fireworks at first, until you heard the screaming. No, not like that: you were not there in one humble and limited spot; you were everywhere there, because that amazing coverage put you everywhere there. You had a sort of God's-eye view.

This is a form of flattery so pervasive, so fundamental to the very nature of representation, that it gets taken for granted. The alchemy that fuses reality and representation gets *carried* into our psyches by the irresistible flattery that goes with being constantly addressed in such fabulous ways. We are so habituated to this flattery that it can be made remarkable only by contrast.

Say your car breaks down in the middle of nowhere—the middle of Saskatchewan, say. You have no radio, no cell phone, nothing to read, no gear to fiddle with. You just have to wait. Pretty soon you notice how everything around you just happens to be there. And it just happens to be there in this very precise but unfamiliar way. You are so not used to this. Every tuft of weed, the scattered pebbles, the lapsing fence, the cracks in the asphalt, the buzz of insects in the field, the flow of cloud against the sky—everything is very specifically exactly the way it is, and none of it is for you. Nothing here was designed to affect you. It isn't arranged so that you can experience it, and you didn't plan to experience it. There is no screen, no display, no entrance, no brochure, nothing special to look at, no dramatic scenery or wildlife, no tour guide, no campsites, no benches, no paths, no viewing platforms with natural-historical information posted under slanted Plexiglas lectern things—whatever is there is just there, and so are you. You begin to get a sense of what it would be like if you weren't the center of it all.

But usually you are. That's why you are a mediated person. Especially if you've been in therapy and done workshops and stuff like that. It's no accident that therapeutic techniques are so akin to that Method developed at The Actor's Studio. Getting in touch with your real feelings so that you can be "in the moment" is the aim in both settings. That's why there is a self-consciousness about you that makes your grandparents look like automatons by comparison. Wonderful people they may have been but, compared with you, utterly without reflexivity. And that puts you on the continuum with Di's mourners. We are all Method actors now. And the cultural consequences are profound.

Virtual Revolution

When historians look back on the twentieth century, will the rise of rock and roll—and TV/pop culture generally—take on a significance comparable to the Reformation? Will "teen/youth" appear as analogue to the bourgeoisie in the seventeenth century or the proletariat in the nineteenth? If so, the great performers of that culture will be seen as the real heroes of this age.

Pop-music stars who stand for something across their appearances come as close as a mediated culture allows to genuine heroic stature. They are performers and they are real. Dylan, Madonna, Selena, Garth Brooks, Sinatra—these people helped millions of people define themselves. They instilled and reinforced values and conditioned people's life choices, especially style, the attitude that gets you through the day. These star-types posit and reflect the selves their fans have chosen to be. That's how it works; that's how the circle closes.

For consider what this means. It means that these performer/heroes are all about us. There is no cause they are summoning their fans to serve—other than the cause of being whoever you are.

That's big-time flattery—and a pivot point in the dialectic of mediation.

Those stars on the stage, being adored, being pursued, they may be the ones most obviously at the center while we, the fans, are individually invisible. But consider the totality of the relationship, not just between you and your particular performer/hero but between you and all those celebrities, vying for your attention. Is it not ultimately the spectators, in their hiddenness, who hold sway, who have the last word? All the gratifications of voyeurism accrue to a judge nobody knows, passing sentence upon the celebrated, the mighty, and the fallen, from that central position in the Panopticon of representation. And those celebrities, competing for the judge's attention and approval, are in effect inviting the treatment they get. They are so needy, actually—dressing up, dieting, touring, posing, exposing privacies, cavorting desperately, endlessly, before us.

We should not underestimate the unconscious sense of sovereignty that has been the lot of spectators. The hidden blandishments of representation implanted a sense of entitlement, an envy, a desire for public significance commensurate with our unconscious sense of centrality. Celebrities held a monopoly on the most scarce and precious resource in a mediated society: attention. For spectators, the most basic of specifically human needs—the need for acknowledgment, for significance—was left unsatisfied. Unlike premodern monarchs, who were openly flattered when minstrels and jesters postured before them, postmodern fans, implicitly flattered, had to take action if they were going to make their covert centrality apparent—as only seems fair.

All that was lacking were the means. Until recently. This is the ultimate significance of all the technology: cable, satellite, the web, camcorders, video phones—all the usual suspects. They were the means to virtual revolution.

Coached by performer heroes, seeking the recognition to which they felt entitled, spectators pushed themselves forward as the technological venues opened up, and not only in what we call the "reality show." Other reality shows, under other names, sprang up everywhere. What they all had in common was the celebration of people refusing to be spectators—all the mini-celebrities, for example, who dominate chat rooms and game sites, and the blogs, the intimate "life journals." Think also of raves and flash mobbing, marathon running, karaoke bars, focus groups, talk-radio call-in shows, homemade porn, sponsored sports teams for tots—and every would-be band in the world can now burn a CD and produce cool cover art and posters.

Being famous isn't what it used to be.

Has it ever struck you, watching interviews with people in clips from the 1940s and 1950s, say, or even just looking at them in photographs, how stiff and unnatural they seem? Even prominent people, but especially regular folk, the way they lean into the mike and glance awkwardly around as they say whatever they have to say in semi-formal tones, almost as if reciting; and the way they raise their voices, as if they can't quite trust the technology to reach an absent audience. But nowadays? Every man on the street, every girl on the subway platform, interviewed about the snowstorm or the transit strike—they are total pros, laughing in the right places, looking directly at the interviewer or into the camera, fluid, colloquial, comments and mannerisms pitched just right for the occasion, completely at ease.

Method actors all.

It's All About You

Reality shows of all kinds accomplish the virtual revolution, but so do those ubiquitous memoirs—and all the fiction that mimics the memoir, the whole *Bridget Jones's Diary* genre. We are inundated with stories of ordinary folk as protagonists in extreme circumstances—shattered by drugs, stricken by disease, stranded in the wild, captured by the mullahs, spending Tuesdays with Morrie, giving kidneys to their sisters, awakened from comas. But starring also in more mundane situations—being dumped by clueless boyfriends, worried about the size of their thighs, and on and on. What is it with these stories?

Identification. Self-recognition. It may be fact, it may be fiction, it may be comedy or tragedy, but it's all aimed at eliciting responses that go, "I'm *exactly* like that" or, "Imagine how I would feel if . . ."

It's all about you.

Notice especially how people identify with confessional suffering even when they can't identify with the particular condition. There is a huge fan base out there for trauma stories, and it goes way beyond the constituency that shares the specific malady. Why? Well, partly it's morbid curiosity, a ghoulish investment in gazing upon the misfortunes of others, of course that's part of it—that's the disdainful high-brow analysis, and there is some truth to it. But there are other reasons. When you witness these public confessionals, how often do you hear this refrain, "I felt so alone, I thought no one would understand what I was going through"? That's the mantra. And it's the key to understanding how people who haven't been, say, abused by their Siamese twin can nevertheless identify with someone who has.

The fact is that a lot of people who have not had some problematic condition thrust upon them by fate *feel as if they have.* They feel alone and misunderstood. They feel unacknowledged, unappreciated. So they identify with a saga of redemption through recognition, which transforms the anonymous victim into the heroic survivor. They respond projectively with something that borders on envy. The specifics of the case are symbolic condensations of the amorphous afflictions that burden them, especially the pain of anonymity, and its public resolution is their own vindication.

These public forms of therapy serve to leaven necessity with reflexivity, just as private therapy has always done. And personal intimacies, morphing into public identities, inevitably get absorbed into performative categories. The process is relatively superficial on the talk-show circuit compared with therapy itself, but the structure and function are the same.

And the aim of all these therapeutic missions? A particular sensation, cherished by all the participants in this mediated ritual of self-overcoming, a feeling that wells up, wells up and overflows when at last it finds expression in words and sobs, freed at last from repression and self-loathing and self-doubt, admitted, at last, into the light of self-acceptance made public, acknowledged, recognized—and, yes, celebrated.

Just for being you.

Reviewing in Contexts

Transgression and Transformation

Leaving Las Vegas

bell hooks

Six years ago I published a book of essays, *Yearning: race, gender, and cultural politics*, which included this dedication: "for you to whom i surrender—to you for whom i wait." When the book was about to go to press, several feminist editors working on the project expressed concern about this dedication. They found the use of the word "surrender" problematic, disempowering to women. It suggested for them a loss of control, powerlessness. While I agreed that the word "surrender" has this connotation, it also means to give up, to submit. I argued that there are moments when submission is a gesture of agency and power, that a distinction has to be made between conscious surrender, an act of choice and the submission of someone who is victimized and without choice. It seemed to me then, as it does now that women would need to know the difference if we were ever to be capable of self-actualization within patriarchal culture.

To love fully one must be able to surrender—to give up control. If we are to know love, then we cannot escape the practice of surrender. In patriarchal culture women who love men take a risk that our willingness to surrender may create a space of vulnerability where we can be wounded, violated. This is why there was such a critique of romantic love in early radical feminist discussions and why it was believed that it was difficult for any woman to fully realize feminist practice in a heterosexual relationship. Hence the saying: "feminism is the theory and lesbianism is the practice." Women active in the feminist movement who continued relating to men sexually had to grapple with the meaning of a politics of surrender in the context of heterosexual love in patriarchal society.

Unfortunately, feminist thinkers have to a grave extent abandoned radical discussions of sexuality and the meaning of love in heterosexual relationships. At times these concerns are dismissed as irrelevant and the issues are addressed by simply calling attention to male sexism as though acknowledgement of that reality precludes any need to understand the construction of female and female sexual agency within this context. These issues are raised by Mike Figgis's film *Leaving Las Vegas*. Many feminist viewers simply dismissed this film as another example of the male pornographic imagination at work. Despite the ways in which sexism informs female sexuality is in this film, *Leaving Las Vegas* is a daring work in so far as it suggests that within patriarchy female masochism need not be disempowering, that it can be the space of abjection and surrender wherein the powerless regain a sense of agency. However utopian, this vision does not condemn women to play forever the role of victim.

Leaving Las Vegas chronicles the story of Sera, a prostitute who falls in love with a washed up movie executive named Ben who is drinking himself to death. Ben chooses to travel to Las Vegas to abandon himself to dying. When the film begins we witness him bottoming out at work and in relationships. The film makes it clear that he is not seeking help (this is not about recovery). Addressing the issue of alcoholism in his popular work *Further Along the Road Less Traveled*, psychologist M. Scott Peck contends: "Alcoholics are not any more broken than people who are not alcoholic. We all have our griefs and our terrors, we may not be conscious of them, but we all have them. We are all broken people, but alcoholics can't hide it anymore, whereas the rest of us can hide behind our masks of composure. We are not able to talk with each other about the things that are most important to us, about the way our hearts are breaking. So the great lesson of alcoholism is the nature of the disease. It puts people into visible crisis." Yet Figgis creates an alcoholic in crisis who is not seeking redemption. He has surrendered to his fate. He is courting death.

In the midst of this flirtation, he seeks community and finds it with Sera. Mistakenly, reviewers of the film talk about it as a romantic love story between two individuals who are both broken. The sign of Sera's brokenness is presumably that she is a sex worker. However, audiences and critics arrive at this assessment of her through the lens of their own morality, their own sense that to work as a prostitute means that one is a loser. In actuality, the film disturbs many feminist viewers precisely because Sera is not presented as a victim. In *Leaving Las Vegas* Sera is depicted as a prostitute who enjoys her work. She likes the power to take charge, to use sexuality as a means of making money. Like the actual prostitute in Sallie Tisdale's *Talk Dirty to Me* who states that she would like to be able to display the material comforts of her life and say to people: "See? I am really good in bed! Look at this apartment! Look at what my pussy got me!" It is this assertion of female agency in relation to her body that Sera's character exhibits in the film that is so unsettling for viewers. Many of them choose to see this characterization as male fantasy rather than accept that there are women in the sex industry who feel this way about their work.

Unlike Ben, the alcoholic male, Sera is not washed up. Her vulnerability lies not in her profession but in her longing to be seen as more than her job.

In fact, she is resisting the dehumanization that working as a prostitute in patriarchal culture would have her succumb to. It is this resistance, this refusal to be a victim, or object without choices that attracts her to Ben. He seduces her by recognizing her humanity, by seeing that she is not defined by her work and the stigma attached to it. This recognition enables Sera to share with someone critical awareness of the burden of having other people treat you as a loser when you do not see yourself that way. Sera responds to this recognition, to Ben's willingness to address her in the complexity of her being, by falling in love. Yet later, once she has trusted him, he continually reminds her, "We both know that I am a drunk and you are a hooker." Love matters to Sera more than to Ben.

Wary of her and love, instead of returning that love fully, Ben violates the trust she shows him by swiftly becoming an intimate terrorist. While Sera can express her need for Ben without shame, he resists. It is his resistance that turns the potential love relationship into a torturous sadomasochistic bond. Michael Miller argues in *Intimate Terrorism* that when the psychological fate of the self becomes enmeshed with erotic passion, individuals panic: "When people fear what they need, they become angry both at themselves and at those from whom they seek to get their needs met . . . Often you see a man and a woman in an intimate relationship . . . treat one another with cruelty that they would never consider directing toward anyone who meant less to them." This is precisely what happens with Ben in *Leaving Las Vegas*.

Having made the decision to surrender to death, Ben resists the pull of eros—the call to return to life that sexual longing and connection make on his psyche. His impotence is the sign of that resistance. Hence his insistence that Sera never suggest that he seek help. He demands that she completely surrender any longing for him to be well—to stay alive. It is the unequal demand in the relationship that creates the sadomasochistic dynamic. Sera becomes the slave of love. In the end it is she who confesses in therapy that "We realized we didn't have much time and I accepted him for what he was."

Throughout the film, Ben remains enthralled by his flirtation with death. In the forward to *The Tears of Eros* George Bataille celebrates a love affair like Ben's, declaring: "The essence of man as given in sexuality—which is his origin and beginning—poses a problem for him that has no other outcome than wild turmoil. This turmoil is given in the 'little death.' How can I fully live the 'little death' if not as a foretaste of the final death? The violence of spasmodic joy lies deep in my heart. This violence, at the same time, and I tremble as I say it, is the heart of death: it opens itself up to me." To a grave extent, Ben, the wasted lost male soul, is the personification of the patriarchal betrayal of masculinity. Before he leaves for Las Vegas, everyone he reaches out to for connection is male. His friend Peter tells him "Never contact me again." Once he is broken, the world of homosocial patriarchal bonding that once sustained him shuns him. Lost to himself and others precisely because his lust for death is the extreme living out of the patriarchal masculine ethos, he is naked and exposed.

As Sera's sense of wholeness is restored by the act of loving Ben, he loses his power over her. She begins to long for him to be well. When she expresses that longing he violently rejects her. Later he violates her home by bringing another woman prostitute there and sharing with her the erotic passion he withholds from Sera. Even though she has willingly surrendered to love, Sera refuses violation, especially in the domestic space that is her sanctuary and refuge. Despite her love for Ben, she demands that he leave. It is at this filmic moment that the misogynist pornographic imagination rears its ugly head and we see that Sera's refusal to be a victim in romantic love sets the stage for her to be brutally raped. This is the sequence in the film that appears as pure, unadulterated sexist male fantasy. Up until this point in the movie, Sera has been a savvy, tough woman of the streets who can take care of herself. Suddenly, she is portrayed as dumb, as blinded by the sight of three college males with money seeking sexual servicing. In this sequence Sera is triply betrayed: First by the men who rape her, then by the lover who has violated her in the first place, and ultimately by the filmmaker who succumbs to the usual stereotypes and has the "bad" girl punished. This male punishment of the sexually assertive woman who refuses to be a victim gives the film a conventional, predictable patriarchal pornographic slant.

Indeed, this brutal anal rape sequence undermines the more progressive narrative in the film wherein Sera's sense of self is restored by having a healthy interaction with a male she loves. Interviewed in *The Power to Dream*, writer Maxine Hong Kingston states: "I believe that in order to truly grow up, women must love men. That has to be the next stage of feminism. I can't believe that feminism just breaks off at the point where we get to join the Marines." Significantly, Sera is the quintessentially sexually liberated woman in modern society. Her overactive sexuality serves to mask her desire to be loved. It is in the act of loving that Sera risks vulnerability, not in being sexual with men. In sex she can be indifferent—in control. To love she must let go. It is this letting go that makes it possible for her to be redeemed. Unlike Ben, she begins a love affair with life. Loving him makes her want to live. In *Rituals of Love* Ted Polhemus and Housk Randall suggest that in the sadomasochistic power ritual the submissive believes that by "submitting to humiliating indignity she will discover in herself a 'sublime dignity' and that by the loss of control over her own actions (the will that wills self-abandon) she will discover a greater self-hood." This is Sera's quest.

After she has gained recognition of her selfhood through the reciprocal bond she forms with Ben, she finds it impossible to reinhabit a social space where she is not being truly seen. Although she has asked Ben to leave, she continues to love him. Throughout their affair she has felt powerless because she cannot sexually seduce him. Seduction is the way that she previously controlled men. Describing the power relations embedded in the process of seduction, Jean Baudrillard in *Seduction* states: "There is something impersonal in every process of seduction, as in every crime, something ritualistic, something supra-subjective and supra-sensual, the lived experience, whether of the seducer or his victim, being only its unconscious reflection." Sera the experienced seducer is seduced. Baudrillard claims that "seduction always seeks to overturn and exorcise a power. If seduction is artificial, it is also sacrificial. One is playing with death, it always being a matter of capturing or immolating the desire of the other." When Ben calls Sera, like the slave of love she is, she obeys. Entering the sleazy hotel room where he lies in the throes of death, she gives him the mingling of tears and eros Georges Bataille extols in his work. For Ben ecstasy is merely a preparation for death. Meditating on death, on the "last instant," Bataille observed: "When there is physical pain, a high degree of what may be termed narcissistic cathexis of the painful place occurs: this cathexis continues to increase and tends, as it were, to 'empty' the ego." It is this state of emptiness that gives Ben his aura of blissful indifference. That bliss would be eradicated at the moment of death, were it not for Sera's presence. As Bataille testifies: "In myself, the satisfaction of a desire is often opposed to my interests. But I give in to it, for in a brutal way it has become for me the ultimate end . . . the end of reason, which exceeds reason, is not opposed to the overcoming of reason! In the violence of the overcoming, in the disorder of my laughter and my sobbing, in the excess of raptures that shatter me, I seize on the similarity between a horror and a voluptuousness that goes beyond me, between an ultimate pain and an unbearable joy!" Ben fails in his quest to meet death alone. The desire for connection triumphs. He is able to go—to truly leave Las Vegas—only when he is connected, only when he has a witness.

Sera gives him the recognition he needs before dying, just as he has given her the recognition that restores her to full humanity, that brings her back to life. Coming back to life for Sera means acknowledging pain and suffering. To cope with the very realties Ben has failed to cope with, she seeks connection and healing. The wounds of passion in her life become the source of that healing.

As a witness to death, Sera is ultimately transformed. She experiences a world that is deeper than the one she knows every day. All experiences are essential for self-actualization, including those of suffering, degradation, and pain. Through her acceptance of Ben and of herself, Sera finds a way to experience unity. In *On the Way to the Wedding*, the Jungian therapist Linda Leonard shares this insight: "As Heidegger has said, our being is to 'be there' where Being opens up and reveals itself, and our task is to open to the revelation and to try to preserve it through expression. For Heidegger, the fundamental opening-up of experience for the human being occurs when one is able to accept and affirm the mystery of death within one's being. For in the acceptance of our 'being-unto-death' we surrender our desire to control reality and thus are able to accept whatever offers itself to us. . . . For death is the ultimate transformation and threshold." Sera crosses the threshold of death and enters life. She is born again through her redemptive love. The tragedy of *Leaving Las Vegas* lies in the way in which Ben's transgression of boundaries does not lead to redemption. This is the danger of being seduced by transgression. At the end of her essay "Is Transgression Transgressive?" Elizabeth Wilson concludes: "We transgress in order to insist that we are, that we exist, and to place a distance between ourselves and the dominant culture. But we have to go further—we have to have an idea of how things could be different, otherwise transgression is mere posturing. In other words, transgression on its own leads eventually to entropy, unless we carry within us some idea of transformation. It is therefore not transgression that should be our watchword, but transformation." If audiences watching *Leaving Las Vegas* are merely enthralled by sexual scenarios of pleasure and danger, by alcoholic hedonistic excess, by the various tropes of transgression, they will feast on the tragedy and ignore the call to love—to be transformed utterly. To love is to endure.

The Melodramatic Moment

Daniel Mendelsohn

Was it in quotation marks, or was it not? A few months ago, I found myself arguing with an old friend about "Far From Heaven." This was before it started appearing on critics' 10-best lists, and at the time I'd dismissed it as a clever but ultimately empty exercise in camp: a knowing parody that lovingly, even obsessively, quotes the look, feel and rhythms of the kind of 50s melodramas that featured second-rate actresses in first-rate outfits. My friend wasn't so sure. Yes, the costumes and wigs and camera angles all betrayed an exactitude that only a true obsessive would worry about; but she was convinced that there was more here than just an uncannily sharp eye for midcentury modern. Beneath all that Heywood-Wakefield, she argued, there was something real, something authentic. "It's not just a pair of quotation marks," she said, making that little gesture with the first and second fingers of both hands that had become the intellectual tic of the 80s and 90s—the "ironic" sign meant to signal the speaker's awareness that, culturally speaking, everything was a rerun.

It may well be that the most interesting thing about our argument wasn't my take on the film, or hers, but rather that we were having it at all. This was a disagreement that couldn't have taken place two years before. If you were to reincarnate a Douglas Sirk movie in, say, 2001—at the height, or perhaps the exhausted depth, of the Age of Irony, the summer of Lizzie Grubman—would you have doubted for an instant that it was an elaborate, artful gag, a tongue-in-cheek cinematic hors d'oeuvre for the cultural cognoscenti? That's what I thought it was, too, at first; but my friend and millions of others clearly disagree, and the fact that I seem to have been wrong, that a cinematic reincarnation of a classic melodrama is meant to be taken straight, suggests that the cultural ground has shifted radically. After at least two full decades of ironic pop culture, ironic intellectual discourse, post-this, post-that—during which a sense of been-there, done-that permeated every level of mass culture—it was as if we were all ironied out. Sept. 11 was the catalyst for a change that was already in the works.

But a change to what? On the public stage, a solemn if not deadly earnestness has set in: words that would have provoked a collective giggle five years ago—"hero," "villain," "evil"—are bandied about by straight-faced anchors, to say nothing of elected officials. On the artistic front, this earnestness has been mirrored by an aesthetic mode that's been making a gradual comeback and suddenly seems here to stay. "Far From Heaven" is only the tip of an iceberg that's slowly coming into view. In film, a gamut running from art-house fixtures like Pedro Almodóvar's "Talk to Her" to huge hits like "Chicago" to crossover successes like "The Hours"—to say nothing of everything from the new season of "Six Feet Under" to reality TV shows and the latest Beck album—suggests that the dominant cultural mode for the "Ought" decade might well be the New Melodrama. If so, it's cause for both optimism and concern.

Melodrama has always suffered in comparison to its older, more respectable sibling, drama. Drama, in classical Greek, is derived from the word dran, "to do," and literally means "an action"; that it became synonymous with "play" suggests the extent to which classical Greek theater prized precisely engineered action—action that was seamlessly the result of character, that was "organic." "Melodrama," on the other hand, is a much later coinage, one that gives plain old drama a little something more: in this case, a melos, a flowery lyric song. The way in which melos dresses up drama in the word "melodrama" is, in fact, a perfect reflection of the difference between straight drama and melodrama: if the former values economy of expression and tight logic, the latter revels in excess and synthetically produced emotion. It's perfectly happy to paint the artistic lily with anything that will generate more emotions—more disasters, more traumas, more crises, more incident, and to hell with character and motivation. Sophocles was satisfied to leave his Oedipus with the soul-crushing knowledge that he'd killed his father and married his mother; Douglas Sirk would have given him a brain tumor to boot, and filmed the whole thing in a thunderstorm. Given melodrama's penchant for synthetic, and what some might even regard as dishonest, means of stimulating response, it's remarkable now to see it at work in the same aesthetic realms that used to regard austere emotional reserve as the hallmark of "high" artistic achievement.

Baz Luhrmann's "Moulin Rouge!" started the ball rolling. You don't have to love it (and many did not), but you can't deny that its sheer excessiveness—the unabashed opulence of its design; the lavishness of its production numbers, with their loonily anachronistic song-and-dance routines (as soon as these 19th-century Frenchmen break into an a cappella rendering of "The Sound of Music," you know you're in the presence of a new kind of film); the show-must-go-on, heroine-dying-of-consumption plot, like a bizarre literary love child of "Summer Stock" and "La Traviata"—served, ultimately, a rather sweet and definitely earnest vision of Love. Five or 10 years ago, all you would have cared about were the quotations—of "Traviata" and "Bohème"

and "Lady Marmalade" and "The Sound of Music" and God knows what else. Today, what strikes you is the sincerity and purity, even, of its emotions. When Luhrmann puts big signs saying "L'amour" on his movie and stage sets, he's not being cute: this guy believes in Love!

This year, a number of films followed suit, with the same willing embrace of melodramatic excess: the stylized overemotionality, the penchant for formal elements that overwhelm, in wild disproportion, the actual plot or "theme" of a movie. The French director François Ozon—whose taut study of grief and existential helplessness, "Under the Sand," was so underwritten and subtle that it made "L'Avventura" look like a Busby Berkeley musical—took on as his next project, a musical, "Eight Women," whose oscillation between camp parody, stylistic excess and real emotion recalled "Moulin Rouge!" in more ways than one. This year's biggest Oscar contender, "Chicago," may raise its sequined eyebrows in sardonic amusement at the corruption of the world, but there's no denying its belief—a rather corny one, shared by all musicals—in the redemptive power of show biz itself, of starring in musicals just like this one.

But what may be far more interesting, and significant, than these all-singing, all-emoting film extravaganzas are recent works that use melodrama to achieve what we think of as being more sober and "serious" artistic aims. Among these you could certainly count Almodóvar's latest film, which has the deceptively restrained title "Talk to Her." (Restrained, that is, in comparison to his 1988 breakout film, "Women on the Verge of a Nervous Breakdown.") Perhaps because two of its main characters spend most of the film in a coma, critics have taken to referring to this movie as the director's most mature and quiet work—"gentle," in one description. But everything is relative: this is, after all, a gentle film that takes audiences through a car accident, a goring of a toreador by a maddened bull, a rape, a suicide and a snake infestation. The thematic excess is reflected in gleeful stylistic hyperbole that never leaves you in doubt about what to feel. A movie-within-a-movie—in which an incredible shrinking man disappears into a giant vagina—a tragic ballet-within-a-movie, a freestanding musical interlude and those endless close-ups of tear-stained faces. Weep! the film tells you; and you do.

This isn't to say that "Talk to Her" isn't in its way subtle, or rather subtly interested in exploring delicate (and not so delicate) emotions: grief, loyalty, obsession, passion. It's merely to note what has always been obvious, which is that this director has no qualms about self-consciously using the kinds of overkill that we normally associate with that bastard genre, melodrama, to achieve the insights we think of as being reserved for high tragedy. That so many critics find "Talk to Her" an understated and even elegiac work suggests, perhaps, less about Almodóvar's supposed evolution than it does about the serious film's evolution—about its willingness to countenance melodrama, as well as drama, as a legitimate aesthetic ethos.

In another very serious-minded Oscar-nominated film, "The Hours," three scenes are already hardening into cinematic icons—Meryl Streep crumpling to the kitchen floor, moaning "I feel like I'm unraveling"; Julianne Moore driving manically en route to a hotel room to commit suicide; and an impassioned Nicole Kidman, as Virginia Woolf, declaring that it is "the right of every human being!" to choose the violent and possibly fatal excitement of the city over "the suffocating anaesthetic of the suburbs." Perhaps it's no coincidence that these defining moments, which are not in the novel on which the film was based, happen to be the most melodramatic in the film.

Still, no film in recent memory has used melodrama as earnestly, or as knowingly, to achieve its artistic ends as Todd Haynes's "Far From Heaven" does. The title alone puts you squarely in the territory of the great cinematic master of 1940s and 50s Hollywood schmaltz, Sirk, the director whose penchant for the distraught was reflected in everything from the oversaturated palettes of his sets and costumes to his Miltonian titles ("All That Heaven Allows," "Magnificent Obsession"). In Sirk's best-known films, illicit passions seemed not to be the point of the movie but merely the excuse to dye those fabrics and swirl those leaves. "Far From Heaven"—the story of a picture-perfect housewife whose husband turns out to be gay and who finds herself falling for the black handyman—is also acutely alert to the emotional potential of stylistic elements: the swoony score, the almost surreally 50s costumes (more 50s than actual 50s clothes, you can't help feeling), the swooping camera angles in moments of high tension.

What fascinates about "Far From Heaven" is the tentativeness with which it tiptoes along the line between camp parody and melodrama's effortful self-seriousness—a very fine line indeed. That tentativeness—as if the film is embarrassed by its own emotional and sociological yearnings—is, I now see, what generated my argument with my friend. The first time I saw "Far From Heaven," I suppose I was still thinking like a child of the 80s and found it empty—an arch homage to Sirk, one that sent up the conventions of 50s melodramas while retaining what I thought of as an unpleasant smugness about the moral and political cluelessness of its heroine. But subsequent viewings persuaded me that "Far From Heaven" is, after all, in earnest—it really thinks it has something more to tell us. More, that is, than about the cleverness of its own allusive style, something perhaps about women and repression and race. If that's true—if "Far From Heaven" is more straight than it first appears—then it's not an arty riff on melodrama, but melodrama itself.

"Straight" may be the crucial word. Both Almodóvar and Haynes are gay directors and emerge from a culture steeped in the traditions of camp—of knowing parody (and self-parody). It's the knowingness that makes something campy—the archness, the irony, the (finger-wiggle here) quotation marks. What's remarkable about these directors' latest films is, in fact, how utterly unironic they are: they make you realize that camp is just melodrama with the addition of irony (and, conversely, that melodrama is camp minus irony). It's as if Haynes—whose first feature, let us not forget, was about Karen Carpenter and featured Barbie dolls instead of actors—and Almodóvar are working backward in terms of genre. Both began squarely in the traditions of gay camp, which itself was an ironic comment on melodramatic models, and ever since then have been moving toward a more purely melodramatic style. That this new style has made them surprisingly popular—has relocated them away from the periphery to the center of popular taste—might be considered an irony, if you were prone to such thoughts.

These recent films' ambivalence, if not embarrassment, about their lack of irony may be the true hallmark of the new cultural mode. You feel it in pop music too: Beck and Wilco put out highly successful CDs that won over audiences and critics alike with a kind of sentimental earnestness far removed from the more familiar effort to be clever or arch or hip. Similarly, what strikes you about best-selling behemoths like Dave Eggers's "Heartbreaking Work of Staggering Genius" or Jonathan Franzen's "Corrections" is not how elaborate their carapaces of knowing self-consciousness are (the pomo marginalia, the insider allusiveness) but how desperately those carapaces are trying to cover up what is, in the end, some very old-fashioned sentimentality. (You feel, as you read Eggers's metamemoir, that he's embarrassed about having a classic, four-hankie, orphans-in-the-storm story to tell.)

The uneasiness about just how unironic we're now allowed to be is evident on some cutting-edge TV, too. When it first started, "Six Feet Under" looked as if it was going to be the campiest show since "Twin Peaks": the funeral-parlor setting seemed to call for nothing less. But from the start it was clear that the weird stylistic excess—the nutty dream sequences, superhip and up-to-the-minute cultural references, the talking corpses and grotesque camera angles—was jostling awkwardly with earnestness. That scene, last season, in which the guy with the brain disease lovingly looks at his assembled family (who at that point know nothing of his condition), left you feeling uneasy not because it was bitter, but because it was so unabashedly sweet—so "straight." The show's swift devolution in the course of three seasons from real funk to the usual soapy assortment of crises—the new season has brought subplots concerning the cliché angst of the artsy daughter and some drearily contrived domestic crises between the gay brother and his abusive partner—suggests a parallel to culture's own paradigm shift from ironic edge to effortful feeling.

It's no accident that the triumphant return of melodrama, a drama that shuns irony, is happening right now. If irony deadens feeling, melodrama can be thought of as a kind of emotional shock treatment—a useful way, for a public that has been in the habit of distancing itself from sincerity, to feel its way back to some kind of unabashed authenticity.

Yet the very emphasis on emotion has historically made melodrama a marker of a kind of political decay. It's no accident that tragedy first flourished in the world's first democracy: tragedy, you could say, is democracy's genre. Like democracy, classical tragedy must stoically confront insoluble dilemmas between valid alternative visions of how the world could work. (Tragedies wouldn't be as gripping if they were about right versus wrong; what makes them anguishing is that they're often about one noble conviction coming into conflict with another.) Melodrama, which values emotions and cares little where they originate, couldn't care less about issues. Amid the crisp dialectics and rhetorical brilliance of classical Athenian politics, wrenching, austere plays like "Oedipus" were esteemed. But much later in antiquity, when democratic city-states were a thing of the past, the cosmopolitan bourgeoisie canonized the bizarrely overplotted farce "Orestes," by Euripides, with its murderous teenage villains, pathetic girlish victims, last-minute hostage crises and improbable 11th-hour divine rescue. Similarly, the mordant political comedies of Aristophanes devolved into the pleasantly amusing situational comedies called "New Comedy." If you zip forward a few millennia, it's the same-old same-old: in the 1950s, another comfortable bourgeoisie retreated from a recent real-life tragedy into the bathos of Sirkian melodrama, with its highly manufactured emotions; that was also the decade that brought us another new comedy form: the TV sitcom.

Today's resurgence of melodramatic impulses may indeed just be the least disturbing aspect of a larger trend. Reality television, from humiliation-oriented quiz shows like "The Weakest Link" to "Survivor" to "The Bachelor," is just melodrama in a different mode—as desperate as any Sirk weepy to generate emotions, and to use any means possible to do so. In the case of Sirk, however, the emotions are the good old cathartic ones that Aristotle pegged: pity, fear. In the case of reality TV, the emotions are, predictably, the lower ones: not pity but disdain, not fear but a gross-out. Here another classical civilization suggests itself as an analogue. Like reality TV, the Roman games were, in essence, elaborate entertainments designed to get the audiences riled up—emotional, but emotional about something that had no larger significance. Now, as then, "reality" entertainments—people dropped in bowls of worms, real Christians being fed to lions—are just the flip, dark side of melodrama: desperate entertainments for emotionally exhausted times. The culture that feasts on one will happily eat the other.

Or will swallow anything else. Until a few weeks ago, you could almost laugh at the way television news coverage of the Iraq crisis had itself become an exercise in melodramatic overkill: the intentional enhancement of emotions grossly disproportionate to any actual event yet in question, the fancy graphics, the dramatic theme songs, the high-tech wizardry, the elaborate orchestrations. But what happens when it's not just TV (or film or record) producers who show a penchant for the new mode? Melodrama, let's remember, believes fervently in its special effects, and it will stop at nothing to generate a plot twist to justify them. That's fine when you're talking about popular culture, but once you leave entertainment for politics, that kind of melodrama can swiftly become tragedy.

The Pleasure of Flinching

Nicholas Sautin

From two hundred yards, a handheld digital camera tracks a Humvee down a desolate road. Voices, in Arabic: "Keep the camera on it!" "*Allahu akbar.*" Most of the audience at last year's MoMA screening of Mauro Andrizzi's documentary *Iraqi Short Films* was probably thinking what I was. It was hardly surprising that many of them got up to leave before the conclusion of the film. *I am going to watch these American soldiers die.* The Humvee and the soldiers trundle along, perfectly in the center of the crosshairs of the camera. Then, unceremoniously, the Humvee explodes into a ball of flame. There is an audible gasp from the person sitting behind me. A few seconds later—and here is where many in the audience got up to leave—a second vehicle inches its way, in excruciating real time, to the crash site before also bursting into flame.

Those who stayed until the end of the film witnessed a collage of sorts, a barrage of short clips of increasingly and astonishingly bloody footage. Soldiers and insurgents filming themselves firing machine guns at each other, tanks crushing cars and reducing buildings to rubble, graphic close-ups of dead and dying civilians, snipers on both sides recording their hits ("I got him, I got him" translates remarkably well from Arabic, as does "Shoot the mother-fucker!"), KBR trucks ambushed, helicopters shot down, bombs dropping from the sky freeze-framed the moment before impact ("See you in fucking hell, dude," one U.S. soldier offers in voiceover), masked insurgents and American soldiers alike mugging before the camera, British soldiers making amateur dance videos, alleged spies executed on the street by handgun, dead children, and many, many car bombs, IEDs, and people bursting into flame. Above all, it was war as obscene spectacle, slowed down and mesmerizingly, shamefully violent. Interspersed throughout the film are interludes of ironic commentary—quotes from T.E. Lawrence, Dick Cheney ("I think for us to get American military personnel involved in a civil war inside Iraq would literally be a quagmire"), C. Wright Mills, and Mark Twain—that highlight the absurdity, cynicism, and hopelessness of armed conflict. Like comedy in a horror film, these interludes allowed the audience to catch its breath only to dread what would come next. That's about it. Ninety minutes of carnage and irony. Yet if the violence of Andrizzi's footage seemed shocking and incomprehensible, and the urge to look away in anger, shame, or sadness strong, I also had the uncanny sense of having seen these images already. In many cases, I actually had.

Ostensibly an impassioned critique of mainstream media coverage of the war, Andrizzi's film contained no original footage—Andrizzi, a twenty-nine-year-old filmmaker from Argentina, has never been to Afghanistan or Iraq or, as far as I can tell from his biography, any other warzone. The film instead appropriates and consolidates images that have found a second life on the Internet as short and seemingly unfiltered acts of violence. Such footage—YouTube slideshows, passionate pro- and anti-war pleas, insurgent recruitment videos, crudely satirical musical mash-ups, amateur documentaries by soldiers themselves—has become an increasingly popular sub-genre in the viral video phenomenon, ranking somewhere behind pornography, the drunken exploits of celebrities, police videos, and shark attacks in online popularity. Images both mundane (soldiers goofing off) and obscene (dead children) have found a second life within a digital landscape that has spawned no shortage of academic theorization, much of which is devoted to the idea that digital media has rendered the world unknowable. Digital atrocity footage, it seems, has created a new blindness toward the war through which aesthetic shock has replaced critical understanding.

The footage that rankled the audience at MoMA has been seen by thousands, and the best known videos—of beheadings, particularly gruesome deaths, spectacular explosions—by hundreds of thousands, even millions. The self-censoring moral logic of Internet pornography can be traced in the number of views each video receives. Compare the 41,081 views for "Little Iraqi Girl Hit By Car Tossed Like Rag Doll" to the 91,308 views of "Apache Helicopter Stalks and Obliterates Suicide Bomber." On YouTube, where both users and administrators exercise some control over horrific content (generally meaning that the site's archive of sniper-cam footage is confined unequally to the stalking and obliterating of Iraqis), over ten million people have witnessed Yagsiecapsym's (read it backwards) "US MARINES in Iraq Real Footage Warning Graphic," which appropriates many of Andrizzi's safer images to the tune of 009 Sound System's "With a Spirit."

Such images are double acts of representation. While its perspective necessarily extends beyond the field of vision of an individual soldier, the photographer, or the victim, the technological process of capturing the image on film and screening it for a passive audience creates a further distance between the traditionally "real" and what is seen on the screen. *Iraqi Short Films* merely couples such "unreal" images with a vague and not entirely persuasive anti-war message—war is crazy, war is unknowable, war is spectacle. Yet even if its hollow ironies fail, the film's fractured obscenities, made lovingly strange on the big screen, remain unsettling and nearly unwatchable.

In short, the proliferation of atrocity footage on the Internet has complicated the ethical and aesthetic landscape of how and why we watch the suffering of others. If technology grants every war a dominant representational medium (consider the role of television during the Vietnam War), the digital aesthetic associated with Internet video perhaps most closely inhabits our contemporary anxiety about the wars fought in our name—our ability to see and not see, and our desire both to know and not know. The Internet passively collects the visual dregs of a world where anything and everything can be captured on film. In *Regarding the Pain of Others*, Susan Sontag argued that to be a spectator of calamity has become quintessential to modern experience, with photographs of atrocity haunting modern consciousness. Visual understanding, though, is also an ever-changing experience, and it may be that digital Internet footage has in many ways overtaken the photograph as the modern form of technological representation that most closely approaches the intolerable; there exists on every screen the possibility to see what no one should see. This is no longer the case with photography. Digital footage is not framed in somber gallery exhibitions, mounted on museum walls, or filtered through any editorial process. Such images now belong to the public domain, for better or worse. They have lost almost all sense of origin, and function as a kind of traumatic global currency. The same images are recycled countless times for wildly divergent aesthetic and ideological purposes. For Sontag, there is always a moral need to question our right to witness atrocity: "Perhaps the only people with the right to look at images of suffering of this extreme order are those who could do something to alleviate it . . . or those who could learn from it. The rest of us are voyeurs, whether or not we mean to be."

The problem with voyeurism and the Internet, though, is that the idea of "the right to look" may have become obsolete. Atrocity footage has been taken out of the hands of those who would previously have held such moral responsibility—governments, journalists, censors, teachers, etc. The images are simply there for anyone who wishes to look. We imagine their existence, haunted by glimpses of what we have actually seen, and often choose not to look further.

At their core, such images remain visible traces of what has happened, even if they seem incomprehensible. In their democratic lack of artifice and ornamentation, they suggest the closest approximation we have to reality; this makes them intolerable. In this, such video has played a role in the upheaval of traditional journalism. How can a reporter with even total access compete with a soldier attaching a camera to his helmet during a firefight? This immediacy fuels journalism's increased obsolescence; despite the American media's remarkably successful attempts to shield its viewers from gruesome images of the wars in Iraq and Afghanistan, the ease with which digital photos and videos can be recorded and disseminated has largely antiquated traditional military censorship. While mainstream networks were still fretting over whether to show flag-draped coffins on the nightly news, wrestling internally over the complicated ethics of embedded journalism, and creating ever more extravagant banners and catchphrases, camera phones quietly and permanently altered the journalistic landscape.

In their anguished and provocative memoirs, it is telling that both Richard Engel and Dexter Filkins confess to the sickening helplessness they felt upon first seeing images of atrocity emerging from a city too dangerous even to enter. In his *War Journal*, Engel, already numbed by his role in packaging "aftermath pix" for a largely uncaring public, describes the spring and summer of 2005 as a "blur of murders, bombings, shootings, and kidnappings"—unknown and unknowable. It is not surprising that Engel should resort to a visual metaphor of unseeing. Engel is trapped in his hotel as images of Nicholas Berg's beheading spread nearly instantaneously across the globe.

Filkins's much-lauded *The Forever War* follows a similar path, casting the miasma of the war in the language of impassioned, gonzo-inflected journalese—the writer as witness, participant, and victim. And yet despite the power of their angry memoirs, what is striking is just how much the war seems to overwhelm their ability to make sense of it in traditional narrative. Like Sontag, their despair privileges experience—those who know, those who have the right to know—over our voyeurism, but I'm not sure that our contemporary war culture respects such a distinction.

There is something in the accidental and arbitrary nature of amateur digital footage that seems deeply real. This accounts for its continuing power to shock. There is no room for making sense of what you are seeing, no aesthetic consideration of framing or composition—you can only look. Although the Abu Ghraib photos are paradigmatic to our conversation, it is the largely anonymous quality of amateur digital video that marks the footage. Its amateurishness heightens its authenticity and erodes the boundaries between spectator and participant. From afar, you are there, without context and commentary getting in the way. At their worst, such images appropriate the queasy aesthetics of first-person shooter video games, the camera fusing with the gun-barrel—snuff films for the joystick and *Jackass* era. Yet it would be foolish to dismiss such rambunctious images as simply pornographic. The power of these images lies in our perception that they best convey the chaotic reality of postmodern warfare to an audience that takes the fractured, the obscene, and the unknowable for granted. *Who* is killed, *where*, and *why* are no longer relevant questions. We entertain the notion that we are too sophisticated even to ask. We are looking at the war, and we are looking at ourselves looking.

All that remains is what Sontag calls "the pleasure of flinching." Whether or not we choose to look at these images (and for the most part we choose not to look at them), these images are the closest things we have to a war that has become increasingly, and perhaps comfortingly, unreal. It is this comfortable unreality that drives Sontag's insistence that spectators of atrocity think past their sympathy, grief, and shock, the sheer sense of amazement that such horror exists, to think critically—to reach what she calls "moral or psychological adulthood." This is for Sontag the only imperative contained within images of horror: "To set aside the sympathy we extend to others beset by war and murderous politics for a reflection on how our privileges are located on the same map as their suffering, and may—in ways we prefer not to imagine—be linked to their suffering, as the wealth of some may imply the destitution of others, is a task for which the painful, stirring images supply only an initial spark."

What is at stake here is precisely the ethics of shock and incomprehension, which in popular Internet footage have become aesthetically entangled. The more the footage revels in the insanity—the sheer mindlessness and bloodlust of combat—the more viewers respond, feeling closer to the real, ultimately fetishizing the spark and ignoring the flame.

One result of this has been a surge of fictional films that appropriate the aesthetics of Internet atrocity for often dubious storytelling purposes. Think of the near-beheadings that punctuate such Hollywood tripe as *The Kingdom* or *Body of Lies*, soft-core snuff, so to speak, that titillates through the haunted digital memory of Nicholas Berg. Or Brian De Palma's vicious, brilliant, and unwatchable film *Redacted*, which repeatedly implicates its audience's capacity to rationalize atrocity. Recasting the plot of his own *Casualties of War* as a series of short Internet clips, the film's increasingly ludicrous framing devices highlight the changing visual landscape of digital technology. The film ends with a brash intertitle that reads "Collateral

Damage." What follows are horrific (and real) photos of dead children, their eyes "redacted" by black marker to protect their identities. As a last fuck-you to his audience, though, the final, heartbreaking photo is of the corpse of a young girl we assume is the real-life victim that inspired the story. The photo is actually a fake (I had to look it up), and in blurring the line between fact and fiction, the film ultimately risks emptying its outrage, focusing its gaze on the profession of filmmaking rather than the profession of war-making.

Even Paul Haggis's unusually sober *In The Valley of Elah,* which traces the aftermath of war in miniature, engages in the hazy moral calculus that *Redacted* so savagely tries to bury. Tommy Lee Jones plays Hank Deerfield, a grieving father trying to decipher a corrupted bit of digital video in order to explain his son's murder upon returning to America from Iraq. The plot structure is that of the classic detective story. He discovers that his son had committed a war crime, the torture of a wounded prisoner, but *In the Valley of Elah* makes the crime itself a moment of allegorical incomprehension; what is even worse, it elevates this incomprehension to the level of tragedy. Movingly, it casts the torture of prisoners as a symptom of post-traumatic stress rather than a symptom of war; Jones's son hurts a nameless other because he himself is hurting. His victim is incidental to the mechanics of the plot, a fictional counterpart to *Redacted*'s young victim. Deerfield's son's death is metaphorical; like wounded soldiers returning from the occupation, he is destroyed—cast aside, dismembered, and incinerated like trash on the side of the road. The film's deep empathy for returning soldiers abandoned by their government is no doubt sincere, but the film's conflation of aggression and victimhood dubiously replaces difficult questions about complicity and torture with emotional drama, shielding its viewers from critical awareness by elevating its narrative into a tragedy that engulfs all of America; but it is ultimately a tragedy that only America is given the right to own.

In *On Photography,* Susan Sontag despaired that the proliferation of atrocity photos risked taking away from their power to shock us into outrage and political action. Instead of changing the world, she argued, photography invites us, passively, to collect it. This is the reaction, she feared, to a world that had become unknowable except in its photographic aftermath. In *Regarding the Pain of Others,* Sontag further insisted that the right to look be earned in the service of political change; anything else is voyeurism.

It may be then that the Internet, with its ability to make such atrocity images available everywhere in an instant, has created a global collection for which no one can take responsibility. *Iraqi Short Films* brought these images to MoMA, but to what end? What did I gain by staying as others walked out?

Such images unsettle our visual understanding of the world just enough to stimulate us with the pornography of their violence. If the spectacle, though, simply becomes a vehicle for incomprehension and disgust, it can only further fuel political complacency. By tickling our desire for the real—or for the hardcore, to be more precise—these images quietly invite us to say, *Yes, yes I know* while looking away, turning off the computer, walking out of the theater, or flipping the channel.

On Reading a Video Text

Robert Scholes

The moments of surrender proposed to us by video texts come in many forms, but all involve a complex dynamic of power and pleasure. We are, for instance, offered a kind of power through the enhancement of our vision. Close-ups position us where we could never stand. Slow motion allows us an extraordinary penetration into the mechanics of movement, and, combined with music, lends a balletic grace to ordinary forms of locomotion. Filters and other devices cause us to see the world through jaundiced or rose-colored optics, coloring events with emotion more effectively than verbal pathetic fallacy and less obtrusively. These derangements of normal visual processing can be seen as either constraints or extensions of visual power—that is, as power over the viewer or as extensions of the viewer's own optical power, or both. Either way they offer us what is perhaps the greatest single virtue of art: change from the normal, a defense against the ever-present threat of boredom. Video texts, like all except the most utilitarian forms of textuality, are constructed upon a base of boredom, from which they promise us relief.

Visual fascination—and I have mentioned only a few of its obvious forms—is just one of the matrices of power and pleasure that are organized by video texts. Others include narrativity and what I should like to call, at least tentatively, cultural reinforcement. By narrativity, of course, I mean the pleasures and powers associated with the reception of stories presented in video texts. By cultural reinforcement, I mean the process through which video texts confirm viewers in their ideological positions and reassure them as to their membership in a collective cultural body. This function, which operates in the ethical-political realm, is an extremely important element of video textuality and, indeed, an extremely important dimension of all the mass media. This is a function performed throughout much of human history by literature and the other arts, but now, as the arts have become more estranged from their own culture and even opposed to it, the mass media have come to perform this role. What the epic poem did for ancient cultures, the romance for feudalism, and the novel for bourgeois society, the media—and especially television—now do for the commodified, bureaucratized world that is our present environment.

It is time, now, to look at these processes as they operate in some specific texts. Let us begin with a well-known Budweiser commercial, which tells—most frequently in a format of twenty-eight seconds, though a longer version also exists—the life story of a black man pursuing a career as a baseball umpire. In this brief period of time, we are given enough information to construct an entire life story—provided we have the cultural knowledge upon which this construction depends. The story we construct is that of a young man from the provinces, who gets his "big break," his chance to make it in the big city, to rise to the top of his profession. We see him working hard in the small-time, small-town atmosphere of the minor leagues, where the pace of events is slower and more relaxed than it is "at the top." He gets his chance for success—the voice-over narrator says, "In the minors you got to make all the calls, and then one day you *get* the call"—after which we see him face his first real test. He must call an important and "close" play correctly and then withstand the pressure of dispute, neither giving ground by changing his mind (which would be fatal) nor reacting too vigorously to the challenge of his call by an offended manager. His passing of this test and being accepted is presented through a later scene in a bar, in which the manager who had staged the protest "toasts" the umpire with a bottle of Budweiser beer, with a chorus in the background singing, "You keep America working. This Bud's for you." From this scene we conclude that the ump has now "made it" and will live happily ever after. From a few scenes, then, aided by the voice-over narration and a music track, we construct an entire life. How do we do this? We draw upon a storehouse of cultural information that extends from fairy tales and other basic narrative structures to knowledge about the game and business of baseball.

In processing a narrative text we actually construct the story, bringing a vast repertory of cultural knowledge to bear upon the text that we are contemplating. Our pleasure in the narrative is to some extent a constructive pleasure, based upon the sense of accomplishment we achieve by successfully completing this task. By "getting" the story, we prove our competence and demonstrate our membership in a cultural community. And what is the story that we "get"? It is the myth of America itself, of the racial melting pot, of upward mobility, of justice done without fear or favor. The corporate structure of baseball, with minor leagues offering a path for the talented to the celebrity and financial rewards of the majors, embodies values that we all possess, we Americans, as one of the deepest parts of our cultural heritage or ideology. It is, of course, on the playing field that talent triumphs most easily over racial or social barriers. Every year in baseball new faces arrive. Young men, having proved themselves in the minors, get their chance to perform at the highest level. Yale graduates and high-school dropouts who speak little or no English are judged equally by how well they hit, run, throw, and react to game situations. If baseball is still the national pastime, it is because in it our cherished myths materialize—or appear to materialize.

The commercial we are considering is especially interesting because it shows us a black man competing not with his body but with his mind, his judgment and his emotions, in a cruelly testing public arena. Americans who attend to sports are aware that black athletes are just beginning to find acceptance at certain "leadership" positions, such as quarterback in professional football, and that there is still an active scandal over the slender representation of blacks at baseball's managerial and corporate levels. The case of the black umpire reminds viewers of these problems, even as it suggests that here, too, talent will finally prevail. The system works, America works. We can take pride in this. The narrative reduces its story to the absolutely bare essentials, making a career turn, or seem to turn, on a single decision. The ump must make a close call, which will be fiercely contested by a manager who is deliberately testing him. This is a story of initiation, in that respect, an ordeal that the ump must meet successfully. The text ensures that we know this is a test, by showing us the manager plotting in his dugout, and it gives us a manager with one of those baseball faces (Irish? German?) that have the history of the game written on them. This is not just partisan versus impartial judge, it is old man against youth, and white against black. We root for the umpire because we want the system to work—not just baseball but the whole thing: America. For the story to work, of course, the ump must make the right call, and we must know it to be right. Here, the close-up and slow motion come into play—just as they would in a real instant replay—to let us see both how close the call is and that the umpire has indeed made the right call. The runner is out. The manager's charge from the dugout is classic baseball protest, and the ump's self-control and slow walk away from the angry manager are gestures in a ritual we all know. That's right, we think, that's the way it's done. We know these moves the way the contemporaries of Aeschylus and Sophocles knew the myths upon which the Greek tragedies were based. Baseball is already a ritual, and a ritual we partake of mostly through the medium of television. The commercial has only to organize these images in a certain way to create a powerful narrative.

At the bar after the game, we are off stage, outside that ritual of baseball, but we are still in the world of myth. The manager salutes the ump with his tilted bottle of beer; the old man acknowledges that youth has passed its test. The sword on the shoulder of knighthood, the laying on of hands, the tilted Bud—all these are ritual gestures in the same narrative structure of initiation. To the extent that we have wanted this to happen we are gratified by this closing scene of the narrative text, and many things, as I have suggested, conspire to make us want this ending. We are dealing with an archetypal narrative that has been adjusted for maximum effect within a particular political and social context, and all this has been deployed with a technical skill in casting, directing, acting, photographing, and editing that is of a high order. It is very hard to resist the pleasure of this text, and we cannot accept the pleasure without, for the bewildering minute at least, also accepting the ideology that is so richly and closely entangled with the story that we construct from the video text. To accept the pleasure of this text is to believe that America works; and this is a comforting belief, itself a pleasure of an even higher order—for as long as we can maintain it. Does the text also sell Budweiser? This is something only market research (if you believe it) can tell. But it surely sells the American way first and then seeks to sell its brand of beer by establishing a metonymic connection between the product and the nation: a national beer for the national pastime.

An audience that can understand this commercial, successfully constructing the ump's story from the scenes represented in the text and the comments of the narrative voice, is an audience that understands narrative structure and has a significant amount of cultural knowledge as well, including both data (how baseball leagues are organized, for instance, and how the game is played) and myth (what constitutes success, for example, and what initiation is). At a time when critics such as William Bennett and E. D. Hirsch are bewailing our ignorance of culture, it is important to realize that many Americans are not without culture; they simply have a different culture from that of Bennett and Hirsch. What they really lack, for the most part, is any way of analyzing and criticizing the power of a text like the Budweiser commercial—not its power to sell beer, which is easily resisted, especially once you have tasted better beer—but its power to sell America. For the sort of analysis that I am suggesting, it is necessary to recover (as Eliot says) from the surrender to this text, and it is also necessary to have the tools of ideological criticism. Recovery, in fact, may depend upon critical analysis, which is why the analysis of video texts needs to be taught in all our schools.

Before moving on to the consideration of a more complex textual economy, we would do well to pause and consider the necessity of ideological criticism. One dimension of the conservative agenda for this country has been conspicuously anticritical. The proposals of William Bennett and E. D. Hirsch, for instance, different as they are in certain respects, are both recipes for the indoctrination of young people in certain cultural myths. The great books of past ages, in the eyes of Bennett, Hirsch, and Allan Bloom, are to be mythologized, turned into frozen monuments of Greatness in which our "cultural heritage" is embodied. This is precisely what Bloom does to Plato, for instance, turning the dialectical search for truth into a fixed recipe for "greatness of soul." The irony of this is that Plato can only die in this process.

Plato's work can better be kept alive in our time by such irreverent critiques as that of Jacques Derrida, who takes Plato seriously as an opponent, which is to say, takes him dialectically. In this age of massive manipulation and disinformation, criticism is the only way we have of taking something seriously. The greatest patriots in our time will be those who explore our ideology critically, with particular attention to the gaps between mythology and practice. Above all, we must start with our most beloved icons, not the ones we profess allegiance to, but those that really have the power to move and shake us.

The Track of a Teardrop, a Filmmaker's Path

A. O. Scott

Pedro Almodóvar's new movie, *Talk to Her,* which is likely to cement his somewhat unlikely reputation as one of the leading filmmakers of our time, begins wordlessly, with a performance of "Café Müller," a dance piece by the German choreographer Pina Bausch.

Two women, apparently blind, stumble across the stage as their male companions scramble to clear tables and chairs from their paths and to prevent them from slamming into the walls. In the audience, two men, strangers to each other, sit side by side, one of them watching, with evident curiosity, the progress of a tear down the other's cheek.

The story that follows reunites the two men—a male nurse named Benigno and a journalist named Marco—in a private clinic outside Madrid, and traces the progress of their serendipitously entwined destinies. Benigno, who spent most of his life caring for his invalid mother, now devotes himself to the care of Alicia, a young ballerina left comatose by a car accident. Down the hall, Marco sits at the bedside of his lover, Lydia, a bullfighter who lies in a vegetative state after being gored in the ring. The film's title comes from a bit of advice that Benigno, who regales the silent Alicia with amusing anecdotes, beauty tips, and movie plot summaries, gives to the disconsolate Marco.

"Benigno is not only talkative," Mr. Almodóvar said during an interview in a midtown hotel on a rainy afternoon last month, a few days before *Talk to Her* brought the 40th New York Film Festival to a rapturous close. "He tells a lot of stories—related to ballets, to movies. The movie is a kind of glorification of storytelling."

Mr. Almodóvar, in both Spanish and English, is an eager, serious talker, even though his new movie presents decided conversational challenges. "It's a bit of a contradiction that a movie that talks about words, communication, human voices is a movie that's difficult to talk about without betraying it," he warned at the beginning of the interview. In at least one very concrete sense, he's right. To attempt even a bald, literally accurate plot summary is to risk not only spoiling some keen surprises but, much worse, falsifying the film's delicate tone and heartfelt mood. Events that might sound outlandish, even grotesque if I tried to tell you about them here are presented with warmth, humor, and sympathy. The film's passionate, brightly colored humanity would inevitably be lost in translation.

Talk to Her, which opens on Friday in New York and Los Angeles, is by far the most complex, layered narrative Mr. Almodóvar has attempted—gliding backward and forward in time, examining the knots and permutations of at least a half dozen thorny, passionate relationships. But somehow, for all the swerves and surprises that follow, that initial sequence of nonverbal, inadvertent communication contains the film's emotional core; it functions as a cinematic overture, gesturing toward themes and states of feeling that will be elaborated, embroidered, and brought together in a work of daunting dramatic scope and breathtaking coherence. Most obviously, Ms. Bausch's blind women prefigure Alicia (played by Leonor Watling) and Lydia (Rosario Flores), shut off from sensory contact with the world. But the emotion that filters from the stage to Marco (Darío Grandinetti), and then to Benigno (Javier Cámara), is also an allegory of both Mr. Almodóvar's message and his method. A work of art speaks to us, and invites us to speak to each other.

"I would have liked to call it 'The Man Who Cried,'" Mr. Almodóvar remarked at his Film Festival news conference. That title, had it not already been taken by Sally Potter for her 2000 film starring John Turturro and Christina Ricci, would certainly have been apt. Marco's tears, which so fascinate Benigno, will also resonate with moviegoers who find themselves caught up in the film's swirl of unrestrained, beautifully modulated sentiment. "One of the ideas that I wanted to convey was a man who cried for emotional reasons linked to a work of art—from seeing a work of enormous beauty," Mr. Almodóvar said, and it is an idea carried forward by the film's tone as much as by its content. His previous movie, *All about My Mother* (1999), which won the New York Film Critics Circle Award and the Oscar for best foreign film, was a powerful and unironic tribute to the great Hollywood "women's pictures" of the 1940s and '50s, and to the actresses who brought them to life. *Talk to Her*, which shares its predecessor's interests in grief and in loyalty, is a melodrama in a decidedly masculine key.

Both movies offer audiences something they might not have anticipated from this director: a good, honest cry. In the 1980s, Mr. Almodóvar, who was born in 1951 in the provincial Spanish town of Calzada de Calatrava, seemed to embody the transgressive exuberance of his country's cultural awakening after decades of political repression. Spain's recent history had been lachrymose enough, and there was little time for tears or sighs in the baroque, frenetic world of his films. Of course, there was plenty of sensation—gasps of shock, convulsions of laughter, spasms of liberated desire.

In Mr. Almodóvar's early features, which quickly won him heroic status in Spain and a cult following outside it, the thwarted energies of the Franco era burst out in a riot of color, sex, music, drugs, and decadence. To see *Labyrinth of Passions, Dark Habits,* and *What Have I Done to Deserve This?* was to see the anarchic, libertarian strain in Spanish cinema—long represented by the peripatetic surrealist government-in-exile of Luis Buñuel—restored to its native soil, and to witness both the joys and the dangers of sudden freedom. Those movies were riotous to the point of chaos—pulpy, campy, and gleefully overwrought.

At lunch after the news conference, Mr. Almodóvar happily recalled an early assessment from the American press: "sometimes in bad taste, but never boring." Which was precisely the point: in post-Franco Spain, offending sexual propriety, religious authority, and Fascist family values in the name of pleasure was a therapeutic and a political necessity.

But Mr. Almodóvar has always understood that the pursuit of pleasure is not all about fun. In the early films there were always undercurrents of risk, cruelty, and pain, and an implicit recognition that bodies and feelings, in addition to outmoded social norms, might be damaged by unchained eros. And as the ghost of Franco receded—and the specter of AIDS haunted Europe—he began to explore the darker implications of desire. (In addition to being a central theme in his work, desire is also the name of the production company Mr. Almodóvar founded with his brother and longtime producer Agustín in 1987.) *Matador* (1986) and *Law of Desire* (1987) are still headlong, passionate and funny, but they are also disturbing, even a little frightening, in the way they follow the logic of sensual need—the craving for intensity, for novelty, for physical connection—to the edge of the grave.

Those two films, followed by the smashing international success of *Women on the Verge of a Nervous Breakdown,* his great screwball melodrama of 1988, established Mr. Almodóvar as much more than just a naughty provocateur. The habit of provocation for its own sake, however, may have proved hard to break. In the early '90s, it seemed that Mr. Almodóvar risked slipping into mannerism. The sexual insouciance that was so fresh in, for instance, *Labyrinth of Passions* feels forced in *Tie Me Up! Tie Me Down!* (1990) and *Kika* (1994); their lighthearted treatments of stalking, rape, and sadomasochism are less bracing than abrasive.

There is a sense of incipient fatigue in these two films—the bad taste was threatening to become boring after all—which nonetheless have their moments of vibrancy, humor, and insight. They look now like the last bubblings of the post-Fascist cultural ferment—the cinematic equivalent of Chevy Chase's old *Saturday Night Live* news flash: Generalissimo Francisco Franco is still dead.

By the '90s, however, Almodóvarismo, in Spain and beyond, was very much alive. Traces of his influence began to show up everywhere, a notion that elicited a good-natured wince from Mr. Almodóvar. "I do see my influence in some Spanish films," he said, "and even some American films, but I say that with some embarrassment. I truly would not counsel anyone to imitate me, not because I'm so unique, but because I think the way I work is very personal, and also because the kind of material I work with is often on the verge of being ridiculous, even grotesque. Some of my movies became plays, in Spain and in Italy, and they were very successful, but I didn't like them at all. They were very broad and exaggerated. The mistake is that people will think I'll be very happy to go to a play with a lot of drag queens, and I can't tell them that I'm fed up with drag queens, because it might be offensive or it might not be politically correct."

His would-be followers are not the only ones to miss the nuance and sophistication of his work. Like his characters, who keep copies of Djuna Barnes, Tennessee Williams, or Davis Grubb's *Night of the Hunter* on their bedside tables, Mr. Almodóvar is a passionate reader, and from very early in his career he dreamed of adapting novels as various as *The Accidental Tourist, The Silence of the Lambs* and, more recently, *The Human Stain.* The options on those properties, of course, were taken—just think of what the recent history of American cinema would look like if they had not been—though an adaptation of *The Paperboy,* Peter Dexter's melancholy Southern novel, did reach the early stages of production. When Hollywood studios came calling, it was usually with projects like *Sister Act 2* and *To Wong Foo, Thanks for Everything! Julie Newmar,* as if cuddly, commercialized camp, with men in dresses and women in habits, would have represented the logical next step in Mr. Almodóvar's career, instead of a giant step backward.

The Flower of My Secret, released in 1995, marked not only a return to form, but a new direction, as if Mr. Almodóvar, starting from a parodic, camp sensibility, had found his way back to the full, theatrical emotionalism that camp feeds upon and travesties. "I think that emotions have always been present in my films," he says now, "but I'm conscious of a change, of almost deciding that I will concentrate solely on emotions and take away as much of anything extraneous to them as I can, and that takes place as of *The Flower of My Secret.* I now deal with a completely open heart."

"It's not something I had decided," he continued. "It seems imposed on me by my own life and my own experience. I suppose it comes with age; it doesn't really have to do with an intellectual position. I prefer to be unconscious about the reasons. I think it may have to do with a change of a vision, a vision I wouldn't like to say is pessimistic, but which is sad, mournful about life. When I think about my life, I think more about suffering than about joy."

In his last four films—*The Flower of My Secret, Live Flesh, All about My Mother,* and now *Talk to Her*—this sorrow is transformed into tenderness and beauty. There is something deeply consoling in Mr. Almodóvar's mature vision, and the consolation comes from a deep faith in the power of art. To an extent more unusual in the movies than in life, perhaps, his characters define themselves, and reach each other, through their experience of books, movies, theater, and music. In *High Heels*, Victoria Abril's character expresses her rage toward her mother by citing a scene from Bergman's *Autumn Sonata*. The lovelorn romance novelist in *The Flower of My Secret* dissects her romantic predicament with reference to *The Apartment*. The desperate lovers in *Matador* find their violent passions mirrored and inspired by Gregory Peck and Jennifer Jones in *Duel in the Sun*.

The examples proliferate, and they are not confined to movies, or to actually existing works. (At the center of *Talk to Her* are excerpts from *The Shrinking Lover*, a wonderfully bizarre black and white silent film directed by Mr. Almodóvar himself.) Nor are they displays of erudition for its own sake, or attempts to cannibalize cultural prestige.

Sometimes they operate at an almost subliminal level. At one dramatically crucial point in the new film, Mr. Almodóvar noted, the camera glances at a copy of *The Hours* by Michael Cunningham underneath a telephone. "On the cover," he said, "you see a detail of a painting of a body under water, with her hand resting on the water." This apparently casual image has a deep and complex resonance. "On one hand, this is a confession that I love *The Hours*, and that I would have liked to have made the movie, but they already did it. But it is also about the theme of death and water. Rain becomes for Benigno a point of entry into the world of Alicia's coma. Obviously I don't talk about all these meanings because it's not necessary to understand them, but when I'm making a movie it's necessary to surround myself with a lot of images that have a lot of meaning for me, and to the story."

And the story, as a result, is saturated with meaning and thick with feeling beyond what the viewer is able to analyze or the filmmaker to explain. *Talk to Her*, like the Pina Bausch pieces that serve as its bookends, and the gorgeous Caetano Veloso song that is its centerpiece, seems to possess a soul of its own, compounded of gravity and elegance, not explicable or reducible to anything else. "This movie represents something very intimate of myself," Mr. Almodóvar said at the end of our interview, "something that even I feel embarrassed to talk about, some part of myself that I don't even know how to verbalize."

Yet it communicates perfectly. As I stood up to leave, Mr. Almodóvar offered to autograph my copy of the soundtrack CD, which includes Mr. Veloso's song, as well as Alberto Iglesias's lush, melancholy orchestral score. As the elevator doors closed, I glanced down at the cover and noticed the message Mr. Almodóvar had written above his signature, a private communication I am happy to pass along. "Cry," it said.

The Uncommon Reader

George Steiner

Chardin's *Le Philosophe lisant* was completed on 4 December 1734. It is thought to be a portrait of the painter Aved, a friend of Chardin's. The subject and the pose, a man or a woman reading a book open on a table, are frequent. They form almost a sub-genre of domestic interiors. Chardin's composition has antecedents in medieval illuminations where the figure of St. Jerome or some other reader is itself illustrative of the text which it illumines. The theme remains popular until well into the nineteenth century (witness Courbet's celebrated study of Baudelaire reading or the various readers depicted by Daumier). But the motif of *le lecteur* or *la lectrice* seemed to have enjoyed particular prevalence during the seventeenth and eighteenth centuries and constitutes a link, of which Chardin's whole output was representative, between the great age of Dutch interiors and the treatment of domestic subjects in the French classical manner. Of itself, therefore, and in its historical context, *Le Philosophe lisant* embodies a common topic conventionally handled (though by a master). Considered in respect of our own time and codes of feeling, however, this 'ordinary' statement points, in almost every detail and principle of meaning, to a revolution of values.

Consider first the reader's garb. It is unmistakably formal, even ceremonious. The furred cloak and hat suggest brocade, a suggestion borne out by the matt but aureate sheen of the coloration. Though clearly at home, the reader is 'coiffed'—an archaic word which does convey the requisite note of almost heraldic ceremony (that the shape and treatment of the furred bonnet most likely derive from Rembrandt is a point of mainly art-historical interest). What matters is the emphatic elegance, the sartorial deliberation of the moment. The reader does not meet the book casually or in disarray. He is dressed for the occasion, a proceeding which directs our attention to the construct of values and sensibility which includes both 'vestment' and 'investment'. The primary quality of the act, of the reader's self-investiture before the act of reading, is one of *cortesia*, a term rendered only imperfectly by 'courtesy'. Reading, here, is no haphazard, unpremeditated motion. It is a courteous, almost a courtly encounter, between a private person and one of those 'high guests' whose entrance into mortal houses is evoked by Hölderlin in his hymn 'As on a festive day' and by Coleridge

Le Philosophe lisant, by Jean-Siméon Chardin.
Musée du Louvre, Paris

in one of the most enigmatic glosses he appended to *The Rime of the Ancient Mariner*. The reader meets the book with a courtliness of heart (that is what *cortesia* signifies), with a courtliness, a scruple of welcome and entertainment of which the russet sleeve, possibly of velvet or velveteen, and the furred cloak and bonnet are the external symbols.

The fact that the reader is wearing a hat is of distinct resonance. Ethnographers have yet to tell us what general meanings apply to the distinctions between those religious and ritual practices which demand that the participant be covered, and those in which he is bare-headed. In both the Hebraic and the Graeco-Roman traditions, the worshipper, the consultant of the oracle, the initiate when he approaches the sacred text or augury, is covered. So is Chardin's reader, as if to make evident the numinous character of his access to, of his encounter with, the book. Discreetly—and it is at this point that the echo of Rembrandt may be pertinent—the furred bonnet suggests the headdress of the kabbalist or Talmudic scholar when he seeks the flame of the spirit in the momentary fixity of the letter. Taken together with the furred robe, the reader's bonnet implies precisely those connotations of ceremony of intellect, of the mind's tensed apprehension of meaning, which induce Prospero to put on courtly raiment before he opens his magic books.

Observe next the hourglass beside the reader's right elbow. Again, we are looking at a conventional motif, but one so charged with meaning that an exhaustive commentary would nearly comprise a history of the western sense of invention and of death. As Chardin places it, the hourglass declares the relationship of time and the book. The sand sifts rapidly through the narrow of the hourglass (a sifting whose tranquil finality Hopkins invokes at a key point in the mortal turbulence of 'The Wreck of the Deutschland'). But at the same time, the text endures. The reader's life is measured in hours; that of the book, in millennia. This is the triumphant scandal first proclaimed by Pindar: 'When the city I celebrate shall have perished, when the men to whom I sing shall have vanished into oblivion, my words shall endure'. It is the conceit to which Horace's *exegi monumentum* gave canonic expression and which culminates in Mallarmé's hyperbolic supposition that the object of the universe is *le Livre*, the final book, the text that transcends time. Marble crumbles, bronze decays, but written words—seemingly the most fragile of media—survive. They survive their begetters—Flaubert cried out against the paradox whereby he lay dying like a dog whereas that 'whore' Emma Bovary, his creature, sprung of lifeless letters scratched on a piece of paper, continued alive. So far, only books have circumvented death and have fulfilled what Paul Éluard defined as the artist's central compulsion: *le dur désir de durer* (indeed, books can even survive themselves, leapfrogging out of the shadow of their own initial being: there are vital translations of languages long extinct). In Chardin's painting, the hourglass, itself a twofold form with its iconic suggestion of the torus or figure eight of infinity, modulates exactly and ironically between the *vita brevis* of the reader and the *ars longa* of his book. As he reads, his own existence ebbs. His reading is a link in the chain of performative continuity which underwrites—a term worth returning to—the survivance of the read text.

But even as the shape of the hourglass is a binary one, its import is dialectical. The sand falling through the glass tells both of the time-defying nature of the written word and of how little time there is in which to read. Even the most obsessed of bookmen can read only a minute fraction of the world's totality of texts. He is no true reader, no *philosophe lisant*, who has not experienced the reproachful fascination of the great shelves of unread books, of the libraries at night of which Borges is the fabulist. He is no reader who has not heard, in his inward ear, the call of the hundreds of thousands, of the millions of volumes which stand in the stacks of the British Library or of Widener asking to be read. For there is in each book a gamble against oblivion, a wager against silence, which can be won only when the book is opened again (but in contrast to man, the book can wait centuries for the hazard of resurrection). Every authentic reader, in the sense of Chardin's delineation, carries within him a nagging weight of omission, of the shelves he has hurried past, of the books whose spine his fingers have brushed across in blind haste. I have, a dozen times, slunk by Sarpi's leviathan history of the Council of Trent (one of the pivotal works in the development of western religious-political argument); or the *opera omnia* of Nikolai Hartmann in their stately binding; I shall never manage the sixteen thousand pages of Amiel's (profoundly interesting) journal currently being published. There is so little time in 'the library that is the universe' (Borges's Mallarméen phrase). But the unopened books call to us none the less, in a summoning as noiseless but insistent as is the sift of the sand in the hourglass. That the hourglass is a traditional prop of Death in western art and allegory points up the twofold signification of Chardin's composition: the afterlife of the book, the brevity of the life of man without whom the book lies buried. To repeat: the interactions of meaning between hourglass and book are such as to comprehend much of our inner history.

Note next the three metal discs in front of the book. Almost certainly these are bronze medals or medallions used to weigh down, to keep smooth the page (in folios, pages tend to wrinkle and lift at their corners). It is not, I think, fanciful to think of these medallions as bearing portraits or heraldic devices or mottoes, this being the natural function of the numismatic arts from antiquity to the commemorative coinage or medallions struck today. In the eighteenth century, as in the Renaissance, the sculptor or engraver used these small circumferences to concentrate, to make incisive in the literal sense, a celebration of civic or military renown, to give to a moral-mythological allegory lapidary, enduring pronouncement. Thus we find, in Chardin's painting, the presentment of a second major semantic code. The medallion also is a text. It may date from or recompose words and images of high antiquity. Bronze relief or engraving defies the mordant envy of time. It is stamped with meaning as is the book. It may have returned to the light, as do inscriptions, papyri, Dead Sea Scrolls, from a long sojourn in the dark. This lapidary textuality is perfectly rendered in the eleventh of Geoffrey Hill's *Mercian Hymns*:

> Coins handsome as Nero's; of good substance and weight. *Offa Rex* resonant in silver, and the names of his moneyers. They struck with accountable tact. They could alter the king's face.
>
> Exactness of design was to deter imitation; mutilation if that failed. Exemplary metal, ripe for commerce. Value from a sparse people, scrapers of salt-pans and byres.

But the 'exemplary metal', whose weight, whose literal gravity, keeps down the crinkling, fragile page, is itself, as Ovid said, ephemeral, of brief durance, as compared with the words on the page. *Exegi monumentum*: 'I have reared a monument more lasting than bronze' says the poet (remember Pushkin's matchless reprise of Horace's tag), and by placing the medals before the book Chardin exactly invokes the antique wonder and paradox of the longevity of the word.

This longevity is affirmed by the book itself, which provides the painting with its compositional centre and light-focus. It is a bound folio, in a garb which subtly counterpoints that of the reader. Its format and physique are those of stateliness (in Chardin's period, it is more than likely that a folio-volume would have been bound *for* its proprietor, that it would have carried his device). It is no object for the pocket or the airport lounge. The posture of the other folio behind the hourglass suggests that the reader is perusing a multi-volume work. Serious work may well run to several tomes (the eight volumes, unread, of Sorel's great diplomatic history of Europe and the French Revolution haunt me). Another folio looms behind the *lecteur*'s right shoulder. The constituent values and habits of sensibility are patent: they entail massiveness of format, a private library, the commissioning and subsequent conservation of binding, the life of the letter in a canonic guise.

Immediately in front of the medals and hourglass, we observe the reader's quill. Verticality and the play of light on the feathers emphasize the compositional and substantive role of the object. The quill crystallizes the primary obligation of response. It defines reading as action. To read well is to answer the text, to be answerable to the text, 'answerability' comprising the crucial elements of response and of responsibility. To read well is to enter into answerable reciprocity with the book being read; it is to embark on total exchange ('ripe for commerce' says Geoffrey Hill). The dual compaction of light on the page and on the reader's cheek enacts Chardin's perception of the primal fact: to read well is to be read by that which we read. It is to be answerable to it. The obsolete word 'responsion', signifying, as it still does at Oxford, the process of examination and reply, may be used to shorthand the several and complex stages of active reading inherent in the quill.

The quill is used to set down marginalia. Marginalia are the immediate indices of the reader's response to the text, of the dialogue between the book and himself. They are the active tracers of the inner speech-current—laudatory, ironic, negative, augmentative—which accompanies the process of reading. Marginalia may, in extent and density of organization, come to rival the text itself, crowding not only the margin proper but the top and bottom of the page and the interlinear spaces. In our great libraries, there are counter libraries constituted by the marginalia and marginalia on marginalia which successive generations of true readers stenographed, coded, scribbled or set down with elaborate flourishes alongside, above, below and between the horizontals of the printed text. Often, marginalia are the hinges of aesthetic doctrine and intellectual history (look at Racine's copy of Euripides). Indeed, they may embody a major act of authorship, as do Coleridge's marginalia, soon to be published.

Annotation may well occur in the margin, but it is of a different cast. Marginalia pursue an impulsive, perhaps querulous discourse or disputation with the text. Annotations, often numbered, will tend to be of a more formal, collaborative character. They will, where possible, be made at the bottom of the page. They will elucidate this or that point in the text; they will cite parallel or subsequent authorities. The writer of marginalia is, incipiently, the rival of his text; the annotator is its servant.

This service finds its most exacting and necessary expression in the use of the reader's quill to correct and emend. He who passes over printing errors without correcting them is no mere philistine: he is a perjurer of spirit and sense. It may well be that in a secular culture the best way to define a condition of grace is to say that it is one in which one leaves uncorrected neither literal nor substantive errata in the texts one reads and hands on to those who come after us. If God, as Aby Warburg affirmed, 'lies in the detail', faith lies in the correction of misprints. Emendation, the epigraphical, prosodic, stylistic reconstitution of a valid text in the place of a spurious one, is an infinitely more taxing craft. As A. E. Housman professed in his paper on 'The Application of Thought to Textual Criticism' of 1922, 'this science and this art require more in the learner than a simply receptive mind; and indeed the truth is that they cannot be taught at all: *criticus nascitur, non fit*'. The conjunction of learning and sensitivity, of empathy with the original and imaginative scruple which produce a just emendation is, as Housman went on to say, of the rarest order. The stakes are high and ambiguous: Theobald may have won immortality when he suggested that Falstaff died 'babbling of green fields'—but is the emendation correct? The twentieth-century textual editor who has substituted 'brightness fell from her hair' for Thomas Nashe's 'brightness falls from the air' may be correct, but he is, surely, of the damned.

With his quill *le philosophe lisant* will transcribe from the book he is reading. The excerpts he makes can vary from the briefest of quotations to voluminous transcriptions. The multiplication and dissemination of written material after Gutenberg in fact increases the extent and variousness of personal transcription. The sixteenth- and seventeenth-century clerk or gentleman takes down in his hornbook, commonplace book, personal *florilegium* or breviary the maxims, 'taffeta phrases', *sententiae*, exemplary turns of elocution and tropes from classical and contemporary masters. Montaigne's essays are a living weave of echoes and citations. Until late into the nineteenth century—a fact borne witness to by the recollections of men and women as diverse as John Henry Newman, Abraham Lincoln, George Eliot or Carlyle—it is customary for the young and for committed readers throughout their lives to transcribe lengthy political orations, sermons, pages of verse and prose, encyclopaedia articles and chapters of historical narration. Such recopying had manifold purposes: the improvement of one's own style, the deliberate storage in the mind of ready examples of argument or persuasion, the buttressing of exact memory (a cardinal issue). But, above all, transcription comports a full engagement with the text, a dynamic reciprocity between reader and book.

It is this full engagement which is the sum of the varying modes of response: marginalia, annotation, textual correction and emendation, transcription. Together these generate a continuation of the book being read. The reader's active quill sets down 'a book in answer to' (the root-links between 'reply' and 'replication' are pertinent). This response will range from facsimile—which is total acquiescence—and affirmative development all the way to negation and counter-statement (many books are antibodies to other books). But the principal truth is this: latent in every act of complete reading is the compulsion to write a book in reply. The intellectual is, quite simply, a human being who has a pencil in his or her hand when reading a book.

Enveloping Chardin's reader, his folio, his hourglass, his incised medallions, his ready quill, is silence. Like his predecessors and contemporaries in the schools of interior, nocturnal and still-life painting, particularly in northern and eastern France, Chardin is a virtuoso of silence. He makes it present to us, he gives it tactile weight, in the quality of light and fabric. In his particular painting, silence is palpable: in the thick stuff of the table-cloth and curtain, in the lapidary poise of the background wall, in the muffling fur of the reader's gown and bonnet. Genuine reading demands silence (Augustine, in a famous passage, records that his master, Ambrose, was the first man able to read without moving his lips). Reading, as Chardin portrays it, is silent and solitary. It is a vibrant silence and a solitude crowded by the life of the word. But the curtain is drawn between the reader and the world (the key but eroded term is 'mundanity').

There would be many other elements in the painting to comment on: the alembic or retort, with its implications of scientific inquiry and its obvious compositional thrust; the skull on the shelf, at once a conventional prop in scholars' or philosophers' studies and, perhaps, an additional icon in the articulation of human mortality and textual survival; the possible interplay (I am not at all certain here) between the quill and the sand in the hourglass, sand being used to dry ink on the written page. But even a cursory look at the major components of Chardin's *Le Philosophe lisant* tells us of the classical vision of the act of reading—a vision we can document and detail in western art from medieval representations of St Jerome to the late nineteenth century, from Erasmus at his lectern to Mallarmé's apotheosis of *le Livre*.

What of the act of reading now? How does it relate to the proceedings and values inherent in Chardin's painting of 1734?

The motif of *cortesia*, of ceremonious encounter between reader and book, implicit in the costume worn by Chardin's *philosophe*, is now so remote as to be almost unrecapturable. If we come across it at all, it is in such ritualized, unavoidably archaic functions as the reading of the lesson in church or the solemn access to the Torah, head covered, in the synagogue. Informality is our password—though there is a poignant bite to Mencken's quip that many who think themselves emancipated are merely unbuttoned.

Far more radical and so far-reaching as to inhibit adequate summary are the changes in the values of temporality as these figure in Chardin's placement of hourglass, folio and death's head. The whole relationship between time and word, between mortality and the paradox of literary survivance, crucial to western high culture from Pindar to Mallarmé and self-evidently central to Chardin's painting, has altered. This alteration affects the two essential strands of the classic relation between the author and time on the one hand, and between the reader and the text on the other.

It may well be that contemporary writers continue to harbour the scandalous hope of immortality, that they continue to set down words in the hope that these will last not only beyond their own personal decease but for centuries to come. The conceit—in both its common and its technical sense—echoes still, though with characteristic wryness, in Auden's elegy on Yeats. But if such hopes persist, they are not professed publicly, let alone clarioned to the winds. The Pindaric-Horatian-Ovidian manifesto of literary immortality, with its innumerable repeats in the western syllabus, now grates. The very notion of *fama*, of literary glory achieved in defiance of and as rebuttal to death, embarrasses. There is no greater distance than that between the *exegi monumentum* trope and Kafka's reiterated finding that writing is a leprosy, an opaque and cancerous infirmity which is to be hidden from men of ordinary daylight and good sense. Yet it is Kafka's proposal, ambivalent and strategic as it may have been, which qualifies our apprehension of the unstable, perhaps pathological provenance and status of the modern work of art. When Sartre insists that even the most vital of literary personages is no more than an assemblage of semantic markers, of arbitrary letters of the page, he is seeking to demythologize, once for all, Flaubert's hurt fantasy about the autonomous life, about the life after his death, of Emma Bovary. *Monumentum*: the concept and its connotations ('the monumental') have passed into irony. This passage is marked, with masterly sadness, in Ben Belitt's 'This Scribe, My Hand'—with its reflection on the graves of Keats and Shelley in Rome, by Cestius' Pyramid:

> I write, in the posthumous way,
> on the flat of a headstone
> with a quarrier's ink, like yourself;
>
> an anthologist's date and an asterisk,
> a parenthetical mark in the gas
> of the pyramid-builders,
>
> an obelisk whirling with Vespas
> in a poisonous motorcade.

Note the exactness of 'the posthumous way'; not the *voie sacrée* to Parnassus which the classic poet maps for his works and, by exalted inference, for himself. 'The gas of the pyramid-builders' allows, indeed invites, vulgar interpretation: 'the hot air of the pyramid-builders', their vacant grandiloquence. It is not Plato's bees, carriers of divine rhetoric, that attend the poet, but loud, polluting Vespas ('wasps'), their acid sting decomposing the poet's monument even as the mass-technological values they incarnate decompose the aura of his work. We no longer look to texts, except in mandarin artifice, as negating personal death. 'All is precarious,' says Belitt,

> A maniac
> waits on the streets. Nobody listens. What
> must I do? I am writing on water . . .

The desolate phrase is, of course, Keats's. But it was denied, at once, in Shelley's assurance of immortality in 'Adonais', a denial Keats hoped for and, somehow, anticipated. Today such denials ring hollow ('the gas of the pyramid-builders').

The reader reciprocates this ironic declension. For him, as well, the notion that the book in front of him shall outlast his own life, that it prevails against the hourglass and the *caput mortuum* on the shelf, has lost immediacy. This loss involves the entire theme of *auctoritas*, of the normative, prescriptive status of the written word. It is no oversimplification to identify the classic ideal of culture, of civility, with that of the transmission of a syllabus, with that of the study of sybilline or canonic texts by whose authority successive generations test and validate their conduct of life (Matthew Arnold's 'touchstones'). The Greek *polis* saw itself as the organic medium of the principles, of the felt pressures of heroic-political precedent derived from Homer. At no juncture is the sinew of English culture and history separable from the ubiquity in that culture and history of the King James Bible, of the Book of Common Prayer and of Shakespeare. Collective and individual experience found an ordering mirror in a garland of texts; their self-realization was, in the full sense of the word, 'bookish' (in Chardin's painting the light is drawn to and projected from the open book).

Current literacies are diffuse and irreverent. It is no longer a natural motion to turn to a book for oracular guidance. We distrust *auctoritas*—the commanding script or scripture, the core of the authoritarian in classical authorship—precisely because it aspires to immutability. We did not write the book. Even our most intense, penetrative encounter with it is experience at second hand. This is the crux. The legacy of romanticism is one of strenuous solipsism, of the development of self out of immediacy. A single credo of vitalist spontaneity leads from Wordsworth's assertion that 'one impulse from a vernal wood' outweighs the dusty sum of libraries to the slogan of radical students at the University of Frankfurt in 1968: 'Let there be no more quotations.' In both cases the polemic is that of the 'life of life' against the 'life of the letter', of the primacy of personal experience against the derivativeness of even the most deeply felt of literary emotions. To us, the phrase 'the book of life' is a sophistic antinomy or cliché. To Luther, who used it at a decisive point in his version of Revelation and, one suspects, to Chardin's reader, it was a concrete verity.

As object, the book itself has changed. Except in academic or antiquarian circumstances, few of us will have come across, let alone made use of, the sort of tome being pondered by Chardin's *lecteur*. Who, today, has books privately bound? Implicit in the format and atmosphere of the folio, as we see it in the picture, is the private library, the wall of book-lined shelves, library-steps, lecterns, which is the functional space of the inner lives of Montaigne, of Evelyn, of Montesquieu, of Thomas Jefferson. This space, in turn, entails distinct economic and social relations: as between domestics who dust and oil the books and the master who reads them, as between the sanctified privacy of the scholar and the more vulgar terrain on which the family and outside world conduct their noisy, philistine lives. Few of us know such libraries, fewer still possess them. The entire economy, the architecture of privilege, in which the classic act of reading took place, has become remote (we visit the Morgan Library in New York or one of the great English country houses to view, albeit on a magnified scale, what was once the effective cadre of high bookishness). The modern apartment, notably for the young, simply has no space, no wall-surfaces for rows of books, for the folios, the quartos, the multi-volume *opera omnia* from which Chardin's reader has selected his text. Indeed, it is striking to what extent the cabinet for long-playing records and the record-shelf now occupy spaces formerly reserved for books (the substitution of music for reading is one of the major, most complex factors in the current changes of western feeling). Where there are books, moreover, they will, to a greater or lesser degree, be paperbacks. Now there can be no doubt that the 'paperback revolution' has been a liberating, a creative piece of technology, that it has widened the reach of literature and restored to availability whole areas of material, some of it even esoteric. But there is another side to the coin. The paperback is, physically, ephemeral. To accumulate paperbacks is not to assemble a library. By its very nature, the paperback preselects and anthologizes from the totality of literature and thought. We do not get, or get only very rarely, the complete works of an author. We do not get what current fashion regards as his inferior products. Yet it is only when we know a writer integrally, when we turn with special if querulous solicitude to his 'failures' and thus construe our own vision of his presentness, that the act of reading is authentic. Dog-eared in our pocket, discarded in the airport lounge, lurching between *ad hoc* brick bookends, the paperback is both a marvel of packaging and a denial of the largesse of form and spirit expressly stated in Chardin's scene. 'And I saw in the right hand of him that sat on the throne a book written within and on the back side, sealed with seven seals.' Can a paperback have seven seals?

We underline (particularly if we are students or harried book-reviewers). Sometimes we scribble a note in the margin. But how few of us write marginalia in Erasmus's or Coleridge's sense, how few of us annotate with copious rigour. Today it is only the trained epigrapher or bibliographer or textual scholar who emends, this is to say: who encounters the text as a living presence whose continued vitality, whose quick and radiance of being, depend on collaborative engagement with the reader. How many of us are equipped to correct even the crassest blunder in a classical quotation, to spot and emend even the most puerile error in accent or measure, though such blunders and errata abound in even the most reputed of modern editions? And who among us bothers to transcribe, to set down for personal content and commission to memory, the pages that have spoken to him most directly, that have 'read him' most searchingly?

Memory is, of course, the pivot. 'Answerability to' the text, the understanding and critical response to *auctoritas,* as they inform the classic act of reading and the depiction of this act by Chardin, depend strictly on the 'arts of memory'. *Le Philosophe lisant,* like the cultured men around him in a tradition which runs from classical antiquity to, roughly, the First World War, will know texts *by heart* (an idiom worth thinking about closely). They will know by heart considerable segments of Scripture, of the liturgy, of epic and lyric verse. Macaulay's formidable accomplishments in this respect—even as a schoolboy he had committed to memory a fair measure of Latin and English poetry—were only a heightened instance of a general practice. The ability to cite Scripture, to recite from memory large stretches of Homer, Virgil, Horace or Ovid, to cap on the instant a quotation from Shakespeare, Milton or Pope, generated the shared texture of echoes, of intellectual and emotive recognition and reciprocity, on which the language of British politics, law and letters was founded. Knowledge by heart of the Latin sources, of La Fontaine, of Racine, of the trumpet-calls in Victor Hugo, has given to the entire fabric of French public life its rhetorical stress. The classic reader, Chardin's *philosophe lisant,* locates the text he is reading inside a resonant manifold. Echo answers echo, analogy is precise and contiguous, correction and emendation carry the justification of accurately remembered precedent. The reader replies to the text out of the articulate density of his own store of reference and remembrance. It is an ancient, formidable suggestion that the Muses of memory and of invention are one.

The atrophy of memory is the commanding trait in mid and later twentieth-century education and culture. The great majority of us can no longer identify, let alone quote, even the central biblical or classical passages which not only are the underlying script of western literature (from Caxton to Robert Lowell, poetry in English has carried inside it the implicit echo of previous poetry), but have been the alphabet of our laws and public institutions. The most elementary allusions to Greek mythology, to the Old and the New Testament, to the classics, to ancient and to European history, have become hermetic. Short bits of text now lead precarious lives on great stilts of footnotes. The identification of fauna and flora, of the principal constellations, of the liturgical hours and seasons on which, as C. S. Lewis showed, the barest understanding of western poetry, drama and romance from Boccaccio to Tennyson intimately depends, is now specialized knowledge. We no longer learn by heart. The inner spaces are mute or jammed with raucous trivia. (Do not ask even a relatively well-prepared student to respond to the title of 'Lycidas', to tell you what an eclogue is, to recognize even one of the Horatian allusions and echoes from Virgil and Spenser which give to the four opening lines of the poem their meaning, their meaning of meaning. Schooling today, notably in the United States, is planned amnesia.)

The sinews of memory can only be made taut where there is silence, the silence so explicit in Chardin's portrait. To learn by heart, to transcribe faithfully, to read fully is to be silent and within silence. This order of silence is, at this point in western society, tending to become a luxury. It will require future historians of consciousness (*historiens des mentalités*) to gauge the abridgements in our attention span, the dilutions of concentration, brought on by the simple fact that we may be interrupted by the ring of the telephone, by the ancillary fact that most of us will, except under constraints of stoic resolve, answer the telephone, whatever else we may be doing. We need a history of noise-levels, of the diminution in those natural masses of silence, not only nocturnal, which still enfolded the daily lives of Chardin and his reader. Recent studies suggest that some seventy-five per cent of adolescents in the United States read against a background of sound (a radio, a record-player, a television set at one's back or in the next room). More and more young people and adults confess to being unable to read a serious text without a background of organized sound. We know too little about the ways in which the brain processes and integrates competing simultaneous stimuli to be able to say just what this electronic input does to the centres of attention and conceptualization involved in reading. But it is, at the least, plausible to suppose that the capacities for exact comprehension, for retention and for energetic response which knit our being to that of the book are drastically eroded. We tend to be, as Chardin's *philosophe lisant* was not, part-time readers, readers by half.

It would be fatuous to hope for the restoration of the complex of attitudes and disciplines instrumental in what I have called 'the classic act of reading'. The power relations (*auctoritas*), the economics of leisure and domestic service, the architectonics of private space and guarded silence which sustain and surround this act are largely unacceptable to the egalitarian-populist aims of western consumer societies. This, in point of fact, leads to a troubling anomaly. There is a society or social order in which many of the values and habits of sensibility implicit in Chardin's canvas are still operative; in which the classics are read with passionate attention; in which there are few mass media to compete with the primacy of literature; in which secondary education and the blackmail of censorship induce constant memorization and the transmission of texts from remembrance to remembrance. There is a society which is bookish in the root sense, which argues its destiny by perpetual reference to canonic texts, and whose sense of historical record is at once so compulsive and so vulnerable that it employs a veritable industry of exegetic falsification. I am, of course, alluding to the Soviet Union. And this example alone would suffice to keep before our minds perplexities as old as Plato's dialogues about the affinities between great art and centralized power, between high literacy and political absolutism.

But in the democratic-technological west, so far as one can tell, the die is cast. The folio, the private library, at-homeness in classical tongues, the arts of memory, will belong, increasingly, to the specialized few. The price of silence and of solitude will rise. (Part of the ubiquity and prestige of music derives precisely from the fact that one can listen to it while being with others. Serious reading excludes even one's intimates.) Already, the dispositions and techniques symbolized by *Le Philosophe lisant* are, in the proper sense of the term, academic. They occur in university libraries, in archives, in professors' studies.

The dangers are obvious. Not only much of Greek and Latin literature, but substantial portions of European letters, from the *Commedia* to *Sweeney Agonistes* (a poem which, like so many of T. S. Eliot's, is a palimpsest of echoes), have passed out of natural reach. Subject to the scholar's conservation and to occasional, fragmentary visitation by university students, works which were once immediate to literate recall now lead the dreary half-life of those Stradivari fiddles mute behind glass in the Coolidge collection in Washington. Large tracts of once fertile ground are already beyond reclaim. Who but the specialist reads Boiardo, Tasso and Ariosto, that meshed lineage of the Italian epic without which neither the notion of Renaissance nor that of romanticism makes much sense? Is Spenser still a cardinal presence in our repertoire of feeling, as he was to Milton, to Keats, to Tennyson? Voltaire's tragedies are, literally, a closed book; only the scholar may remember that these plays dominated European taste and styles of public utterance for nearly a century, that it is Voltaire, not Shakespeare or Racine, who holds the serious stage from Madrid to St Petersburg, from Naples to Weimar.

But the loss is not only ours. The essence of the full act of reading is, we have seen, one of dynamic reciprocity, of responsion to the life of the text. The text, however inspired, cannot have significant being if it is unread (what quick of life is there in an unplayed Stradivarius?). The relation of the true reader to the book is creative. The book has need of him as he has need of it—a parity of trust exactly rendered in the composition of Chardin's painting. It is in this perfectly concrete sense that every genuine act of reading, that every *lecture bien faite*, is collaborative with the text. *Lecture bien faite* is a term defined by Charles Péguy in his incomparable analysis of true literacy (in the *Dialogue de l'histoire et de l'âme païenne* of 1912–13):

> Une lecture bien faite . . . n'est pas moins que le vrai, que le véritable et même et surtout que le réel achèvement du texte, que le réel achèvement de l'œuvre; comme un couronnement, comme une grâce particulière et coronale . . . Elle est ainsi littéralement une coopération, une collaboration intime, intérieure . . . aussi, une haute, une suprême et singulière, une déconcertante responsabilité. C'est une destinée merveilleuse, et presqu'effrayante, que tant de grandes œuvres, tant d'œuvres de grands hommes et de si grands hommes puissent recevoir encore un accomplissement, un achèvement, un couronnement de nous . . . de notre lecture. Quelle effrayante responsabilité, pour nous.

As Péguy says: 'what a terrifying responsibility', but also what a measureless privilege; to know that the survival of even the greatest literature depends on *une lecture bien faite, une lecture honnête.* And to know that this act of reading cannot be left in the sole custody of mandarin specialists.

But where are we to find true readers, *des lecteurs qui sachent lire*? We shall, I expect, have to train them.

I carry with me a vision of 'schools of creative reading' ('schools' is far too pretentious a word; a quiet room and table will do). We shall have to begin at the simplest, and therefore most exacting level of material integrity. We must learn to parse sentences and to analyse the grammar of our text, for, as Roman Jakobson has taught us, there is no access to the grammar of poetry, to the nerve and sinew of the poem, if one is blind to the poetry of grammar. We shall have to relearn metrics and those rules of scansion familiar to every literate schoolboy in the Victorian age. We shall have to do so not out of pedantry, but because of the overwhelming fact that in all poetry, and in a fair proportion of prose, metre is the controlling music of thought and of feeling. We shall have to wake the numbed muscles of memory, to rediscover in our quite ordinary selves the enormous resources of precise recollection, and the delight that comes of the texts which have secure lodging within us. We would seek to acquire those rudiments of mythological and scriptural recognition, of shared historical remembrance, without which it is hardly possible, except by constant resort to more and more laboured footnotes, to read adequately a line of Chaucer, of Milton, of Goethe, or, to give a deliberately modernist instance, of Mandelstam (who turns out to be one of the masters of echo).

A class in 'creative reading' would proceed step by step. It would begin with the near-dyslexia of current reading habits. It would hope to attain the level of informed competence prevalent among the well-educated in Europe and the United States at, say, the end of the nineteenth century. It would aspire, ideally, to that *achèvement*, to that fulfilling and crowning involvement in the text of which Péguy speaks and of which such complete acts of reading as Mandelstam on Dante or Heidegger on Sophocles are exemplary.

The alternatives are not reassuring: vulgarization and loud vacancies of intellect on the one hand, and the retreat of literature into museum cabinets on the other. The tawdry 'plot outline' or predigested and trivialized version of the classic on the one hand, and the illegible variorum on the other. Literacy must strive to regain the middle ground. If it fails to do so, if *une lecture bien faite* becomes a dated artifice, a great emptiness will enter our lives, and we shall experience no more the quiet and the light in Chardin's painting.

Transcending Argument

Argument as Emergence, Rhetoric as Love

Jim W. Corder

In a recent review in the *New York Times Book Review*, A. G. Mojtabai said, "We are all authors. Adding here, deleting there, we people the world with our needs: with friends, lovers, ciphers, enemies, villains—and heroes" (March 3, 1985: 7). All authors, to be sure, we are more particularly narrators, historians, taletellers. Going through experience, hooking some version of it to ourselves, accumulating what we know as evidence and insight, ignoring what does not look like evidence and insight to us, finding some pieces of life that become life for us, failing to find others, or choosing not to look, each of us creates the narrative that he or she is. We tell our lives and live our tales, enjoying where we can, tolerating what we must, turning away to re-tell, or sinking into madness and disorder if we cannot make (or remake) our tale into a narrative we can live in. Each of us forms conceptions of the world, its institutions, its public, private, wide, or local histories, and each of us is the narrative that shows our living in and through the conceptions that are always being formed as the tales of our lives take their shape. In this history-making, as E. L. Doctorow says, "there is no fiction or non-fiction as we commonly understand the distinction" ("False Documents," *American Review* 26 [1977]: 215–32). There is only our making, sometimes by design, sometimes not. None of us lives without a history; each of us is a narrative. We're always standing some place in our lives, and there is always a tale of how we came to stand there, though few of us have marked carefully the dimensions of the place where we are or kept time with the tale of how we came to be there.

The catch is that, though we are all fiction-makers/historians, we are seldom all that good at the work. Sometimes we can't find all that's needed to make the narrative we want of ourselves, though we still make our narrative. Sometimes we don't see enough. Sometimes we find enough and see enough and still tell it wrong. Sometimes we fail to judge either the events within our narrative or the people, places, things, and ideas that might enter our narrative. Sometimes we judge dogmatically, even ignorantly, holding only to standards that we have already accepted or established. We see only what our eyes will let us see at a given moment, but eventually make a narrative of ourselves that we can enjoy, tolerate, or at least not have to think about too much. Every so often, we will see something we have not seen before, and then we have to nudge, poke, and remake our narrative, or we decide we can either ignore the thing seen or whittle into shape the narrative we already have. We are always seeing, hearing, thinking, living, and saying the fiction that we and our times make possible and tolerable, a fiction that is the history we can assent to at a given time. But not only can we not always be good narrators/historians, we also cannot be thorough at the work. We never quite get the narrative all said: we're always making a fiction/history that always has to be remade, unless we are so bound by dogma, arrogance, and ignorance that we cannot see a new artifact, hear a new opinion, or enter a new experience in our narrative.

When I say that we make the fictions that are our lives, I mean to identify a human activity, not a foolish or evil one. History as fiction may become evil, of course, if we refuse to see any history except the one we've already accepted or if we try to force that history upon others. At any rate, making the fiction of our lives—not at all the same as discovering a way to present an objective, externally verifiable history, which is not possible, anywhere—is not by nature limited, valueless, ignorant, despicable, or "merely subjective." It is human. It is what we do and are, even if we think we are doing and being something else. Even if we imagine that we are learning what can be known "our there," some truths that are fixed and forever, we are after all creating our narratives "in here," ourselves always agents for what can be known. We are always, as the rhetorician might say, inventing the narratives that are our lives.

As I have already suggested, we are always standing somewhere in our narratives when we speak to others or to ourselves. When we use language, some choices have already been made and others must be made. Our narratives, which include our pasts, accompany us and exist in our statements and exercise their influence whether or not we are aware of the influence. Before we speak, we have lived; when we speak, we must continually choose because our mouths will not say two words simultaneously. Whether consciously or not, we always station ourselves somewhere in our narratives when we use language. This means that invention always occurs. The process of invention may occur in a conscious, deliberate way, but it will occur, even if at some subterranean level. Any statement carries its history with it. We may speak without knowing all of our narratives, but the history is there. If the history of a statement someone else makes isn't apparent to us as hearers, then we have to go and find it. If we are talking to someone and that person says something we don't understand, or something that offends us, or something we cannot easily agree to, then we have to start searching that person's history until we begin to understand what led him or her to speak just so. Sometimes we do less well: if the history isn't there for us, we don't learn it, but instead make it up to suit ourselves. If we learn or make up another's narrative so that it becomes part of our narrative, then we can live in some peace with the other. If the other's narrative will not enter our own, then something else happens, to which I'll return in a moment.

While the language that lets us invent our narratives and be human is a great gift, its capacities will not extend infinitely. Language comes out of us a word at a time; we cannot get all said at once. We open ourselves as we can to insight and experience and say what we can, but what we say will invariably be incomplete. Two words cannot occupy the same space at the same time; two messages cannot fully occupy the same space at the same time. Language enforces a closure: we must say one thing or the other; we choose, and make our narrative. To be sure, having lived, thought, and spoken, we can open ourselves again to insight and experience and evidence and try to say it all again. But what will come out will be the fiction we can make at the time. We cannot make all that was and is and shall be into an is of the moment's speaking. Whatever we can get into our heads we will make into the narratives that will be our truths unless we learn again.

2

Each of us is a narrative. A good part of the time we can live comfortably adjacent to or across the way from other narratives. Our narratives can be congruent with other narratives, or untouched by other narratives. But sometimes another narrative impinges upon ours, or thunders around and down into our narratives. We can't build this other into our narratives without harm to the tales we have been telling. This other is a narrative in another world; it is disruptive, shocking, initially at least incomprehensible, and, as Carl Rogers has shown us, threatening.

When this happens, our narratives become indeed what they are perpetually becoming—arguments. The choosing we do to make our narratives (whether or not we are aware of the nature of our choosing) also makes our narratives into arguments. The narratives we tell (ourselves) create and define the worlds in which we hold our beliefs. Our narratives are the evidence we have of ourselves and of our convictions. Argument, then, is not something we *make* outside ourselves; argument is what we are. Each of us is an argument. We always live in, through, around, over, and under argument. All the choices we've made, accidentally or on purpose, in creating our histories/narratives have also made us arguments, or, I should go on to say, sets of congruent arguments, or in some instances, sets of conflicting arguments.

3

Each of us is an argument, evidenced by our narrative. What happens, then, if the narrative of another crushes up against our own—disruptive, shocking, incomprehensible, threatening, suddenly showing us into a narrative not our own? What happens if a narrative not our own reveals to us that our own narrative was wanting all along, though it is the only evidence for our identity? What happens if the merest glimpse into another narrative sends us lurching, stunned by its differentness, either alarmed that such differentness could exist or astonished to see that our own narrative might have been or might yet be radically otherwise than it is? Do we hold our narratives? Keep telling the story we have been telling? At all costs?

We react, of course, in many different ways. Sometimes we turn away from other narratives. Sometimes we teach ourselves not to know that there are other narratives. Sometimes—probably all too seldom—we encounter another narrative and learn to change our own. Sometimes we lose our plot, and our convictions as well; since our convictions belong to our narratives, any strong interference with our narrative or sapping of its way of being will also interrupt or sap our convictions. Sometimes we go to war. Sometimes we sink into madness, totally unable to manage what our wit or judgment has shown us—a contending narrative that has force to it and charm and appeal and perhaps justice and beauty as well, a narrative compelling us to attention and toward belief that we cannot ultimately give, a contending narrative that shakes and cracks all foundations and promise to alter our identity, a narrative that would educate us to be wholly other than what we are. Any narrative exists in time; any narrative is made of the past, the present, and the future. We cannot without potential harm shift from the past of the one narrative into the present and future of another, or from the past and present of one narrative into the future of another, or from the future we are narrating into a past that is not readily ours. How can we take that one chance I mentioned just now and learn to change when change is to be cherished? How can we expect another to change when we are ourselves that other's contending narrative?

4

Let there be no mistake: a contending narrative, that is, an argument of genuine consequence because it confronts one life with another, is a threat, whether it is another's narrative become argument impinging upon or thundering into ours, or our own, impinging upon the other's. A contending narrative, I'd suggest, is a threat more consequential than Carl Rogers has shown us.

In *On Becoming a Person* (Boston: Houghton Mifflin, 1961), Rogers proposes that "significant learning . . . takes place when five conditions are met":

- When the client perceives himself as faced by a serious problem;
- When the therapist is a congruent person in the relationship, able to *be* the person he is;
- When the therapist feels an unconditional positive regard for the client;
- When the therapist experiences an accurate emphatic understanding of the client's private world and communicates this;
- When the client to some degree experiences the therapist's congruence, acceptance, and empathy.

Rogers had earlier applied his thinking more directly to rhetoric, announcing his belief that a sense of threat usually blocks successful communication. As he put it, "the major barrier to mutual interpersonal communication is our very natural tendency to judge, to evaluate, to approve or disapprove, the statement of the other person" ("Communication: Its Blocking and Its Facilitation," paper delivered at Northwestern University's Centennial Conference on Communication, Oct. 11, 1951, reprinted in Richard E. Young, Alton L. Becker, and Kenneth L. Pike, *Rhetoric: Discovery and Change* [New York: Harcourt, Brace, and World, 1979]: 284–89). If we refrain from evaluating and instead "listen with understanding," according to Rogers, we will "see the expressed idea and attitude from the other person's point of view . . . sense how it feels to him . . . achieve his frame of reference in regard to the thing he is talking about" (285). When we are immersed in the attitudes, ideas, and beliefs of the other person, we "will find the emotion going out of the discussion, the differences being reduced, and those differences which remain being of a rational and understandable sort" (286).

Such insights have been enormously valuable in recent years. Some (Maxine Hairston, for example) believe that Rogers's work has brought a new dimension to rhetoric after all these centuries, changing our way of thinking about argument. Others believe that Rogers's views are assumed by Aristotle, as Andrea Lunsford put it, to be "the foundation which is necessary before successful argumentation begins" ("Aristotelian vs. Rogerian Argument: A Reassessment," *College Composition and Communication* [May, 1979]: 146–51). Lunsford singles out two texts that propose methods of organizing Rogerian argument. Young, Becker, and Pike (283) suggest the following method:

First: an introduction to the problem and a demonstration that the opponent's position is understood.

Second: a statement of the contexts in which the opponent's position may be valid.

Third: a statement of the writer's position, including the contexts in which it is valid.

Fourth: a statement of how the opponent's position would benefit if he were to adopt elements of the writer's position.

In *A Contemporary Rhetoric* (Boston: Houghton Mifflin, 1974 [210–11]), Maxine Hairston presents another Rogerian pattern:

1. A brief, objectively phrased statement of the issue.
2. A complete and impartially worded summary of your audience's opinion on the issue, demonstrating that you have made an honest effort to understand how they feel and why they feel that way. It would be useful to mention the values that underlie these opinions.
3. An objective statement of your opinions on the issue, along with your reasons for feeling as you do. Here again it would be useful to give the values on which you base your opinions.
4. An analysis of what your opinions have in common.
5. A proposal for resolving the issue in a way that injures neither party.

Such insights added to those of Carl Rogers, I'll say again, have been highly valuable. They lead to patterns of argument that may even work, part of the time, in some settings. But they won't do. They do not, I believe, face the flushed, feverish, quaky, shaky, angry, scared, hurt, shocked, disappointed, alarmed, outraged, even terrified condition that a person comes to when his or her narrative is opposed by a genuinely contending narrative. Then it is one life or another, perhaps this life or none.

I want to pause a little to suggest some of the reasons that I think Rogers and others who have applied his work have not gone far enough, though this is not the place for a full critique, even if I could give it. First, we should remember, Rogers is talking about the therapist-client relationship, and much of what he says rises from that context. Since it takes two to tango, and since at least one of the participants in this context is already intent upon *not* being an adversary, then conflict may be resolved and mutual communication may ensue. The therapist-client relationship, I'd suggest, even at its prickliest, is simply not going to produce the stress and pain that can occur when contending narratives meet. It is by its nature more amenable to discussion and resolution, and the rules or conditions I cited earlier are, at any rate, game rules, as my colleague, Professor James Baumlin, has pointed out. In the passage I cited earlier, Rogers is talking about a client who already has a need (he or she is faced by a serious problem), and the therapist is already a congruent person in the relationship. Rogers proposes for the therapist an "unconditional positive regard," but straight away recommends that all take emotion out of discussions and reduce differences. If one holds another in "unconditional positive regard," that regard, I believe, includes both emotions and differences. They cannot be reduced, though their force may be diminished for a moment; such energy is always conserved. If emotions do go out of the discussion—and I don't think they do—it is only after time and care. What each must face in contention before emotions and differences dwindle is something in the other altogether more startling: a horror, a wrong, a dishonesty (as each sees the other), a shock, an outrage, or perhaps a beauty too startling and stunning to see. As for the texts that propose patterns of Rogerian arguments, I'd say that the recommended designs are altogether commendable and will sometimes work, so long as the argument isn't crucial to the nature of the narratives involved. Where arguments entail identity, the presentation of "a statement of how the opponent's position would benefit if he were to adopt elements of the writer's position" is about as efficacious as storming Hell with a bucket of water or trying to hide the glories of Heaven with a torn curtain. If I cannot accept the identity of the other, his kindness in offering me benefits will be of no avail. As for offering a "proposal for resolving the issue in a way that injures neither party," I'd say that in the arguments that grip us most tightly, we *do* injure the other, or the other injures us, or we seem about to injure each other, except we take the tenderest, strongest care. Paul Bator ("Aristotelian and Rogerian Argument," *College Composition and Communication* [1980]: 427–32) acknowledges that Rogerian strategy works most effectively when students "encounter non-adversary writing situations." "Under the Rogerian schema," he continues, "students can be encouraged to view their writing as a communicative first step—one designed to build bridges and win over minds—rather than being prompted to view the essay only as a finished product serving as an ultimate weapon for conversion."

I am suggesting that the arguments most significant to us are just where threat occurs and continues, just where emotions and differences do not get calmly talked away, just where we are plunged into that flushed, feverish, quaky, shaky, angry, scared, hurt, shocked, disappointed, alarmed, outraged, even terrified condition I spoke of a little earlier. Then what do we do?

5

To make the kind of contention or opposition I am trying to discuss a little clearer, I should add another term. I have been talking about contending narratives, or identities. Let me now add what I hope has been suggested all along: let us suppose that in this contention each narrator is entirely *steadfast*, wholly intent upon preserving the nature and movement of his or her narrative, earnest and zealous to keep its identity. I think we have not fully considered what happens in argument when the arguers are steadfast.

If Ms. Smith is steadfast in conviction and is outfitted with what she takes to be good evidence and sound reasoning, that means that she is living a narrative that is congruent with her expectations and satisfying to her needs. But if she speaks to Mr. Jones, who is at opposites and equally steadfast, who is his own satisfying narrative, then it's likely that Ms. Smith's evidence will not look like evidence to Mr. Jones, and Ms. Smith's reasoning will not look like reasoning. Evidence and reason are evidence and reason only if one lives in the narrative that creates and regards them.

That seems to picture a near-hopeless prospect.

Sometimes it is, at least for long periods of time. Sometimes we don't resolve oppositions, but must either remain apart or live as adversaries with the other. But the prospect doesn't have to be hopeless, at least not permanently.

What can change it? What can free us from the apparent hopelessness of steadfast arguments opposing each other? I have to start with a simple answer and hope that I can gradually give it the texture and capacity it needs: we have *to see* each other, *to know* each other, *to be present to* each other, *to embrace* each other.

What makes that possible? We have to change the way we talk about argument and conceive of argument.

6

I'm not ready to go on yet. I want to try to place my interest in argument, and perhaps I can do that by comparing my interest to those of Carl Rogers, to whom I am clearly much indebted. Rogers extrapolates from therapist-client relationships to public communication relationships. The base from which he works (the therapist-client relationship) gives him a setting in which civil understanding is a goal to be reached through mutual communication transactions. He does recognize the potentially threatening effect of alien insights and ideas. Young, Becker, and Pike show that the Rogerian strategy "rests on the assumption that a man holds to his beliefs about who he is and what the world is like because other beliefs threaten his identity and integrity" (7). In the Rogerian view, as Paul Bator puts it, carefully reasoned arguments "may be totally ineffectual when employed in a rhetorical situation where the audience feels its beliefs or values are being threatened. No amount of reasoned argument will prompt the audience to consider the speaker's point of view if the audience senses that its opinions are somehow being 'explained away'" (428). Followers of Rogers see in Aristotle's *Rhetoric* an antagonistic speaker-audience relationship; they do not find this in Rogers, for, as Bator says, "Generation and control of audience expectation do not attract Rogers" (428). As I have already suggested, given the therapist-client relationship he starts from, Rogers is appropriately enough interested in rhetorical contexts that do not involve advocacy. As Rogers says, "If I can listen to what [the other person] can tell me, if I can understand how it seems to him, if I can see its personal meaning for him, if I can sense the emotional flavor which it has for him, then I will be releasing potent forces of change in him" (285–86). Since he is customarily talking about a mutual communication transaction, Rogers is often as concerned with the audience as with the speaker. A speaker, Bator says, "must be willing to achieve the frame of reference of the listener even if the values or views held by the other are antithetical to the speaker's personal code of ethics. A necessary correlate of acceptance (of the other's view) is understanding, an understanding which implies that the listener accepts the views of the speaker without knowing cognitively what will result. Such understanding, in turn, encourages the speaker to explore untried avenues of exchange" (428). Looking for the therapist-client relationship, Rogers sees the therapist/communicator as an understanding audience. He expects that the therapist-as-audience will not only accept, but also understand the feelings and thoughts of the client-as-speaker. When the therapist understands the feelings and thoughts that seem so horrible or weak or sentimental or bizarre to the client, when the therapist understands and accepts the client, then the therapist frees the client to explore deep experience freely. As each understands and accepts the other, then they may move toward the truth.

This, I would gladly agree, is the way we ought to argue, each accepting, understanding, and helping the other. However, I think the significant arguments that crowd us into each other are somewhat less kindly composed. I want to get to the place where we are threatened and where the setting doesn't seem to give us opportunity to reduce threat and to enter a mutual search for congruence and regard. I want to get to the place where we are advocates of contending narratives (with their accompanying feelings and thoughts), where we are adversaries, each seeming to propose the repudiation or annihilation of what the other lives, values, and is, where we are beyond being adversaries in that strange kind of argument we seldom attend to, where one offers the other a rightness so demanding, a beauty so stunning, a grace so fearful as to call the hearer to forego one identity for a startling new one.

7

What can free us from the apparent hopelessness of steadfast arguments contending with each other, of narratives come bluntly up against each other? Can the text of one narrative become the text of another narrative without sacrifice? If there is to be hope, we have to see each other, to know each other, to be present to each other, embrace each other.

What makes that possible? I don't know. We can start toward these capacities by changing the way we talk about argument and conceive of argument.

It may be helpful, before I go on, if I try to explain a little more fully the kind of occasion I mean to refer to, the kind of setting in which contention generates the flushed, feverish, quaky, shaky, angry, scared, hurt, shocked, disappointed, alarmed, outraged, even terrified condition I have mentioned. Of course I cannot imagine, let alone explain or describe, all the oppositions that can occur. Perhaps I can by illustration at least suggest the kind of occasion that I want to talk about. I mean such occasions as these: let two people confront each other, each holding views antithetical to the sacred values and images of the other, one an extreme advocate of the current pro-life movement, the other an extreme advocate of the current movement to leave free choice open to women in the matter of abortion, each a mockery of the other; let two parties confront each other, zealous advocates of one contending that farmers must learn to stand on their own without government support, and zealous advocates of the other contending that the government, by withdrawing support, will literally kill farmers; let two tribes go to war for ancient reasons not entirely explicable to themselves or to outsiders, each a denial of the other, as in various current Middle East crises; let two nations confront each other in what sometimes appears to be a shocked and total inability to understand or even to recognize each other, as in continuing conflicts between the United States and Russia, wherever these conflicts happen to be located, whether in East Germany or in Nicaragua; let a beautiful Jewish woman encounter an aged captain of guards for Dachau; let some man confront an affirmation of life he has not been able to achieve; let an honest woman encounter cruel dishonesty; let a man encounter a narrative so beautiful but different that he cannot look; let two quite different narratives converge in conflict inside the head of a single lonely man or woman.

Given such occasions, what do we do in argument? Can we hope for happy resolution? I don't know. I do think the risk in argument is greater than we have learned from Aristotle or Rogers. What can we do, then?

We can start, as I suggested earlier, by changing the way we talk about argument.

As we presently understand, talk about, and teach argument, it is, whatever our intentions, *display* and *presentation*. We entice with an exordium and lay in a background. We present a proposition. We display our proofs, our evidence. We show that we can handle and if need be refute opposing views. We offer our conclusion. That is display and presentation. The same thing is true of proposed plans for Rogerian argument, as in the passages I cited earlier from Young, Becker, and Pike and from Maxine Hairston.

But argument is not something to *present* or *to display*. It is something *to be*. It is what we *are*, as I suggested earlier.

We are the argument over against another. Another is the argument over against us. We live in, through, around, and against arguments. To display or to present them is to pretend a disengagement that we cannot actually achieve and probably should not want to achieve. Argument is not display or presentation, for our engagement in it, or identity with it, will out. When argument is taken as display or presentation, then it eventually becomes a matter of my poster against yours, with the prize to the slickest performance.

If we are to hope for ourselves and to value all others, we must learn that argument is emergence.

8

Argument is emergence toward the other. That requires a readiness to testify to an identity that is always emerging, a willingness to dramatize one's narrative in progress before the other; it calls for an untiring stretch toward the other, a reach toward unfolding the other. It is a risky revelation of the self, for the arguer is asking for an acknowledgement of his or her identity, is asking for witness from the other. In argument, the arguer must plunge on alone, with no assurance of welcome from the other, with no assurance whatever of unconditional positive regard from the other. In argument, the arguer must, with no assurance, go out, inviting the other to enter a world that the arguer tries to make commodious, inviting the other to emerge as well, but with no assurance of kind or even thoughtful response. How does this happen? Better, how can it happen?

It can happen if we learn to love before we disagree. Usually, it's the other way around: if we learn to love, it is only after silence or conflict or both. In ancient times, I was in the United States Army. I spent the better part of 1951 and 1952 in Germany. In those years, American troops were still officially regarded as an Occupation Force, with certain privileges extended, such as free transportation. One service provided was a kind of rental agency in many large cities. On pass or on leave, one could go to this agency and be directed to a room for rent (very cheap) in a private home. Since I was stationed only ten or twelve miles away, I often went to Heidelberg when I had just a weekend pass or a three-day pass. On one such occasion I went to Heidelberg, stopped in at the agency, and got directions to a room that was available. I found the address, a large brownstone just a block off the main street, met the matron of the house, and was taken to a small bedroom on the third floor that would be mine for a couple of days. I left shortly thereafter to go places and do things, paying no particular attention to the room except to notice it was clean and neat. The next morning was clear and bright and cool; I opened the windows and finally began to see the room. A picture on one wall startled me, more, stunned me.

On the kitchen wall in my parents' home in Texas there was a picture of my older brother, taken while he was in what was known as the Air Corps in World War II. It was a posed shot of the sort that I suppose most airmen had taken at one time or another to send home to the folks. In the picture, my brother is wearing the airman's favorite of that time, a leather jacket with knit cuffs and a knit band about the waist. He is wearing the old-fashioned leather cap with ear flaps and goggles, and there is a white scarf around his neck, one end tossed over his shoulder. Behind him there is a Consolidated-Vultee B-24.

The picture on the wall in the bedroom in Heidelberg showed a young man wearing a leather jacket with knit cuffs and a knit band about the waist. He wore an old-fashioned leather cap with ear flaps and goggles, and there is a white scarf around his neck, one end tossed over his shoulder. Behind him there was an air-plane; it was a Focke-Wulf 190. He might have been my brother. After a while, I guess I realized that he *was* my brother.

The television news on March 7, 1985, showed a memorial service at Remagen, Germany, marking the fortieth anniversary of the American troops' capture of the Remagen bridge, which let them cross the Rhine. No major world leaders were there, but veterans from both sides had come to look and take notice of the day. American and German veterans who had fought there wept and hugged each other and shook hands.

In the mid-fifties, another group of veterans met, to commemorate the fortieth anniversary of the end of battle at Verdun, that hellish landscape where over a million men died to gain or to preserve two or three miles of scrubby country, where no birds sang. They shook hands; they embraced; they wept; they sang an old song that begins, "Ich hatte ein kamaraden."

After a while, the hated dead can be mourned, and the old enemy can be embraced.

In these instances, we waited to love (or at least to accept) until long after silence and grim conflict. (I've not lost my head altogether: some conflicts will not be resolved in time and love—there's always that captain of guards from Dachau.) Often, we don't learn to love (or at least to accept) at all. All precedents and examples notwithstanding, I'll still insist that argument—that rhetoric itself—must begin, proceed, and end in love.

9

But how is this to happen? How will we argue, or teach argument taken in this way? I don't know, but I'll chance some suggestions.

A. The arguer has to go alone. When argument has gone beyond attempts made by the arguer and by the other to accept and understand, when those early exploratory steps toward mutual communication are over, or when all of these stages have been bypassed altogether—as they often will be—then the arguer is alone, with no assurance at all that the other or any audience will be kindly disposed. When argument comes to advocacy or to adversarial confrontation, the mutuality that Rogers describes will probably not occur. At the point of advocacy, most particularly at the crisis point in adversarial relationships, the burden is on the maker of the argument as he or she is making the argument. At the moment of heat (which may last twenty seconds or twenty years and which may be feverish and scary), the arguer in all likelihood will not know whether or not the other, the audience, will choose to take the role of the well-disposed listener or the kindly therapist. The arguer, alone, must see in the reverence owed to the other, discover and offer all grace that he or she can muster, and, most especially, extend every liberty possible to the other. The arguer must hold the other wholly in mind and yet cherish his or her own identity. *Then,* perhaps, the arguer and the other may be able to break into mutuality.

B. The arguer must at once hold his or her identity and give it to the other, learning to live—and argue—provisionally. In "Supposing History Is a Woman—What Then?" (*The American Scholar,* Autumn, 1984), Gertrude Himmelfarb remarks:

> Whatever "truth or validity" adheres to history ... does not derive, as the conventional historian might assume, from an "objective" world, a world of past events waiting to be discovered and reconstructed by the historian. For there is no objective world, no historical events independent of the experience of the historian, no events or facts which are not also ideas.

We must keep learning as speakers/narrators/arguers (and as hearers). We can learn to dispense with what we imagined was absolute truth and to pursue the reality of things only partially knowable. We can learn to keep adding pieces of knowledge here, to keep rearranging pieces over yonder, to keep standing back and turning to see how things look elsewhere. We can learn that our narrative/argument doesn't exist except as it is composed and that the "act of composition can never end," as Doctorow has said.

C. As I have just suggested, we arguers can learn to abandon authoritative positions. They cannot be achieved, at any rate, except as in arrogance, ignorance, and dogma we convince ourselves that we have reached authority. We should not want to achieve an authoritative position, anyway. An authoritative position is a prison both to us and to any audience.

D. We arguers can learn the lessons that rhetoric itself wants to teach us. By its nature, invention asks us to open ourselves to the richness of creation, to plumb its depths, search its expanses, and track its chronologies. But the moment we speak (or write), we are no longer open; we have chosen, whether deliberately or not, and so have closed ourselves off from some possibilities. Invention wants openness; structure and style demand closure. We are asked to perpetually open and always closing. If we stay open, we cannot speak or act; if we stand closed, we have succumbed to dogma and rigidity. Each utterance may deplete the inventive possibilities if a speaker falls into arrogance, ignorance, or dogma. But each utterance, if the speaker having spoken opens again, may also nurture and replenish the speaker's inventive world and enable him or her to reach out around the other. Beyond any speaker's bound inventive world lies another: there lie the riches of creation, the great, unbounded possible universe of invention. All time is there, past, present, and future. The natural and the supernatural are there. All creation is there, ground and source for invention. The knowledge we have is formed out of the plenitude of creation, which is all before us, but must be sought again and again through the cycling process of rhetoric, closing to speak, opening again to invent again. In an unlimited universe of meaning, we can never foreclose on interpretation and argument. Invention is a name for great miracle—the attempt to unbind time, to loosen the capacities of time and space into our speaking. This copiousness is eternally there, a plenitude for all. Piaget remarked that the more an infant sees and hears, the more he or she wants to see and hear. Just this is what the cycling of rhetoric offers us: opening to invention, closing to speak, opening again to a richer invention. Utterances may thus be elevated, may grow to hold both arguer and other.

E. We still need to study. There is much about argument that we still have not learned, or that we have not acknowledged. If we are accurate in our evaluation of what happens in conflict, I think we will have to concede that most of what happens is bad. If we know that accurately, we'll be a step farther than we were toward knowing how to deal with contention and the hurts that rise from conflict and argument. We have not at any time in our public or personal histories known consistently how to deal with conflicts, especially when each side or party or view arises normally according to its own variety of thought—and there is no arguer who does not believe that his or her view is a just consequence of normal thought and need. In discourse and behavior, our ways of resolving conflicts have typically been limited and unsatisfactory. When opposing views, each issuing by its own normal processes from its own inventive world, come together in conflict because each wants the same time and space, we usually have only a few ways of handling the conflict:

1. one view prevails, the other subsides;
2. advocates of the two views compromise;

3. the need for action prompts arbitrary selection of one of the two views, even if both are appealing and attractive;
4. we are paralyzed, unable to choose;
5. we go to war; or
6. occasionally, the advocates of one side learn gladly from those of the other and gladly lay down their own views in favor of the other.

To be sure, there are other patterns for resolving conflicts that I haven't had wit enough to recognize; I'd reckon, however, that most are unrewarding to some or all. Once a view emerges—that is, once an inventive process has become structure and style—it cannot wholly subside, as in 1, though it must seem to do so; required by force or expediency to subside, it does not subside but persists underground, festering. Compromise, as in 2, is likely to leave parts of both views hidden away and festering. Deliberate choice between two appealing views, as in 3, leaves the unchosen to grow and compete underground, generating a cynicism that undercuts the chosen argument. Paralysis, as in 4, clearly gives no view gain, though each remains, eating away at the paralyzed agent. War, physical or psychological, is plainly not an appropriate human resolution. In most of these instances there is a thwarted or misplaced or submerged narrative, a normality that may grow wild because it is thwarted, misplaced, or submerged. We have not learned how to let competing normalities live together in the same time and space. We're not sure, we frail humans, that it is possible.

F. The arguer must go alone, unaided by any world of thought, value, and belief except the one that he or she composes in the process of arguing, unassisted by the other because the other is over in a different place, being realized in a different narrative. In my mind, this means that the burden of argument is upon the *ethos* of the arguer. *Ethos*, of course, is a term still poorly understood. Among others, Bator objects to any concentration upon *ethos* because it seems to be "related primarily to adversary situations calling for argumentative strategies designed to persuade others," because "the speaker may be concerned particularly with enhancing her own image or character rather than addressing the issue at hand" (428). Ideally, Bator believes, the subject or problem "is viewed within the audience's framework of values, not simply from the writer's assumptions or premises. The *ethos* of the writer is not the main focus of attention, nor is it the primary means of appeal" (431). This view omits considering the likelihood that *ethos* occurs in various ways; the term does not require to be defined as it has formerly been defined. A genuinely provocative and evocative *ethos* does, in fact, hold the audience wholly in mind, does view matters both as the arguer sees them and as others see them. The self-authenticating language of such an *ethos* issues an invitation into a commodious universe. Argument is partial; when a speaker argues a proposition or develops a theme or makes an assertion, he or she has knowingly or not chosen one proposition, one theme, one assertion from all available. When we speak, we stand somewhere, and our standing place makes both known and silent claims upon us. We make truth, if at all, out of what is incomplete or partial. Language is a closure, but the generative *ethos* I am trying to identify uses language to shove back the restraints of closure, like a commodious universe, to stretch words out beyond our private universe.

G. We must pile time into argumentative discourse. Earlier, I suggested that in our most grievous and disturbing conflicts, we need time to accept, to understand, to love the other. At crisis points in adversarial relationships, we do not, however, have time; we are already in opposition and confrontation. Since we don't have time, we must rescue time by putting it into our discourses and holding it there, learning to speak and write not argumentative displays and presentations, but arguments full of the anecdotal, personal, and cultural reflections that will make us plain to all others, thoughtful histories and narratives that reveal us as we're reaching for the others. The world, of course, doesn't want time in its discourses. The world wants the quick memo, the rapid-fire electronic mail service; the world wants speed, efficiency, and economy of motion, all goals that, when reached, have given the world less than it wanted or needed. We must teach the world to want otherwise, to want time for care.

10

Rhetoric is love, and it must speak a commodious language, creating a world full of space and time that will hold our diversities. Most failures of communication result from some willful or inadvertent but unloving violation of the space and time we and others live in, and most of our speaking is tribal talk. But there is more to us than that. We can learn to speak a commodious language, and we can learn to hear a commodious language.

Sentimental Journeys

Joan Didion

1

We know her story, and some of us, although not all of us, which was to become one of the story's several equivocal aspects, know her name. She was a twenty-nine-year-old unmarried white woman who worked as an investment banker in the corporate finance department at Salomon Brothers in downtown Manhattan, the energy and natural resources group. She was said by one of the principals in a Texas oil-stock offering on which she had collaborated as a member of the Salomon team to have done "top-notch" work. She lived alone in an apartment on East 83rd Street, between York and East End, a sublet cooperative she was thinking about buying. She often worked late and when she got home she would change into jogging clothes and at eight-thirty or nine-thirty in the evening would go running, six or seven miles through Central Park, north on the East Drive, west on the less traveled road connecting the East and West Drives at approximately 102nd Street, and south on the West Drive. The wisdom of this was later questioned by some, by those who were accustomed to thinking of the Park as a place to avoid after dark, and defended by others, the more adroit of whom spoke of the citizen's absolute right to public access ("That park belongs to us and this time nobody is going to take it from us," Ronnie Eldridge, at the time a Democratic candidate for the City Council of New York, declared on the op-ed page of the *New York Times*), others of whom spoke of "running" as a preemptive right. "Runners have Type A controlled personalities and they don't like their schedules interrupted," one runner, a securities trader, told the *Times* to this point. "When people run is a function of their lifestyle," another runner said. "I am personally very angry," a third said. "Because women should have the right to run anytime."

For this woman in this instance these national rights did not prevail. She was found, with her clothes torn off, not far from the 102nd Street connecting road at one-thirty on the morning of April 20, 1989. She was taken near death to Metropolitan Hospital on East 97th Street. She had lost 75 percent of her blood. Her skull had been crushed, her left eyeball pushed back through its socket, the characteristic surface wrinkles of her brain flattened. Dirt and twigs were found in her vagina, suggesting rape. By May 2, when she first woke from coma, six black and Hispanic teenagers, four of whom had made videotaped statements concerning their roles in the attack and another of whom had described his role in an unsigned verbal statement, had been charged with her assault and rape and she had become, unwilling and unwitting, a sacrificial player in the sentimental narrative that is New York public life.

Nightmare in Central Park, the headlines and display type read. *Teen Wolfpack Beats and Rapes Wall Street Exec on Jogging Path. Central Park Horror. Wolf Pack's Prey. Female Jogger Near Death After Savage Attack by Roving Gang. Rape Rampage. Park Marauders Call It "Wilding," Street Slang for Going Berserk. Rape Suspect: "It Was Fun." Rape Suspect's Jailhouse Boast: "She Wasn't Nothing." The teenagers were back in the holding cell, the confessions gory and complete. One shouted "hit the beat" and they all started rapping to "Wild Thing." The Jogger and the Wolf Pack. An Outrage and a Prayer.* And, on the Monday morning after the attack, on the front page of the *New York Post,* with a photograph of Governor Mario Cuomo and the headline "*None of Us Is Safe,*" this italic text: "A visibly shaken Governor Cuomo spoke out yesterday on the vicious Central Park rape: 'The people are angry and frightened—my mother is, my family is. To me, as a person who's lived in this city all of his life, this is the ultimate shriek of alarm.' "

Later it would be recalled that 3,254 other rapes were reported that year, including one the following week involving the near decapitation of a black woman in Fort Tryon Park and one two weeks later involving a black woman in Brooklyn who was robbed, raped, sodomized, and thrown down an air shaft of a four-story building, but the point was rhetorical, since crimes are universally understood to be news to the extent that they offer, however erroneously, a story, a lesson, a high concept. In the 1986 Central Park death of Jennifer Levin, then eighteen, at the hands of Robert Chambers, then nineteen, the "story," extrapolated more or less from thin air but left largely uncorrected, had to do not with people living wretchedly and marginally on the underside of where they wanted to be, not with the Dreiserian pursuit of "respectability" that marked the revealed details (Robert Chambers's mother was a private-duty nurse who worked twelve-hour night shifts to enroll her son in private schools and the Knickerbocker Greys), but with "preppies," and the familiar "too much too soon."

Susan Brownmiller, during a year spent monitoring newspaper coverage of rape as part of her research for *Against Our Will: Men, Women and Rape,* found, not surprisingly, that "although New York City police statistics showed that black women were more frequent victims of rape than white women, the favored victim in the tabloid headline . . . was young, white, middle class and 'attractive'." In its quite extensive coverage of rape-murders during the year 1971, according to Ms. Brownmiller, the *Daily News* published in its four-star final edition only two stories in which the victim was not described in the lead paragraph as "attractive": one of these stories involved an eight-year-old child, the other was a second-day follow-up on a first-day story that had in fact described the victim as "attractive." The *Times*, she found, covered rapes only infrequently that year, but what coverage they did "concerned victims who had some kind of middle-class status, such as 'nurse,' 'dancer' or 'teacher,' and with a favored setting of Central Park."

As a news story, "Jogger" was understood to turn on the demonstrable "difference" between the victim and her accused assailants, four of whom lived in Schomburg Plaza, a federally subsidized apartment complex at the northeast corner of Fifth Avenue and 110th Street in East Harlem, and the rest of whom lived in the projects and rehabilitated tenements just to the north and west of Schomburg Plaza. Some twenty-five teenagers were brought in for questioning; eight were held. The six who were finally indicted ranged in age from fourteen to sixteen. That none of the six had previous police records passed, in this context, for achievement; beyond that, one was recalled by his classmates to have taken pride in his expensive basketball shoes, another to have been "a follower." *I'm a smooth type of fellow, cool, calm, and mellow,* one of the six, Yusef Salaam, would say in the rap he presented as part of his statement before sentencing.

> *I'm kind of laid back, but now I'm speaking so that you know/I got used and abused and even was put on the news. . . .*
>
> *I'm not dissing them all, but the some that I called.*
>
> *They tried to dis me like I was an inch small, like a midget, a mouse, something less than a man.*

The victim, by contrast, was a leader, part of what the *Times* would describe as "the wave of young professionals who took over New York in the 1980s," one of those who were "handsome and pretty and educated and white," who, according to the *Times*, not only "believed they owned the world" but "had reason to." She was from a Pittsburgh suburb, Upper St. Clair, the daughter of a retired Westinghouse senior manager. She had been Phi Beta Kappa at Wellesley, a graduate of the Yale School of Management, a congressional intern, nominated for a Rhodes Scholarship, remembered by the chairman of her department at Wellesley as "probably one of the top four or five students of the decade." She was reported to be a vegetarian, and "fun-loving," although only "when time permitted," and also to have had (these were the *Times'* details) "concerns about the ethics of the American business world."

In other words she was wrenched, even as she hung between death and life and later between insentience and sentience, into New York's ideal sister, daughter, Bacharach bride: a young woman of conventional middle-class privilege and promise whose situation was such that many people tended to overlook the fact that the state's case against the accused was not invulnerable. The state could implicate most of the defendants in the assault and rape in their own videotaped words, but had none of the incontrovertible forensic evidence—no matching semen, no matching fingernail scrapings, no matching blood—commonly produced in this kind of case. Despite the fact that jurors in the second trial would eventually mention physical evidence as having been crucial in their bringing guilty verdicts against one defendant, Kevin Richardson, there was not actually much physical evidence at hand. Fragments of hair "similar [to] and consistent" with that of the victim were found on Kevin Richardson's clothing and underwear, but the state's own criminologist had testified that hair samples were necessarily inconclusive since, unlike fingerprints, they could not be traced to a single person. Dirt samples found on the defendants' clothing were, again, similar to dirt found in that part of the park where the attack took place, but the state's criminologist allowed that the samples were also similar to dirt found in other uncultivated areas of the park. To suggest, however, that this minimal physical evidence could open the case to an aggressive defense—to, say, the kind of defense that such celebrated New York criminal lawyers as Jack Litman and Barry Slotnick typically present—would come to be construed, during the weeks and months to come, as a further attack on the victim.

She would be Lady Courage to the *New York Post*, she would be A Profile in Courage to the *Daily News* and *New York Newsday*. She would become for Anna Quindlen in the *New York Times* the figure of "New York rising above the dirt, the New Yorker who has known the best, and the worst, and has stayed on, living somewhere in the middle." She would become for David Dinkins, the first black mayor of New York, the emblem of his apparently fragile hopes for the city itself: "I hope the city will be able to learn a lesson from this event and be inspired by the young woman who was assaulted in the case," he said. "Despite tremendous odds, she is rebuilding her life. What a human life can do, a human society can do as well." She was even then for John Gutfreund, at that time the chairman and chief executive officer of Salomon Brothers, the personification of "what makes this city so vibrant and so great," now "struck down by a side of our city that is as awful and terrifying as the creative side is wonderful." It was precisely in this conflation of victim and city, this confusion of personal woe with public distress, that the crime's "story" would be found, its lesson, its encouraging promise of narrative resolution.

One reason the victim in this case could be so readily abstracted, and her situation so readily made to stand for that of the city itself, was that she remained, as a victim of rape, unnamed in most press reports. Although the American and English press convention of not naming victims of rape (adult rape victims are named in French papers) derives from the understandable wish to protect the victim, the rationalization of this special protection rests on a number of doubtful, even magical, assumptions. The convention assumes, by providing a protection for victims of rape not afforded victims of other assaults, that rape involves a violation absent from other kinds of assault. The convention assumes that this violation is of a nature best kept secret, that the rape victim feels, and would feel still more strongly were she identified, a shame and self-loathing unique to this form of assault; in other words that she has been in an unspecified way party to her own assault, that a special contract exists between this one kind of victim and her assailant. The convention assumes, finally, that the victim would be, were this special contract revealed, the natural object of prurient interest; that the act of male penetration involves such potent mysteries that the woman so penetrated (as opposed, say, to having her face crushed with a brick or her brain penetrated with a length of pipe) is permanently marked, "different," even—especially if there is a perceived racial or social "difference" between victim and assailant, as in nineteenth-century stories featuring white women taken by Indians—"ruined."

These quite specifically masculine assumptions (women do not want to be raped, nor do they want to have their brains smashed, but very few mystify the difference between the two) tend in general to be self-fulfilling, guiding the victim to define her assault as her protectors do. "Ultimately we're doing women a disservice by separating rape from other violent crimes," Deni Elliott, the director of Dartmouth's Ethics Institute, suggested in a discussion of this custom in *Time*. "We are participating in the stigma of rape by treating victims of this crime differently," Geneva Overholser, the editor of the *Des Moines Register*, said about her decision to publish in February of 1990 a five-part piece about a rape victim who agreed to be named. "When we as a society refuse to talk openly about rape, I think we weaken our ability to deal with it." Susan Estrich, a professor of criminal law at Harvard Law School and the manager of Michael Dukakis's 1988 presidential campaign, discussed, in *Real Rape*, the conflicting emotions that followed her own 1974 rape:

> At first, being raped is something you simply don't talk about. Then it occurs to you that people whose houses are broken into or who are mugged in Central Park talk about it *all* the time. . . . If it isn't my fault, why am I supposed to be ashamed? If I'm not ashamed, if it wasn't "personal," why look askance when I mention it?

There were, in the 1989 Central Park attack, specific circumstances that reinforced the conviction that the victim should not be named. She had clearly been, according to the doctors who examined her at Metropolitan Hospital and to the statements made by the suspects (she herself remembered neither the attack nor anything that happened during the next six weeks), raped by one or more assailants. She had also been beaten so brutally that, fifteen months later, she could not focus her eyes or walk unaided. She had lost all sense of smell. She could not read without experiencing double vision. She was believed at the time to have permanently lost function in some areas of her brain.

Given these circumstances, the fact that neither the victim's family nor, later, the victim herself wanted her name known struck an immediate chord of sympathy, seemed a belated way to protect her as she had not been protected in Central Park. Yet there was in this case a special emotional undertow that derived in part from the deep and allusive associations and taboos attaching, in American black history, to the idea of the rape of white women. Rape remained, in the collective memory of many blacks, the very core of their victimization. Black men were accused of raping white women, even as black women were, Malcolm X wrote in *The Autobiography of Malcolm X*, "raped by the slave-master white man until there had begun to emerge a homemade, handmade, brainwashed race that was no longer even of its true color, that no longer even knew its true family names." The very frequency of sexual contact between white men and black women increased the potency of the taboo on any such contact between black men and white women. The abolition of slavery, W. J. Cash wrote in *The Mind of the South*,

> . . . in destroying the rigid fixity of the black at the bottom of the scale, in throwing open to him at least the legal opportunity to advance, had inevitably opened up to the mind of every Southerner a vista at the end of which stood the overthrow of this taboo. If it was given to the black to advance at all, who could say (once more the logic of the doctrine of his inherent inferiority would not hold) that he would not one day advance the whole way and lay claim to complete equality, including, specifically, the ever crucial right of marriage?
>
> What Southerners felt, therefore, was that any assertion of any kind on the part of the Negro constituted in a perfectly real manner an attack on the Southern woman. What they saw, more or less consciously, in the conditions of Reconstruction was a passage toward a condition for her as degrading, in their view, as rape itself. And a condition, moreover, which, logic or no logic, they infallibly thought of as being as absolutely forced upon her as rape, and hence a condition for which the term "rape" stood as truly as for the *de facto* deed.

Nor was the idea of rape the only potentially treacherous undercurrent in this case. There has historically been, for American blacks, an entire complex of loaded references around the question of "naming": slave names, masters' names, African names, call me by my rightful name, nobody knows my name; stories, in which the specific gravity of naming locked directly into that of rape, of black men whipped for addressing white women by their given names. That, in this case, just such an interlocking of references could work to fuel resentments and inchoate hatreds seemed clear, and it seemed equally clear that some of what ultimately occurred—the repeated references to lynchings, the identification of the defendants with the Scottsboro boys, the insistently provocative repetition of the victim's name, the weird and self-defeating insistence that no rape had taken place and little harm been done the victim—derived momentum from this historical freight. "Years ago, if a white woman said a Black man looked at her lustfully, he could be hung higher than a magnolia tree in bloom, while a white mob watched joyfully sipping tea and eating cookies," Yusef Salaam's mother reminded readers of the *Amsterdam News*. "The first thing you do in the United States of America when a white woman is raped is round up a bunch of black youths, and I think that's what happened here," the Reverend Calvin O. Butts III of the Abyssinian Baptist Church in Harlem told the *New York Times*. "You going to arrest me now because I said the jogger's name?" Gary Byrd asked rhetorically on his WLIB show, and was quoted by Edwin Diamond in *New York* magazine:

> I mean, she's obviously a public figure, and a very mysterious one, I might add. Well, it's a funny place we live in called America, and should we be surprised that they're up to their usual tricks? It was a trick that got us here in the first place.

This reflected one of the problems with not naming this victim: she was in fact named all the time. Everyone in the courthouse, everyone who worked for a paper or a television station or who followed the case for whatever professional reason, knew her name. She was referred to by name in all court records and in all court proceedings. She was named, in the days immediately following the attack, on some local television stations. She was also routinely named—and this was part of the difficulty, part of what led to a damaging self-righteousness among those who did not name her and to an equally damaging embattlement among those who did—in Manhattan's black-owned newspapers, the *Amsterdam News* and the *City Sun*, and she was named as well on WLIB, the Manhattan radio station owned by a black partnership that included Percy Sutton and, until 1985, when he transferred his stock to his son, Mayor Dinkins.

That the victim in this case was identified on Centre Street and north of 96th Street but not in between made for a certain cognitive dissonance, especially since the names of even the juvenile suspects had been released by the police and the press before any suspect had been arraigned, let alone indicted. "The police normally withhold the names of minors who are accused of crimes," the *Times* explained (actually the police normally withhold the names of accused "juveniles," or minors under age sixteen, but not of minors sixteen or seventeen), "but officials said they made public the names of the youths charged in the attack on the woman because of the seriousness of the incident." There seemed a debatable point here, the question of whether "the seriousness of the incident" might not have in fact seemed a compelling reason to avoid any appearance of a rush to judgment by preserving the anonymity of a juvenile suspect; one of the names released by the police and published in the *Times* was of a fourteen-year-old who was ultimately not indicted.

There were, early on, certain aspects of this case that seemed not well handled by the police and prosecutors, and others that seemed not well handled by the press. It would seem to have been tactically unwise, since New York State law requires that a parent or guardian be present when children under sixteen are questioned, for police to continue the interrogation of Yusef Salaam, then fifteen, on the grounds that his Transit Authority bus pass said he was sixteen, while his mother was kept waiting outside. It would seem to have been unwise for Linda Fairstein, the assistant district attorney in charge of Manhattan sex crimes, to ignore, at the precinct house, the mother's assertion that the son was fifteen, and later to suggest, in court, that the boy's age had been unclear to her because the mother had used the word "minor."

It would also seem to have been unwise for Linda Fairstein to tell David Nocenti, the assistant U.S. Attorney who was paired with Yusef Salaam in a "Big Brother" program and who had come to the precinct house at the mother's request, that he had "no legal standing" there and that she would file a complaint with his supervisors. It would seem in this volatile a case imprudent of the police to follow their normal procedure by presenting Raymond Santana's initial statement in their own words, cop phrases that would predictably seem to some in the courtroom, as the expression of a fourteen-year-old held overnight and into the next afternoon for interrogation, unconvincing:

> On April 19, 1989, at approximately 20:30 hours, I was at the Taft Projects in the vicinity of 113th St. and Madison Avenue. I was there with numerous friends. . . . At approximately 21:00 hours, we all (myself and approximately 15 others) walked south on Madison Avenue to E. 110th Street, then walked westbound to Fifth Avenue. At Fifth Avenue and 110th Street, we met up with an additional group of approximately 15 other males, who also entered Central Park with us at that location with the intent to rob cyclists and joggers . . .

In a case in which most of the defendants had made videotaped statements admitting at least some role in the assault and rape, this less than meticulous attitude toward the gathering and dissemination of information seemed peculiar and self-defeating, the kind of pressured or unthinking standard procedure that could not only exacerbate the fears and angers and suspicions of conspiracy shared by many blacks but open what seemed, on the basis of the confessions, a conclusive case to the kind of doubt that would eventually keep juries out, in the trial of the first three defendants, ten days, and, in the trial of the next two defendants, twelve days. One of the reasons the jury in the first trial could not agree, *Manhattan Lawyer* reported in its October 1990 issue, was that one juror, Ronald Gold, remained "deeply troubled by the discrepancies between the story [Antron] McCray tells on his videotaped statement and the prosecution's scenario":

> Why did McCray place the rape at the reservoir, Gold demanded, when all evidence indicated it happened at the 102 Street cross-drive? Why did McCray say the jogger was raped where she fell, when the prosecution said she'd been dragged 300 feet into the woods first? Why did McCray talk about having to hold her arms down, if she was found bound and gagged?
>
> The debate raged for the last two days, with jurors dropping in and out of Gold's acquittal [for McCray] camp. . . .
>
> After the jurors watched McCray's video for the fifth time, Miranda [Rafael Miranda, another juror] knew it well enough to cite the time-code numbers imprinted at the bottom of the videotape as he rebuffed Gold's arguments with specific statements from McCray's own lips. [McCray, on the videotape, after admitting that he had held the victim by her left arm as her clothes were pulled off, volunteered that he had "got on top" of her, and said that he had rubbed against her without an erection "so everybody would . . . just know I did it."] The pressure on Gold was mounting. Three jurors agree that it was evident Gold, worn down perhaps by his own displays of temper as much as anything else, capitulated out of exhaustion. While a bitter Gold told other jurors he felt terrible about ultimately giving in, Brueland [Harold Brueland, another juror who had for a time favored acquittal for McCray] believes it was all part of the process.
>
> "I'd like to tell Ronnie someday that nervous exhaustion is an element built into the court system. They know that," Brueland says of court officials. "They know we're only going to be able to take it for so long. It's just a matter of, you know, who's got the guts to stick with it."

So fixed were the emotions provoked by this case that the idea that there could have been, for even one juror, even a moment's doubt in the state's case, let alone the kind of doubt that could be sustained over ten days, seemed, to many in the city, bewildering, almost unthinkable: the attack on the jogger had by then passed into narrative, and the narrative was about confrontation, about what Governor Cuomo had called "the ultimate shriek of alarm," about what was wrong with the city and about its solution. What was wrong with the city had been identified, and its names were Raymond Santana, Yusef Salaam, Antron McCray, Kharey Wise, Kevin Richardson, and Steve Lopez. "They never could have thought of it as they raged through Central Park, tormenting and ruining people," Bob Herbert wrote in the *News* after the verdicts came in on the first three defendants.

> There was no way it could have crossed their vicious minds. Running with the pack, they would have scoffed at the very idea. They would have laughed.
>
> And yet it happened. In the end, Yusef Salaam, Antron McCray and Raymond Santana were nailed by a woman.
>
> Elizabeth Lederer stood in the courtroom and watched Saturday night as the three were hauled off to jail. . . . At times during the trial, she looked about half the height of the long and lanky Salaam, who sneered at her from the witness stand. Salaam was apparently too dumb to realize that Lederer—this petite, soft-spoken, curly-haired prosecutor—was the jogger's avenger. . . .
>
> You could tell that her thoughts were elsewhere, that she was thinking about the jogger.
>
> You could tell that she was thinking: I did it.
>
> I did it for you.

Do this in remembrance of me: the solution, then, or so such pervasive fantasies suggested, was to partake of the symbolic body and blood of The Jogger, whose idealization was by this point complete, and was rendered, significantly, in details stressing her "difference," or superior class. The Jogger was someone who wore, according to *Newsday*, "a light gold chain around her slender neck" as well as, according to the *News*, a "modest" gold ring and "a thin sheen" of lipstick. The Jogger was someone who would not, according to the *Post*, "even dignify her alleged attackers with a glance." The Jogger was someone who spoke, according to the *News*, in accents "suited to boardrooms," accents that might therefore seem "foreign to many native New Yorkers." In her first appearance on the witness stand she had been subjected, the *Times* noted, "to questions that most people do not have to answer publicly during their lifetimes," principally about her use of a diaphragm on the Sunday preceding the attack, and had answered these questions, according to an editorial in the *News*, with an "indomitable dignity" that had taught the city a lesson "about courage and class."

This emphasis on perceived refinements of character and of manner and of taste tended to distort and to flatten, and ultimately to suggest not the actual victim of an actual crime but a fictional character of a slightly earlier period, the well-brought-up virgin who briefly graces the city with her presence and receives in turn a taste of "real life." The defendants, by contrast, were seen as incapable of appreciating these marginal distinctions, ignorant of both the norms and accoutrements of middle-class life. "Did you have jogging clothes on?" Elizabeth Lederer asked Yusef Salaam, by way of trying to discredit his statement that he had gone into the park that night only to "walk around." Did he have "jogging clothes," did he have "sports equipment," did he have "a bicycle." A pernicious nostalgia had come to permeate the case, a longing for the New York that had seemed for a while to be about "sports equipment," about getting and spending rather than about having and not having: the reason that this victim must not be named was so that she could go unrecognized, it was astonishingly said, by Jerry Nachman, the editor of the *New York Post*, and then by others who seemed to find in this a particular resonance, to Bloomingdale's.

Some New York stories involving young middle-class white women do not make it to the editorial pages, or even necessarily to the front pages. In April 1990, a young middle-class white woman named Laurie Sue Rosenthal, raised in an Orthodox Jewish household and at age twenty-nine still living with her parents in Jamaica, Queens, happened to die, according to the coroner's report from the accidental toxicity of Darvocet in combination with alcohol, in an apartment at 36 East 68th Street in Manhattan. The apartment belonged to the man she had been, according to her parents, seeing for about a year, a minor city assistant commissioner named Peter Franconeri. Peter Franconeri, who was at the time in charge of elevator and boiler inspections for the Buildings Department and married to someone else, wrapped Laurie Sue Rosenthal's body in a blanket; placed it, along with her handbag and ID, outside the building with the trash; and went to his office at 60 Hudson Street. At some point an anonymous call was made to 911. Franconeri was identified only after Laurie Sue Rosenthal's parents gave the police his beeper number, which they found in her address book. According to *Newsday*, which covered the story more extensively than the *News*, the *Post*, or the *Times*.

> Initial police reports indicated that there were no visible wounds on Rosenthal's body. But Rosenthal's mother, Ceil, said yesterday that the family was told the autopsy revealed two "unexplained bruises" on her daughter's body.
>
> Larry and Ceil Rosenthal said those findings seemed to support their suspicions that their daughter was upset because they received a call from their daughter at 3 A.M. Thursday "saying that he had beaten her up." The family reported the conversation to police.
>
> "I told her to get into a cab and get home," Larry Rosenthal said yesterday. "The next I heard was two detectives telling me terrible things."
>
> "The ME [medical examiner] said the bruises did not constitute a beating but they were going to examine them further," Ceil Rosenthal said.

"There were some minor bruises," a spokeswoman for the Office of the Chief Medical Examiner told *Newsday* a few days later, but the bruises "did not in any way contribute to her death." This is worth rerunning: A young woman calls her parents at three in the morning, "distraught." She says that she has been beaten up. A few hours later, on East 68th Street between Madison and Park avenues, a few steps from Porthault and Pratesi and Armani and Saint Laurent and the Westbury Hotel, at a time of day in this part of New York 10021 when Jim Buck's dog trainers are assembling their morning packs and Henry Kravis's Bentley is idling outside his Park Avenue apartment and the construction crews are clocking in over near the Frick at the multimillion-dollar houses under reconstruction for Bill Cosby and for the owner of The Limited, this young middle-class white woman's body, showing bruises, gets put out with the trash.

"Everybody got upside down because of who he was," an unidentified police officer later told Jim Dwyer of *Newsday*, referring to the man who put the young woman out with the trash. "If it had happened to anyone else, nothing would have come of it. A summons would have been issued and that would have been the end of it." In fact nothing did come of the death of Laurie Sue Rosenthal, which might have seemed a natural tabloid story but failed, on several levels, to catch the local imagination. For one thing she could not be trimmed into the role of the preferred tabloid victim, who is conventionally presented as fate's random choice (Laurie Sue Rosenthal had, for whatever reason, taken the Darvocet instead of a taxi home, her parents reported treatment for a previous Valium dependency, she could be presumed to have known over the course of a year that Franconeri was married and yet continued to see him); for another, she seemed not to have attended an expensive school or to have been employed in a glamour industry (no Ivy Grad, no Wall Street Exec), which made it hard to cast her as part of "what makes this city so vibrant and so great."

In August 1990, Peter Franconeri pled guilty to a misdemeanor, the unlawful removal of a body, and was sentenced by Criminal Court judge Peter Benitez to seventy-five hours of community service. This was neither surprising nor much of a story (only twenty-three lines even in *Newsday*, on page twenty-nine of the city edition), and the case's lenient resolution was for many people a kind of relief. The district attorney's office had asked for "some incarceration," the amount usually described as a "touch," but no one wanted, it was said, to crucify the guy: Peter Franconeri was somebody who knew a lot of people, understood how to live in the city, who had for example not only the apartment on East 68th Street between Madison and Park but a house in Southampton and who also understood that putting a body outside with the trash was nothing to get upside down about, if it was handled right. Such understandings may in fact have been the city's true "ultimate shriek of alarm," but it was not a shriek the city wanted to recognize.

2

Perhaps the most arresting collateral news to surface, during the first few days after the attack on the Central Park jogger, was that a significant number of New Yorkers apparently believed the city sufficiently well-ordered to incorporate Central Park into their evening fitness schedules. "Prudence" was defined, even after the attack, as "staying south of 90th Street," or having "an awareness that you need to think about planning your routes," or, in the case of one woman interviewed by the *Times*, deciding to quit her daytime job (she was a lawyer) because she was "tired of being stuck out there, running later and later at night." "I don't think there's a runner who couldn't describe the silky, gliding feeling you get running at night," an editor of *Runner's World* told the *Times*. "You see less of what's around you and you become centered on your running."

The notion that Central Park at night might be a good place to "see less of what's around you" was recent. There were two reasons why Frederick Law Olmsted and Calvert Vaux, when they devised their winning entry in the 1858 competition for a Central Park design, decided to sink the transverse roads below grade level. One reason, the most often cited, was aesthetic, a recognition on the part of the designers that the four crossings specified by the terms of the competition, at 65th, 79th, 85th, and 97th streets, would intersect the sweep of the landscape, be "at variance with those agreeable sentiments which we should wish the park to inspire." The other reason, which appears to have been equally compelling, had to do with security. The problem with grade-level crossings, Olmsted and Vaux wrote in their "Greensward" plan, would be this:

> The transverse roads will . . . have to be kept open, while the park proper will be useless for any good purpose after dusk; for experience has shown that even in London, with its admirable police arrangements, the public cannot be assured safe transit through large open spaces of ground after nightfall.
>
> These public throughfares will then require to be well-lighted at the sides, and, to restrain marauders pursued by the police from escaping into the obscurity of the park, strong fences or walls, six or eight feet high, will be necessary.

The park, in other words, was seen from its conception as intrinsically dangerous after dark, a place of "obscurity," "useless for any good purpose," a refuge only for "marauders." The parks of Europe closed at nightfall, Olmsted noted in his 1882 pamphlet. *The Spoils of the Park: With a Few Leaves from the Deep-laden Note-books of "A Wholly Unpractical Man,"* "but one surface road is kept open across Hyde Park, and the superintendent of the

Metropolitan Police told me that a man's chances of being garrotted or robbed were, because of the facilities for concealment to be found in the Park, greater in passing at night along this road than anywhere else in London."

In the high pitch of the initial "jogger" coverage, suggesting as it did a city overtaken by animals, this pragmatic approach to urban living gave way to a more ideal construct, one in which New York either had once been or should be "safe," and now, as in Governor Cuomo's "none of us is safe," was not. It was time, accordingly, to "take it back," time to "say no"; time, as David Dinkins would put it during his campaign for the mayoralty in the summer of 1989, to "draw the line." What the line was to be drawn against was "crime," an abstract, a free-floating specter that could be dispelled by certain acts of personal affirmation, by the kind of moral rearmament that later figured in Mayor Dinkins's plan to revitalize the city by initiating weekly "Tuesday Night Out Against Crime" rallies.

By going into the park at night, Tom Wicker wrote in the *Times*, the victim in this case had "affirmed the primacy of freedom over fear." A week after the assault, Susan Chace suggested on the op-ed page of the *Times* that readers walk into the park at night and join hands. "A woman can't run in the park at an offbeat time," she wrote. "Accept it, you say. I can't. It shouldn't be like this in New York City, in 1989, in spring." Ronnie Eldridge also suggested that readers walk into the park at night, but to light candles. "Who are we that we allow ourselves to be chased out of the most magnificent part of our city?" she asked, and also: "If we give up the park, what are we supposed to do: fall back to Columbus Avenue and plant grass?" This was interesting, suggesting as it did that the city's not inconsiderable problems could be solved by the willingness of its citizens to hold or draw some line, to "say no"; in other words that a reliance on certain magical gestures could affect the city's fate.

The insistent sentimentalization of experience, which is to say the encouragement of such reliance, is not new in New York. A preference for broad strokes, for the distortion and flattening of character and the reduction of events to narrative, has been for well over a hundred years the heart of the way the city presents itself: Lady Liberty, huddled masses, ticker-tape parades, heroes, gutters, bright lights, broken hearts, 8 million stories in the naked city; 8 million stories and all the same story, each devised to obscure not only the city's actual tensions of race and class but also, more significantly, the civic and commercial arrangements that rendered those tensions irreconcilable.

Central Park itself was such a "story," an artificial pastoral in the nineteenth-century English romantic tradition, conceived, during a decade when the population of Manhattan would increase by 58 percent, as a civic project that would allow the letting of contracts and the employment of voters on a scale rarely before undertaken in New York. Ten million cartloads of dirt would need to be shifted during the twenty years of its construction. Four to five million trees and shrubs would need to be planted, half a million cubic yards of topsoil imported, 114 miles of ceramic pipe laid.

Nor need the completion of the park mean the end of the possibilities: in 1870, once William Marcy Tweed had revised the city charter and invented his Department of Public Parks, new roads could be built whenever jobs were needed. Trees could be dug up, and replanted. Crews could be set loose to prune, to clear, to hack at will. Frederick Law Olmsted, when he objected, could be overridden, and finally eased out. "A 'delegation' from a great political organization called on me by appointment," Olmsted wrote in *The Spoils of the Park*, recalling the conditions under which he had worked:

> After introductions and handshakings, a circle was formed, and a gentleman stepped before me, and said, "We know how much pressed you must be . . . but at your convenience our association would like to have you determine what share of your patronage we can expect, and make suitable arrangements for our using it. We will take the liberty to suggest, sir, that there could be no more convenient way than that you should send us our due quota of tickets, if you will please, sir, in this form, *leaving us to fill in the name.*" Here a packet of printed tickets was produced, from which I took one at random. It was a blank appointment and bore the signature of Mr. Tweed.
>
> As superintendent of the Park, I once received in six days more than seven thousand letters of advice as to appointments, nearly all from men in office. . . . I have heard a candidate for a magisterial office in the city addressing from my doorsteps a crowd of such advice-bearers, telling them that I was bound to give them employment, and suggesting plainly, that, if I was slow about it, a rope round my neck might serve to lessen my reluctance to take good counsel. I have had a dozen men force their way into my house before I had risen from bed on a Sunday morning, and some break into my drawing room in their eagerness to deliver letters of advice.

Central Park, then, for its underwriters if not for Olmsted, was about contracts and concrete and kickbacks, about pork, but the sentimentalization that worked to obscure the pork, the "story," had to do with certain dramatic contrasts, or extremes, that were believed to characterize life in this as in no other city. These "contrasts," which have since become the very spine of the New York narrative, appeared early on: Philip Hone, the mayor of New York in 1826 and 1827, spoke in 1843 of a city "overwhelmed with population, and where the two extremes of costly luxury in living, expensive establishments and improvident wastes are presented in daily and hourly contrast with squalid mixing and hapless destruction." Given this narrative, Central Park could be and ultimately would be seen the way Olmsted himself saw it, as an essay in democracy, a social experiment meant to socialize a new immigrant population and to ameliorate the perilous separation of rich and poor. It was the duty and the interest of the city's privileged class, Olmsted had suggested some years before he designed Central Park, to "get up parks, gardens, music, dancing schools, reunions which will be so attractive as to force into contact the good and the bad, the gentleman and the rowdy."

The notion that the interests of the "gentleman" and the "rowdy" might be at odds did not intrude: then as now, the preferred narrative worked to veil actual conflict, to cloud the extent to which the condition of being rich was predicated upon the continued neediness of a working class; to confirm the responsible stewardship of "the gentleman" and to forestall the possibility of a self-conscious, or politicized, proletariat. Social and economic phenomena, in this narrative, were personalized. Politics were exclusively electoral. Problems were best addressed by the emergence and election of "leaders," who could in turn inspire the individual citizen to "participate," or "make a difference." "Will you help?" Mayor Dinkins asked New Yorkers, in a September 1990 address from St. Patrick's Cathedral intended as a response to the "New York crime wave" stories then leading the news. "Do you care? Are you ready to become part of the solution?"

"Stay," Governor Cuomo urged the same New Yorkers. "Believe. Participate. Don't give up." Manhattan borough president Ruth Messinger, at the dedication of a school flagpole, mentioned the importance of "getting involved" and "participating," or "pitching in to put the shine back on the Big Apple." In a discussion of the popular "New York" stories written between 1902 and 1910 by William Sidney Porter, or "O. Henry," William R. Taylor of the State University of New York at Stony Brook spoke of the way in which these stories, with their "focus on individuals' plights," their "absence of social or political implications" and "ideological neutrality," provided "a miraculous form of social glue":

> These sentimental accounts of relations between classes in the city have a specific historical meaning: empathy without political compassion. They reduce the scale of human suffering to what atomized individuals endure as their plucky, sad lives were recounted week after week for almost a decade . . . their sentimental reading of oppression, class differences, human suffering, and affection helped create a new language for interpreting the city's complex society, a language that began to replace the threadbare moralism that New Yorkers inherited from 19th-century readings of the city. This language localized suffering in particular moments and confined it to particular occasions; it smoothed over differences because it could be read almost the same way from either end of the social scale.

Stories in which terrible crimes are inflicted on innocent victims, offering as they do a similarly sentimental reading of class differences and human suffering, a reading that promises both resolution and retribution, have long performed as the city's endorphins, a built-in source of natural morphine working to blur the edges of real and to a great extent insoluble problems. What is singular about New York, and remains virtually incomprehensible to people who live in less rigidly organized parts of the country, is the minimal level of comfort and opportunity its citizens have come to accept. The romantic capitalist pursuit of privacy and security and individual freedom, so taken for granted nationally, plays, locally, not much role. A city where virtually every impulse has been to stifle rather than to encourage normal competition, New York works, when it does work, not on a market economy but on little deals, payoffs, accommodations, *baksheesh* arrangements that circumvent the direct exchange of goods and services and prevent what would be, in a competitive economy, the normal ascendance of the superior product.

There were in the five boroughs in 1990 only 581 supermarkets (a supermarket, as defined by the trade magazine *Progressive Grocer*, is a market that does an annual volume of $2 million), or, assuming a population of 8 million, one supermarket for every 13,769 citizens. Groceries, costing more than they should because of this absence of competition and also because of the proliferation of payoffs required to ensure this absence of competition (produce, we have come to understand, belongs to the Gambinos, and fish to the Lucheses and the Genoveses, and a piece of the construction of the market to each of the above, but keeping the door open belongs finally to the inspector here, the inspector there), are carried home or delivered, as if in Jakarta, by pushcart.

It has historically taken, in New York as if in Mexico City, ten years to process and specify and bid and contract and construct a new school; twenty or thirty years to build or, in the cases of Bruckner Boulevard and the West Side Highway, to not quite build a highway. A recent public scandal revealed that a batch of city-ordered Pap smears had gone unread for more than a year (in the developed world the Pap smear, a test for cervical cancer, is commonly read within a few days); what did not become a public scandal, what is still accepted as the way things are, is that even Pap smears ordered by Park Avenue gynecologists can go unread for several weeks.

Such resemblances to cities of the third world are in no way casual, or based on the "color" of a polyglot population: these are all cities arranged primarily not to improve the lives of their citizens but to be labor-intensive, to accommodate, ideally at the subsistence level, since it is at the subsistence level that the work force is most apt to be captive and loyalty assured, a third-world population. In some ways New York's very attractiveness, its promises of opportunity and improved wages, its commitments as a city in the developed world, were what seemed destined to render it ultimately unworkable. Where the vitality of such cities in the less developed world had depended on their ability to guarantee low-cost labor and an absence of regulation, New York had historically depended instead on the constant welling up of new businesses, of new employers to replace those phased out, like the New York garment manufacturers who found it cheaper to make their clothes in Hong Kong or Kuala Lumpur or Taipei, by rising local costs.

It had been the old pattern of New York, supported by an expanding national economy, to lose one kind of business and gain another. It was the more recent error of New York to misconstrue this history of turnover as an indestructible resource, there to be taxed at will, there to be regulated whenever a dollar could be seen in doing so, there for the taking. By 1977, New York had lost some 600,000 jobs, most of them in manufacturing and in the kinds of small businesses that could no longer maintain their narrow profit margins inside the city. During the "recovery" years, from 1977 until 1988, most of these jobs were indeed replaced, but in a potentially perilous way: of the 500,000 new jobs created, most were in the area most vulnerable to a downturn, that of financial and business services, and many of the rest in an area not only equally vulnerable to bad times but dispiriting to the city even in good, that of tourist and restaurant services.

The demonstration that many kinds of businesses were finding New York expendable had failed to prompt real efforts to make the city more competitive. Taxes grew still more punitive, regulation more Byzantine. Forty-nine thousand new jobs were created in New York's city agencies between 1983 and 1990, even as the services provided by those agencies were widely perceived to decline. Attempts at "reform" typically tended to create more jobs: in 1988, in response to the length of time it was taking to build or repair a school, a new agency, the School Construction Authority, was formed. A New York City school, it was said, would now take only five years to build. The head of the School Construction Authority was to receive $145,000 a year and each of the three vice presidents $110,000 a year. An executive gym, with Nautilus equipment, was contemplated for the top floor of the agency's new headquarters at the International Design Center in Long Island City. Two years into this reform, the backlog on repairs to existing schools stood at 33,000 outstanding requests. "To relieve the charity of friends of the support of a half-blind and half-witted man by employing him at the public expense as an inspector of cement may not be practical with reference to the permanent firmness of a wall," Olmsted noted after his Central Park experience, "while it is perfectly so with reference to the triumph of sound doctrine at an election."

In fact the highest per capita taxes of any city in the United States (and, as anyone running a small business knows, the widest variety of taxes) provide, in New York, unless the citizen is prepared to cut a side deal here and there, only the continuing multiplication of regulations designed to benefit the contractors and agencies and unions with whom the regulators have cut their own deals. A kitchen appliance accepted throughout the rest of the United States as a basic postwar amenity, the in-sink garbage disposal unit, is for example illegal in New York. Disposals, a city employee advised me, not only encourage rats, and "bacteria," presumably in a way that bags of garbage sitting on the sidewalk do not ("Because it is," I was told when I asked how this could be), but also encourage people "to put their babies down them."

On the one hand this illustrates how a familiar urban principle, that of patronage (the more garbage there is to be collected, the more garbage collectors can be employed), can be reduced, in the bureaucratic wilderness that is any third-world city, to voodoo; on the other it reflects this particular city's underlying criminal ethic, its acceptance of graft and grift as the bedrock of every transaction. "Garbage costs are outrageous," an executive of Supermarkets General, which owns Pathmark, recently told *City Limits* about why the chains preferred to locate in the suburbs. "Every time you need to hire a contractor, it's a problem." The problem, however, is one from which not only the contractor but everyone with whom the contractor does business—a chain of direct or indirect patronage extending deep into the fabric of the city—stands to derive one or another benefit, which was one reason the death of a young middle-class white woman in the East 68th Street apartment of the assistant commissioner in charge of boiler and elevator inspections flickered so feebly on the local attention span.

It was only within the transforming narrative of "contrasts" that both the essential criminality of the city and its related absence of civility could become points of pride, evidence of "energy": if you could make it here you could make it anywhere, hello sucker, get smart. Those who did not get the deal, who bought retail, who did not know what it took to get their electrical work signed off, were dismissed as provincials, bridge-and-tunnels, out-of-towners who did not have what it took not to get taken. "Every tourist's nightmare became a reality for a Maryland couple over the weekend when the husband was beaten and robbed on Fifth Avenue in front of Trump Tower," began a story in the *New York Post* during the summer of 1990. "Where do you think we're from, Iowa?" The prosecutor who took Robert Chambers's statement said on videotape by way of indicating that he doubted Chambers's version of Jennifer Levin's death. "They go after poor people like you from out of town, they prey on the tourists," a clerk explained in the West 46th Street computer store where my husband and I had taken refuge to escape three muggers. My husband said that we lived in New York. "That's why they didn't get you," the clerk said, effortlessly incorporating this change in the data. "That's how you could move fast."

The narrative comforts us, in other words, with the assurance that the world is knowable, even flat, and New York its center, its motor, its dangerous but vital "energy." "Family in Fatal Mugging Loved New York" was the *Times* headline on a story following the September 1990 murder, in the Seventh Avenue IND station, of a twenty-two-year-old tourist from Utah. The young man, his parents, his brother, and his sister-in-law had attended the U.S. Open and were reportedly on their way to dinner at a Moroccan restaurant downtown. "New York, to them, was the greatest place in the world," a family friend from Utah was quoted as having said. Since the narrative requires that the rest of the country provide a dramatic contrast to New York, the family's hometown in Utah was characterized by the *Times* as a place where "life revolves around the orderly rhythms of Brigham Young University" and "there is only about one murder a year." The town was in fact Provo, where Gary Gilmore shot the motel manager, both in life and in *The Executioner's Song.* "She loved New York, she just loved it," a friend of the assaulted jogger told the *Times* after the attack. "I think she liked the fast pace, the competitiveness."

New York, the *Times* concluded, "invigorated" the jogger, "matched her energy level." At a time when the city lay virtually inert, when forty thousand jobs had been wiped out in the financial markets and former traders were selling shirts at Bergdorf Goodman for Men, when the rate of mortgage delinquencies had doubled, when 50 or 60 million square feet of office space remained unrented (60 million square feet of unrented office space is the equivalent of fifteen darkened World Trade Towers) and even prime commercial blocks on Madison Avenue in the Seventies were boarded up, empty; at a time when the money had dropped out of all the markets and the Europeans who had lent the city their élan and their capital during the eighties had moved on, vanished to more cheerful venues, this notion of the city's "energy" was sedative, as was the commandeering of "crime" as the city's central problem.

3

The extent to which the October 1987 crash of the New York financial markets damaged the illusions of infinite recovery and growth on which the city had operated during the 1980s had been at first hard to apprehend. "Ours is a time of New York ascendant," the New York City Commission on the Year 2000, created during the mayoralty of Edward Koch to reflect the best thinking of the city's various business and institutional establishments, had declared in its 1987 report. "The city's economy is stronger than it has been in decades, and is driven both by its own resilience and by the national economy; New York is more than ever the international capital of finance, and the gateway to the American economy."

And then, its citizens had come gradually to understand, it was not. This perception that something was "wrong" in New York had been insidious, a slow-onset illness at first noticeable only in periods of temporary remission. Losses that might have seemed someone else's problem (or even comeuppance) as the markets were in their initial 1987 free-fall, and that might have seemed more remote still as the markets regained the appearance of strength, had come imperceptibly but inexorably to alter the tone of daily life. By April of 1990, people who lived in and around New York were expressing, in interviews with the *Times*, considerable anguish and fear that they did so: "I feel very resentful that I've lost a lot of flexibility in my life," one said. "I often wonder, 'Am I crazy for coming here?'" "People feel a sense of impending doom about what may happen to them," a clinical psychologist said. People were "frustrated," "feeling absolutely desolate," "trapped," "angry," "terrified," and "on the verge of panic."

It was a panic that seemed in many ways specific to New York, and inexplicable outside it. Even later, when the troubles of New York had become a common theme, Americans from less depressed venues had difficulty comprehending the nature of those troubles, and tended to attribute them, as New Yorkers themselves had come to do, to "crime." "Escape From New York" was the headline on the front page of the *New York Post* on September 10, 1990. "Rampaging Crime Wave Has 59 percent of Residents Terrified. Most Would Get Out of the City, Says Time/CNN Poll." This poll appeared in the edition of *Time* dated September 17, 1990, which carried the cover legend "The Rotting of the Big Apple." "Reason: a surge of drugs and violent crime that government officials seem utterly unable to combat," the story inside explained. Columnists referred, locally, to "this sewer of a city." The *Times* ran a plaintive piece about the snatch of Elizabeth Rohatyn's Hermès handbag outside Arcadia, a restaurant on East 62nd Street that had for a while seemed the very heart of the New York everyone now missed, the New York where getting and spending could take place without undue reference to having and not having, the duty-free New York; that this had occurred to the wife of Felix Rohatyn, who was widely perceived to have saved the city from its fiscal crisis in the midseventies, seemed to many a clarion irony.

This question of crime was tricky. There were in fact eight American cities with higher homicide rates, and twelve with higher overall crime rates. Crime had long been taken for granted in the less affluent parts of the city, and had become in the midseventies, as both unemployment and the costs of maintaining property rose and what had once been functioning neighborhoods were abandoned and burned and left to whoever claimed them, endemic. "In some poor neighborhoods, crime became almost a way of life," Jim Sleeper, an editor at *Newsday* and the author of *The Closest of Strangers:*

Liberalism and the Politics of Race in New York, noted in his discussion of the social disintegration that occurred during this period:

> . . . a subculture of violence with complex bonds of utility and affection within families and the larger, "law-abiding" community. Struggling merchants might "fence" stolen goods, for example, thus providing quick cover and additional incentive for burglaries and robberies; the drug economy became more vigorous, reshaping criminal lifestyles and tormenting the loyalties of families and friends. A walk down even a reasonably busy street in a poor, minority neighborhood at high noon could become an unnerving journey into a landscape eerie and grim.

What seemed markedly different a decade later, what made crime a "story," was that the more privileged, and especially the more privileged white, citizens of New York had begun to feel unnerved at high noon in even their own neighborhoods. Although New York City Police Department statistics suggested that white New Yorkers were not actually in increased mortal danger (the increase in homicides between 1977 and 1989, from 1,557 to 1,903, was entirely among what the NYPD classified as Hispanic, Asian, and black victims; the number of white murder victims had steadily declined, from 361 in 1977 to 227 in 1984 and 190 in 1989), the apprehension of such danger, exacerbated by street snatches and muggings and the quite useful sense that the youth in the hooded sweatshirt with his hands jammed in his pockets might well be a predator, had become general. These more privileged New Yorkers now felt unnerved not only on the street, where the necessity for evasive strategies had become an exhausting constant, but in even the most insulated and protected apartment buildings. As the residents of such buildings, the owners of twelve- and sixteen- and twenty-four-room apartments, watched the potted ficus trees disappear from outside their doors and the graffiti appear on their limestone walls and the smashed safety glass from car windows get swept off their sidewalks, it had become increasingly easy to imagine the outcome of a confrontation between, say, the relief night doorman and six dropouts from Julia Richman High School on East 67th Street.

And yet those New Yorkers who had spoken to the *Times* in April of 1990 about their loss of flexibility, about their panic, their desolation, their anger, and their sense of impending doom, had not been talking about drugs, or crime, or any of the city's more publicized and to some extent inflated ills. These were people who did not for the most part have twelve- and sixteen-room apartments and doormen and the luxury of projected fears. These people were talking instead about an immediate fear, about money, about the vertiginous plunge in the value of their houses and apartments and condominiums, about the possibility or probability of foreclosure and loss; about, implicitly, their fears of being left, like so many they saw every day, below the line, out in the cold, on the street.

This was a climate in which many of the questions that had seized the city's attention in 1987 and 1988, for example that of whether Mortimer Zuckerman should be "allowed" to build two fifty-nine-story office towers on the site of what is now the Coliseum, seemed in retrospect wistful, the baroque concerns of better times. "There's no way anyone would make a sane judgment to go into the ground now," a vice president at Cushman and Wakefield told the *New York Observer* about the delay in the Coliseum project, which had in fact lost its projected major tenant, Salomon Brothers, shortly after Black Monday, 1987. "It would be suicide. You're better off sitting in a tub of water and opening your wrists." Such fears were, for a number of reasons, less easy to incorporate into the narrative than the fear of crime.

The imposition of a sentimental, or false, narrative on the disparate and often random experience that constitutes the life of a city or a country means, necessarily, that much of what happens in that city or country will be rendered merely illustrative, a series of set pieces, or performance opportunities. Mayor Dinkins could, in such a symbolic substitute for civic life, "break the boycott" (the Flatbush boycott organized to mobilize resentment of Korean merchants in black neighborhoods) by purchasing a few dollars' worth of produce from a Korean grocer on Church Avenue. Governor Cuomo could "declare war on crime" by calling for five thousand additional police; Mayor Dinkins could "up the ante" by calling for sixty-five hundred. "White slut comes into the park looking for the African man," a black woman could say, her voice loud but still conversational, in the corridor outside the courtroom where, during the summer of 1990, the first three defendants in the Central Park attack, Antron McCray, Yusef Salaam, and Raymond Santana, were tried on charges of attempted murder, assault, sodomy, and rape. "Boyfriend beats shit out of her, they blame it on our boys," the woman could continue, and then, referring to a young man with whom the victim had at one time split the cost of an apartment: "How about the roommate, anybody test his semen? No. He's white. They don't do it to each other."

Glances could then flicker among those reporters and producers and courtroom sketch artists and photographers and cameramen and techs and summer interns who assembled daily at 111 Centre Street. Cellular phones could be picked up, a show of indifference. Small talk could be exchanged with the marshals, a show of solidarity. The woman could then raise her voice: "White folk, all of them are devils, even those that haven't been born yet, they are *devils*. Little *demons*. I don't understand these devils, I guess they think this is *their court*." The reporters could gaze beyond her, faces blank, no eye contact, a more correct form of hostility and also more lethal. The woman could hold her ground but avert her eyes, letting her gaze fall on another black, in this instance a black *Daily News* columnist, Bob Herbert. "You," she could say. "You are a *disgrace*. Go ahead. Line up there. Line up with the white folk. Look at them, lining up for their first-class seats while *my* people are downstairs behind *barricades* . . . kept behind barricades like *cattle* . . . not even allowed in the room to see their sons lynched . . . is that an *African* I see in that line? Or is that a *Negro*. Oh, oh, sorry, shush, white folk didn't know, he was *passing* . . ."

In a city in which grave and disrupting problems had become general—problems of not having, problems of not making it, problems that demonstrably existed, among the mad and the ill and the under-equipped and the overwhelmed, with decreasing reference to color—the case of the Central Park jogger provided more than just a safe, or structured, setting in which various and sometimes only marginally related rages could be vented. "This trial," the *Daily News* announced on its editorial page one morning in July 1990, midway through the trial of the first three defendants, "is about more than the rape and brutalization of a single woman. It is about the rape and the brutalization of a city. The jogger is a symbol of all that's wrong here. And all that's right, because she is nothing less than an inspiration."

The *News* did not define the ways in which "the rape and the brutalization of the city" manifested itself, nor was definition necessary: this was a city in which the threat or the fear of brutalization had become so immediate that citizens were urged to take up their own defense, to form citizen patrols or militia, as in Beirut. This was a city in which between twenty and thirty neighborhoods had already given over their protection, which was to say the right to determine who belonged in the neighborhood and who did not and what should be done about it, to the Guardian Angels. This was a city in which a Brooklyn vigilante group, which called itself Crack Busters and was said to be trying to rid its Bedford-Stuyvesant neighborhood of drugs, would before September was out "settle an argument" by dousing with gasoline and setting on fire an abandoned van and the three homeless citizens inside. This was a city in which the *Times* would soon perceive, in the failing economy, "a bright side for the city at large," the bright side being that while there was believed to have been an increase in the number of middle-income and upper-income families who wanted to leave the city, "the slumping market is keeping many of those families in New York."

In this city rapidly vanishing into the chasm between its actual life and its preferred narratives, what people said when they talked about the case of the Central Park jogger came to seem a kind of poetry, a way of expressing, without directly stating, different but equally volatile and similarly occult visions of the same disaster. One vision, shared by those who had seized upon the attack on the jogger as an exact representation of what was wrong with the city, was of a city systematically ruined, violated, raped by its underclass. The opposing vision, shared by those who had seized upon the arrest of the defendants as an exact representation of their own victimization, was of a city in which the powerless had been systematically ruined, violated, raped by the powerful. For so long as this case held the city's febrile attention, then, it offered a narrative for the city's distress, a frame in which the actual social and economic forces wrenching the city could be personalized and ultimately obscured.

Or rather it offered two narratives, mutually exclusive. Among a number of blacks, particularly those whose experience with or distrust of the criminal justice system was such that they tended to discount the fact that five of the six defendants had to varying degrees admitted taking part in the attack, and to focus instead on the absence of any supporting forensic evidence incontrovertibly linking this victim to these defendants, the case could be read as a confirmation not only of their victimization but of the white conspiracy they saw at the heart of that victimization. For the *Amsterdam News*, which did not veer automatically to the radical analysis (a typical issue in the fall of 1990 lauded the FBI for its minority recruiting and the Harlem National Guard for its high morale and readiness to go to the Gulf), the defendants could in this light be seen as victims of "a political trial," of a "legal lynching," of a case "rigged from the very beginning" by the decision of "the white press" that "whoever was arrested and charged in this case of the attempted murder, rape and sodomy of a well-connected, bright, beautiful, and promising white woman was guilty, pure and simple."

For Alton H. Maddox, Jr., the message to be drawn from the case was that the American criminal justice system, which was under any circumstances "inherently and unabashedly racist," failed "to function equitably at any level when a Black male is accused of raping a white female." For others the message was more general, and worked to reinforce the fragile but functional mythology of a heroic black past, the narrative in which European domination could be explained as a direct and vengeful response to African superiority. "Today the white man is faced head-on with what is happening on the Black Continent, Africa," Malcolm X wrote.

> Look at the artifacts being discovered there, that are proving over and over again, how the black man had great, fine, sensitive civilizations before the white man was out of the caves. Below the Sahara, in the places where most of America's Negroes' foreparents were kidnapped, there is being unearthed some of the finest craftsmanship, sculpture and other objects, that has ever been seen by modern man. Some of these things now are on view in such places as New York City's Museum of Modern Art. Gold work of such fine tolerance and workmanship that it has no rival. Ancient objects produced by black hands . . . refined by those black hands with results that no human hand today can equal.

> History has been so "whitened" by the white man that even the black professors have known little more than the most ignorant black man about the talents and rich civilizations and cultures of the black man of millenniums ago . . .

"Our proud African queen," the Reverend Al Sharpton had said of Tawana Brawley's mother, Glenda Brawley: "She stepped out of anonymity, stepped out of obscurity, and walked into history." It was said in the corridors of the courthouse where Yusuf Salaam was tried that he carried himself "like an African king."

"It makes no difference anymore whether the attack on Tawana happened," William Kunstler had told *New York Newsday* when the alleged rape and torture of Tawana Brawley by a varying number of white police officers seemed, as an actual prosecutable crime if not as a window on what people needed to believe, to have dematerialized. "If her story was a concoction to prevent her parents from punishing her for staying out all night, that doesn't disguise the fact that a lot of young black women are treated the way she said she was treated." The importance of whether or not the crime had occurred was, in this view, entirely resident in the crime's "description," which was defined by Stanley Diamond in *The Nation* as "a crime that did not occur" but was "described with skill and controlled hysteria by the black actors as the epitome of degradation, a repellent model of what actually happens to too many black women."

A good deal of what got said around the edges of the jogger case, in the corridors and on the call-in shows, seemed to derive exclusively from the suspicions of conspiracy increasingly entrenched among those who believe themselves powerless. A poll conducted in June of 1990 by the *New York Times* and WCBS-TV News determined that 77 percent of blacks polled believed either that it was "true" or "might possibly be true" (as opposed to "almost certainly not true") that the government of the United States "singles out and investigates black elected officials in order to discredit them in a way it doesn't do with white officials." Sixty percent believed that it was true or might possibly be true that the government "deliberately makes sure that drugs are easily available in poor black neighborhoods in order to harm black people." Twenty-nine percent believed that it was true or might possibly be true that "the virus which causes AIDS was deliberately created in a laboratory in order to infect black people." In each case, the alternative response to "true" or "might possibly be true" was "almost certainly not true," which might have seemed in itself to reflect a less than ringing belief in the absence of conspiracy. "The conspiracy to destroy Black boys is very complex and interwoven," Jawanza Kunjufu, a Chicago educational consultant, wrote in his *Countering the Conspiracy to Destroy Black Boys*, a 1982 pamphlet that has since been extended to three volumes.

> There are many contributors to the conspiracy, ranging from the very visible who are more obvious, to the less visible and silent partners who are more difficult to recognize.
>
> Those people who adhere to the doctrine of white racism, imperialism, and white male supremacy are easier to recognize. Those people who actively promote drugs and gang violence are active conspirators, and easier to identify. What makes the conspiracy more complex are those people who do not plot together to destroy Black boys, but, through their indifference, perpetuate it. This passive group of conspirators consists of parents, educators, and white liberals who deny being racists, but through their silence allow institutional racism to continue.

For those who proceeded from the conviction that there was under way a conspiracy to destroy blacks, particularly black boys, a belief in the innocence of these defendants, a conviction that even their own statements had been rigged against them or wrenched from them, followed logically. It was in the corridors and on the call-in shows that the conspiracy got sketched in, in a series of fantasy details that conflicted not only with known facts but even with each other. It was said that the prosecution was withholding evidence that the victim had gone to the park to meet a drug dealer. It was said, alternately or concurrently, that the prosecution was withholding evidence that the victim had gone to the park to take part in a satanic ritual. It was said that the forensic photographs showing her battered body were not "real" photographs, that "they," the prosecution, had "brought in some corpse for the pictures." It was said that the young woman who appeared on the witness stand and identified herself as the victim was not the "real" victim, that "they" had in this case brought in an actress.

What was being expressed in each instance was the sense that secrets must be in play, that "they," the people who had power in the courtroom, were in possession of information systematically withheld—since information itself was power—from those who did not have power. On the day the first three defendants were sentenced, C. Vernon Mason, who had formally entered the case in the penalty phase as Antron McCray's attorney, filed a brief that included the bewildering and untrue assertion that the victim's boyfriend, who had not at that time been called to testify, was black. That some whites jumped to engage this assertion on its own terms (the *Daily News* columnist Gail Collins referred to it as Mason's "slimiest argument of the hour—an announcement that the jogger had a black lover") tended only to reinforce the sense of racial estrangement that was the intended subtext of the assertion, which was without meaning or significance except in that emotional deep where whites are seen as conspiring in secret to sink blacks in misery. "Just answer me, who got addicted?" I recall one black spectator asking another as they left the courtroom. "I'll tell you who got addicted, the inner city got addicted." He had with him a pamphlet that laid out a scenario in which the government had conspired to exterminate blacks by flooding their neighborhoods with drugs, a scenario touching all the familiar points, Laos, Cambodia, the Golden Triangle, the CIA, more secrets, more poetry.

"From the beginning I have insisted that this was not a racial case," Robert Morgenthau, the Manhattan district attorney, said after the verdicts came in on the first jogger trial. He spoke of those who, in his view, wanted "to divide the races and advance their own private agendas," and of how the city was "ill-served" by those who had so "sought to exploit" this case. "We had hoped that the racial tensions surrounding the jogger trial would begin to dissipate soon after the jury arrived at a verdict," a *Post* editorial began a few days later. The editorial spoke of an "ugly claque of 'activists'," of the "divisive atmosphere" they had created, and of the anticipation with which the city's citizens had waited for "mainstream black leaders" to step forward with praise for the way in which the verdicts had brought New York "back from the brink of criminal chaos":

> Alas, in the jogger case, the wait was in vain. Instead of praise for a verdict which demonstrated that sometimes criminals are caught and punished, New Yorkers heard charlatans like the Rev. Al Sharpton claim the case was fixed. They heard that C. Vernon Mason, one of the engineers of the Tawana Brawley hoax—the attorney who thinks Mayor Dinkins wears "too many yarmulkes"—was planning to appeal the verdicts . . .

To those whose preferred view of the city was of an inherently dynamic and productive community ordered by the natural play of its conflicting elements, enriched, as in Mayor Dinkins's "gorgeous mosaic," by its very "contrasts," this case offered a number of useful elements. There was the confirmation of "crime" as the canker corroding the life of the city. There was, in the random and feral evening described by the East Harlem attackers and the clear innocence of and damage done to the Upper East Side and Wall Street victim, an eerily exact and conveniently personalized representation of what the *Daily News* had called "the rape and the brutalization of a city." Among the reporters on this case, whose own narrative conventions involved "hero cops" and "brave prosecutors" going hand to hand against "crime" (the "Secret Agony of Jogger DA," we learned in the *Post* a few days after the verdicts in the first trial, was that "Brave Prosecutor's Marriage Failed as She Put Rapists Away"), there seemed an unflagging enthusiasm for the repetition and reinforcement of these elements, and an equally unflagging resistance, even hostility, to exploring the point of view of the defendants' families and friends and personal or political allies (or, as they were called in news reports, the "supporters") who gathered daily at the other end of the corridor from the courtroom.

This seemed curious. Criminal cases are widely regarded by American reporters as windows on the city or culture in which they take place, opportunities to enter not only households but parts of the culture normally closed, and yet this was a case in which indifference to the world of the defendants extended even to the reporting of names and occupations. Yusuf Salaam's mother, who happened to be young and photogenic and to have European features, was pictured so regularly that she and her son became the instantly recognizable "images" of Jogger One, but even then no one got her name quite right. For a while in the papers she was "Cheroney," or sometimes "Cheron*a*y," McEllhonor, then she became Cheroney McEllhonor Salaam. After she testified, the spelling of her first name was corrected to "Sharonne," although, since the byline on a piece she wrote for the *Amsterdam News* spelled it differently, "Sharrone," this may have been another misunderstanding. Her occupation was frequently given as "designer" (later, after her son's conviction, she went to work as a paralegal for William Kunstler), but no one seemed to take this seriously enough to say what she designed or for whom; not until after she testified, when *Newsday* reported her testimony that on the evening of her son's arrest she had arrived at the precinct house late because she was an instructor at the Parsons School of Design, did the notion of "designer" seem sufficiently concrete to suggest an actual occupation.

The Jogger One defendants were referred to repeatedly in the news columns of the *Post* as "thugs." The defendants and their families were often said by reporters to be "sneering." (The reporters, in turn, were said at the other end of the corridor to be "smirking.") "We don't have nearly so strong a question as to the guilt or innocence of the defendants as we did at Bensonhurst," a *Newsday* reporter covering the first jogger trial said to the *New York Observer*, well before the closing arguments, by way of explaining why *Newsday's* coverage may have seemed less extensive on this trial than on the Bensonhurst trials. "There is not a big question as to what happened in Central Park that night. Some details are missing, but it's fairly clear who did what to whom."

In fact this came close to the heart of it: that it seemed, on the basis of the videotaped statements, fairly clear who had done what to whom was precisely the case's liberating aspect, the circumstance that enabled many of the city's citizens to say and think what they might otherwise have left unexpressed. Unlike other recent high visibility cases in New York, unlike Bensonhurst and unlike Howard Beach and unlike Bernhard Goetz, here was a case in which the issue not exactly of race but of an increasingly visible underclass could be confronted by the middle-class, both white and black, without guilt. Here was a case that gave this middle-class a way to transfer and express what had clearly become a growing and previously inadmissible rage with the city's disorder, with the entire range of ills and uneasy guilts that came to mind in a city where entire families slept in the discarded boxes in which new Sub-Zero refrigerators were delivered, at twenty-six hundred per, to more affluent families. Here was also a case, most significantly, in which even that transferred rage could be transferred still further, veiled, personalized: a case in which the city's distress could be seen to derive not precisely from its underclass but instead from certain identifiable individuals who claimed to speak for this underclass, individuals who, in Robert Morgenthau's words, "sought to exploit" this case, to "advance their own private agendas"; individuals who wished even to "divide the races."

If the city's problems could be seen as deliberate disruptions of a naturally cohesive and harmonious community, a community in which, undisrupted, "contrasts" generated a perhaps dangerous but vital "energy," then those problems were tractable, and could be addressed, like "crime," by the call for "better leadership." Considerable comfort could be obtained, given this story line, through the demonization of the Reverend Al Sharpton, whose presence on the edges of certain criminal cases that interested him had a polarizing effect that tended to reinforce the narrative. Jim Sleeper, in *The Closet of Strangers*, described one of the fifteen marches Sharpton led through Bensonhurst after the 1989 killing of an East New York sixteen-year-old, Yusuf Hawkins, who had come into Bensonhurst and been set upon, with baseball bats and ultimately with bullets, by a group of young whites.

> An August 27, 1989, *Daily News* photo of the Reverend Al Sharpton and a claque of black teenagers marching in Bensonhurst to protest Hawkins's death shows that they are not really "marching." They are stumbling along, huddled together, heads bowed under the storm of hatred breaking over them, eyes wide, hanging on to one another and to Sharpton, scared out of their wits. They, too, are innocents—or were until that day, which they will always remember. And because Sharpton is with them, his head bowed, his face showing that he knows what they're feeling, he is in the hearts of black people all over New York.
>
> Yet something is wrong with this picture. Sharpton did not invite or coordinate with Bensonhurst community leaders who wanted to join the march. Without the time for organizing which these leaders should have been given in order to rein in the punks who stood waving watermelons; without an effort by black leaders more reputable than Sharpton to recruit whites citywide and swell the march, Sharpton was assured that the punks would carry the day. At several points he even baited them by blowing kisses . . .

"I knew that Bensonhurst would clarify whether it had been a racial incident or not," Sharpton said by way of explaining, on a recent "Frontline" documentary, his strategy in Bensonhurst. "The fact that I was so controversial to Bensonhurst helped them forget that the cameras were there," he said. "So I decided to help them . . . I would throw kisses to them, and they would go nuts." *Question*, began a joke told in the aftermath of the first jogger trial. *You're in a room with Hitler, Saddam Hussein, and Al Sharpton. You have only two bullets. Who do you shoot? Answer: Al Sharpton. Twice.*

Sharpton did not exactly fit the roles New York traditionally assigns, for maximum audience comfort, to prominent blacks. He seemed in many ways a phantasm, someone whose instinct for the connections between religion and politics and show business was so innate that he had been all his life the vessel for other people's hopes and fears. He had given his first sermon at age four. He was touring with Mahalia Jackson at eleven. As a teenager, according to Robert D. McFadden, Ralph Blumenthal, M. A. Farber, E. R. Shipp, Charles Strum, and Craig Wolff, the *New York Times* reporters and editors who collaborated on *Outrage: The Story Behind the Tawana Brawley Hoax*, Sharpton was tutored first by Adam Clayton Powell, Jr. ("You got to know when to hit it and you got to know when to quit it and when it's quittin' time, don't push it," Powell told him), then by the Reverend Jesse Jackson ("Once you turn on the gas, you got to cook or burn 'em up," Jackson told him), and eventually, after obtaining a grant from Bayard Rustin and campaigning for Shirley Chisholm, by James Brown. "Once, he trailed Brown down a corridor, through a door, and, to his astonishment, onto a stage flooded with spotlights," the authors of *Outrage* reported. "He immediately went into a wiggle and dance."

It was perhaps this talent for seizing the spotlight and the moment, this fatal bent for the wiggle and the dance, that most clearly disqualified Sharpton from casting as the Good Negro, the credit to the race, the exemplary if often imagined figure whose refined manners and good grammar could be stressed and who could be seen to lay, as Jimmy Walker said of Joe Louis, "a rose on the grave of Abraham Lincoln." It was left, then, to cast Sharpton, and for Sharpton to cast himself, as the Outrageous Nigger, the familiar role—assigned sixty years ago to Father Divine and thirty years later to Adam Clayton Powell—of the essentially manageable fraud whose first concern is his own well-being. It was for example repeatedly mentioned, during the ten days the jury was out on the first jogger trial, that Sharpton had chosen to wait out the verdict not at 111 Centre Street but "in the airconditioned comfort" of C. Vernon Mason's office, from which he could be summoned by beeper.

Sharpton, it was frequently said by whites and also by some blacks, "represented nobody," was "self-appointed" and "self-promoting." He was an "exploiter" of blacks, someone who "did them more harm than good." It was pointed out that he had been indicted by the state of New York in June of 1989 on charges of grand larceny. (He was ultimately acquitted.) It was pointed out that *New York Newsday*, working on information that appeared to have been supplied by federal law-enforcement agencies, had in January 1988 named him as a federal informant, and that he himself admitted to having let the government tap his phone in a drug-enforcement effort. It was routinely said, most tellingly of all in a narrative based on the magical ability of "leaders" to improve the commonweal, that he was "not the right leader," "not at all the leader the black community needs." His clothes and his demeanor were ridiculed (my husband was asked by *Esquire* to do a piece predicated on interviewing Sharpton while he was having his hair processed), his motives derided, and his tactics, which were those of an extremely sophisticated player who counted being widely despised among his stronger cards, not very well understood.

Whites tended to believe, and to say, that Sharpton was "using" the racial issue—which, in the sense that all political action is based on "using" one issue or another, he clearly was. Whites also tended to see him as destructive and irresponsible, indifferent to the truth or to the sensibilities of whites—which, most notoriously in the nurturing of the Tawana Brawley case, a primal fantasy in which white men were accused of a crime Sharpton may well have known to be a fabrication, he also clearly was. What seemed not at all understood was that for Sharpton, who had no interest in making the problem appear more tractable ("The question is, do you want to 'ease' it or do you want to 'heal' it," he had said when asked if his marches had not worked against "easing tension" in Bensonhurst), the fact that blacks and whites could sometimes be shown to have divergent interests by no means suggested the need for an ameliorative solution. Such divergent interests were instead a lucky break, a ready-made organizing tool, a dramatic illustration of who had the power and who did not, who was making it and who was falling below the line; a metaphor for the sense of victimization felt not only by blacks but by all those Sharpton called "the left-out opposition." *We got the power*, the chants go on "Sharpton and Fulani in Babylon: Volume I, The Battle of New York City," a tape of the speeches of Sharpton and of Leonora Fulani, a leader of the New Alliance Party. *We are the chosen people. Out of the pain. We that can't even talk together. Have learned to walk together.*

"I'm no longer sure what I thought about Al Sharpton a year or two ago still applies," Jerry Nachman, the editor of the *New York Post*, who had frequently criticized Sharpton, told Howard Kurtz of the *Washington Post* in September of 1990. "I spent a lot of time on the street. There's a lot of anger, a lot of frustration. Rightly or wrongly, he may be articulating a great deal more of what typical attitudes are than some of us thought." Wilbert Tatum, the editor and publisher of the *Amsterdam News*, tried to explain to Kurtz how, in his view, Sharpton had been cast as "a caricature of black leadership":

> He was fat. He wore jogging suits. He wore a medallion and gold chains. And the unforgivable of unforgivables, he had processed hair. The white media, perhaps not consciously, said, "We're going to promote this guy

> because we can point up the ridiculousness and paucity of black leadership." Al understood precisely what they were doing, precisely. Al is probably the most brilliant tactician this country has ever produced . . .

Whites often mentioned, as a clinching argument, that Sharpton paid his demonstrators to appear; the figure usually mentioned was five dollars (by November 1990, when Sharpton was fielding demonstrators to protest the killing of a black woman alleged to have grabbed a police nightstick in the aftermath of a domestic dispute, a police source quoted in the *Post* had jumped the payment to twenty dollars), but the figure floated by a prosecutor on the jogger case was four dollars. This seemed on many levels a misunderstanding, or an estrangement, or as blacks would say a disrespect, too deep to address, but on its simplest level it served to suggest what value was placed by whites on what they thought of as black time.

In the fall of 1990, the fourth and fifth of the six defendants in the Central Park attack, Kevin Richardson and Kharey Wise, went on trial. Since this particular narrative had achieved full resolution, or catharsis, with the conviction of the first three defendants, the city's interest in the case had by then largely waned. Those "charlatans" who had sought to "exploit" the case had been whisked, until they could next prove useful, into the wings. Even the verdicts in this second trial, coinciding as they did with yet another arrest of John ("The Dapper Don") Gotti, a reliable favorite on the New York stage, did not lead the local news. It was in fact the economy itself that had come center stage in the city's new, and yet familiar, narrative work: a work in which the vital yet beleaguered city would or would not weather yet another "crisis" (the answer was a resounding yes); a work, or a dreamwork, that emphasized not only the cyclical nature of such "crises" but the regenerative power of the city's "contrasts." "With its migratory population, its diversity of cultures and institutions, and its vast resources of infrastructure, capital, and intellect, New York has been the quintessential modern city for more than a century, constantly reinventing itself," Michael Stone concluded in his *New York* magazine cover story, "Hard Times." "Though the process may be long and painful, there's no reason to believe it won't happen again."

These were points commonly made in support of a narrative that tended, with its dramatic line of "crisis" and resolution, or recovery, only to further obscure the economic and historical groundwork for the situation in which the city found itself: that long unindictable conspiracy of criminal and semi-criminal civic and commercial arrangements, deals, negotiations, gimmes and getmes, graft and grift, pipe, topsoil, concrete, garbage; the conspiracy of those in the know, those with a connection, those with a rabbi at the Department of Sanitation or the Buildings Department or the School

Construction Authority or Foley Square, the conspiracy of those who believed everybody got upside down because of who it was, it happened to anybody else, a summons gets issued and that's the end of it. On November 12, 1990, in its page-one analysis of the city's troubles, the *New York Times* went so far as to locate, in "public spending," not the drain on the city's vitality and resources it had historically been but "an important positive factor":

> Not in decades has so much money gone for public works in the area—airports, highways, bridges, sewers, subways and other projects. Roughly $12 billion will be spent in the metropolitan region in the current fiscal year. Such government outlays are a healthy counterforce to a 43 percent decline since 1987 in the value of new private construction, a decline related to the sharp drop in real estate prices. . . . While nearly every industry in the private sector has been reducing payrolls since spring, government hiring has risen, maintaining an annual growth rate of 20,000 people since 1987 . . .

That there might well be, in a city in which the proliferation of and increase in taxes were already driving private-sector payrolls out of town, hardly anyone left to tax for such public works and public-sector jobs was a point not too many people wished seriously to address: among the citizens of a New York come to grief on the sentimental stories told in defense of its own lazy criminality, the city's inevitability remained the given, the heart, the first and last word on which all the stories rested. We love New York, the narrative promises, because it matches our energy level.

Troublemakers

What Pit Bulls Can Teach Us about Profiling

Malcolm Gladwell

One afternoon last February, Guy Clairoux picked up his two-and-a half-year-old son, Jayden, from day care and walked him back to their house in the west end of Ottawa, Ontario. They were almost home. Jayden was straggling behind, and, as his father's back was turned, a pit bull jumped over a back-yard fence and lunged at Jayden. "The dog had his head in its mouth and started to do this shake," Clairoux's wife, JoAnn Hartley, said later. As she watched in horror, two more pit bulls jumped over the fence, joining in the assault. She and Clairoux came running, and he punched the first of the dogs in the head, until it dropped Jayden, and then he threw the boy toward his mother. Hartley fell on her son, protecting him with her body. "JoAnn!" Clairoux cried out, as all three dogs descended on his wife. "Cover your neck, cover your neck." A neighbor, sitting by her window, screamed for help. Her partner and a friend, Mario Gauthier, ran outside. A neighborhood boy grabbed his hockey stick and threw it to Gauthier. He began hitting on the dogs over the head, until the stick broke. "They wouldn't stop," Gauthier said. "As soon as you'd stop, they'd attack again. I've never seen a dog go so crazy. They were like Tasmanian devils." The police came. The dogs were pulled away, and the Clairouxes and one of the rescuers were taken to the hospital. Five days later, the Ontario legislature banned the ownership of pit bulls. "Just as we wouldn't let a great white shark in a swimming pool," the province's attorney general, Michael Bryant, had said, "maybe we shouldn't have these animals on the civilized streets."

Pit bulls, descendants of the bulldogs used in the nineteenth century for bull baiting and dogfighting, have been bred for "gameness," and thus a lowered inhibition to aggression. Most dogs fight as a last resort, when starting and growling fail. A pit bull is willing to fight with little or no provocation. Pit bulls seem to have a high tolerance for pain, making it possible for them to fight to the point of exhaustion. Whereas guard dogs like German shepherds usually attempt to restrain those they perceive to be threats by biting and holding, pit bulls try to inflict the maximum amount of damage on an opponent. They bite, hold, shake, and tear. They don't growl or assume an aggressive facial expression as warning. They just attack. "They are often insensitive to behaviors that usually stop aggression," one scientific review of the breed states. "For example, dogs not bred for fighting usually display defeat in combat by rolling over and exposing a light underside. On several occasions, pit bulls have been reported to disembowel dogs offering this signal of submission." In epidemiological studies of dog bites, the pit bull is overrepresented among dogs known to have seriously injured or killed human beings, and, as a result, pit bulls have been banned or restricted in several Western European countries, China, and numerous cities and municipalities across North America. Pit bulls are dangerous.

Of course, not all pit bulls are dangerous. Most don't bite anyone. Meanwhile, Dobermans and Great Danes and German shepherds and Rottweilers are frequent biters as well, and the dog that recently mauled a Frenchwoman so badly that she was given the world's first face transplant was, of all things, a Labrador retriever. When we say that pit bulls are dangerous, we are making a generalization, just as insurance companies use generalizations when they charge young men more for car insurance than the rest of us (even though many young men are perfectly good drivers), and doctors use generalizations when they tell overweight middle-aged men to get their cholesterol checked (even though many overweight middle-aged men won't experience heart trouble). Because we don't know which dog will bite someone or who will have a heart attack or which drivers will get in an accident, we can make predictions only by generalizing. As the legal scholar Frederick Schauer has observed, "painting with a broad brush" is "an often inevitable and frequently desirable dimension of our decision-making lives."

Another word for generalization, though, is "stereotype," and stereotypes are usually not considered desirable dimensions of our decision-making lives. The process of moving from the specific to the general is both necessary and perilous. A doctor could, with some statistical support, generalize about men of a certain age and weight. But what if generalizing from other traits—such as high blood pressure, family history, and smoking—saved more lives? Behind each generalization is a choice of what factors to leave in and what factors to leave out, and those choices can prove surprisingly complicated. After the attack on Jayden Clairoux, the Ontario government chose to make a generalization about pit bulls. But it could also have chosen to generalize about powerful dogs, or about the kinds of people who own powerful dogs, or about small children, or about back-yard fences—or, indeed, about any number of other things to do with dogs and people and places. How do we know when we've made the right generalization?

5 In July of last year, following the transit bombings in London, the New York City Police Department announced that it would send officers into the subways to conduct random searches of passengers' bags. On the face of it, doing random searches in the hunt for terrorists—as opposed to being guided by generalizations—seems like a silly idea. As a columnist in *New York* wrote at the time, "Not just 'most' but nearly every jihadi who has attacked a Western European or American target is a young Arab or Pakistani man. In other words, you can predict with a fair degree of certainty what an Al Qaeda terrorist looks like. Just as we have always known what Mafiosi look like—even as we understand that only an infinitesimal fraction of Italian-Americans are members of the mob."

6 But wait: do we really know what mafiosi look like? In "The Godfather," where most of us get our knowledge of the Mafia, the male members of the Corleone family were played by Marlon Brando, who was of Irish and French ancestry, James Caan, who is Jewish, and two Italian-Americans, Al Pacino and John Cazale. To go by "The Godfather," mafiosi look like white men of European descent, which, as generalizations go, isn't terribly helpful. Figuring out what an Islamic terrorist looks like isn't any easier. Muslims are not like the Amish: they don't come dressed in identifiable costumes. And they don't look like basketball players; they don't come in predictable shapes and sizes. Islam is a religion that spans the globe.

"We have a policy against racial profiling," Raymond Kelly, New York City's police commissioner, told me. "I put it in here in March of the first year I was here. It's the wrong thing to do, and it's also ineffective. If you look at the London bombings, you have three British citizens of Pakistani descent. You have Germaine Lindsay, who is Jamaican. You have the next crew, on July 21st, who are East African. You have a Chechen woman in Moscow in early 2004 who blows herself up in the subway station. So whom do you profile? Look at New York City. Forty per cent of New Yorkers are born outside the country. Look at the diversity here. Who am I supposed to profile?"

Kelly was pointing out what might be called profiling's "category problem." Generalizations involve matching a category of people to a behavior or trait—overweight middle-aged men to heart-attack risk, young men to bad driving. But, for that process to work, you have to be able both to define and to identify the category you are generalizing about. "You think that terrorists aren't aware of how easy it is to be characterized by ethnicity?" Kelly went on. "Look at the 9/11 hijackers. They came here. They shaved. They went to topless bars. They wanted to blend in. They wanted to look like they were part of the American dream. These are not dumb people. Could a terrorist dress up as a Hasidic Jew and walk into the subway, and not be profiled? Yes. I think profiling is just nuts."

Pit-bull bans involve a category problem, too, because pit bulls, as it happens, aren't a single breed. The name refers to dogs belonging to a number of related breeds, such as the American staffordshire terrier, the Staffordshire bull terrier, and the American pit bull terrier—all of which share a square and muscular body, a short snout, and a sleek, short-haired coat. Thus the Ontario ban prohibits not only these three breeds but any "dog that has an appearance and physical characteristics that are substantially similar" to theirs; the term of art is "pit bull-type" dogs. But what does that mean? Is a cross between an American pit bull terrier and a golden retriever a pit bull-type dog or a golden retriever-type dog? If thinking about muscular terriers as pit bulls is a generalization, then thinking about dangerous dogs as anything substantially similar to a pit bull is a generalization about a generalization. "The way a lot of these laws are written, pit bulls are whatever they say they are," Lora Brashears, a kennel manager in Pennsylvania, says. "And for most people it just means big, nasty, scary dog that bites."

The goal of pit-bull bans, obviously, isn't to prohibit dogs that look like pit bulls. The pit-bull appearance is a proxy for the pit-bull temperament—for some trait that these dogs share. But "pit bullness" turns out to be elusive as well. The supposedly troublesome characteristics of the pit-bull type—its gameness, its determination, its insensitivity to pain—are chiefly directed toward other dogs. Pit bulls were not bred to fight humans. On the contrary: a dog that went after spectators, or its handler, or the trainer, or any of the other people involved in making a dogfighting dog a good dogfighter was usually put down. (The rule in the pit-bull world was "Man-eaters die.")

A Georgia-based group called the American Temperament Test Society has put twenty-five thousand dogs through a ten-part standardized drill designed to assess a dog's stability, shyness, aggressiveness, and friendliness in the company of people. A handler takes a dog on a six-foot lead and judges its reaction to stimuli such as gunshots, an umbrella opening, and a weirdly dressed stranger approaching in a threatening way. Eighty-four per cent of the pit bulls that have been given the test have passed, which ranks pit bulls ahead of beagles, Airedales, bearded collies, and all but one variety of dachshund. "We have tested somewhere around a thousand pit-bull-type dogs," Carl Herkstroeter, the president of the A.T.T.S., says. "I've tested half of them. And of the number I've tested I have disqualified one pit bull because of aggressive tendencies. They have done extremely well. They have a good temperament. They are very good with children." It can even be argued that the same traits that make the pit bull so aggressive toward other dogs are what make it so nice to humans. "There are a lot of pit bulls these days who are licensed therapy dogs," the writer Vicki Hearne points out. "Their stability and resoluteness make them excellent for work with people who might not like a more bouncy, flibbertigibbet sort of dog. When pit bulls set out to provide comfort, they are as resolute as they are when they fight, but what they are resolute about is being gentle. And, because they are fearless, they can be gentle with anybody."

Then which are the pit bulls that get into trouble? "The ones that the legislation is geared toward have aggressive tendencies that are either bred in by the breeder, trained in by the trainer, or reinforced in by the owner," Herkstroeter says. A mean pit bull is a dog that has been turned mean, by selective breeding, by being cross-bred with a bigger, human-aggressive breed like German shepherds or Rottweilers, or by being conditioned in such a way that it begins to express hostility to human beings. A pit bull is dangerous to people, then, not to the extent that it expresses its essential pit bullness but to the extent that it deviates from it. A pit-bull ban is a generalization about a generalization about a trait that is not, in fact, general. That's a category problem.

One of the puzzling things about New York City is that, after the enormous and well-publicized reductions in crime in the mid-nineteen-nineties, the crime rate has continued to fall. In the past two years, for instance, murder in New York has declined by almost ten percent, rape by twelve percent, and burglary by more than eighteen percent. Just in the last year, auto theft went down 11.8 percent. On a list of two hundred and forty cities in the United States with a population of a hundred thousand or more, New York City now ranks two hundred-and-twenty-second in crime, down near the bottom with Fontana, California, and Port St. Lucie, Florida. In the nineteen-nineties, the crime decrease was attributed to big obvious changes in city life and government—the decline of the drug trade, the gentrification of Brooklyn, the successful implementation of "broken windows" policing. But all those big changes happened a decade ago. Why is crime *still* falling?

The explanation may have to do with a shift in police tactics. The N.Y.P.D. has a computerized map showing, in real time, precisely where serious crimes are being reported, and at any moment the map typically shows a few dozen constantly shifting high-crime hot spots, some as small as two or three blocks square. What the N.Y.P.D. has done, under Commissioner Kelly, is to use the map to establish "impact zones," and to direct newly graduated officers—who used to be distributed proportionally to precincts across the city—to these zones, in some cases doubling the number of officers in the immediate neighborhood. "We took two-thirds of our graduating class and linked them with experienced officers, and focussed on those areas," Kelly said. "Well, what has happened is that over time we have averaged about a thirty-five-per-cent crime reduction in impact zones."

For years, experts have maintained that the incidence of violent crime is "inelastic" relative to police presence—that people commit serious crimes because of poverty and psychopathology and cultural dysfunction, along with spontaneous motives and opportunities. The presence of a few extra officers down the block, it was thought, wouldn't make much difference. But the N.Y.P.D. experience suggests otherwise. More police means that some crimes are prevented, others are more easily solved, and still others are displaced—pushed out of the troubled neighborhood—which Kelly says is a good thing, because it disrupts the patterns and practices and social networks that serve as the basis for lawbreaking. In other words, the relation between New York City (a category) and criminality (a trait) is unstable, and this kind of instability is another way in which our generalizations can be derailed.

Why, for instance, is it a useful rule of thumb that Kenyans are good distance runners? It's not just that it's statistically supportable today. It's that it has been true for almost half a century, and that in Kenya the tradition of distance running is sufficiently rooted that something cataclysmic would have to happen to dislodge it. By contrast, the generalization that New York City is a crime-ridden place was once true and now, manifestly, isn't. People who moved to sunny retirement communities like Port St. Lucie because they thought they were much safer than New York are suddenly in the position of having made the wrong bet.

The instability issue is a problem for profiling in law enforcement as well. The law professor David Cole once tallied up some of the traits that Drug Enforcement Administration agents have used over the years in making generalizations about suspected smugglers. Here is a sample:

> Arrived late at night; arrived early in the morning; arrived in afternoon; one of the first to deplane; one of the last to deplane; deplaned in the middle; purchased ticket at the airport; made reservation on short notice; bought coach ticket; bought first-class ticket; used one-way ticket; used round-trip ticket; paid for ticket with cash; paid for ticket with small denomination currency; paid for ticket with large denomination currency; made local telephone calls after deplaning; made long distance telephone call after deplaning; pretended to make telephone call; traveled from New York to Los Angeles; traveled to Houston; carried no luggage; carried brand-new luggage; carried a small bag; carried a medium-sized bag; carried two bulky garment bags; carried two heavy suitcases; carried four pieces of luggage; overly protective of luggage; disassociated self from luggage; traveled alone; traveled with a companion; acted too nervous; acted too calm; made eye contact with officer; avoided making eye contact with officer; wore expensive clothing and jewelry; dressed casually; went to restroom after deplaning; walked rapidly through airport; walked slowly through airport; walked aimlessly through airport; left airport by taxi; left airport by limousine; left airport by private car; left airport by hotel courtesy van.

Some of these reasons for suspicion are plainly absurd, suggesting that there's no particular rationale to the generalizations used by D.E.A. agents in stopping suspected drug smugglers. A way of making sense of the list, though, is to think of it as a catalogue of unstable traits. Smugglers may once have tended to buy one-way tickets in cash and carry two bulky suitcases. But they don't have to. They can easily switch to round-trip tickets bought with a credit card, or a single carry-on bag, without losing their capacity to smuggle. There's a second kind of instability here as well. Maybe the reason some of them switched from one-way tickets and two bulky suitcases was that law enforcement got wise to those habits, so the smugglers did the equivalent of what the jihadis seemed to have done in London, when they switched to East Africans because the scrutiny of young Arab and Pakistani men grew too intense. It doesn't work to generalize about a relationship between a category and a trait when that relationship isn't stable—or when the act of generalizing may itself change the basis of the generalization.

Before Kelly became the New York police commissioner, he served as the head of the U.S. Customs Service, and while he was there he overhauled the criteria that border-control officers use to identify and search suspected smugglers. There had been a list of forty-three suspicious traits. He replaced it with a list of six broad criteria. Is there something suspicious about their physical appearance? Are they nervous? Is there specific intelligence targeting this person? Does the drug-sniffing dog raise an alarm? Is there something amiss in their paperwork or explanations? Has contraband been found that implicates this person?

You'll find nothing here about race or gender or ethnicity, and nothing here about expensive jewelry or deplaning at the middle or the end, or walking briskly or walking aimlessly. Kelly removed all the unstable generalizations, forcing customs officers to make generalizations about things that don't change from one day or one month to the next. Some percentage of smugglers will *always* be nervous, will *always* get their story wrong, and will *always* be caught by the dogs. That's why those kinds of inferences are more reliable than the ones based on whether smugglers are white or black, or carry one bag or two. After Kelly's reforms, the number of searches conducted by the Customs Service dropped by about seventy-five percent, but the number of successful seizures improved by twenty-five percent. The officers went from making fairly lousy decisions about smugglers to making pretty good ones. "We made them more efficient and more effective at what they were doing," Kelly said.

Does the notion of a pit-bull menace rest on a stable or an unstable generalization? The best data we have on breed dangerousness are fatal dog bites, which serve as a useful indicator of just how much havoc certain kinds of dogs are causing. Between the late nineteen-seventies and the late nineteen-nineties, more than twenty-five breeds were involved in fatal attacks in the United States. Pit-bull breeds led the pack, but the variability from year to year is considerable. For instance, in the period from 1981 to 1982 fatalities were caused by five pit bulls, three mixed breeds, two St. Bernards, two

German-shepherd mixes, a pure-bred German shepherd, a husky type, a Doberman, a Chow Chow, a Great Dane, a wolf-dog hybrid, a husky mix, and a pit-bull mix—but no Rottweilers. In 1995 and 1996, the list included ten Rottweilers, four pit bulls, two German shepherds, two huskies, two Chow Chows, two wolf-dog hybrids, two shepherd mixes, a Rottweiler mix, a mixed breed, a Chow Chow mix, and a Great Dane. The kinds of dogs that kill people change over time, because the popularity of certain breeds changes over time. The one thing that doesn't change is the total number of the people killed by dogs. When we have more problems with pit bulls, it's not necessarily a sign that pit bulls are more dangerous than other dogs. It could just be a sign that pit bulls have become more numerous.

"I've seen virtually every breed involved in fatalities, including Pomeranians and everything else, except a beagle or a basset hound," Randall Lockwood, a senior vice-president of the A.S.P.C.A. and one of the country's leading dog-bite experts, told me. "And there's always one or two deaths attributable to malamutes or huskies, although you never hear people clamoring for a ban on those breeds. When I first started looking at fatal dog attacks, they largely involved dogs like German shepherds and shepherd mixes and St. Bernards—which is probably why Stephen King chose to make Cujo a St. Bernard, not a pit bull. I haven't seen a fatality involving a Doberman for decades, whereas in the nineteen-seventies they were quite common. If you wanted a mean dog, back then, you got a Doberman. I don't think I even saw my first pit-bull case until the middle to late nineteen-eighties, and I didn't start seeing Rottweilers until I'd already looked at a few hundred fatal dog attacks. Now those dogs make up the preponderance of fatalities. The point is that it changes over time. It's a reflection of what the dog of choice is among people who want to own an aggressive dog."

There is no shortage of more stable generalizations about dangerous dogs, though. A 1991 study in Denver, for example, compared a hundred and seventy-eight dogs with a history of biting people with a random sample of a hundred and seventy-eight dogs with no history of biting. The breeds were scattered: German shepherds, Akitas, and Chow Chows were among those most heavily represented. (There were no pit bulls among the biting dogs in the study, because Denver banned pit bulls in 1989.) But a number of other, more stable factors stand out. The biters were 6.2 times as likely to be male than female, and 2.6 times as likely to be intact than neutered. The Denver study also found that biters were 2.8 times as likely to be chained as unchained. "About twenty per cent of the dogs involved in fatalities were chained at the time, and had a history of long-term chaining," Lockwood said. "Now, are they chained because they are aggressive or aggressive because they are chained? It's a bit of both. These are animals that have not had an opportunity to become socialized to people. They don't necessarily even know that children are small human beings. They tend to see them as prey."

In many cases, vicious dogs are hungry or in need of medical attention. Often, the dogs had a history of aggressive incidents, and, overwhelmingly, dog-bite victims were children (particularly small boys) who were physically vulnerable to attack and may also have unwittingly done things to provoke the dog, like teasing it, or bothering it while it was eating. The strongest connection of all, though, is between the trait of dog viciousness and certain kinds of dog owners. In about a quarter of fatal dog-bite cases, the dog owners were previously involved in illegal fighting. The dogs that bite people are, in many cases, socially isolated because their owners are socially isolated, and they are vicious because they have owners who want a vicious dog. The junk-yard German shepherd—which looks as if it would rip your throat out—and the German-shepherd guide dog are the same breed. But they are not the same dog, because they have owners with different intentions.

"A fatal dog attack is not just a dog bite by a big or aggressive dog," Lockwood went on. "It is usually a perfect storm of bad human-canine interactions—the wrong dog, the wrong background, the wrong history in the hands of the wrong person in the wrong environmental situation. I've been involved in many legal cases involving fatal dog attacks, and, certainly, it's my impression that these are generally cases where everyone is to blame. You've got the unsupervised three-year-old child wandering in the neighborhood killed by a starved, abused dog owned by the dogfighting boyfriend of some woman who doesn't know where her child is. It's not old Shep sleeping by the fire who suddenly goes bonkers. Usually there are all kinds of other warning signs."

Jayden Clairoux was attacked by Jada, a pit-bull terrier, and her two pit-bull-bullmastiff puppies, Agua and Akasha. The dogs were owned by a twenty-one-year-old man named Shridev Café, who worked in construction and did odd jobs. Five weeks before the Clairoux attack, Café's three dogs got loose and attacked a sixteen-year-old boy and his four-year-old half brother while they were ice skating. The boys beat back the animals with a snow shovel and escaped into a neighbor's house. Café was fined, and he moved the dogs to his seventeen-year-old girlfriend's house. This was not the first time that he ran into trouble last year; a few months later, he was charged with domestic assault, and, in another incident, involving a street brawl, with aggravated assault. "Shridev has personal issues," Cheryl Smith, a canine-behavior specialist who consulted on the case, says. "He's certainly not a very mature person." Agua and Akasha were now about seven months old. The court order in the wake of the first attack required that they be muzzled when they were outside the home and kept in an enclosed yard. But Café did not muzzle them, because, he said later, he couldn't afford muzzles, and apparently no one from the city ever came by to force him to comply. A few times, he talked about taking his dogs to obedience classes, but never did. The subject of neutering them also came up—particularly Agua, the male—but neutering cost a hundred dollars, which he evidently thought was too much money, and when the city temporarily confiscated his animals after the first attack it did not neuter them, either, because Ottawa does not have a policy of preëmptively neutering dogs that bite people.

On the day of the second attack, according to some accounts, a visitor came by the house of Café's girlfriend, and the dogs got wound up. They were put outside, where the snowbanks were high enough so that the back-yard fence could be readily jumped. Jayden Clairoux stopped and stared at the dogs, saying "Puppies, puppies." His mother called out to his father. His father came running, which is the kind of thing that will rile up an aggressive dog. The dogs jumped the fence, and Agua took Jayden's head in his mouth and started to shake. It was a textbook dog-biting case: unneutered, ill-trained, charged-up dogs, with a history of aggression and an irresponsible owner, somehow get loose, and set upon a small child. The dogs had already passed through the animal bureaucracy of Ottawa, and the city could easily have prevented the second attack with the right kind of generalization—a generalization based not on breed but on the known and meaningful connection between dangerous dogs and negligent owners. But that would have required someone to track down Shridev Café, and check to see whether he had bought muzzles, and someone to send the dogs to be neutered after the first attack, and an animal-control law that insured that those whose dogs attack small children forfeit their right to have a dog. It would have required, that is, a more exacting set of generalizations to be more exactingly applied. It's always easier just to ban the breed.

On the Rights of Molotov Man

Appropriation and the Art of Context

Joy Garnett and Susan Meiselas

JOY GARNETT: In the spring of 2003, soon after the United States invaded Iraq, I embarked on a new project having to do with the human figure *in extremis.* It was a project born of frustration and anger. All of my paintings are based on photographs, and so for this project—which I came to think of as the Riot series—I searched the Web for images of figures in extreme emotional or physical states. I saved the most promising images in folders on my computer desktop, and I let them sit for a while so I could forget where I found them. I wanted my choices to be based more on aesthetic criteria than on my emotional attachment to their narratives. Eventually I would look through the folders again to see what struck me.

After a few months of this, I decided to go ahead and make the paintings. A photo of a man throwing a Molotov cocktail grabbed my attention, and he became my first subject. I rendered him larger than life—the painting is nearly six feet tall—and I was sufficiently pleased with the results. I went to work on other paintings: shouting demonstrators, angry skinheads, an Air Force pilot and his girl in an emotional embrace, frat boys jumping over bonfires, screaming punk rockers.

When a gallery in New York City offered to exhibit the Riot paintings in January 2004, the directors and I agreed that the "Molotov" painting was emblematic of the series, and so we chose it for the image on the announcement card.

Partway through the exhibition, I received an email from an acquaintance who had received the card. He said, "That image is from a photograph by Susan Meiselas. Is she aware of your use? And if not, are you going to ask her permission?" He also sent me the link to the website of the Magnum Photo Agency, which represents Susan. The original photograph was different from the fragment I had found. The man with the Molotov cocktail was the central figure of a larger scene, for one thing, and he was also brandishing a rifle. The man, it turned out, was a Nicaraguan rebel. The photograph was from *Nicaragua,* Susan's celebrated photo essay on the revolution, published by Pantheon in 1981. I was fascinated by the original image and the

richness of the narrative behind it, but it didn't make any difference to me in terms of permission or credit.

Shortly after the exhibit closed, though, I received a letter sent by a lawyer on Susan's behalf. The letter informed me that I had infringed upon Susan's copyright and that I was "sailing under the flag of piracy." It asked that I give credit to the source in any exhibition of the painting and that I agree to seek written permission from her before I made any further reproductions of the painting.

I immediately made an appointment with a lawyer, and I also went online to an artists' discussion group I had long been frequenting, a virtual place hosted by a not-for-profit arts organization called Rhizome.org. Subscribers to this group were given to discussing their philosophies of appropriation, sampling, remixing, and current copyright controversies. To open my situation to public discussion was, for me, a natural thing to do. I thought that if there was an argument to be made this would be the place to make it. I was feeling paranoid, though, so I did not name names or post a link to Susan's photograph. Instead, we limited ourselves to looking at the image of my painting and discussing the reasons why this might be happening to me.

Air Strip and *Emo* by Joy Garnett. Courtesy the artist.

Within a few days I was ready to respond. I wrote a letter to Susan's lawyer. As requested, I would include a credit line in all current and future displays of the painting itself, as well as on any reproductions, citing Susan's photograph as its source. But I would not, I said, agree to seek written approval from Susan anytime my painting might be reproduced somewhere. I thought this was too difficult a burden to accept under the circumstances. Susan's lawyer responded with a much longer letter that cited cases to support Susan's position and requested a $2,000 licensing fee for the additional uses.

I was frightened, and so I decided to remove the image of *Molotov* from my website. When I announced this decision to my online discussion group at Rhizome, though, something unexpected—something interesting—happened.

First, I learned that an artist named Tim Whidden had copied the *Molotov* webpage and uploaded it to his own website, creating a "mirror" page. After he posted the link to Rhizome, several other artists followed suit. Mirrors of *Molotov* started popping up all over the place.

Then things took an even odder turn. An artist named Mark River appropriated a portion of *Molotov* and made a collage depicting this act of mirroring:

Artwork courtesy of M. River of MTAA.

Artwork courtesy of Ryan Griffis.

Artwork courtesy of Patrick Lichty.

This was the green light: soon, dozens of artists were making "copyfight" agitprop based on *Molotov* in a kind of solidarity campaign. Before long, the campaign came to be known as "Joywar," a play on words referring to an infamous, earlier legal battle—between etoy, the arts collective, and eToys, the online toy retailer—known as "Toywar."

Over the course of the next few days, many *Molotov* appropriations were posted on Rhizome.

Then my story hit the blogs and Joywar went global. The story was translated—and mistranslated—onto various blogs and e-zines in French, Italian, Chinese, and Czech. The Italians were especially horrified, absolutely certain as they were that Pepsi was suing me.

"The American artist Joy Garnett, whose paintings a
images, is faced with a legal action for thousands of

This has nothing to do with the protection of livelih
the suppression of free speech and free artistic practi

Don't let the schoolyard bullies win!

Show your solidarity with Joy by grabbing this imag
website or by making your own artwork derived fro
this or this or this or this or this or this or this or this
or this or this or this or this or this or this."

Posted by Adam at March 25, 2004 09:15 PM

Comments

Please fix the links...

+LINK Posted by: FRANK* at March 26, 2004 10:05 AM

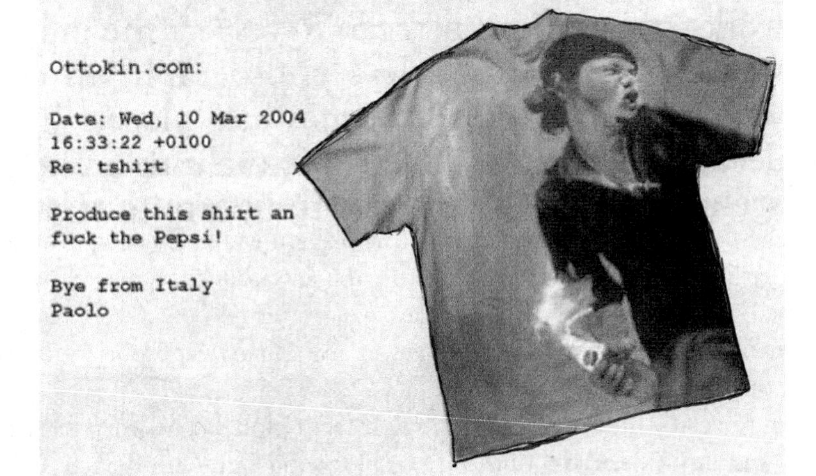

Ottokin.com:

Date: Wed, 10 Mar 2004
16:33:22 +0100
Re: tshirt

Produce this shirt an
fuck the Pepsi!

Bye from Italy
Paolo

Artwork (top) courtesy of Pau Waelder.

In this swirl of creative agitprop and commentary, several questions came to the fore: Does the author of a documentary photograph—a document whose mission is, in part, to provide the public with a record of events of social and historical value—have the right to control the content of this document for all time? Should artists be allowed to decide who can comment on their work and how? Can copyright law, as it stands, function in any way except as a gag order? These remain open questions for many people. It was a blogger named "nmazca," however, who posed what has, for me, become the central question in all of the activity surrounding *Molotov*. Referring to the lone figure of that Sandinista rebel, nmazca asked, "Who owns the rights to this man's struggle?"

SUSAN MEISELAS: My own relationship to this picture obviously is very different from Joy's. No one can "control" art, of course, but it is important to me—in fact, it is central to my work—that I do what I can to respect the individuality of the people I photograph, all of whom exist in specific times and places. Indeed, Joy's practice of decontextualizing an image as a painter is precisely the opposite of my own hope as a photographer to contextualize an image. So here is some context: I took the picture below in Nicaragua, which had been ruled by the Somoza family since before World War II. The FSLN, popularly known as the Sandinistas, had opposed that regime since the early Sixties. I took the picture below on a hillside known as the place where Anastasio Somoza's national guard would execute suspected rebels.

And more context: I made the image in question on July 16, 1979, the eve of the day that Somoza would flee Nicaragua forever. What is happening is anything but a "riot." In fact, the man is throwing his bomb at a Somoza national

Photograph © Susan Meiselas/Magnum Photos.

Photograph © Susan Meiselas/Magnum Photos.

guard garrison, one of the last such garrisons remaining in Somoza's hands. It was an important moment in the history of Nicaragua—the Sandinistas would soon take power and hold that power for another decade—and this image ended up representing that moment for a long time to come. I don't think it was published anywhere at that time, and it was only published in my book a year or so later, but in the years since, the image has been subjected to many kinds of reappropriations, most of which, far from condemning, I have welcomed.

The first time I re-encountered "Molotov Man"—as I had come to think of him—was in 1980, when I saw these matchbox covers celebrating the first anniversary of the Sandinista revolution.

Photograph © Susan Meiselas/Magnum Photos.

Photograph © Susan Meiselas/Magnum Photos.

Over the years, though, Molotov Man kept appearing and reappearing, used by different players for different purposes. The leaders of Nicaragua's Catholic Church, for instance, noticed that he had been wearing a crucifix, so they reproduced his image on the cover of this magazine in tribute to Gaspar García Laviana, a Jesuit priest killed in 1978 while fighting the Somoza regime. (This was before the Church itself turned against the Sandinistas.)

In 1983, as CIA-funded Contras flooded across the Honduran border and the counterrevolution gathered strength, the Sandinistas attempted a kind

Photograph © Susan Meiselas/Magnum Photos.

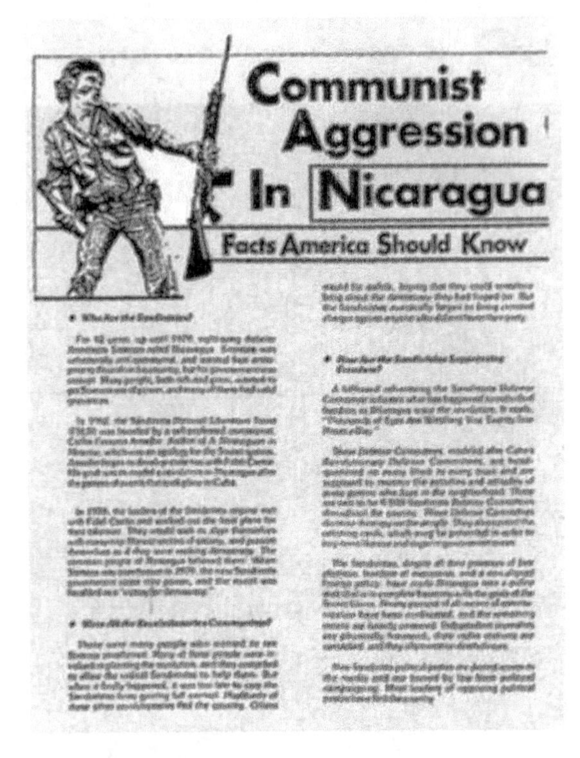

Communist Aggression In Nicaragua

Facts America Should Know

Photograph © Susan Meiselas/Magnum Photos.

of viral campaign, pre-Internet, on the walls all over Nicaragua to raise a popular militia. They hoped to associate Molotov Man's image with the Spanish Civil War–era anti-fascist slogan NO PASARÁN—"they shall not pass."

At the same time, the Contras themselves used Molotov Man in their fund-raising campaign to gain further support in the United States to fight the Sandinistas.

Photograph © Susan Meiselas/Magnum Photos.

Photograph © Susan Meiselas/Magnum Photos.

In 1990, I returned to Nicaragua with two filmmakers to document what had happened to the people in my earlier photographs. I learned that "Molotov Man" was Pablo Arauz, who was known as "Bareta" during the war, still identified himself as a Sandinista, and had ended up with a family and a pretty good job delivering lumber. (He owned his own truck.)

Photograph © Susan Meiselas/Magnum Photos.

Photograph © Susan Meiselas/Magnum Photos.

Meanwhile, the Sandinistas continued to paint Molotov Man on the walls of Nicaragua, along with other heroes of the revolution, including Daniel Ortega's brother Camilo (in glasses), who was killed by Somoza forces in 1978.

Interestingly, when the Sandinistas were voted from office in 1990, that same wall in the province of Masaya was blackened over as if you could just erase history.

Yet when I returned to Nicaragua in 1999, on the twentieth anniversary of the revolution, that same image of Molotov Man was all over the plazas of Managua, only now it was in T-shirt form.

Photograph © Susan Meiselas/Magnum Photos.

Photograph © Susan Meiselas/Magnum Photos.

Bareta remained the symbol of that uprising for the twenty-fifth-anniversary celebration in 2004.

That same year, I decided to explore and document how the people of Nicaragua were interacting with this history, and so I brought nineteen mural-sized prints—Molotov Man among them—back to the places I had shot the original images.

In November 2006, Daniel Ortega was elected president of Nicaragua, and the Sandinistas were once again set to take power. The following month, Robert Gates, the number-two man at the CIA when it was funding the Contras, was confirmed by Congress as secretary of defense. He will now prosecute the very war that Joy says caused her to claim the image of Pablo Arauz.

There is no denying in this digital age that images are increasingly dislocated and far more easily decontextualized. Technology allows us to do many things, but that does not mean we must do them. Indeed, it seems to me that if history is working against context, then we must, as artists, work all the harder to reclaim that context. We owe this debt of specificity not just to one another but to our subjects, with whom we have an implicit contract.

I never did sue Joy in the end, nor did I collect any licensing fees. But I still feel strongly, as I watch Pablo Arauz's context being stripped away—as I watch him being converted into the emblem of an abstract riot—that it would be a betrayal of him if I did not at least protest the diminishment of his act of defiance.

Letter from Birmingham Jail

Martin Luther King, Jr.

April 16, 1963

My Dear Fellow Clergymen:

While confined here in the Birmingham city jail, I came across your recent statement calling my present activities "unwise and untimely." Seldom do I pause to answer criticism of my work and ideas. If I sought to answer all the criticisms that cross my desk, my secretaries would have little time for anything other than such correspondence in the course of the day, and I would have no time for constructive work. But since I feel that you are men of genuine good will and that your criticisms are sincerely set forth, I want to try to answer your statement in what I hope will be patient and reasonable terms.

I think I should indicate why I am here in Birmingham, since you have been influenced by the view which argues against "outsiders coming in." I have the honor of serving as president of the Southern Christian Leadership Conference, an organization operating in every southern state, with headquarters in Atlanta, Georgia. We have some eighty-five affiliated organizations across the South, and one of them is the Alabama Christian Movement for Human Rights. Frequently we share staff, educational, and financial resources with our affiliates. Several months ago the affiliate here in Birmingham asked us to be on call to engage in a nonviolent direct-action program if such were deemed necessary. We readily consented, and when the hour came we lived up to our promise. So I, along with several members of my staff, am here because I was invited here. I am here because I have organizational ties here.

But more basically, I am in Birmingham because injustice is here. Just as the prophets of the eighth century B.C. left their villages and carried their "thus saith the Lord" far beyond the boundaries of their home towns, and just as the Apostle Paul left his village of Tarsus and carried the gospel of Jesus Christ to the far corners of the GrecoRoman world, so am I compelled to carry the gospel of freedom beyond my own home town. Like Paul, I must constantly respond to the Macedonian call for aid.

Moreover, I am cognizant of the interrelatedness of all communities and states. I cannot sit idly by in Atlanta and not be concerned about what happens in Birmingham. Injustice anywhere is a threat to justice everywhere. We are caught in an inescapable network of mutuality, tied in a single garment of destiny. Whatever affects one directly, affects all indirectly. Never again can we afford to live with the narrow, provincial, "outside agitator" idea. Anyone who lives inside the United States can never be considered an outsider anywhere within its bounds.

You deplore the demonstrations taking place in Birmingham. But your statement, I am sorry to say, fails to express a similar concern for the conditions that brought about the demonstrations. I am sure that none of you would want to rest content with the superficial kind of social analysis that deals merely with effects and does not grapple with underlying causes. It is unfortunate that demonstrations are taking place in Birmingham, but it is even more unfortunate that the city's white power structure left the Negro community with no alternative.

In any nonviolent campaign there are four basic steps: collection of the facts to determine whether injustices exist; negotiation; self-purification; and direct action. We have gone through all these steps in Birmingham. There can be no gainsaying the fact that racial injustice engulfs this community. Birmingham is probably the most thoroughly segregated city in the United States. Its ugly record of brutality is widely known. Negroes have experienced grossly unjust treatment in courts. There have been more unsolved bombings of Negro homes and churches in Birmingham than in any other city in the nation. These are the hard, brutal facts of the case. On the basis of these conditions, Negro leaders sought to negotiate with the city fathers. But the latter consistently refused to engage in good-faith negotiation.

Then, last September, came the opportunity to talk with leaders of Birmingham's economic community. In the course of the negotiations, certain promises were made by the merchants—for example, to remove the stores' humiliating racial signs. On the basis of these promises, the Reverend Fred Shuttlesworth and the leaders of the Alabama Christian Movement for Human Rights agreed to a moratorium on all demonstrations. As the weeks and months went by, we realized that we were the victims of a broken promise. A few signs, briefly removed, returned; the others remained.

As in so many past experiences, our hopes had been blasted, and the shadow of deep disappointment settled upon us. We had no alternative except to prepare for direct action, whereby we would present our very bodies as means of laying our case before the conscience of the local and the national community. Mindful of the difficulties involved, we decided to undertake a process of self-purification. We began a series of workshops on nonviolence, and we repeatedly asked ourselves: "Are you able to accept blows without retaliating?"

"Are you able to endure the ordeal of jail?" We decided to schedule our direct-action program for the Easter season, realizing that except for Christmas, this is the main shopping period of the year. Knowing that a strong economic-withdrawal program would be the by-product of direct action, we felt that this would be the best time to bring pressure to bear on the merchants for the needed change.

Then it occurred to us that Birmingham's mayoral election was coming up in March, and we speedily decided to postpone action until after election day. When we discovered that the Commissioner of Public Safety, Eugene "Bull" Connor, had piled up enough votes to be in the run-off, we decided again to postpone action until the day after the run-off so that the demonstrations could not be used to cloud the issues. Like many others, we waited to see Mr. Connor defeated, and to this end we endured postponement after postponement. Having aided in this community need, we felt that our direct-action program could be delayed no longer.

You may well ask, "Why direct action? Why sit-ins, marches, and so forth? Isn't negotiation a better path?" You are quite right in calling for negotiation. Indeed, this is the very purpose of direct action. Nonviolent direct action seeks to create such a crisis and foster such a tension that a community which has constantly refused to negotiate is forced to confront the issue. It seeks so to dramatize the issue that it can no longer be ignored. My citing the creation of tension as part of the work of the nonviolent-resistor may sound rather shocking. But I must confess that I am not afraid of the word "tension." I have earnestly opposed violent tension, but there is a type of constructive, nonviolent tension which is necessary for growth. Just as Socrates felt that it was necessary to create a tension in the mind so that individuals could rise from the bondage of myths and half-truths to the unfettered realm of creative analysis and objective appraisal, so must we see the need for nonviolent gadflies to create the kind of tension in society that will help men rise from the dark depths of prejudice and racism to the majestic heights of understanding and brotherhood.

The purpose of our direct-action program is to create a situation so crisis-packed that it will inevitably open the door to negotiation. I therefore concur with you in your call for negotiation. Too long has our beloved Southland been bogged down in a tragic effort to live in monologue rather than dialogue.

One of the basic points in your statement is that the action that I and my associates have taken in Birmingham is untimely. Some have asked: "Why didn't you give the new city administration time to act?" The only answer that I can give to this query is that the new Birmingham administration must be prodded about as much as the outgoing one, before it will act. We are sadly mistaken if we feel that the election of Albert Boutwell as mayor will bring the millennium to Birmingham. While Mr. Boutwell is a much more gentle

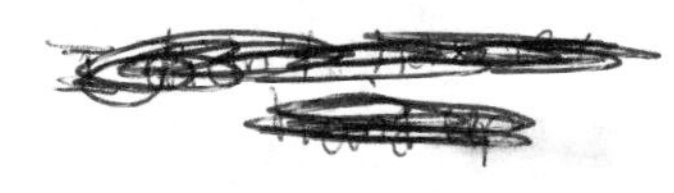

person than Mr. Connor, they are both segregationists, dedicated to maintenance of the status quo. I have hoped that Mr. Boutwell will be reasonable enough to see the futility of massive resistance to desegregation. But he will not see this without pressure from devotees of civil rights. My friends, I must say to you that we have not made a single gain in civil rights without determined legal and nonviolent pressure. Lamentably, it is an historical fact that privileged groups seldom give up their privileges voluntarily. Individuals may see the moral light and voluntarily give up their unjust posture; but, as Reinhold Niebuhr has reminded us, groups tend to be more immoral than individuals.

We know through painful experience that freedom is never voluntarily given by the oppressor; it must be demanded by the oppressed. Frankly, I have yet to engage in a direct-action campaign that was "well-timed" in the view of those who have not suffered unduly from the disease of segregation. For years now I have heard the word "Wait!" It rings in the ear of every Negro with piercing familiarity. This "Wait" has almost always meant "Never." We must come to see, with one of our distinguished jurists, that "justice too long delayed is justice denied."

We have waited for more than 340 years for our constitutional and God-given rights. The nations of Asia and Africa are moving with jetlike speed toward gaining political independence, but we still creep at horse-and-buggy pace toward gaining a cup of coffee at a lunch counter. Perhaps it is easy for those who have never felt the stinging darts of segregation to say, "Wait." But when you have seen vicious mobs lynch your mothers and fathers at will and drown your sisters and brothers at whim; when you have seen hate-filled policemen curse, kick, and even kill your black brothers and sisters; when you see the vast majority of your twenty million Negro brothers smothering in an airtight cage of poverty in the midst of an affluent society; when you suddenly find your tongue twisted and your speech stammering as you seek to explain to your six-year-old daughter why she can't go to the public amusement park that has just been advertised on television, and see tears welling up in her eyes when she is told that Funtown is closed to colored children, and see ominous clouds of inferiority beginning to form in her little mental sky, and see her beginning to distort her personality by developing an unconscious bitterness toward white people; when you have to concoct an answer for a five-year-old son who is asking, "Daddy, why do white people treat colored people so mean?"; when you take a cross-country drive and find it necessary to sleep night after night in the uncomfortable corners of your automobile because no motel will accept you; when you are humiliated day in and day out by nagging signs reading "white" and "colored"; when your first name becomes "nigger," your middle name becomes "boy" (however old you are) and your last name becomes "John," and your wife and mother are never given the respected title "Mrs."; when you are harried by day and haunted by night by the fact that you are a Negro, living constantly at tiptoe stance, never quite knowing what to expect next, and are plagued with inner fears and outer resentments; when you are forever fighting a degenerating sense of "nobodiness"—then you will understand why we find it difficult to wait. There comes a time when the cup of endurance runs over, and men are no longer willing to be plunged into the abyss of despair. I hope, sirs, you can understand our legitimate and unavoidable impatience.

You express a great deal of anxiety over our willingness to break laws. This is certainly a legitimate concern. Since we so diligently urge people to obey the Supreme Court's decision of 1954 outlawing segregation in the public schools, at first glance it may seem rather paradoxical for us consciously to break laws. One may well ask: "How can you advocate breaking some laws and obeying others?" The answer lies in the fact that there are two types of laws: just and unjust. I would be the first to advocate obeying just laws. One has not only a legal but a moral responsibility to obey just laws. Conversely, one has a moral responsibility to disobey unjust laws. I would agree with St. Augustine that "an unjust law is no law at all."

Now, what is the difference between the two? How does one determine whether a law is just or unjust? A just law is a man-made code that squares with the moral law or the law of God. An unjust law is a code that is out of harmony with the moral law. To put it in the terms of St. Thomas Aquinas: An unjust law is a human law that is not rooted in eternal law and natural law. Any law that uplifts human personality is just. Any law that degrades human personality is unjust. All segregation statutes are unjust because segregation distorts the soul and damages the personality. It gives the segregator a false sense of superiority and the segregated a false sense of inferiority. Segregation, to use the terminology of the Jewish philosopher Martin Buber, substitutes an "I-it" relationship for an "I-thou" relationship and ends up relegating persons to the status of things. Hence segregation is not only politically, economically, and sociologically unsound, it is morally wrong and sinful. Paul Tillich has said that sin is separation. Is not segregation an existential expression of man's tragic separation, his awful estrangement, his terrible sinfulness? Thus it is that I can urge men to obey the 1954 decision of the Supreme Court, for it is morally right; and I can urge them to disobey segregation ordinances, for they are morally wrong.

Let us consider a more concrete example of just and unjust laws. An unjust law is a code that a numerical or power majority group compels a minority group to obey but does not make binding on itself. This is *difference* made legal. By the same token, a just law is a code that a majority compels a minority to follow and that it is willing to follow itself. This is *sameness* made legal.

Let me give another explanation. A law is unjust if it is inflicted on a minority that, as a result of being denied the right to vote, had no part in enacting or devising the law. Who can say that the legislature of Alabama which set up that state's segregation laws was democratically elected? Throughout Alabama all sorts of devious methods are used to prevent Negroes from becoming registered voters, and there are some counties in which, even though Negroes constitute a majority of the population, not a single Negro is registered. Can any law enacted under such circumstances be considered democratically structured?

Sometimes a law is just on its face and unjust in its application. For instance, I have been arrested on a charge of parading without a permit. Now, there is nothing wrong in having an ordinance which requires a permit for a parade. But such an ordinance becomes unjust when it is used to maintain segregation and to deny citizens the First-Amendment privilege of peaceful assembly and protest.

I hope you are able to see the distinction I am trying to point out. In no sense do I advocate evading or defying the law, as would the rabid segregationist. That would lead to anarchy. One who breaks an unjust law must do so openly, lovingly, and with a willingness to accept the penalty. I submit that an individual who breaks a law that conscience tells him is unjust, and who willingly accepts the penalty of imprisonment in order to arouse the conscience of the community over its injustice, is in reality expressing the highest respect for law.

Of course, there is nothing new about this kind of civil disobedience. It was evidenced sublimely in the refusal of Shadrach, Meshach, and Abednego to obey the laws of Nebuchadnezzar, on the ground that a higher moral law was at stake. It was practiced superbly by the early Christians, who were willing to face hungry lions and the excruciating pain of chopping blocks rather than submit to certain unjust laws of the Roman Empire. To a degree, academic freedom is a reality today because Socrates practiced civil disobedience. In our own nation, the Boston Tea Party represented a massive act of civil disobedience.

We should never forget that everything Adolph Hitler did in Germany was "legal" and everything the Hungarian freedom fighters did in Hungary was "illegal." It was "illegal" to aid and comfort a Jew in Hitler's Germany. Even so, I am sure that, had I lived in Germany at the time, I would have aided and comforted my Jewish brothers. If today I lived in a Communist country where certain principles dear to the Christian faith are suppressed, I would openly advocate disobeying that country's anti-religious laws.

I must make two honest confessions to you, my Christian and Jewish brothers. First, I must confess that over the past few years I have been gravely disappointed with the white moderate. I have almost reached the regrettable conclusion that the Negro's great stumbling block in his stride toward freedom is not the White Citizens Counciler or the Ku Klux Klanner, but the white moderate, who is more devoted to "order" than to justice; who prefers a negative peace which is the absence of tension to a positive peace which is the presence of justice; who constantly says, "I agree with you in the goal you seek, but I cannot agree with your methods of direct action"; who paternalistically believes he can set the timetable for another man's freedom; who lives by a mythical concept of time and who constantly advises the Negro to wait for a "more convenient season." Shallow understanding from people of good will is more frustrating than absolute misunderstanding from people of ill will. Lukewarm acceptance is much more bewildering than outright rejection.

I had hoped that the white moderate would understand that law and order exist for the purpose of establishing justice and that when they fail in this purpose they become the dangerously structured dams that block the flow of social progress. I had hoped that the white moderate would understand that the present tension in the South is a necessary phase of the transition from an obnoxious negative peace, in which the Negro passively accepted his unjust plight, to a substantive and positive peace, in which all men will respect the dignity and worth of human personality. Actually, we who engage in nonviolent direct action are not the creators of tension. We merely bring to the surface the hidden tension that is already alive. We bring it out in the open, where it can be seen and dealt with. Like a boil that can never be cured so long as it is covered up but must be opened with all its ugliness to the natural medicines of air and light, injustice must be exposed, with all the tension its exposure creates, to the light of human conscience and the air of national opinion, before it can be cured.

In your statement you assert that our actions, even though peaceful, must be condemned because they precipitate violence. But is this a logical assertion? Isn't this like condemning a robbed man because his possession of money precipitated the evil act of robbery? Isn't this like condemning Socrates because his unswerving commitment to truth and his philosophical inquiries precipitated the act by the misguided populace in which they made him drink hemlock? Isn't this like condemning Jesus because his unique God-consciousness and never-ceasing devotion to God's will precipitated the evil act of crucifixion? We must come to see that, as the federal courts have consistently affirmed, it is wrong to urge an individual to cease his efforts to gain his basic constitutional rights because the quest may precipitate violence. Society must protect the robbed and punish the robber.

I had also hoped that the white moderate would reject the myth concerning time in relation to the struggle for freedom. I have just received a letter from a white brother in Texas. He writes: "All Christians know that the colored people will receive equal rights eventually, but it is possible that you are in too great a religious hurry. It has taken Christianity almost two thousand years to accomplish what it has. The teachings of Christ take time to come to earth." Such an attitude stems from a tragic misconception of time, from the strangely irrational notion that there is something in the very flow of time that will inevitably cure all ills. Actually, time itself is neutral; it can be used either destructively or constructively. More and more I feel that the people of ill will have used time much more effectively than have the people of good will. We will have to repent in this generation not merely for the hateful words and actions of the bad people, but for the appalling silence of the good people. Human progress never rolls in on wheels of inevitability; it comes through the tireless efforts of men willing to be coworkers with God, and without his hard work, time itself becomes an ally of the forces of social stagnation. We must use time creatively, in the knowledge that the time is always ripe to do right. Now is the time to make real the promise of democracy and transform our pending national elegy into a creative psalm of brotherhood. Now is the time to lift our national policy from the quicksand of racial injustice to the solid rock of human dignity.

You speak of our activity in Birmingham as extreme. At first I was rather disappointed that fellow clergymen would see my nonviolent efforts as those of an extremist. I began thinking about the fact that I stand in the middle of two opposing forces in the Negro community. One is a force of complacency, made up in part of Negroes who, as a result of long years of oppression, are so drained of self-respect and a sense of "somebodiness" that they have adjusted to segregation; and in part of a few middle-class Negroes who, because of a degree of academic and economic security and because in some ways they profit by segregation, have become insensitive to the problems of the masses. The other force is one of bitterness and hatred, and it comes perilously close to advocating violence. It is expressed in the various black nationalist groups that are springing up across the nation, the largest and best-known being Elijah Muhammad's Muslim movement. Nourished by the Negro's frustration over the continued existence of racial discrimination, this movement is made up of people who have lost faith in America, who have absolutely repudiated Christianity, and who have concluded that the white man is an incorrigible "devil."

I have tried to stand between these two forces, saying that we need emulate neither the "do-nothingism" of the complacent nor the hatred and despair of the black nationalist. For there is the more excellent way of love and nonviolent protest. I am grateful to God that, through the influence of the Negro church, the way of nonviolence became an integral part of our struggle.

If this philosophy had not emerged, by now many streets of the South would, I am convinced, be flowing with blood. And I am further convinced that if our white brothers dismiss as "rabble-rousers" and "outside agitators" those of us who employ nonviolent direct action, and if they refuse to support our nonviolent efforts, millions of Negroes will, out of frustration and despair, seek solace and security in black-nationalist ideologies—a development that would inevitably lead to a frightening racial nightmare.

Oppressed people cannot remain oppressed forever. The yearning for freedom eventually manifests itself, and that is what has happened to the American Negro. Something within has reminded him of his birthright of freedom, and something without has reminded him that it can be gained. Consciously or unconsciously, he has been caught up by the *Zeitgeist,* and with his black brothers of Africa and his brown and yellow brothers of Asia, South America, and the Caribbean, the United States Negro is moving with a sense of great urgency toward the promised land of racial justice. If one recognizes this vital urge that has engulfed the Negro community, one should readily understand why public demonstrations are taking place. The Negro has many pent-up resentments and latent frustrations, and he must release them. So let him march; let him make prayer pilgrimages to the city hall; let him go on freedom rides—and try to understand why he must do so. If his repressed emotions are not released in nonviolent ways, they will seek expression through violence; this is not a threat but a fact of history. So I have not said to my people, "Get rid of your discontent." Rather, I have tried to say that this normal and healthy discontent can be channeled into the creative outlet of nonviolent direct action. And now this approach is being termed extremist.

But though I was initially disappointed at being categorized as an extremist, as I continued to think about the matter I gradually gained a measure of satisfaction from the label. Was not Jesus an extremist for love: "Love your enemies, bless them that curse you, do good to them that hate you, and pray for them which despitefully use you, and persecute you." Was not Amos an extremist for justice: "Let justice roll down like waters and righteousness like an ever-flowing stream." Was not Paul an extremist for the Christian gospel: "I bear in my body the marks of the Lord Jesus." Was not Martin Luther an extremist: "Here I stand; I cannot do otherwise, so help me God." And John Bunyan: "I will stay in jail to the end of my days before I make a butchery of my conscience." And Abraham Lincoln: "This nation cannot survive half slave and half free." And Thomas Jefferson: "We hold these truths to be self-evident, that all men are created equal. . . ." So the question is not whether we will be extremists, but what kind of extremists we will be. Will we be extremists for hate or for love? Will we be extremists for the preservation of injustice or for the extension of justice? In that dramatic scene on Calvary's hill three men were crucified. We must never forget that all three were crucified for the same crime—the crime of extremism. Two were extremists for immorality, and thus fell below their environment. The other, Jesus

Christ, was an extremist for love, truth, and goodness, and thereby rose above his environment. Perhaps the South, the nation, and the world are in dire need of creative extremists.

I had hoped that the white moderate would see this need. Perhaps I was too optimistic; perhaps I expected too much. I suppose I should have realized that few members of the oppressor race can understand the deep groans and passionate yearnings of the oppressed race, and still fewer have the vision to see that injustice must be rooted out by strong, persistent, and determined action. I am thankful, however, that some of our white brothers in the South have grasped the meaning of this social revolution and committed themselves to it. They are still all too few in quantity, but they are big in quality. Some—such as Ralph McGill, Lillian Smith, Harry Golden, James McBride Dabbs, Ann Braden, and Sarah Patton Boyle—have written about our struggle in eloquent and prophetic terms. Others have marched with us down nameless streets of the South. They have languished in filthy, roach-infested jails, suffering the abuse and brutality of policemen who view them as "dirty nigger-lovers." Unlike so many of their moderate brothers and sisters, they have recognized the urgency of the moment and sensed the need for powerful "action" antidotes to combat the disease of segregation.

Let me take note of my other major disappointment. I have been so greatly disappointed with the white church and its leadership. Of course, there are some notable exceptions. I am not unmindful of the fact that each of you has taken some significant stands on this issue. I commend you, Reverend Stallings, for your Christian stand on this past Sunday, in welcoming Negroes to your worship service on a nonsegregated basis. I commend the Catholic leaders of this state for integrating Spring Hill College several years ago.

But despite these notable exceptions, I must honestly reiterate that I have been disappointed with the church. I do not say this as one of those negative critics who can always find something wrong with the church. I say this as a minister of the gospel, who loves the church; who was nurtured in its bosom; who has been sustained by its spiritual blessings and who will remain true to it as long as the cord of life shall lengthen.

When I was suddenly catapulted into the leadership of the bus protest in Montgomery, Alabama, a few years ago, I felt we would be supported by the white church. I felt that the white ministers, priests, and rabbis of the South would be among our strongest allies. Instead, some have been outright opponents, refusing to understand the freedom movement and misrepresenting its leaders; all too many others have been more cautious than courageous and have remained silent behind the anesthetizing security of stained-glass windows.

In spite of my shattered dreams, I came to Birmingham with the hope that the white religious leadership of this community would see the justice of our cause and, with deep moral concern, would serve as the channel through which our just grievances could reach the power structure. I had hoped that each of you would understand. But again I have been disappointed.

There was a time when the church was very powerful—in the time when the early Christians rejoiced at being deemed worthy to suffer for what they believed. In those days the church was not merely a thermometer that recorded the ideas and principles of popular opinion; it was a thermostat that transformed the mores of society. Whenever the early Christians entered a town, the people in power became disturbed and immediately sought to convict the Christians for being "disturbers of the peace" and "outside agitators." But the Christians pressed on, in the conviction that they were "a colony of heaven," called to obey God rather than man. Small in number, they were big in commitment. They were too God-intoxicated to be "astronomically intimidated." By their effort and example they brought an end to such ancient evils as infanticide and gladiatorial contests.

Things are different now. So often the contemporary church is a weak, ineffectual voice with an uncertain sound. So often it is an archdefender of the status quo. Far from being disturbed by the presence of the church, the power structure of the average community is consoled by the church's silent—and often even vocal—sanction of things as they are.

But the judgment of God is upon the church as never before. If today's church does not recapture the sacrificial spirit of the early church, it will lose its authenticity, forfeit the loyalty of millions, and be dismissed as an irrelevant social club with no meaning for the twentieth century. Every day I meet young people whose disappointment with the church has turned into outright disgust.

Perhaps I have once again been too optimistic. Is organized religion too inextricably bound to the status quo to save our nation and the world? Perhaps I must turn my faith to the inner spiritual church, the church within the church, as the true *ekklesia* and the hope of the world. But again I am thankful to God that some noble souls from the ranks of organized religion have broken loose from the paralyzing chains of conformity and joined us as active partners in the struggle for freedom. They have left their secure congregations and walked the streets of Albany, Georgia, with us. They have gone down the highways of the South on torturous rides for freedom. Yes, they have gone to jail with us. Some have been dismissed from their churches, have lost the support of their bishops and fellow ministers. But they have acted in the faith that right defeated is stronger than evil triumphant. Their witness has been the spiritual salt that has preserved the true meaning of the gospel in these troubled times. They have carved a tunnel of hope through the dark mountain of disappointment.

I hope the church as a whole will meet the challenge of this decisive hour. But even if the church does not come to the aid of justice, I have no despair about the future. I have no fear about the outcome of our struggle in Birmingham, even if our motives are at present misunderstood. We will reach the goal of freedom in Birmingham and all over the nation, because the goal of America is freedom. Abused and scorned though we may be, our destiny is tied up with America's destiny. Before the pilgrims landed at Plymouth, we were here. Before the pen of Jefferson etched the majestic words of the Declaration of Independence across the pages of history, we were here. For more than two centuries our forebears labored in this country without wages; they made cotton king; they built the homes of their masters while suffering gross injustice and shameful humiliation—and yet out of a bottomless vitality they continued to thrive and develop. If the inexpressible cruelties of slavery could not stop us, the opposition we now face will surely fail. We will win our freedom because the sacred heritage of our nation and the eternal will of God are embodied in our echoing demands.

Before closing I feel impelled to mention one other point in your statement that has troubled me profoundly. You warmly commended the Birmingham police for keeping "order" and "preventing violence." I doubt that you would have so warmly commended the police force if you had seen its dogs sinking their teeth into unarmed, nonviolent Negroes. I doubt that you would so quickly commend the policemen if you were to observe their ugly and inhumane treatment of Negroes here in the city jail; if you were to watch them push and curse old Negro women and young Negro girls; if you were to see them slap and kick old Negro men and young boys; if you were to observe them, as they did on two occasions, refuse to give us food because we wanted to sing our grace together. I cannot join you in your praise of the Birmingham police department.

It is true that the police have exercised a degree of discipline handling the demonstrators. In this sense they have conducted themselves rather "nonviolently" in public. But for what purpose? To preserve the evil system of segregation. Over the past few years I have consistently preached that nonviolence demands that the means we use must be as pure as the ends we seek. I have tried to make clear that it is wrong to use immoral means to attain moral ends. But now I must affirm that it is just as wrong, or perhaps even more so, to use moral means to preserve immoral ends. Perhaps Mr. Connor and his policemen have been rather nonviolent in public, as was Chief Pritchett in Albany, Georgia, but they have used the moral means of nonviolence to maintain the immoral end of racial injustice. As T. S. Eliot has said, "The last temptation is the greatest treason: To do the right deed for the wrong reason."

I wish you had commended the Negro sit-inners and demonstrators of Birmingham for their sublime courage, their willingness to suffer, and their amazing discipline in the midst of great provocation. One day the South will recognize its real heroes. They will be the James Merediths, with the noble sense of purpose that enables them to face jeering and hostile mobs, and with the agonizing loneliness that characterizes the life of the pioneer. They will be old, oppressed, battered Negro women, symbolized in a seventy-two-year-old woman in Montgomery, Alabama, who rose up with a sense of dignity and with her people decided not to ride segregated buses, and who responded with ungrammatical profundity to one who inquired about her weariness: "My feets is tired, but my soul is at rest." They will be the young high school and college students, the young ministers of the gospel and a host of their elders, courageously and nonviolently sitting in at lunch counters and willingly going to jail for conscience' sake. One day the South will know that when these disinherited children of God sat down at lunch counters, they were in reality standing up for what is best in the American dream and for the most sacred values in our Judaeo-Christian heritage, thereby bringing our nation back to those great wells of democracy which were dug deeply by the founding fathers in their formulation of the Constitution and the Declaration of Independence.

Never before have I written so long a letter. I'm afraid it is much too long to take your precious time. I can assure you that it would have been much shorter if I had been writing from a comfortable desk, but what else can one do when he is alone in a narrow jail cell, other than write long letters, think long thoughts, and pray long prayers?

If I have said anything in this letter that overstates the truth and indicates an unreasonable impatience, I beg you to forgive me. If I have said anything that understates the truth and indicates my having a patience that allows me to settle for anything less than brotherhood, I beg God to forgive me.

I hope this letter finds you strong in the faith. I also hope that circumstances will soon make it possible for me to meet each of you, not as an integrationist or a civil-rights leader but as a fellow clergyman and a Christian brother. Let us all hope that the dark clouds of racial prejudice will soon pass away and the deep fog of misunderstanding will be lifted from our fear-drenched communities, and in some not too distant tomorrow the radiant stars of love and brotherhood will shine over our great nation with all their scintillating beauty.

Yours for the cause of Peace and Brotherhood,
Martin Luther King, Jr.

A Fist in the Eye of God

Barbara Kingsolver

In the slender shoulders of the myrtle tree outside my kitchen window, a hummingbird built her nest. It was in April, the sexiest month, season of budburst and courtship displays, though I was at the sink washing breakfast dishes and missing the party, or so you might think. Then my eye caught a flicker of motion outside, and there she was, hovering uncertainly. She held in the tip of her beak a wisp of wadded spiderweb so tiny I wasn't even sure it was there, until she carefully smoodged it onto the branch. She vanished then, but in less than a minute she was back with another tiny white tuft that she stuck on top of the first. For more than an hour she returned again and again, increasingly confident of her mission, building up by infinitesimal degrees a whitish lump on the branch—and leaving me plumb in awe of the supply of spiderwebbing on the face of the land.

I stayed at my post, washing everything I could find, while my friend did her own housework out there. When the lump had grown big enough—when some genetic trigger in her small brain said, "Now, that will do"—she stopped gathering and sat down on her little tuffet, waggling her wings and tiny rounded underbelly to shape the blob into a cup that would easily have fit inside my cupped hand. Then she hovered up to inspect it from this side and that, settled and waddled with greater fervor, hovered and appraised some more, and dashed off again. She began now to return with fine filaments of shredded bark, which she wove into the webbing along with some dry leaflets and a slap-dab or two of lichen pressed onto the outside for curb appeal. When she had made of all this a perfect, symmetrical cup, she did the most surprising thing of all: She sat on it, stretched herself forward, extended the unbelievable length of her tongue, and *licked* her new nest in a long upward stroke from bottom to rim. Then she rotated herself a minute degree, leaned forward, and licked again. I watched her go all the way around, licking the entire nest in a slow rotation that took ten minutes to complete and ended precisely back at her starting point. Passed down from hummingbird great-grandmothers immemorial, a spectacular genetic map in her mind had instructed her at every step, from snipping out with her beak the first spiderweb tuft to laying down whatever salivary secretion was needed to accrete and finalize her essential creation.

Then, suddenly, that was that. Her busy urgency vanished, and she settled in for the long stillness of laying and incubation.

If you had been standing with me at my kitchen sink to witness all this, you would likely have breathed softly, as I did, "My God." The spectacular perfection of that nest, that tiny tongue, that beak calibrated perfectly to the length of the tubular red flowers from which she sucks nectar and takes away pollen to commit the essential act of copulation for the plant that feeds her—every piece of this thing and all of it, my God. You might be expressing your reverence for the details of a world created in seven days, 4,004 years ago (according to some biblical calculations), by a divine being approximately human in shape. Or you might be revering the details of a world created by a billion years of natural selection acting utterly without fail on every single life-form, one life at a time. For my money the latter is the greatest show on earth, and a church service to end all. I have never understood how anyone could have the slightest trouble blending religious awe with a full comprehension of the workings of life's creation.

Charles Darwin himself was a religious man, blessed with an extraordinary patience for observing nature's details, as well as the longevity and brilliance to put it all together. In his years of studying animate life he noticed four things, which any of us could notice today if we looked hard enough. They are:

1. Every organism produces more seeds or offspring than will actually survive to adulthood.
2. There is variation among these seeds or offspring.
3. Traits are passed down from one generation to the next.
4. In each generation the survivors succeed—that is, they survive—because they possess some advantage over the ones that don't succeed, and *because* they survive, they will pass that advantage on to the next generation. Over time, therefore, the incidence of that trait will increase in the population.

Bingo: the greatest, simplest, most elegant logical construct ever to dawn across our curiosity about the workings of natural life. It is inarguable, and it explains everything.

Most people have no idea that this, in total, is Darwin's theory of evolution. Furthermore, parents who tell their children not to listen to such talk because "it's just a theory" are ignorant of what that word means. A theory, in science, is a coherent set of principles used to explain and predict a class of phenomena. Thus, gravitational theory explains why objects fall when you drop them, even though it, too, is "just a theory." Darwin's has proven to be the most robust unifying explanation ever devised in biological science. It's stunning that he could have been so right—scientists of Darwin's time knew absolutely nothing about genetics—but he was. After a century and a half, during which time knowledge expanded boundlessly in genetics, geology, paleontology, and all areas of natural science, his simple logical construct continues to explain and predict perfectly the existence and behavior of every earthly life form we have ever studied. As the unifying principle of natural sciences, it is no more doubted among modern biologists than gravity is questioned by physicists. Nevertheless, in a bizarre recent trend, a number of states have limited or even outright banned the teaching of evolution in high schools, and many textbooks for the whole country, in turn, have wimped out on the subject. As a consequence, an entire generation of students is arriving in college unprepared to comprehend or pursue good science. Many science teachers I know are nostalgic for at least one aspect of the Cold War days, when *Sputnik* riveted us to the serious business of training our kids to real science, instead of allowing it to be diluted or tossed out to assuage the insecurities of certain ideologues.

We dilute and toss at our peril. Scientific illiteracy in our population is leaving too many of us unprepared to discuss or understand much of the damage we are wreaking on our atmosphere, our habitat, and even the food that enters our mouths. Friends of mine who opted in school for English lit instead of microbiology (an option I myself could easily have taken) sometimes come to me and ask, "In two hundred words or less, can you explain to me why I should be nervous about genetic engineering?" I tell them, "Sit down, I'll make you a cup of tea, and then get ready for more than two hundred words."

A sound-bite culture can't discuss science very well. Exactly what we're losing when we reduce biodiversity, the causes and consequences of global warming—these traumas can't be adequately summarized in an evening news wrap-up. Arguments *in favor* of genetically engineered food, in contrast, are dangerously simple: A magazine ad for an agribusiness touts its benevolent plan to "feed the world's hungry with our vitamin-engineered rice!" To which I could add in reply my own snappy motto: "If you thought that first free hit of heroin was a good idea. . . ." But before you can really decide whether or not you agree, you may need the five hundred words above and a few thousand more. If so, then sit down, have a cup of tea, and bear with me. This is important.

At the root of everything, Darwin said, is that wonder of wonders, genetic diversity. You're unlike your sister, a litter of pups is its own small Rainbow Coalition, and every grain of wheat in a field holds inside its germ a slightly separate destiny. You can't see the differences until you cast the seeds on the ground and grow them out, but sure enough, some will grow into taller plants and some shorter, some tougher, some sweeter. In a good year all or most of them will thrive and give you wheat. But in a bad year a spate of high winds may take down the tallest stalks and leave standing at harvest time only, say, the 10 percent of the crop that had a "shortness" gene. And if that wheat comprises your winter's supply of bread, plus the only seed you'll have for next year's crop, then you'll be almighty glad to have that small, short harvest. Genetic diversity, in domestic populations as well as wild ones, is nature's sole insurance policy. Environments change: Wet years are followed by droughts, lakes dry up, volcanoes rumble, ice ages dawn. It's a big, bad world out there for a little strand of DNA. But a population will persist over time if, deep within the scattered genetics of its ranks, it is literally prepared for anything. When the windy years persist for a decade, the wheat population will be overtaken by a preponderance of shortness, but if the crop maintains its diversity, there will always be recessive aspirations for height hiding in there somewhere, waiting to have their day.

How is the diversity maintained? That old black magic called sex. Every seed has two parents. Plants throw their sex to the wind, to a hummingbird's tongue, to the knees of a bee—in April you are *inhaling* sex, and sneezing—and in the process, each two parents put their scrambled genes into offspring that represent whole new genetic combinations never before seen on Earth. Every new outfit will be ready for *something*, and together—in a large enough population—the whole crowd will be ready for *anything*. Individuals will die, not at random but because of some fatal misfit between what an organism *has* and what's *required*. But the population will live on, moving always in the direction of fitness (however "fitness" is at the moment defined), not because anyone has a master plan but simply because survival carries fitness forward, and death doesn't.

People have railed at this reality, left and right, since the evening when a British ambassador's wife declared to her husband, "Oh dear, let us hope Mr. Darwin isn't right, and if he is, let us hope no one finds out about it!" Fundamentalist Christians seem disturbed by a scenario in which individual will is so irrelevant. They might be surprised to learn that Stalin tried to ban the study of genetics and evolution in Soviet universities for the opposite reason, attacking the idea of natural selection—which acts only at the level of the individual—for being anti-Communist. Through it all, the little engines of evolution have kept on turning as they have done for millennia, delivering us here and passing on, untouched by politics or what anybody thinks.

Nikolai Vavilov was an astounding man of science, and probably the greatest plant explorer who has ever lived. He spoke seven languages and could recite books by Pushkin from memory. In his travels through sixty-four countries between 1916 and 1940, he saw more crop diversity than anyone had known existed, and founded the world's largest seed collection.

As he combed continents looking for primitive crop varieties, Vavilov noticed a pattern: Genetic variation was not evenly distributed. In a small region of Ethiopia he found hundreds of kinds of ancient wheat known only to that place. A single New World plateau is astonishingly rich in corn varieties, while another one is rolling in different kinds of potatoes. Vavilov mapped the distribution of what he found and theorized that the degree of diversity of a crop indicated how long it had been grown in a given region, as farmers saved their seeds through hundreds and thousands of seasons. They also saved more *types* of seed for different benefits; thus popcorn, tortilla corn, roasting corn, and varieties of corn with particular colors and textures were all derived, over centuries, from one original strain. Within each crop type, the generations of selection would also yield a breadth of resistance to all types of pest and weather problems encountered through the years. By looking through his lens of genetics, Vavilov began to pinpoint the places in the world where human agriculture had originated. More modern genetic research has largely borne out his hypothesis that agriculture emerged independently in the places where the most diverse and ancient crop types, known as land races, are to be found: in the Near East, northern China, Mesoamerica, and Ethiopia.

The industrialized world depends entirely on crops and cultivation practices imported from what we now call the Third World (though evidently it was actually First). In an important departure from older traditions, the crops we now grow in the United States are extremely uniform genetically, due to the fact that our agriculture is controlled primarily by a few large agricultural corporations that sell relatively few varieties of seeds. Those who know the seed business are well aware that our shallow gene bank is highly vulnerable; when a crop strain succumbs all at once to a new disease, all across the country (as happened with our corn in 1970), researchers must return to the more diverse original strains for help. So we still rely on the gigantic insurance policy provided by the genetic variability in the land races, which continue to be hand-sown and harvested, year in and year out, by farmers in those mostly poor places from which our crops arose.

Unbelievably, we are now engaged in a serious effort to cancel that insurance policy.

It happens like this. Let's say you are an Ethiopian farmer growing a land race of wheat—a wildly variable, husky mongrel crop that has been in your family for hundreds of years. You always lose some to wind and weather, but the rest still comes through every year. Lately, though, you've been hearing about a kind of Magic Wheat that grows six times bigger than your crop, is easier to harvest, and contains vitamins that aren't found in ordinary wheat. And amazingly enough, by special arrangement with the government, it's free.

Readers who have even the slightest acquaintance with fairy tales will already know there is trouble ahead in this story. The Magic Wheat grows well the first year, but its rapid, overly green growth attracts a startling number of pests. You see insects on this crop that never ate wheat before, in the whole of your family's history. You watch, you worry. You realize that you're going to have to spray a pesticide to get this crop through to harvest. You're not so surprised to learn that by special arrangement with the government, the same company that gave you the seed for free can sell you the pesticide you need. It's a good pesticide, they use it all the time in America, but it costs money you don't have, so you'll have to borrow against next year's crop.

The second year, you will be visited by a terrible drought, and your crop will not survive to harvest at all; every stalk dies. Magic Wheat from America doesn't know beans about Ethiopian drought. The end.

Actually, if the drought arrived in year two and the end came that quickly, in this real-life fairy tale you'd be very lucky, because chances are good you'd still have some of your family-line seed around. It would be much more disastrous if the drought waited until the eighth or ninth year to wipe you out, for then you'd have no wheat left at all, Magic or otherwise. Seed banks, even if they're eleven thousand years old, can't survive for more than a few years on the shelf. If they aren't grown out as crops year after year, they die—or else get ground into flour and baked and eaten—and then this product of a thousand hands and careful selection is just gone, once and for all.

This is no joke. The infamous potato famine or Southern Corn Leaf Blight catastrophe could happen again any day now, in any place where people are once again foolish enough, or poor enough to be coerced (as was the case in Ireland), to plant an entire country in a single genetic strain of a food crop.

While agricultural companies have purchased, stored, and patented certain genetic materials from old crops, they cannot engineer a crop, *ever*, that will have the resilience of land races under a wide variety of conditions of moisture, predation, and temperature. Genetic engineering is the antithesis of variability because it removes the wild card—that beautiful thing called sex—from the equation.

This is our new magic bullet: We can move single genes around in a genome to render a specific trait that nature can't put there, such as ultrarapid growth or vitamin A in rice. Literally, we could put a wolf in sheep's clothing. But solving agricultural problems this way turns out to be far less broadly effective than the old-fashioned multigenic solutions derived through programs of selection and breeding. Crop predators evolve in quick and mysterious ways, while gene splicing tries one simple tack after another, approaching its goal the way Wile E. Coyote tries out each new gizmo from Acme only once, whereupon the roadrunner outwits it and Wile E. goes crestfallen back to the drawing board.

Wendell Berry, with his reliable wit, wrote that genetic manipulation in general and cloning in particular: ". . . besides being a new method of sheep-stealing, is only a pathetic attempt to make sheep predictable. But this is an affront to reality. As any shepherd would know, the scientist who thinks he has made sheep predictable has only made himself eligible to be outsmarted."

I've heard less knowledgeable people comfort themselves on the issue of genetic engineering by recalling that humans have been pushing genes around for centuries, through selective breeding of livestock and crops. I even read one howler of a quote that began, "Ever since Mendel spliced those first genes. . . ." These people aren't getting it, but I don't blame them—I blame the religious fanatics who kept basic biology out of their grade-school textbooks. Mendel did not *splice* genes, he didn't actually control anything at all; he simply watched peas to learn how their natural system of genetic recombination worked. The farmers who select their best sheep or grains to mother the next year's crop are working with the evolutionary force of selection, pushing it in the direction of their choosing. Anything produced in this way will still work within its natural evolutionary context of variability, predators, disease resistance, and so forth. But tampering with genes outside of the checks and balances you might call the rules of God's laboratory is an entirely different process. It's turning out to have unforeseen consequences, sometimes stunning ones.

To choose one example among many, genetic engineers have spliced a bacterium into a corn plant. It was arguably a good idea. The bacterium was *Bacillus thuringensis*, a germ that causes caterpillars' stomachs to explode. It doesn't harm humans, birds, or even ladybugs or bees, so it's one of the most useful pesticides we've ever discovered. Organic farmers have worked for years to expedite the path of the naturally occurring "Bt" spores from the soil, where the bacterium lives, onto their plants. You can buy this germ in a can at the nursery and shake it onto your tomato plants, where it makes caterpillars croak before sliding back into the soil it came from. Farmers have always used nature to their own ends, employing relatively slow methods circumscribed by the context of natural laws. But genetic engineering took a giant step and spliced part of the bacterium's DNA into a corn plant's DNA chain, so that as the corn grew, each of its cells would contain the bacterial function of caterpillar killing. When it produced pollen, each grain would have a secret weapon against the corn worms that like to crawl down the silks to ravage the crop. So far, so good.

But when the so-called Bt corn sheds its pollen and casts it to the wind, as corn has always done (it's pollinated by wind, not by bees), it dusts a fine layer of Bt pollen onto every tree and bush in the neighborhood of every farm that grows it—which is rapidly, for this popular crop, becoming the territory known as the United States. There it may explode the stomach of any butterfly larva in its path. The populations of monarch butterflies, those bold little pilgrims who migrate all the way to Mexico and back on wings the consistency of pastry crust, are plummeting fast. While there are many reasons for this (for example, their winter forests in Mexico are being burned), no reasonable person can argue that dusting them with a stomach explosive is going to help matters. So, too, go other butterflies more obscure, and more endangered. And if that doesn't happen to break your heart, just wait awhile, because something that pollinates your food and builds the soil underneath it may also be slated for extinction. And there's another practical problem: The massive exposure to Bt, now contained in every cell of this corn, is killing off all crop predators except those few that have mutated a resistance to this long-useful pesticide. As a result, those superresistant mutants are taking over, in exactly the same way that overexposure to antibiotics is facilitating the evolution of antibiotic-resistant diseases in humans.

In this context of phenomenal environmental upsets, with even larger ones just offstage awaiting their cue, it's a bit surprising that the objections to genetic engineering we hear most about are the human health effects. It is absolutely true that new combinations of DNA can create proteins we aren't prepared to swallow; notably, gene manipulations in corn unexpectedly created some antigens to which some humans are allergic. The potential human ills caused by ingestion of engineered foods remain an open category—which is scary enough in itself, and I don't mean to minimize it. But there are so many ways for gene manipulation to work from the inside to destroy our habitat and our food systems that the environmental challenges loom as something on the order of a cancer that might well make personal allergies look like a sneeze. If genetically reordered organisms escape into natural populations, they may rapidly change the genetics of an entire species in a way that could seal its doom. One such scenario is the "monster salmon" with genes for hugely rapid growth, which are currently poised for accidental release into open ocean. Another scenario, less cinematic but dangerously omnipresent, is the pollen escaping from crops, creating new weeds that we cannot hope to remove from the earth's face. Engineered genes don't play by the rules that have organized life for three billion years (or, if you prefer, 4,004). And in this case, winning means loser takes all.

Huge political question marks surround these issues: What will it mean for a handful of agribusinesses to control the world's ever-narrowing seed banks? What about the chemical dependencies they're creating for farmers in developing countries, where government deals with multinational corporations are inducing them to grow these engineered crops? What about the business of patenting and owning genes? Can there be any good in this for the flat-out concern of people trying to feed themselves? Does it seem *safe*, with the world now being what it is, to give up self-sustaining food systems in favor of dependency on the global marketplace? And finally, would *you* trust a guy in a suit who's never given away a nickel in his life, but who now tells you he's made you some *free* Magic Wheat? Most people know by now that corporations can do only what's best for their quarterly bottom line. And anyone who still believes governments ultimately do what's best for their people should be advised that the great crop geneticist Nikolai Vavilov died in a Soviet prison camp.

These are not questions to take lightly, as we stand here in the epicenter of corporate agribusiness and look around at the world asking, "Why on earth would they hate us?" The general ignorance of U.S. populations about who controls global agriculture reflects our trust in an assured food supply. Elsewhere, in places where people grow more food, watch less TV, and generally encounter a greater risk of hunger than we do, they mostly know what's going on. In India, farmers have persisted in burning to the ground trial crops of transgenic cotton, and they forced their government to ban Monsanto's "terminator technology," which causes plants to kill their own embryos so no viable seeds will survive for a farmer to replant in the next generation (meaning he'd have to buy new ones, of course). Much of the world has already refused to import genetically engineered foods or seeds from the United States. But because of the power and momentum of the World Trade Organization, fewer and fewer countries have the clout to resist the reconstruction of their food supply around the scariest New Deal ever.

Even standing apart from the moral and political questions—if a scientist *can* stand anywhere without stepping on the politics of what's about to be discovered—there are question marks enough in the science of the matter. There are consequences in it that no one knew how to anticipate. When the widely publicized Human Genome Project completed its mapping of human chromosomes, it offered an unsettling, not-so-widely-publicized conclusion: Instead of the 100,000 or more genes that had been expected, based on the number of proteins we must synthesize to be what we are, we have only about 30,000—about the same number as a mustard plant. This evidence undermined the central dogma of how genes work; that is, the assumption of a clear-cut chain of processes leading from a single gene to the appearance of the trait it controls. Instead, the mechanism of gene expression appears vastly more complicated than had been assumed since Watson and Crick discovered the structure of DNA in 1953. The expression of a gene may be altered by its context, such as the presence of other genes on the chromosome near it. Yet, genetic engineering operates on assumptions based on the simpler model. Thus, single transplanted genes often behave in startling ways in an engineered organism, often proving lethal to themselves, or, sometimes, neighboring organisms. In light of newer findings, geneticists increasingly concede that gene-tinkering is to some extent shooting in the dark. Barry Commoner, senior scientist at the Center for the Biology of Natural Systems at Queens College, laments that while the public's concerns are often derided by industry scientists as irrational and uneducated, the biotechnology industry is—ironically—conveniently ignoring the latest results in the field "which show that there are strong reasons to fear the potential consequences of transferring a DNA gene between species."

Recently I heard Joan Dye Gussow, who studies and writes about the energetics, economics, and irrationalities of global food production, discussing some of these problems in a radio interview. She mentioned the alarming fact that pollen from genetically engineered corn is so rapidly contaminating all other corn that we may soon have no naturally bred corn left in the United States. "This is a fist in the eye of God," she said, adding with a sad little laugh, "and I'm not even all that religious." Whatever you believe in—whether God for you is the watchmaker who put together the intricate workings of this world in seven days or seven hundred billion days—you'd be wise to believe the part about the fist.

Religion has no place in the science classroom, where it may abridge students' opportunities to learn the methods, discoveries, and explanatory hypotheses of science. Rather, its place is in the hearts of the men and women who study and then practice scientific exploration. Ethics can't influence the outcome of an experiment, but they can serve as a useful adjunct to the questions that get asked in the first place, and to the applications thereafter. (One must wonder what chair God occupied, if any, in the Manhattan Project.) In the halls of science there is often an unspoken sense that morals and objectivity can't occupy the same place. That is balderdash—they always have cohabited. Social norms and judgments regarding gender, race, the common good, cooperation, competition, material gain, and countless other issues reside in every active human mind, so they were hovering somewhere in the vicinity of any experiment ever conducted by a human. That is precisely why science invented the double-blind experiment, in which, for example, experimental subjects don't know whether they're taking the drug or the placebo, and neither does the scientist recording their responses, so as to avoid psychological bias in the results. But it's not possible to double-blind the scientist's approach to the task in the first place, or to the way results will be used. It is probably more scientifically constructive to acknowledge our larger agenda than to pretend it doesn't exist. Where genetic engineering is concerned, I would rather have ethics than profitability driving the program.

I was trained as a biologist, and I can appreciate the challenge and the technical mastery involved in isolating, understanding, and manipulating genes. I can think of fascinating things I'd like to do as a genetic engineer. But I only have to stand still for a minute and watch the outcome of thirty million years' worth of hummingbird evolution transubstantiated before my eyes into nest and egg to get knocked down to size. I have held in my hand the germ of a plant engineered to grow, yield its crop, and then murder its own embryos, and there I glimpsed the malevolence that can lie in the heart of a profiteering enterprise. There once was a time when Thoreau wrote, "I have great faith in a seed. Convince me that you have a seed there, and I am prepared to expect wonders." By the power vested in everything living, let us keep to that faith. I'm a scientist who thinks it wise to enter the doors of creation not with a lion tamer's whip and chair, but with the reverence humankind has traditionally summoned for entering places of worship: a temple, a mosque, or a cathedral. A sacred grove, as ancient as time.

The Moral Instinct

Steven Pinker

Which of the following people would you say is the most admirable: Mother Teresa, Bill Gates or Norman Borlaug? And which do you think is the least admirable? For most people, it's an easy question. Mother Teresa, famous for ministering to the poor in Calcutta, has been beatified by the Vatican, awarded the Nobel Peace Prize and ranked in an American poll as the most admired person of the 20th century. Bill Gates, infamous for giving us the Microsoft dancing paper clip and the blue screen of death, has been decapitated in effigy in "I Hate Gates" Web sites and hit with a pie in the face. As for Norman Borlaug . . . who the heck is Norman Borlaug?

Yet a deeper look might lead you to rethink your answers. Borlaug, father of the "Green Revolution" that used agricultural science to reduce world hunger, has been credited with saving a billion lives, more than anyone else in history. Gates, in deciding what to do with his fortune, crunched the numbers and determined that he could alleviate the most misery by fighting everyday scourges in the developing world like malaria, diarrhea and parasites. Mother Teresa, for her part, extolled the virtue of suffering and ran her well-financed missions accordingly: their sick patrons were offered plenty of prayer but harsh conditions, few analgesics and dangerously primitive medical care.

It's not hard to see why the moral reputations of this trio should be so out of line with the good they have done. Mother Teresa was the very embodiment of saintliness: white-clad, sad-eyed, ascetic and often photographed with the wretched of the earth. Gates is a nerd's nerd and the world's richest man, as likely to enter heaven as the proverbial camel squeezing through the needle's eye. And Borlaug, now 93, is an agronomist who has spent his life in labs and nonprofits, seldom walking onto the media stage, and hence into our consciousness, at all.

I doubt these examples will persuade anyone to favor Bill Gates over Mother Teresa for sainthood. But they show that our heads can be turned by an aura of sanctity, distracting us from a more objective reckoning of the actions that make people suffer or flourish. It seems we may all be vulnerable to moral illusions the ethical equivalent of the bending lines that trick the eye on cereal boxes and in psychology textbooks. Illusions are a favorite tool of perception scientists for exposing the workings of the five senses, and of philosophers for shaking people out of the naïve belief that our minds give us a transparent window onto the world (since if our eyes can be fooled by an illusion, why should we trust them at other times?). Today, a new field is using illusions to unmask a sixth sense, the moral sense. Moral intuitions are being drawn out of people in the lab, on Web sites and in brain scanners, and are being explained with tools from game theory, neuroscience and evolutionary biology.

"Two things fill the mind with ever new and increasing admiration and awe, the oftener and more steadily we reflect on them," wrote Immanuel Kant, "the starry heavens above and the moral law within." These days, the moral law within is being viewed with increasing awe, if not always admiration. The human moral sense turns out to be an organ of considerable complexity, with quirks that reflect its evolutionary history and its neurobiological foundations.

These quirks are bound to have implications for the human predicament. Morality is not just any old topic in psychology but close to our conception of the meaning of life. Moral goodness is what gives each of us the sense that we are worthy human beings. We seek it in our friends and mates, nurture it in our children, advance it in our politics and justify it with our religions. A disrespect for morality is blamed for everyday sins and history's worst atrocities. To carry this weight, the concept of morality would have to be bigger than any of us and outside all of us.

So dissecting moral intuitions is no small matter. If morality is a mere trick of the brain, some may fear, our very grounds for being moral could be eroded. Yet as we shall see, the science of the moral sense can instead be seen as a way to strengthen those grounds, by clarifying what morality is and how it should steer our actions.

The Moralization Switch

The starting point for appreciating that there *is* a distinctive part of our psychology for morality is seeing how moral judgments differ from other kinds of opinions we have on how people ought to behave. Moralization is a psychological state that can be turned on and off like a switch, and when it is on, a distinctive mind-set commandeers our thinking. This is the mind-set that makes us deem actions immoral ("killing is wrong"), rather than merely disagreeable ("I hate brussels sprouts"), unfashionable ("bell-bottoms are out") or imprudent ("don't scratch mosquito bites").

The first hallmark of moralization is that the rules it invokes are felt to be universal. Prohibitions of rape and murder, for example, are felt not to be matters of local custom but to be universally and objectively warranted. One can easily say, "I don't like brussels sprouts, but I don't care if you eat them," but no one would say, "I don't like killing, but I don't care if you murder someone."

The other hallmark is that people feel that those who commit immoral acts deserve to be punished. Not only is it allowable to inflict pain on a person who has broken a moral rule; it is wrong *not* to, to "let them get away with it." People are thus untroubled in inviting divine retribution or the power of the state to harm other people they deem immoral. Bertrand Russell wrote, "The infliction of cruelty with a good conscience is a delight to moralists—that is why they invented hell."

We all know what it feels like when the moralization switch flips inside us—the righteous glow, the burning dudgeon, the drive to recruit others to the cause. The psychologist Paul Rozin has studied the toggle switch by comparing two kinds of people who engage in the same behavior but with different switch settings. Health vegetarians avoid meat for practical reasons, like lowering cholesterol and avoiding toxins. Moral vegetarians avoid meat for ethical reasons: to avoid complicity in the suffering of animals. By investigating their feelings about meat-eating, Rozin showed that the moral motive sets off a cascade of opinions. Moral vegetarians are more likely to treat meat as a contaminant—they refuse, for example, to eat a bowl of soup into which a drop of beef broth has fallen. They are more likely to think that other people ought to be vegetarians, and are more likely to imbue their dietary habits with other virtues, like believing that meat avoidance makes people less aggressive and bestial.

Much of our recent social history, including the culture wars between liberals and conservatives, consists of the moralization or amoralization of particular kinds of behavior. Even when people agree that an outcome is desirable, they may disagree on whether it should be treated as a matter of preference and prudence or as a matter of sin and virtue. Rozin notes, for example, that smoking has lately been moralized. Until recently, it was understood that some people didn't enjoy smoking or avoided it because it was hazardous to their health. But with the discovery of the harmful effects of secondhand smoke, smoking is now treated as immoral. Smokers are ostracized; images of people smoking are censored; and entities touched by smoke are felt to be contaminated (so hotels have not only nonsmoking rooms but nonsmoking *floors*). The desire for retribution has been visited on tobacco companies, who have been slapped with staggering "punitive damages."

At the same time, many behaviors have been amoralized, switched from moral failings to lifestyle choices. They include divorce, illegitimacy, being a working mother, marijuana use and homosexuality. Many afflictions have been reassigned from payback for bad choices to unlucky misfortunes. There used to be people called "bums" and "tramps"; today they are "homeless." Drug addiction is a "disease"; syphilis was rebranded from the price of wanton behavior to a "sexually transmitted disease" and more recently a "sexually transmitted infection."

This wave of amoralization has led the cultural right to lament that morality itself is under assault, as we see in the group that anointed itself the Moral Majority. In fact there seems to be a Law of Conservation of Moralization, so that as old behaviors are taken out of the moralized column, new ones are added to it. Dozens of things that past generations treated as practical matters are now ethical battlegrounds, including disposable diapers, I.Q. tests, poultry farms, Barbie dolls and research on breast cancer. Food alone has become a minefield, with critics sermonizing about the size of sodas, the chemistry of fat, the freedom of chickens, the price of coffee beans, the species of fish and now the distance the food has traveled from farm to plate.

Many of these moralizations, like the assault on smoking, may be understood as practical tactics to reduce some recently identified harm. But whether an activity flips our mental switches to the "moral" setting isn't just a matter of how much harm it does. We don't show contempt to the man who fails to change the batteries in his smoke alarms or takes his family on a driving vacation, both of which multiply the risk they will die in an accident. Driving a gas-guzzling Hummer is reprehensible, but driving a gas-guzzling old Volvo is not; eating a Big Mac is unconscionable, but not imported cheese or crème brûlée. The reason for these double standards is obvious: people tend to align their moralization with their own lifestyles.

Reasoning and Rationalizing

It's not just the content of our moral judgments that is often questionable, but the way we arrive at them. We like to think that when we have a conviction, there are good reasons that drove us to adopt it. That is why an older approach to moral psychology, led by Jean Piaget and Lawrence Kohlberg, tried to document the lines of reasoning that guided people to moral conclusions. But consider these situations, originally devised by the psychologist Jonathan Haidt:

Julie is traveling in France on summer vacation from college with her brother Mark. One night they decide that it would be interesting and fun if they tried making love. Julie was already taking birth-control pills, but Mark uses a condom, too, just to be safe. They both enjoy the sex but decide not to do it again. They keep the night as a special secret, which makes them feel closer to each other. What do you think about that—was it O.K. for them to make love?

A woman is cleaning out her closet and she finds her old American flag. She doesn't want the flag anymore, so she cuts it up into pieces and uses the rags to clean her bathroom.

A family's dog is killed by a car in front of their house. They heard that dog meat was delicious, so they cut up the dog's body and cook it and eat it for dinner.

Most people immediately declare that these acts are wrong and then grope to justify *why* they are wrong. It's not so easy. In the case of Julie and Mark, people raise the possibility of children with birth defects, but they are reminded that the couple were diligent about contraception. They suggest that the siblings will be emotionally hurt, but the story makes it clear that they weren't. They submit that the act would offend the community, but then recall that it was kept a secret. Eventually many people admit, "I don't know, I can't explain it, I just know it's wrong." People don't generally engage in moral reasoning, Haidt argues, but moral *rationalization*: they begin with the conclusion, coughed up by an unconscious emotion, and then work backward to a plausible justification.

The gap between people's convictions and their justifications is also on display in the favorite new sandbox for moral psychologists, a thought experiment devised by the philosophers Philippa Foot and Judith Jarvis Thomson called the Trolley Problem. On your morning walk, you see a trolley car hurtling down the track, the conductor slumped over the controls. In the path of the trolley are five men working on the track, oblivious to the danger. You are standing at a fork in the track and can pull a lever that will divert the trolley onto a spur, saving the five men. Unfortunately, the trolley would then run over a single worker who is laboring on the spur. Is it permissible to throw the switch, killing one man to save five? Almost everyone says "yes."

Consider now a different scene. You are on a bridge overlooking the tracks and have spotted the runaway trolley bearing down on the five workers. Now the only way to stop the trolley is to throw a heavy object in its path. And the only heavy object within reach is a fat man standing next to you. Should you throw the man off the bridge? Both dilemmas present you with the option of sacrificing one life to save five, and so, by the utilitarian standard of what would result in the greatest good for the greatest number, the two dilemmas are morally equivalent. But most people don't see it that way: though they would pull the switch in the first dilemma, they would not heave the fat man in the second. When pressed for a reason, they can't come up with anything coherent, though moral philosophers haven't had an easy time coming up with a relevant difference, either.

When psychologists say "most people" they usually mean "most of the two dozen sophomores who filled out a questionnaire for beer money." But in this case it means most of the 200,000 people from a hundred countries who shared their intuitions on a Web-based experiment conducted by the psychologists Fiery Cushman and Liane Young and the biologist Marc Hauser. A difference between the acceptability of switch-pulling and man-heaving, and an inability to justify the choice, was found in respondents from Europe, Asia and North and South America; among men and women, blacks and whites, teenagers and octogenarians, Hindus, Muslims, Buddhists, Christians, Jews and atheists; people with elementary-school educations and people with Ph.D.'s.

Joshua Greene, a philosopher and cognitive neuroscientist, suggests that evolution equipped people with a revulsion to manhandling an innocent person. This instinct, he suggests, tends to overwhelm any utilitarian calculus that would tot up the lives saved and lost. The impulse against roughing up a fellow human would explain other examples in which people abjure killing one to save many, like euthanizing a hospital patient to harvest his organs and save five dying patients in need of transplants, or throwing someone out of a crowded lifeboat to keep it afloat.

By itself this would be no more than a plausible story, but Greene teamed up with the cognitive neuroscientist Jonathan Cohen and several Princeton colleagues to peer into people's brains using functional M.R.I. They sought to find signs of a conflict between brain areas associated with emotion (the ones that recoil from harming someone) and areas dedicated to rational analysis (the ones that calculate lives lost and saved).

When people pondered the dilemmas that required killing someone with their bare hands, several networks in their brains lighted up. One, which included the medial (inward-facing) parts of the frontal lobes, has been implicated in emotions about other people. A second, the dorsolateral (upper and outer-facing) surface of the frontal lobes, has been implicated in ongoing mental computation (including nonmoral reasoning, like deciding whether to get somewhere by plane or train). And a third region, the anterior cingulate cortex (an evolutionarily ancient strip lying at the base of the inner surface of each cerebral hemisphere), registers a conflict between an urge coming from one part of the brain and an advisory coming from another.

But when the people were pondering a hands-off dilemma, like switching the trolley onto the spur with the single worker, the brain reacted differently: only the area involved in rational calculation stood out. Other studies have shown that neurological patients who have blunted emotions because of damage to the frontal lobes become utilitarians: they think it makes perfect sense to throw the fat man off the bridge. Together, the findings corroborate Greene's theory that our nonutilitarian intuitions come from the victory of an emotional impulse over a cost-benefit analysis.

A Universal Morality?

The findings of trolleyology—complex, instinctive and worldwide moral intuitions—led Hauser and John Mikhail (a legal scholar) to revive an analogy from the philosopher John Rawls between the moral sense and language. According to Noam Chomsky, we are born with a "universal grammar" that forces us to analyze speech in terms of its grammatical structure, with no conscious awareness of the rules in play. By analogy, we are born with a universal moral grammar that forces us to analyze human action in terms of its moral structure, with just as little awareness.

The idea that the moral sense is an innate part of human nature is not far-fetched. A list of human universals collected by the anthropologist Donald E. Brown includes many moral concepts and emotions, including a distinction between right and wrong; empathy; fairness; admiration of generosity; rights and obligations; proscription of murder, rape and other forms of violence; redress of wrongs; sanctions for wrongs against the community; shame; and taboos.

The stirrings of morality emerge early in childhood. Toddlers spontaneously offer toys and help to others and try to comfort people they see in distress. And according to the psychologists Elliot Turiel and Judith Smetana, preschoolers have an inkling of the difference between societal conventions and moral principles. Four-year-olds say that it is not O.K. to wear pajamas to school (a convention) and also not O.K. to hit a little girl for no reason (a moral principle). But when asked whether these actions would be O.K. if the teacher allowed them, most of the children said that wearing pajamas would now be fine but that hitting a little girl would still not be.

Though no one has identified genes for morality, there is circumstantial evidence they exist. The character traits called "conscientiousness" and "agreeableness" are far more correlated in identical twins separated at birth (who share their genes but not their environment) than in adoptive siblings raised together (who share their environment but not their genes). People given diagnoses of "antisocial personality disorder" or "psychopathy" show signs of morality blindness from the time they are children. They bully younger children, torture animals, habitually lie and seem incapable of empathy or remorse, often despite normal family backgrounds. Some of these children grow up into the monsters who bilk elderly people out of their savings, rape a succession of women or shoot convenience-store clerks lying on the floor during a robbery.

Though psychopathy probably comes from a genetic predisposition, a milder version can be caused by damage to frontal regions of the brain (including the areas that inhibit intact people from throwing the hypothetical fat man off the bridge). The neuroscientists Hanna and Antonio Damasio and their colleagues found that some children who sustain severe injuries to their frontal lobes can grow up into callous and irresponsible adults, despite normal intelligence. They lie, steal, ignore punishment, endanger their own children and can't think through even the simplest moral dilemmas, like what two people should do if they disagreed on which TV channel to watch or whether a man ought to steal a drug to save his dying wife.

The moral sense, then, may be rooted in the design of the normal human brain. Yet for all the awe that may fill our minds when we reflect on an innate moral law within, the idea is at best incomplete. Consider this moral dilemma: A runaway trolley is about to kill a schoolteacher. You can divert the trolley onto a sidetrack, but the trolley would trip a switch sending a signal to a class of 6-year-olds, giving them permission to name a teddy bear Muhammad. Is it permissible to pull the lever?

This is no joke. Last month a British woman teaching in a private school in Sudan allowed her class to name a teddy bear after the most popular boy in the class, who bore the name of the founder of Islam. She was jailed for blasphemy and threatened with a public flogging, while a mob outside the prison demanded her death. To the protesters, the woman's life clearly had less value than maximizing the dignity of their religion, and their judgment on whether it is right to divert the hypothetical trolley would have differed from ours. Whatever grammar guides people's moral judgments can't be all *that* universal. Anyone who stayed awake through Anthropology 101 can offer many other examples.

Of course, languages vary, too. In Chomsky's theory, languages conform to an abstract blueprint, like having phrases built out of verbs and objects, while the details vary, like whether the verb or the object comes first. Could we be wired with an abstract spec sheet that embraces all the strange ideas that people in different cultures moralize?

The Varieties of Moral Experience

When anthropologists like Richard Shweder and Alan Fiske survey moral concerns across the globe, they find that a few themes keep popping up from amid the diversity. People everywhere, at least in some circumstances and with certain other folks in mind, think it's bad to harm others and good to help them. They have a sense of fairness: that one should reciprocate favors, reward benefactors and punish cheaters. They value loyalty to a group, sharing and solidarity among its members and conformity to its norms. They believe that it is right to defer to legitimate authorities and to respect people with high status. And they exalt purity, cleanliness and sanctity while loathing defilement, contamination and carnality.

The exact number of themes depends on whether you're a lumper or a splitter, but Haidt counts five—harm, fairness, community (or group loyalty), authority and purity—and suggests that they are the primary colors of our moral sense. Not only do they keep reappearing in cross-cultural surveys, but each one tugs on the moral intuitions of people in our own culture. Haidt asks us to consider how much money someone would have to pay us to do hypothetical acts like the following:

Stick a pin into your palm.

Stick a pin into the palm of a child you don't know. (Harm.)

Accept a wide-screen TV from a friend who received it at no charge because of a computer error.

Accept a wide-screen TV from a friend who received it from a thief who had stolen it from a wealthy family. (Fairness.)

Say something bad about your nation (which you don't believe) on a talk-radio show in your nation.

Say something bad about your nation (which you don't believe) on a talk-radio show in a foreign nation. (Community.)

Slap a friend in the face, with his permission, as part of a comedy skit.

Slap your minister in the face, with his permission, as part of a comedy skit. (Authority.)

Attend a performance-art piece in which the actors act like idiots for 30 minutes, including flubbing simple problems and falling down on stage.

Attend a performance-art piece in which the actors act like animals for 30 minutes, including crawling around naked and urinating on stage. (Purity.)

In each pair, the second action feels far more repugnant. Most of the moral illusions we have visited come from an unwarranted intrusion of one of the moral spheres into our judgments. A violation of community led people to frown on using an old flag to clean a bathroom. Violations of purity repelled the people who judged the morality of consensual incest and prevented the moral vegetarians and nonsmokers from tolerating the slightest trace of a vile contaminant. At the other end of the scale, displays of extreme purity lead people to venerate religious leaders who dress in white and affect an aura of chastity and asceticism.

The Genealogy of Morals

The five spheres are good candidates for a periodic table of the moral sense not only because they are ubiquitous but also because they appear to have deep evolutionary roots. The impulse to avoid harm, which gives trolley ponderers the willies when they consider throwing a man off a bridge, can also be found in rhesus monkeys, who go hungry rather than pull a chain that delivers food to them and a shock to another monkey. Respect for authority is clearly related to the pecking orders of dominance and appeasement that are widespread in the animal kingdom. The purity-defilement contrast taps the emotion of disgust that is triggered by potential disease vectors like bodily effluvia, decaying flesh and unconventional forms of meat, and by risky sexual practices like incest.

The other two moralized spheres match up with the classic examples of how altruism can evolve that were worked out by sociobiologists in the 1960s and 1970s and made famous by Richard Dawkins in his book "The Selfish Gene." Fairness is very close to what scientists call reciprocal altruism, where a willingness to be nice to others can evolve as long as the favor helps the recipient more than it costs the giver and the recipient returns the favor when fortunes reverse. The analysis makes it sound as if reciprocal altruism comes out of a robotlike calculation, but in fact Robert Trivers, the biologist who devised the theory, argued that it is implemented in the brain as a suite of moral emotions. Sympathy prompts a person to offer the first favor, particularly to someone in need for whom it would go the furthest. Anger protects a person against cheaters who accept a favor without reciprocating, by impelling him to punish the ingrate or sever the relationship. Gratitude impels a beneficiary to reward those who helped him in the past. Guilt prompts a cheater in danger of being found out to repair the relationship by redressing the misdeed and advertising that he will behave better in the future (consistent with Mencken's definition of *conscience* as "the inner voice which warns us that someone might be looking"). Many experiments on who helps whom, who likes whom, who punishes whom and who feels guilty about what have confirmed these predictions.

Community, the very different emotion that prompts people to share and sacrifice without an expectation of payback, may be rooted in nepotistic altruism, the empathy and solidarity we feel toward our relatives (and which evolved because any gene that pushed an organism to aid a relative would have helped copies of itself sitting inside that relative). In humans, of course, communal feelings can be lavished on nonrelatives as well. Sometimes it pays people (in an evolutionary sense) to love their companions because their interests are yoked, like spouses with common children, in-laws with common relatives, friends with common tastes or allies with common enemies. And sometimes it doesn't pay them at all, but their kinship-detectors have been tricked into treating their groupmates as if they were relatives by tactics like kinship metaphors (*blood brothers, fraternities, the fatherland*), origin myths, communal meals and other bonding rituals.

Juggling the Spheres

All this brings us to a theory of how the moral sense can be universal and variable at the same time. The five moral spheres are universal, a legacy of evolution. But how they are ranked in importance, and which is brought in to moralize which area of social life—sex, government, commerce, religion, diet and so on—depends on the culture. Many of the flabbergasting practices in faraway places become more intelligible when you recognize that the same moralizing impulse that Western elites channel toward violations of harm and fairness (our moral obsessions) is channeled elsewhere to violations in the other spheres. Think of the Japanese fear of nonconformity (community), the holy ablutions and dietary restrictions of Hindus and Orthodox Jews (purity), the outrage at insulting the Prophet among Muslims (authority). In the West, we believe that in business and government, fairness should trump community and try to root out nepotism and cronyism. In other parts of the world this is incomprehensible—what heartless creep would favor a perfect stranger over his own brother?

The ranking and placement of moral spheres also divides the cultures of liberals and conservatives in the United States. Many bones of contention, like homosexuality, atheism and one-parent families from the right, or racial imbalances, sweatshops and executive pay from the left, reflect different weightings of the spheres. In a large Web survey, Haidt found that liberals put a lopsided moral weight on harm and fairness while playing down group loyalty, authority and purity. Conservatives instead place a moderately high weight on all five. It's not surprising that each side thinks it is driven by lofty ethical values and that the other side is base and unprincipled.

Reassigning an activity to a different sphere, or taking it out of the moral spheres altogether, isn't easy. People think that a behavior belongs in its sphere as a matter of sacred necessity and that the very act of questioning an assignment is a moral outrage. The psychologist Philip Tetlock has shown that the mentality of taboo—a conviction that some thoughts are sinful to think—is not just a superstition of Polynesians but a mind-set that can easily be triggered in college-educated Americans. Just ask them to think about applying the sphere of reciprocity to relationships customarily governed by community or authority. When Tetlock asked subjects for their opinions on whether adoption agencies should place children with the couples willing to pay the most, whether people should have the right to sell their organs and whether they should be able to buy their way out of jury duty, the subjects not only disagreed but felt personally insulted and were outraged that anyone would raise the question.

The institutions of modernity often question and experiment with the way activities are assigned to moral spheres. Market economies tend to put everything up for sale. Science amoralizes the world by seeking to understand phenomena rather than pass judgment on them. Secular philosophy is in the business of scrutinizing all beliefs, including those entrenched by authority and tradition. It's not surprising that these institutions are often seen to be morally corrosive.

Is Nothing Sacred?

And "morally corrosive" is exactly the term that some critics would apply to the new science of the moral sense. The attempt to dissect our moral intuitions can look like an attempt to debunk them. Evolutionary psychologists seem to want to unmask our noblest motives as ultimately self-interested—to show that our love for children, compassion for the unfortunate and sense of justice are just tactics in a Darwinian struggle to perpetuate our genes. The explanation of how different cultures appeal to different spheres could lead to a spineless relativism, in which we would never have grounds to criticize the practice of another culture, no matter how barbaric, because "we have our kind of morality and they have theirs." And the whole enterprise seems to be dragging us to an amoral nihilism, in which morality itself would be demoted from a transcendent principle to a figment of our neural circuitry.

In reality, none of these fears are warranted, and it's important to see why not. The first misunderstanding involves the logic of evolutionary explanations. Evolutionary biologists sometimes anthropomorphize DNA for the same reason that science teachers find it useful to have their students imagine the world from the viewpoint of a molecule or a beam of light. One shortcut to understanding the theory of selection without working through the math is to imagine that the genes are little agents that try to make copies of themselves.

Unfortunately, the meme of the selfish gene escaped from popular biology books and mutated into the idea that organisms (including people) are ruthlessly self-serving. And this doesn't follow. Genes are not a reservoir of our dark unconscious wishes. "Selfish" genes are perfectly compatible with selfless organisms, because a gene's metaphorical goal of selfishly replicating itself can be implemented by wiring up the brain of the organism to do unselfish things, like being nice to relatives or doing good deeds for needy strangers. When a mother stays up all night comforting a sick child, the genes that endowed her with that tenderness were "selfish" in a metaphorical sense, but by no stretch of the imagination is *she* being selfish.

Nor does reciprocal altruism—the evolutionary rationale behind fairness—imply that people do good deeds in the cynical expectation of repayment down the line. We all know of unrequited good deeds, like tipping a waitress in a city you will never visit again and falling on a grenade to save platoonmates. These bursts of goodness are not as anomalous to a biologist as they might appear.

In his classic 1971 article, Trivers, the biologist, showed how natural selection could push in the direction of true selflessness. The emergence of tit-for-tat reciprocity, which lets organisms trade favors without being cheated, is just a first step. A favor-giver not only has to avoid blatant cheaters (those who would accept a favor but not return it) but also prefer generous reciprocators (those who return the biggest favor they can afford) over stingy ones (those who return the smallest favor they can get away with). Since it's good to be chosen as a recipient of favors, a competition arises to be the most generous partner around. More accurately, a competition arises to *appear* to be the most generous partner around, since the favor-giver can't literally read minds or see into the future. A reputation for fairness and generosity becomes an asset.

Now this just sets up a competition for potential beneficiaries to inflate their reputations without making the sacrifices to back them up. But it also pressures the favor-giver to develop ever-more-sensitive radar to distinguish the genuinely generous partners from the hypocrites. This arms race will eventually reach a logical conclusion. The most effective way to *seem* generous and fair, under harsh scrutiny, is to be generous and fair. In the long run, then, reputation can be secured only by commitment. At least some agents evolve to be genuinely high-minded and self-sacrificing—they are moral not because of what it brings them but because that's the kind of people they are.

Of course, a theory that predicted that everyone always sacrificed themselves for another's good would be as preposterous as a theory that predicted that no one ever did. Alongside the niches for saints there are niches for more grudging reciprocators, who attract fewer and poorer partners but don't make the sacrifices necessary for a sterling reputation. And both may coexist with outright cheaters, who exploit the unwary in one-shot encounters. An ecosystem of niches, each with a distinct strategy, can evolve when the payoff of each strategy depends on how many players are playing the other strategies. The human social environment does have its share of generous, grudging and crooked characters, and the genetic variation in personality seems to bear the fingerprints of this evolutionary process.

Is Morality a Figment?

So a biological understanding of the moral sense does not entail that people are calculating maximizers of their genes or self-interest. But where does it leave the concept of morality itself?

Here is the worry. The scientific outlook has taught us that some parts of our subjective experience are products of our biological makeup and have no objective counterpart in the world. The qualitative difference between red and green, the tastiness of fruit and foulness of carrion, the scariness of heights and prettiness of flowers are design features of our common nervous system, and if our species had evolved in a different ecosystem or if we were missing a few genes, our reactions could go the other way. Now, if the distinction between right and wrong is also a product of brain wiring, why should we believe it is any more real than the distinction between red and green? And if it is just a collective hallucination, how could we argue that evils like genocide and slavery are wrong for everyone, rather than just distasteful to us?

Putting God in charge of morality is one way to solve the problem, of course, but Plato made short work of it 2,400 years ago. Does God have a good reason for designating certain acts as moral and others as immoral? If not—if his dictates are divine whims—why should we take them seriously? Suppose that God commanded us to torture a child. Would that make it all right, or would some other standard give us reasons to resist? And if, on the other hand, God was forced by moral reasons to issue some dictates and not others—if a command to torture a child was never an option—then why not appeal to those reasons directly?

This throws us back to wondering where those reasons could come from, if they are more than just figments of our brains. They certainly aren't in the physical world like wavelength or mass. The only other option is that moral truths exist in some abstract Platonic realm, there for us to discover, perhaps in the same way that mathematical truths (according to most mathematicians) are there for us to discover. On this analogy, we are born with a rudimentary concept of number, but as soon as we build on it with formal mathematical reasoning, the nature of mathematical reality forces us to discover some truths and not others. (No one who understands the concept of two, the concept of four and the concept of addition can come to any conclusion but that 2 + 2 = 4.) Perhaps we are born with a rudimentary moral sense, and as soon as we build on it with moral reasoning, the nature of moral reality forces us to some conclusions but not others.

Moral realism, as this idea is called, is too rich for many philosophers' blood. Yet a diluted version of the idea—if not a list of cosmically inscribed Thou-Shalts, then at least a few If-Thens—is not crazy. Two features of reality point any rational, self-preserving social agent in a moral direction. And they could provide a benchmark for determining when the judgments of our moral sense are aligned with morality itself.

One is the prevalence of nonzero-sum games. In many arenas of life, two parties are objectively better off if they both act in a nonselfish way than if each of them acts selfishly. You and I are both better off if we share our surpluses, rescue each other's children in danger and refrain from shooting at each other, compared with hoarding our surpluses while they rot, letting the other's child drown while we file our nails or feuding like the Hatfields and McCoys. Granted, I might be a bit better off if I acted selfishly at your expense and you played the sucker, but the same is true for you with me, so if each of us tried for these advantages, we'd both end up worse off. Any neutral observer, and you and I if we could talk it over rationally, would have to conclude that the state we should aim for is the one in which we both are unselfish. These spreadsheet projections are not quirks of brain wiring, nor are they dictated by a supernatural power; they are in the nature of things.

The other external support for morality is a feature of rationality itself: that it cannot depend on the egocentric vantage point of the reasoner. If I appeal to you to do anything that affects me—to get off my foot, or tell me the time or not run me over with your car—then I can't do it in a way that privileges my interests over yours (say, retaining my right to run you over with my car) if I want you to take me seriously. Unless I am Galactic Overlord, I have to state my case in a way that would force me to treat you in kind. I can't act as if my interests are special just because I'm me and you're not, any more than I can persuade you that the spot I am standing on is a special place in the universe just because I happen to be standing on it.

Not coincidentally, the core of this idea—the interchangeability of perspectives—keeps reappearing in history's best-thought-through moral philosophies, including the Golden Rule (itself discovered many times); Spinoza's Viewpoint of Eternity; the Social Contract of Hobbes, Rousseau and Locke; Kant's Categorical Imperative; and Rawls's Veil of Ignorance. It also underlies Peter Singer's theory of the Expanding Circle—the optimistic proposal that our moral sense, though shaped by evolution to overvalue self, kin and clan, can propel us on a path of moral progress, as our reasoning forces us to generalize it to larger and larger circles of sentient beings.

Doing Better by Knowing Ourselves

Morality, then, is still something larger than our inherited moral sense, and the new science of the moral sense does not make moral reasoning and conviction obsolete. At the same time, its implications for our moral universe are profound.

At the very least, the science tells us that even when our adversaries' agenda is most baffling, they may not be amoral psychopaths but in the throes of a moral mind-set that appears to them to be every bit as mandatory and universal as ours does to us. Of course, some adversaries really are psychopaths, and others are so poisoned by a punitive moralization that they are beyond the pale of reason. (The actor Will Smith had many historians on his side when he recently speculated to the press that Hitler thought he was acting morally.) But in any conflict in which a meeting of the minds is not completely hopeless, a recognition that the other guy is acting from moral rather than venal reasons can be a first patch of common ground. One side can acknowledge the other's concern for community or stability or fairness or dignity, even while arguing that some other value should trump it in that instance. With affirmative action, for example, the opponents can be seen as arguing from a sense of fairness, not racism, and the defenders can be seen as acting from a concern with community, not bureaucratic power. Liberals can ratify conservatives' concern with families while noting that gay marriage is perfectly consistent with that concern.

The science of the moral sense also alerts us to ways in which our psychological makeup can get in the way of our arriving at the most defensible moral conclusions. The moral sense, we are learning, is as vulnerable to illusions as the other senses. It is apt to confuse morality per se with purity, status and conformity. It tends to reframe practical problems as moral crusades and thus see their solution in punitive aggression. It imposes taboos that make certain ideas indiscussible. And it has the nasty habit of always putting the self on the side of the angels.

Though wise people have long reflected on how we can be blinded by our own sanctimony, our public discourse still fails to discount it appropriately. In the worst cases, the thoughtlessness of our brute intuitions can be celebrated as a virtue. In his influential essay "The Wisdom of Repugnance," Leon Kass, former chair of the President's Council on Bioethics, argued that we should disregard reason when it comes to cloning and other biomedical technologies and go with our gut: "We are repelled by the prospect of cloning human beings . . . because we intuit and feel, immediately and without argument, the violation of things that we rightfully hold dear. . . . In this age in which everything is held to be permissible so long as it is freely done . . . repugnance may be the only voice left that speaks up to defend the central core of our humanity. Shallow are the souls that have forgotten how to shudder."

There are, of course, good reasons to regulate human cloning, but the shudder test is not one of them. People have shuddered at all kinds of morally irrelevant violations of purity in their culture: touching an untouchable, drinking from the same water fountain as a Negro, allowing Jewish blood to mix with Aryan blood, tolerating sodomy between consenting men. And if our ancestors' repugnance had carried the day, we never would have had autopsies, vaccinations, blood transfusions, artificial insemination, organ transplants and in vitro fertilization, all of which were denounced as immoral when they were new.

There are many other issues for which we are too quick to hit the moralization button and look for villains rather than bug fixes. What should we do when a hospital patient is killed by a nurse who administers the wrong drug in a patient's intravenous line? Should we make it easier to sue the hospital for damages? Or should we redesign the IV fittings so that it's physically impossible to connect the wrong bottle to the line?

And nowhere is moralization more of a hazard than in our greatest global challenge. The threat of human-induced climate change has become the occasion for a moralistic revival meeting. In many discussions, the cause of climate change is overindulgence (too many S.U.V.'s) and defilement (sullying the atmosphere), and the solution is temperance (conservation) and expiation (buying carbon offset coupons). Yet the experts agree that these numbers don't add up: even if every last American became conscientious about his or her carbon emissions, the effects on climate change would be trifling, if for no other reason than that two billion Indians and Chinese are unlikely to copy our born-again abstemiousness. Though voluntary conservation may be one wedge in an effective carbon-reduction pie, the other wedges will have to be morally boring, like a carbon tax and new energy technologies, or even taboo, like nuclear power and deliberate manipulation of the ocean and atmosphere. Our habit of moralizing problems, merging them with intuitions of purity and contamination, and resting content when we feel the right feelings, can get in the way of doing the right thing.

Far from debunking morality, then, the science of the moral sense can advance it, by allowing us to see through the illusions that evolution and culture have saddled us with and to focus on goals we can share and defend. As Anton Chekhov wrote, "Man will become better when you show him what he is like."

Locked Horns

Rebecca Solnit

One day not long ago, I went to see a show of animal skulls at the local science museum. I like skulls. What's ordinarily hidden under the upholstery of flesh, skin, hair, and other tissue is revealed in bones, the foundations of bodies and, in the size of craniums, perhaps the seat of consciousness, a sort of naked essence of what makes each animal so distinctly itself. The barn-size room was full of them, from the gray throne of an elephant's head to the yellowish hacksaws of crocodile smiles, all the same raw ingredients of teeth and craniums and eye sockets in spectacularly different proportions corresponding to vision and diet and defense and thought. A wall was covered with a grid of hundreds of sea lion skulls to show their subtle variation, and antlered and horned creatures were lined up on other walls, all the splendor of what in that room seemed apt to call the animal kingdom.

Something I'd missed on a previous visit stopped me cold and made me think for days afterward: a glass case containing four stag skulls, or, rather, two pairs of stag skulls. Each pair of opponents had locked antlers and, unable to disentangle themselves, had died face to face, probably of hunger. The antlers were intricately intertwined like branches of trees that had grown together, and it must have taken only an instant of coincidence when the antlers were angled to fit together like two pieces of a puzzle rather than to clash, a moment when the stags sealed their fates. Such a tangle is fairly common among antlered creatures and some horned ones, such as bighorn sheep, and it's given rise to the phrase "lock horns," which I'd never thought about, any more than I had ever thought why a penknife is called a penknife until I came across Wordsworth mentioning that he used one to trim his quill pen.

Language is full of such fossils of the actual and the natural, but what struck me on this visit was the grimness of the stags' fate and the ease with which it turned to metaphor and to warning. I quickly reviewed my own life to see if any conflicts were so intractable and vowed not to let any so consume me. A lot of people have died of being right, and some of them have taken their opponents with them. Everyone's encountered bad divorces, noise-obsessed neighbors, monomaniacs who let a grievance take over their lives to the exclusion of everything else, a sort of psychological starvation. It's not hard to expand this notion to politics, to the locked horns of the cold war between the Soviet Union and the United States. Nor is it hard to extend the idea to the way the United States seems lost without an opponent abroad—an evil empire, an axis of evil—with which to lock horns, so that rather than reap a peace dividend since 1989, we've watched political leaders look for the familiar embrace of an enemy's antlers.

But it's important to remember that it's a metaphor, that stags are no more prone to divorces than to first-strike missile deployment. Theodor Adorno objected to astrology (or, more specifically, to the astrology column in an American newspaper) because people thought that the stars were about them; better to say that we are about the stars. That is, it's not that stags are like us but that we are like stags. One of the uses of the natural world is the generation of striking images and actions that let us define and redefine ourselves and connect ourselves to everything else. That the natural world gives rise to metaphors by which we understand ourselves is, I have long thought, one of the most neglected reasons for protecting it and paying attention to it. It's important to remember too that biological determinism is just bad analogy: all that stuff claiming we are like our primordial selves, therefore we must eat raw food or copulate with those who look this way or act out that way, is just saying that the stars are about us.

The definition is always partial; the door at the far end is always open for something else to happen, for redefinition. "My love is like a red, red rose," wrote the poet Robert Burns; we assume that there is something about roses—sweetness, redness, delicacy, beauty, ephemerality—that he has in mind and do not picture his sweetheart with thorns, roots, and maybe aphids. Partial resemblance, because metaphor takes us only so far; then we must travel by other means.

The same week I saw the skulls of the stags who'd starved of intractable combat, I went downtown to meet my friend Claire and see the last day of a big show of Yoko Ono's art. It was a magnificent show, and Ono's work managed to do all the things the conceptualists of that era most prized, but with a kind of tender hopefulness that wasn't theirs but hers. At the entrance to the exhibition were two tables, each with two chairs, and the tabletop was a chessboard set with chess pieces, ready to play. But all the chessmen—and the tables, and the chairs, and the board—were white, whiter than the stags' antlers, than their skulls, than their teeth, pure white. In Ono's game, your opponent was no longer different from yourself and maybe no longer your opponent. Can you fight yourself? How do you know when you're winning?

Claire, who has gone around the world doing antinuclear and peace work and now heads Oakland's Martin Luther King Jr. Freedom Center, has many surprising talents, and it turned out that she is an avid chess player. I am not, and I was tired, but that was all to the good, because she was delighted that it took only three moves for me to mistake her rook for mine and move it against her—at which point the game was over, we had unhooked antlers, and Ono had firmly suggested that difference is negligible and conflict avoidable, in this artwork that was about remaking the games and metaphors for war into a playful merging. Further in the exhibition was documentation of Ono's billboards and placards from the Vietnam War era, which said things like "The War Is Over If You Want It." Ono makes it clear not only that we could disengage from conflict but also that with open imagination we could transform it into something else—perhaps into love, a word that crops up all over her work. Stags are stags, but chess doesn't have to be war. Neither does war.

Consider the Lobster

David Foster Wallace

The enormous, pungent, and extremely well-marketed Maine Lobster Festival is held every late July in the state's midcoast region, meaning the western side of Penobscot Bay, the nerve stem of Maine's lobster industry. What's called the midcoast runs from Owl's Head and Thomaston in the south to Belfast in the north. (Actually, it might extend all the way up to Bucksport, but we were never able to get farther north than Belfast on Route 1, whose summer traffic is, as you can imagine, unimaginable.) The region's two main communities are Camden, with its very old money and yachty harbor and five-star restaurants and phenomenal B&Bs, and Rockland, a serious old fishing town that hosts the festival every summer in historic Harbor Park, right along the water.[1]

Tourism and lobster are the midcoast region's two main industries, and they're both warm-weather enterprises, and the Maine Lobster Festival represents less an intersection of the industries than a deliberate collision, joyful and lucrative and loud. The assigned subject of this *Gourmet* article is the 56th Annual MLF, 30 July–3 August 2003, whose official theme this year was "Lighthouses, Laughter, and Lobster." Total paid attendance was over 100,000, due partly to a national CNN spot in June during which a senior editor of *Food & Wine* magazine hailed the MLF as one of the best food-themed galas in the world. 2003 festival highlights: concerts by Lee Ann Womack and Orleans, annual Maine Sea Goddess beauty pageant, Saturday's big parade, Sunday's William G. Atwood Memorial Crate Race, annual Amateur Cooking Competition, carnival rides and midway attractions and food booths, and the MLF's Main Eating Tent, where something over 25,000 pounds of fresh-caught Maine lobster is consumed after preparation in the World's Largest Lobster Cooker near the grounds' north entrance. Also available are lobster rolls, lobster turnovers, lobster sauté, Down East lobster salad, lobster bisque, lobster ravioli, and deep-fried lobster dumplings. Lobster thermidor is obtainable at a sit-down restaurant called the Black Pearl on Harbor Park's northwest wharf. A large all-pine booth sponsored by the Maine Lobster Promotion Council has free pamphlets with recipes, eating tips, and Lobster Fun Facts. The winner of Friday's Amateur

[1] There's a comprehensive native apothegm: "Camden by the sea, Rockland by the smell."

Cooking Competition prepares Saffron Lobster Ramekins, the recipe for which is now available for public downloading at www.mainelobsterfestival.com. There are lobster T-shirts and lobster bobblehead dolls and inflatable lobster pool toys and clamp-on lobster hats with big scarlet claws that wobble on springs. Your assigned correspondent saw it all, accompanied by one girlfriend and both his own parents—one of which parents was actually born and raised in Maine, albeit in the extreme northern inland part, which is potato country and a world away from the touristic midcoast.[2]

For practical purposes, everyone knows what a lobster is. As usual, though, there's much more to know than most of us care about—it's all a matter of what your interests are. Taxonomically speaking, a lobster is a marine crustacean of the family Homaridae, characterized by five pairs of jointed legs, the first pair terminating in large pincerish claws used for subduing prey. Like many other species of benthic carnivore, lobsters are both hunters and scavengers. They have stalked eyes, gills on their legs, and antennae. There are a dozen or so different kinds worldwide, of which the relevant species here is the Maine lobster, *Homarus americanus.* The name "lobster" comes from the Old English *loppestre,* which is thought to be a corrupt form of the Latin word for locust combined with the Old English *loppe,* which meant spider.

Moreover, a crustacean is an aquatic arthropod of the class Crustacea, which comprises crabs, shrimp, barnacles, lobsters, and freshwater crayfish. All this is right there in the encyclopedia. And arthropods are members of the phylum Arthropoda, which phylum covers insects, spiders, crustaceans, and centipedes/millipedes, all of whose main commonality, besides the absence of a centralized brain-spine assembly, is a chitinous exoskeleton composed of segments, to which appendages are articulated in pairs.

The point is that lobsters are basically giant sea insects.[3] Like most arthropods, they date from the Jurassic period, biologically so much older than mammalia that they might as well be from another planet. And they are—particularly in their natural brown-green state, brandishing their claws like weapons and with thick antennae awhip—not nice to look at. And it's true that they are garbagemen of the sea, eaters of dead stuff,[4] although they'll also eat some live shellfish, certain kinds of injured fish, and sometimes one another.

But they are themselves good eating. Or so we think now. Up until sometime in the 1800s, though, lobster was literally low-class food, eaten only by the poor and institutionalized. Even in the harsh penal environment of early America, some colonies had laws against feeding lobsters to inmates more than once a

[2] N.B. All personally connected parties have made it clear from the start that they do not want to be talked about in this article.

[3] Midcoasters' native term for a lobster is, in fact, "bug," as in "Come around on Sunday and we'll cook up some bugs."

[4] Factoid: Lobster traps are usually baited with dead herring.

week because it was thought to be cruel and unusual, like making people eat rats. One reason for their low status was how plentiful lobsters were in old New England. "Unbelievable abundance" is how one source describes the situation, including accounts of Plymouth Pilgrims wading out and capturing all they wanted by hand, and of early Boston's seashore being littered with lobsters after hard storms—these latter were treated as a smelly nuisance and ground up for fertilizer. There is also the fact that premodern lobster was cooked dead and then preserved, usually packed in salt or crude hermetic containers. Maine's earliest lobster industry was based around a dozen such seaside canneries in the 1840s, from which lobster was shipped as far away as California, in demand only because it was cheap and high in protein, basically chewable fuel.

Now, of course, lobster is posh, a delicacy, only a step or two down from caviar. The meat is richer and more substantial than most fish, its taste subtle compared to the marine-gaminess of mussels and clams. In the US pop-food imagination, lobster is now the seafood analog to steak, with which it's so often twinned as Surf 'n' Turf on the really expensive part of the chain steakhouse menu.

In fact, one obvious project of the MLF, and of its omni-presently sponsorial Maine Lobster Promotion Council, is to counter the idea that lobster is unusually luxe or unhealthy or expensive, suitable only for effete palates or the occasional blow-the-diet treat. It is emphasized over and over in presentations and pamphlets at the festival that lobster meat has fewer calories, less cholesterol, and less saturated fat than chicken.[5] And in the Main Eating Tent, you can get a "quarter" (industry shorthand for a 1¼-pound lobster), a four-ounce cup of melted butter, a bag of chips, and a soft roll w/ butter-pat for around $12.00, which is only slightly more expensive than supper at McDonald's.

Be apprised, though, that the Maine Lobster Festival's democratization of lobster comes with all the massed inconvenience and aesthetic compromise of real democracy. See, for example, the aforementioned Main Eating Tent, for which there is a constant Disneyland-grade queue, and which turns out to be a square quarter mile of awning-shaded cafeteria lines and rows of long institutional tables at which friend and stranger alike sit cheek by jowl, cracking and chewing and dribbling. It's hot, and the sagged roof traps the steam and the smells, which latter are strong and only partly food-related. It is also loud, and a good percentage of the total noise is masticatory. The suppers come in styrofoam trays, and the soft drinks are iceless and flat, and the coffee is convenience-store coffee in more styrofoam, and the utensils are plastic (there are none of the special long skinny forks for pushing out the tail meat, though a few savvy diners bring their own). Nor do they give you

[5] Of course, the common practice of dipping the lobster meat in melted butter torpedoes all these happy fat-specs, which none of the council's promotional stuff ever mentions, any more than potato industry PR talks about sour cream and bacon bits.

near enough napkins considering how messy lobster is to eat, especially when you're squeezed onto benches alongside children of various ages and vastly different levels of fine-motor development—not to mention the people who've somehow smuggled in their own beer in enormous aisle-blocking coolers, or who all of a sudden produce their own plastic tablecloths and spread them over large portions of tables to try to reserve them (the tables) for their own little groups. And so on. Any one example is no more than a petty inconvenience, of course, but the MLF turns out to be full of irksome little downers like this—see for instance the Main Stage's headliner shows, where it turns out that you have to pay $20 extra for a folding chair if you want to sit down; or the North Tent's mad scramble for the Nyquil-cup-sized samples of finalists' entries handed out after the Cooking Competition; or the much-touted Maine Sea Goddess pageant finals, which turn out to be excruciatingly long and to consist mainly of endless thanks and tributes to local sponsors. Let's not even talk about the grossly inadequate Port-A-San facilities or the fact that there's nowhere to wash your hands before or after eating. What the Maine Lobster Festival really is is a midlevel county fair with a culinary hook, and in this respect it's not unlike Tidewater crab festivals, Midwest corn festivals, Texas chili festivals, etc., and shares with these venues the core paradox of all teeming commercial demotic events: It's not for everyone.[6] Nothing

[6] In truth, there's a great deal to be said about the differences between working-class Rockland and the heavily populist flavor of its festival versus comfortable and elitist Camden with its expensive view and shops given entirely over to $200 sweaters and great rows of Victorian homes converted to upscale B&Bs. And about these differences as two sides of the great coin that is US tourism. Very little of which will be said here, except to amplify the above-mentioned paradox and to reveal your assigned correspondent's own preferences. I confess that I have never understood why so many people's idea of a fun vacation is to don flip-flops and sunglasses and crawl through maddening traffic to loud, hot, crowded tourist venues in order to sample a "local flavor" that is by definition ruined by the presence of tourists. This may (as my festival companions keep pointing out) all be a matter of personality and hardwired taste: the fact that I do not like tourist venues means that I'll never understand their appeal and so am probably not the one to talk about it (the supposed appeal). But, since this FN will almost surely not survive magazine-editing anyway, here goes:

As I see it, it probably really is good for the soul to be a tourist, even if it's only once in a while. Not good for the soul in a refreshing or enlivening way, though, but rather in a grim, steely-eyed, let's-look-honestly-at-the-facts-and-find-some-way-to-deal-with-them way. My personal experience has not been that traveling around the country is broadening or relaxing, or that radical changes in place and context have a salutary effect, but rather that intranational tourism is radically constricting, and humbling in the hardest way—hostile to my fantasy of being a true individual, of living somehow outside and above it all. (Coming up is the part that my companions find especially unhappy and repellent, a sure way to spoil the fun of vacation travel:) To be a mass tourist, for me, is to become a pure late-date American: alien, ignorant, greedy for something you cannot ever have, disappointed in a way you can never admit. It is to spoil, by way of sheer ontology, the very unspoiledness you are there to experience. It is to impose yourself on places that in all non-economic ways would be better, realer, without you. It is, in lines and gridlock and transaction after transaction, to confront a dimension of yourself that is as inescapable as it is painful: As a tourist, you become economically significant but existentially loathsome, an insect on a dead thing.

against the euphoric senior editor of *Food & Wine*, but I'd be surprised if she'd ever actually been here in Harbor Park, amid crowds of people slapping canal-zone mosquitoes as they eat deep-fried Twinkies and watch Professor Paddywhack, on six-foot stilts in a raincoat with plastic lobsters protruding from all directions on springs, terrify their children.

Lobster is essentially a summer food. This is because we now prefer our lobsters fresh, which means they have to be recently caught, which for both tactical and economic reasons takes place at depths less than 25 fathoms. Lobsters tend to be hungriest and most active (i.e., most trappable) at summer water temperatures of 45–50 degrees. In the autumn, most Maine lobsters migrate out into deeper water, either for warmth or to avoid the heavy waves that pound New England's coast all winter. Some burrow into the bottom. They might hibernate; nobody's sure. Summer is also lobsters' molting season—specifically early- to mid-July. Chitinous arthropods grow by molting, rather the way people have to buy bigger clothes as they age and gain weight. Since lobsters can live to be over 100, they can also get to be quite large, as in 30 pounds or more—though truly senior lobsters are rare now because New England's waters are so heavily trapped.[7] Anyway, hence the culinary distinction between hard- and soft-shell lobsters, the latter sometimes a.k.a. shedders. A soft-shell lobster is one that has recently molted. In midcoast restaurants, the summer menu often offers both kinds, with shedders being slightly cheaper even though they're easier to dismantle and the meat is allegedly sweeter. The reason for the discount is that a molting lobster uses a layer of seawater for insulation while its new shell is hardening, so there's slightly less actual meat when you crack open a shedder, plus a redolent gout of water that gets all over everything and can sometimes jet out lemonlike and catch a tablemate right in the eye. If it's winter or you're buying lobster someplace far from New England, on the other hand, you can almost bet that the lobster is a hard-shell, which for obvious reasons travel better.

As an à la carte entrée, lobster can be baked, broiled, steamed, grilled, sautéed, stir-fried, or microwaved. The most common method, though, is boiling. If you're someone who enjoys having lobster at home, this is probably the way you do it, since boiling is so easy. You need a large kettle w/cover, which you fill about half full with water (the standard advice is that you want 2.5 quarts of water per lobster). Seawater is optimal, or you can add two tbsp salt per quart from the tap. It also helps to know how much your lobsters weigh. You get the water boiling, put in the lobsters one at a time, cover the kettle, and bring it back up to a boil. Then you bank the heat and let the kettle simmer—ten minutes

[7] Datum: In a good year, the US industry produces around 80,000,000 pounds of lobster, and Maine accounts for more than half that total.

for the first pound of lobster, then three minutes for each pound after that. (This is assuming you've got hard-shell lobsters, which, again, if you don't live between Boston and Halifax is probably what you've got. For shedders, you're supposed to subtract three minutes from the total.) The reason the kettle's lobsters turn scarlet is that boiling somehow suppresses every pigment in their chitin but one. If you want an easy test of whether the lobsters are done, you try pulling on one of their antennae—if it comes out of the head with minimal effort, you're ready to eat.

A detail so obvious that most recipes don't even bother to mention it is that each lobster is supposed to be alive when you put it in the kettle. This is part of lobster's modern appeal—it's the freshest food there is. There's no decomposition between harvesting and eating. And not only do lobsters require no cleaning or dressing or plucking, they're relatively easy for vendors to keep alive. They come up alive in the traps, are placed in containers of seawater, and can—so long as the water's aerated and the animals' claws are pegged or banded to keep them from tearing one another up under the stresses of captivity[8]—survive right up until they're boiled. Most of us have been in supermarkets or restaurants that feature tanks of live lobsters, from which you can pick out your supper while it watches you point. And part of the overall spectacle of the Maine Lobster Festival is that you can see actual lobstermen's vessels docking at the wharves along the northeast grounds and unloading fresh-caught product, which is transferred by hand or cart 150 yards to the great clear tanks stacked up around the festival's cooker—which is, as mentioned, billed as the World's Largest Lobster Cooker and can process over 100 lobsters at a time for the Main Eating Tent.

So then here is a question that's all but unavoidable at the World's Largest Lobster Cooker, and may arise in kitchens across the US: Is it all right to boil a sentient creature alive just for our gustatory pleasure? A related set of concerns: Is the previous question irksomely PC or sentimental? What does "all right" even mean in this context? Is the whole thing just a matter of personal choice?

As you may or may not know, a certain well-known group called People for the Ethical Treatment of Animals thinks that the morality of lobster-

[8] N.B. Similar reasoning underlies the practice of what's termed "debeaking" broiler chickens and brood hens in modern factory farms. Maximum commercial efficiency requires that enormous poultry populations be confined in unnaturally close quarters, under which conditions many birds go crazy and peck one another to death. As a purely observational side-note, be apprised that debeaking is usually an automated process and that the chickens receive no anesthetic. It's not clear to me whether most *Gourmet* readers know about debeaking, or about related practices like dehorning cattle in commercial feed lots, cropping swine's tails in factory hog farms to keep psychotically bored neighbors from chewing them off, and so forth. It so happens that your assigned correspondent knew almost nothing about standard meat-industry operations before starting work on this article.

boiling is not just a matter of individual conscience. In fact, one of the very first things we hear about the MLF . . . well, to set the scene: We're coming in by cab from the almost indescribably odd and rustic Knox County Airport[9] very late on the night before the festival opens, sharing the cab with a wealthy political consultant who lives on Vinalhaven Island in the bay half the year (he's headed for the island ferry in Rockland). The consultant and cabdriver are responding to informal journalistic probes about how people who live in the midcoast region actually view the MLF, as in is the festival just a big-dollar tourist thing or is it something local residents look forward to attending, take genuine civic pride in, etc. The cabdriver (who's in his seventies, one of apparently a whole platoon of retirees the cab company puts on to help with the summer rush, and wears a US-flag lapel pin, and drives in what can only be called a very *deliberate* way) assures us that locals do endorse and enjoy the MLF, although he himself hasn't gone in years, and now come to think of it no one he and his wife know has, either. However, the demilocal consultant's been to recent festivals a couple times (one gets the impression it was at his wife's behest), of which his most vivid impression was that "you have to line up for an ungodly long time to get your lobsters, and meanwhile there are all these ex–flower children coming up and down along the line handing out pamphlets that say the lobsters die in terrible pain and you shouldn't eat them."

And it turns out that the post-hippies of the consultant's recollection were activists from PETA. There were no PETA people in obvious view at the 2003 MLF,[10] but they've been conspicuous at many of the recent festivals. Since at least the mid-1990s, articles in everything from the *Camden Herald* to the *New York Times* have described PETA urging boycotts of the Maine Lobster

[9] The terminal used to be somebody's house, for example, and the lost-luggage-reporting room was clearly once a pantry.

[10] It turned out that one Mr. William R. Rivas-Rivas, a high-ranking PETA official out of the group's Virginia headquarters, was indeed there this year, albeit solo, working the festival's main and side entrances on Saturday, 2 August, handing out pamphlets and adhesive stickers emblazoned with "Being Boiled Hurts," which is the tagline in most of PETA's published material about lobsters. I learned that he'd been there only later, when speaking with Mr. Rivas-Rivas on the phone. I'm not sure how we missed seeing him *in situ* at the festival, and I can't see much to do except apologize for the oversight—although it's also true that Saturday was the day of the big MLF parade through Rockland, which basic journalistic responsibility seemed to require going to (and which, with all due respect, meant that Saturday was maybe not the best day for PETA to work the Harbor Park grounds, especially if it was going to be just one person for one day, since a lot of diehard MLF partisans were off-site watching the parade (which, again with no offense intended, was in truth kind of cheesy and boring, consisting mostly of slow homemade floats and various midcoast people waving at one another, and with an extremely annoying man dressed as Blackbeard ranging up and down the length of the crowd saying "Arrr" over and over and brandishing a plastic sword at people, etc.; plus it rained)).

Festival, often deploying celebrity spokesmen like Mary Tyler Moore for open letters and ads saying stuff like "Lobsters are extraordinarily sensitive" and "To me, eating a lobster is out of the question." More concrete is the oral testimony of Dick, our florid and extremely gregarious rental-car liaison,[11] to the effect that PETA's been around so much during recent years that a kind of brittlely tolerant homeostasis now obtains between the activists and the festival's locals, e.g.: "We had some incidents a couple years ago. One lady took most of her clothes off and painted herself like a lobster, almost got herself arrested. But for the most part they're let alone. [Rapid series of small ambiguous laughs, which with Dick happens a lot.] They do their thing and we do our thing."

This whole interchange takes place on Route 1, 30 July, during a four-mile, 50-minute ride from the airport[12] to the dealership to sign car-rental papers. Several irreproducible segues down the road from the PETA anecdotes, Dick—whose son-in-law happens to be a professional lobsterman and one of the Main Eating Tent's regular suppliers—explains what he and his family feel is the crucial mitigating factor in the whole morality-of-boiling-lobsters-alive issue: "There's a part of the brain in people and animals that lets us feel pain, and lobsters' brains don't have this part."

Besides the fact that it's incorrect in about nine different ways, the main reason Dick's statement is interesting is that its thesis is more or less echoed by the festival's own pronouncement on lobsters and pain, which is part of a Test Your Lobster IQ quiz that appears in the 2003 MLF program courtesy of the Maine Lobster Promotion Council:

> The nervous system of a lobster is very simple, and is in fact most similar to the nervous system of the grasshopper. It is decentralized with no brain. There is no cerebral cortex, which in humans is the area of the brain that gives the experience of pain.

Though it sounds more sophisticated, a lot of the neurology in this latter claim is still either false or fuzzy. The human cerebral cortex is the brain-part that deals with higher faculties like reason, metaphysical self-awareness, language, etc. Pain reception is known to be part of a much older and more primitive system of nociceptors and prostaglandins that are managed by the

[11] By profession, Dick is actually a car salesman; the midcoast region's National Car Rental franchise operates out of a Chevy dealership in Thomaston.

[12] The short version regarding why we were back at the airport after already arriving the previous night involves lost luggage and a miscommunication about where and what the midcoast's National franchise was—Dick came out personally to the airport and got us, out of no evident motive but kindness. (He also talked nonstop the entire way, with a very distinctive speaking style that can be described only as manically laconic; the truth is that I now know more about this man than I do about some members of my own family.)

brain stem and thalamus.[13] On the other hand, it is true that the cerebral cortex is involved in what's variously called suffering, distress, or the emotional experience of pain—i.e., experiencing painful stimuli as unpleasant, very unpleasant, unbearable, and so on.

Before we go any further, let's acknowledge that the questions of whether and how different kinds of animals feel pain, and of whether and why it might be justifiable to inflict pain on them in order to eat them, turn out to be extremely complex and difficult. And comparative neuroanatomy is only part of the problem. Since pain is a totally subjective mental experience, we do not have direct access to anyone or anything's pain but our own; and even just the principles by which we can infer that other human beings experience pain and have a legitimate interest in not feeling pain involve hardcore philosophy—metaphysics, epistemology, value theory, ethics. The fact that even the most highly evolved nonhuman mammals can't use language to communicate with us about their subjective mental experience is only the first layer of additional complication in trying to extend our reasoning about pain and morality to animals. And everything gets progressively more abstract and convolved as we move farther and farther out from the higher-type mammals into cattle and swine and dogs and cats and rodents, and then birds and fish, and finally invertebrates like lobsters.

The more important point here, though, is that the whole animal-cruelty-and-eating issue is not just complex, it's also uncomfortable. It is, at any rate, uncomfortable for me, and for just about everyone I know who enjoys a variety of foods and yet does not want to see herself as cruel or unfeeling. As far as I can tell, my own main way of dealing with this conflict has been to avoid thinking about the whole unpleasant thing. I should add that it appears to me unlikely that many readers of *Gourmet* wish to think about it, either, or to be queried about the morality of their eating habits in the pages of a culinary monthly. Since, however, the assigned subject of this article is what it was like to attend the 2003 MLF, and thus to spend several days in the midst of a great mass of Americans all eating lobster, and thus to be more or less impelled to think hard about lobster and the experience of buying and eating lobster, it turns out that there is no honest way to avoid certain moral questions.

There are several reasons for this. For one thing, it's not just that lobsters get boiled alive, it's that you do it yourself—or at least it's done specifically

[13] To elaborate by way of example: The common experience of accidentally touching a hot stove and yanking your hand back before you're even aware that anything's going on is explained by the fact that many of the processes by which we detect and avoid painful stimuli do not involve the cortex. In the case of the hand and stove, the brain is bypassed altogether; all the important neurochemical action takes place in the spine.

for you, on-site.[14] As mentioned, the World's Largest Lobster Cooker, which is highlighted as an attraction in the festival's program, is right out there on the MLF's north grounds for everyone to see. Try to imagine a Nebraska Beef Festival[15] at which part of the festivities is watching trucks pull up and the live cattle get driven down the ramp and slaughtered right there on the World's Largest Killing Floor or something—there's no way.

The intimacy of the whole thing is maximized at home, which of course is where most lobster gets prepared and eaten (although note already the semiconscious euphemism "prepared," which in the case of lobsters really means killing them right there in our kitchens). The basic scenario is that we come in from the store and make our little preparations like getting the kettle filled and boiling, and then we lift the lobsters out of the bag or whatever retail container they came home in . . . whereupon some uncomfortable things start to happen. However stuporous a lobster is from the trip home, for instance, it tends to come alarmingly to life when placed in boiling water. If you're tilting it from a container into the steaming kettle, the lobster will sometimes try to cling to the container's sides or even to hook its claws over the kettle's rim like a person trying to keep from going over the edge of a roof. And worse is when the lobster's fully immersed. Even if you cover the kettle and turn away, you can usually hear the cover rattling and clanking as the lobster tries to push it off. Or the creature's claws scraping the sides of the kettle as it thrashes around. The lobster, in other words, behaves very much as you or I would behave if we were plunged into boiling water (with the obvious exception of screaming[16]). A blunter

[14] Morality-wise, let's concede that this cuts both ways. Lobster-eating is at least not abetted by the system of corporate factory farms that produces most beef, pork, and chicken. Because, if nothing else, of the way they're marketed and packaged for sale, we eat these latter meats without having to consider that they were once conscious, sentient creatures to whom horrible things were done. (N.B. "Horrible" here meaning really, really horrible. Write off to PETA or peta.org for their free "Meet Your Meat" video, narrated by Mr. Alec Baldwin, if you want to see just about everything meat-related you don't want to see or think about. (N.B.$_2$ Not that PETA's any sort of font of unspun truth. Like many partisans in complex moral disputes, the PETA people are fanatics, and a lot of their rhetoric seems simplistic and self-righteous. But this particular video, replete with actual factory-farm and corporate-slaughterhouse footage, is both credible and traumatizing.))

[15] Is it significant that "lobster," "fish," and "chicken" are our culture's words for both the animal and the meat, whereas most mammals seem to require euphemisms like "beef" and "pork" that help us separate the meat we eat from the living creature the meat once was? Is this evidence that some kind of deep unease about eating higher animals is endemic enough to show up in English usage, but that the unease diminishes as we move out of the mammalian order? (And is "lamb"/"lamb" the counterexample that sinks the whole theory, or are there special, biblico-historical reasons for that equivalence?)

[16] There's a relevant populist myth about the high-pitched whistling sound that sometimes issues from a pot of boiling lobster. The sound is really vented steam from the layer of seawater between the lobster's flesh and its carapace (this is why shedders whistle more than hard-shells), but the pop version has it that the sound is the lobster's rabbit-like death-scream. Lobsters communicate via pheromones in their urine and don't have anything close to the vocal equipment for screaming, but the myth's very persistent—which might, once again, point to a low-level cultural unease about the boiling thing.

way to say this is that the lobster acts as if it's in terrible pain, causing some cooks to leave the kitchen altogether and to take one of those little lightweight plastic oven-timers with them into another room and wait until the whole process is over.

There happen to be two main criteria that most ethicists agree on for determining whether a living creature has the capacity to suffer and so has genuine interests that it may or may not be our moral duty to consider.[17] One is how much of the neurological hardware required for pain-experience the animal comes equipped with—nociceptors, prostaglandins, neuronal opioid receptors, etc. The other criterion is whether the animal demonstrates behavior associated with pain. And it takes a lot of intellectual gymnastics and behaviorist hairsplitting not to see struggling, thrashing, and lid-clattering as just such pain-behavior. According to marine zoologists, it usually takes lobsters between 35 and 45 seconds to die in boiling water. (No source I could find talks about how long it takes them to die in superheated steam; one rather hopes it's faster.)

There are, of course, other ways to kill your lobster on-site and so achieve maximum freshness. Some cooks' practice is to drive a sharp heavy knife point-first into a spot just above the midpoint between the lobster's eyestalks (more or less where the Third Eye is in human foreheads). This is alleged either to kill the lobster instantly or to render it insensate, and is said at least to eliminate some of the cowardice involved in throwing a creature into boiling water and then fleeing the room. As far as I can tell from talking to proponents of the knife-in-head method, the idea is that it's more violent but ultimately more merciful, plus that a willingness to exert personal agency and accept responsibility for stabbing the lobster's head honors the lobster somehow and entitles one to eat it (there's often a vague sort of Native American spirituality-of-the-hunt flavor to pro-knife arguments). But the problem with the knife method is basic biology: Lobsters' nervous systems operate off not one but several ganglia, a.k.a. nerve bundles, which are sort of wired in series and distributed all along the lobster's underside, from stem to stern. And disabling only the frontal ganglion does not normally result in quick death or unconsciousness.

Another alternative is to put the lobster in cold saltwater and then very slowly bring it up to a full boil. Cooks who advocate this method are going

[17] "Interests" basically means strong and legitimate preferences, which obviously require some degree of consciousness, responsiveness to stimuli, etc. See, for instance, the utilitarian philosopher Peter Singer, whose 1974 *Animal Liberation* is more or less the bible of the modern animal-rights movement:

> It would be nonsense to say that it was not in the interests of a stone to be kicked along the road by a schoolboy. A stone does not have interests because it cannot suffer. Nothing that we can do to it could possibly make any difference to its welfare. A mouse, on the other hand, does have an interest in not being kicked along the road, because it will suffer if it is.

on the analogy to a frog, which can supposedly be kept from jumping out of a boiling pot by heating the water incrementally. In order to save a lot of research-summarizing, I'll simply assure you that the analogy between frogs and lobsters turns out not to hold—plus, if the kettle's water isn't aerated seawater, the immersed lobster suffers from slow suffocation, although usually not decisive enough suffocation to keep it from still thrashing and clattering when the water gets hot enough to kill it. In fact, lobsters boiled incrementally often display a whole bonus set of gruesome, convulsionlike reactions that you don't see in regular boiling.

Ultimately, the only certain virtues of the home-lobotomy and slow-heating methods are comparative, because there are even worse/crueler ways people prepare lobster. Time-thrifty cooks sometimes microwave them alive (usually after poking several vent-holes in the carapace, which is a precaution most shellfish-microwavers learn about the hard way). Live dismemberment, on the other hand, is big in Europe—some chefs cut the lobster in half before cooking; others like to tear off the claws and tail and toss only these parts into the pot.

And there's more unhappy news respecting suffering-criterion number one. Lobsters don't have much in the way of eyesight or hearing, but they do have an exquisite tactile sense, one facilitated by hundreds of thousands of tiny hairs that protrude through their carapace. "Thus it is," in the words of T. M. Prudden's industry classic *About Lobster*, "that although encased in what seems a solid, impenetrable armor, the lobster can receive stimuli and impressions from without as readily as if it possessed a soft and delicate skin." And lobsters do have nociceptors,[18] as well as invertebrate versions of the prostaglandins and major neurotransmitters via which our own brains register pain.

Lobsters do not, on the other hand, appear to have the equipment for making or absorbing natural opioids like endorphins and enkephalins, which are what more advanced nervous systems use to try to handle intense pain. From this fact, though, one could conclude either that lobsters are maybe even *more* vulnerable to pain, since they lack mammalian nervous systems' built-in analgesia, or, instead, that the absence of natural opioids implies an absence of the really intense pain-sensations that natural opioids are designed to mitigate. I for one can detect a marked upswing in mood as I contemplate this latter possibility. It could be that their lack of endorphin/enkephalin hardware means that lobsters' raw subjective experience of pain is so radically different from mammals' that it may not even deserve the term "pain." Perhaps lobsters are more like those frontal-lobotomy patients one reads about who report experiencing pain in a totally different way than you and I. These

[18] This is the neurological term for special pain-receptors that are "sensitive to potentially damaging extremes of temperature, to mechanical forces, and to chemical substances which are released when body tissues are damaged."

patients evidently do feel physical pain, neurologically speaking, but don't dislike it—though neither do they like it; it's more that they feel it but don't feel anything *about* it—the point being that the pain is not distressing to them or something they want to get away from. Maybe lobsters, who are also without frontal lobes, are detached from the neurological-registration-of-injury-or-hazard we call pain in just the same way. There is, after all, a difference between (1) pain as a purely neurological event, and (2) actual suffering, which seems crucially to involve an emotional component, an awareness of pain as unpleasant, as something to fear/dislike/want to avoid.

Still, after all the abstract intellection, there remain the facts of the frantically clanking lid, the pathetic clinging to the edge of the pot. Standing at the stove, it is hard to deny in any meaningful way that this is a living creature experiencing pain and wishing to avoid/escape the painful experience. To my lay mind, the lobster's behavior in the kettle appears to be the expression of a *preference;* and it may well be that an ability to form preferences is the decisive criterion for real suffering.[19] The logic of this (preference ⟶ suffering) relation may be easiest to see in the negative case. If you cut certain kinds of worms in half, the halves will often keep crawling around and going about their vermiform business as if nothing had happened. When we assert, based on their post-op behavior, that these worms appear not to be suffering, what we're really saying is that there's no sign the worms know anything bad has happened or would *prefer* not to have gotten cut in half.

Lobsters, though, are known to exhibit preferences. Experiments have shown that they can detect changes of only a degree or two in water temperature; one reason for their complex migratory cycles (which can often cover 100-plus miles a year) is to pursue the temperatures they like best.[20] And, as

[19] "Preference" is maybe roughly synonymous with "interests," but it is a better term for our purposes because it's less abstractly philosophical—"preference" seems more personal, and it's the whole idea of a living creature's personal experience that's at issue.

[20] Of course, the most common sort of counterargument here would begin by objecting that "like best" is really just a metaphor, and a misleadingly anthropomorphic one at that. The counterarguer would posit that the lobster seeks to maintain a certain optimal ambient temperature out of nothing but unconscious instinct (with a similar explanation for the low-light affinities upcoming in the main text). The thrust of such a counterargument will be that the lobster's thrashings and clankings in the kettle express not unpreferred pain but involuntary reflexes, like your leg shooting out when the doctor hits your knee. Be advised that there are professional scientists, including many researchers who use animals in experiments, who hold to the view that nonhuman creatures have no real feelings at all, merely "behaviors." Be further advised that this view has a long history that goes all the way back to Descartes, although its modern support comes mostly from behaviorist psychology.

To these what-looks-like-pain-is-really-just-reflexes counterarguments, however, there happen to be all sorts of scientific and pro–animal rights counter-counterarguments. And then further attempted rebuttals and redirects, and so on. Suffice it to say that both the scientific and the philosophical arguments on either side of the animal-suffering issue are involved, abstruse, technical, often informed by self-interest or ideology, and in the end so totally inconclusive that as a practical matter, in the kitchen or restaurant, it all still seems to come down to individual conscience, going with (no pun) your gut.

mentioned, they're bottom-dwellers and do not like bright light—if a tank of food-lobsters is out in the sunlight or a store's fluorescence, the lobsters will always congregate in whatever part is darkest. Fairly solitary in the ocean, they also clearly dislike the crowding that's part of their captivity in tanks, since (as also mentioned) one reason why lobsters' claws are banded on capture is to keep them from attacking one another under the stress of close-quarter storage.

In any event, at the MLF, standing by the bubbling tanks outside the World's Largest Lobster Cooker, watching the fresh-caught lobsters pile over one another, wave their hobbled claws impotently, huddle in the rear corners, or scrabble frantically back from the glass as you approach, it is difficult not to sense that they're unhappy, or frightened, even if it's some rudimentary version of these feelings . . . and, again, why does rudimentariness even enter into it? Why is a primitive, inarticulate form of suffering less urgent or uncomfortable for the person who's helping to inflict it by paying for the food it results in? I'm not trying to give you a PETA-like screed here—at least I don't think so. I'm trying, rather, to work out and articulate some of the troubling questions that arise amid all the laughter and saltation and community pride of the Maine Lobster Festival. The truth is that if you, the festival attendee, permit yourself to think that lobsters can suffer and would rather not, the MLF begins to take on the aspect of something like a Roman circus or medieval torture-fest.

Does that comparison seem a bit much? If so, exactly why? Or what about this one: Is it possible that future generations will regard our present agribusiness and eating practices in much the same way we now view Nero's entertainments or Mengele's experiments? My own initial reaction is that such a comparison is hysterical, extreme—and yet the reason it seems extreme to me appears to be that I believe animals are less morally important than human beings;[21] and when it comes to defending such a belief, even to myself, I have to acknowledge that (a) I have an obvious selfish interest in this belief, since I like to eat certain kinds of animals and want to be able to keep doing it, and (b) I haven't succeeded in working out any sort of personal ethical system in which the belief is truly defensible instead of just selfishly convenient.

Given this article's venue and my own lack of culinary sophistication, I'm curious about whether the reader can identify with any of these reactions and acknowledgments and discomforts. I'm also concerned not to come off as shrill or preachy when what I really am is more like confused. For those

[21] Meaning *a lot* less important, apparently, since the moral comparison here is not the value of one human's life vs. the value of one animal's life, but rather the value of one animal's life vs. the value of one human's taste for a particular kind of protein. Even the most diehard carniphile will acknowledge that it's possible to live and eat well without consuming animals.

Gourmet readers who enjoy well-prepared and -presented meals involving beef, veal, lamb, pork, chicken, lobster, etc.: Do you think much about the (possible) moral status and (probable) suffering of the animals involved? If you do, what ethical convictions have you worked out that permit you not just to eat but to savor and enjoy flesh-based viands (since of course refined *enjoyment*, rather than mere ingestion, is the whole point of gastronomy)? If, on the other hand, you'll have no truck with confusions or convictions and regard stuff like the previous paragraph as just so much fatuous navel-gazing, what makes it feel truly okay, inside, to just dismiss the whole thing out of hand? That is, is your refusal to think about any of this the product of actual thought, or is it just that you don't want to think about it? And if the latter, then why not? Do you ever think, even idly, about the possible reasons for your reluctance to think about it? I am not trying to bait anyone here—I'm genuinely curious. After all, isn't being extra aware and attentive and thoughtful about one's food and its overall context part of what distinguishes a real gourmet? Or is all the gourmet's extra attention and sensibility just supposed to be sensuous? Is it really all just a matter of taste and presentation?

we convince ourselves that our behavior is warranted

These last few queries, though, while sincere, obviously involve much larger and more abstract questions about the connections (if any) between aesthetics and morality—about what the adjective in a phrase like "The Magazine of Good Living" is really supposed to mean—and these questions lead straightaway into such deep and treacherous waters that it's probably best to stop the public discussion right here. There are limits to what even interested persons can ask of each other.

we avoid thinking about things that make us feel uncomfortable or immoral

A Room of One's Own, Chapter Six

Virginia Woolf

Next day the light of the October morning was falling in dusty shafts through the uncurtained windows, and the hum of traffic rose from the street. London then was winding itself up again; the factory was astir; the machines were beginning. It was tempting, after all this reading, to look out of the window and see what London was doing on the morning of the twenty-sixth of October 1928. And what was London doing? Nobody, it seemed, was reading *Antony and Cleopatra.* London was wholly indifferent, it appeared, to Shakespeare's plays. Nobody cared a straw—and I do not blame them—for the future of fiction, the death of poetry or the development by the average woman of a prose style completely expressive of her mind. If opinions upon any of these matters had been chalked on the pavement, nobody would have stooped to read them. The nonchalance of the hurrying feet would have rubbed them out in half an hour. Here came an errandboy; here a woman with a dog on a lead. The fascination of the London street is that no two people are ever alike; each seems bound on some private affair of his own. There were the business-like, with their little bags; there were the drifters rattling sticks upon area railings; there were affable characters to whom the streets serve for clubroom, hailing men in carts and giving information without being asked for it. Also there were funerals to which men, thus suddenly reminded of the passing of their own bodies, lifted their hats. And then a very distinguished gentleman came slowly down a doorstep and paused to avoid collision with a bustling lady who had, by some means or other, acquired a splendid fur coat and a bunch of Parma violets. They all seemed separate, self-absorbed, on business of their own.

At this moment, as so often happens in London, there was a complete lull and suspension of traffic. Nothing came down the street; nobody passed. A single leaf detached itself from the plane tree at the end of the street, and in that pause and suspension fell. Somehow it was like a signal falling, a signal pointing to a force in things which one had overlooked. It seemed to point to a river, which flowed past, invisibly, round the corner, down the street, and took people and eddied them along, as the stream at Oxbridge had taken the undergraduate in his boat and the dead leaves. Now it was bringing from one side of the street to the other diagonally a girl in patent leather boots, and then a young man in a maroon overcoat; it was also bringing a taxi-cab; and it brought all three together at a point directly beneath my window; where the taxi stopped; and the girl and the young man stopped; and they got into the taxi; and then the cab glided off as if it were swept on by the current elsewhere.

The sight was ordinary enough; what was strange was the rhythmical order with which my imagination had invested it; and the fact that the ordinary sight of two people getting into a cab had the power to communicate something of their own seeming satisfaction. The sight of two people coming down the street and meeting at the corner seems to ease the mind of some strain, I thought, watching the taxi turn and make off. Perhaps to think, as I had been thinking these two days, of one sex as distinct from the other is an effort. It interferes with the unity of the mind. Now that effort had ceased and that unity had been restored by seeing two people come together and get into a taxi-cab. The mind is certainly a very mysterious organ, I reflected, drawing my head in from the window, about which nothing whatever is known, though we depend upon it so completely. Why do I feel that there are severances and oppositions in the mind, as there are strains from obvious causes on the body? What does one mean by "the unity of the mind," I pondered, for clearly the mind has so great a power of concentrating at any point at any moment that it seems to have no single state of being. It can separate itself from the people in the street, for example, and think of itself as apart from them, at an upper window looking down on them. Or it can think with other people spontaneously, as, for instance, in a crowd waiting to hear some piece of news read out. It can think back through its fathers or through its mothers, as I have said that a woman writing thinks back through her mothers. Again if one is a woman one is often surprised by a sudden splitting off of consciousness, say in walking down Whitehall, when from being the natural inheritor of that civilisation, she becomes, on the contrary, outside of it, alien and critical. Clearly the mind is always altering its focus, and bringing the world into different perspectives. But some of these states of mind seem, even if adopted spontaneously, to be less comfortable than others. In order to keep oneself continuing in them one is unconsciously holding something back, and gradually the repression becomes an effort. But there may be some state of mind in which one could continue without effort because nothing is required to be held back. And this perhaps, I thought, coming in from the window, is one of them. For certainly when I saw the couple get into the taxi-cab the mind felt as if, after being divided, it had come together again in a natural fusion. The obvious reason would be that it is natural for the sexes to co-operate. One has a profound, if irrational, instinct in favour of the theory that the union of man and woman makes for the greatest satisfaction, the most complete happiness. But the sight of the two people getting into the taxi and the satisfaction it gave me made me also ask whether there are two sexes in the mind corresponding to the two sexes in the body, and whether they also require to be united in order to get complete satisfaction and happiness. And I went on amateurishly to sketch a plan of the soul so that in each of us two powers preside, one male, one female; and in the man's brain, the man predominates over the woman, and in the woman's brain, the woman predominates over the man. The normal and comfortable state of being is that when the two live in harmony together, spiritually co-operating. If one is a man, still the woman part of the brain must have effect; and a woman also must have intercourse with the man in her. Coleridge perhaps meant this when he said that a great mind is androgynous. It is when this fusion takes place that the mind is fully fertilised and uses all its faculties. Perhaps a mind that is purely masculine cannot create, any more than a mind that is purely feminine, I thought. But it would be well to test what one meant by man-womanly, and conversely by woman-manly, by pausing and looking at a book or two.

Coleridge certainly did not mean, when he said that a great mind is androgynous, that it is a mind that has any special sympathy with women; a mind that takes up their cause or devotes itself to their interpretation. Perhaps the androgynous mind is less apt to make these distinctions than the single-sexed mind. He meant, perhaps, that the androgynous mind is resonant and porous; that it transmits emotion without impediment; that it is naturally creative, incandescent and undivided. In fact one goes back to Shakespeare's mind as the type of the androgynous, of the man-womanly mind, though it would be impossible to say what Shakespeare thought of women. And if it be true that it is one of the tokens of the fully developed mind that it does not think specially or separately of sex, how much harder it is to attain that condition now than ever before. Here I came to the books by living writers, and there paused and wondered if this fact were not at the root of something that had long puzzled me. No age can ever have been as stridently sex-conscious as our own; those innumerable books by men about women in the British Museum are a proof of it. The Suffrage campaign was no doubt to blame. It must have roused in men an extraordinary desire for self-assertion; it must have made them lay an emphasis upon their own sex and its characteristics which they would not have troubled to think about had they not been challenged. And when one is challenged, even by a few women in black bonnets, one retaliates, if one has never been challenged before, rather excessively. That perhaps accounts for some of the characteristics that I remember to have found here, I thought, taking down a new novel by Mr. A, who is in the prime of life and very well thought of, apparently, by the reviewers. I opened it. Indeed, it was delightful to read a man's writing again. It was so direct, so straightforward after the writing of women. In indicated such freedom of mind, such liberty of person, such confidence in himself. One had a sense of physical well-being in the presence of this well-nourished, well-educated, free mind, which had never been thwarted or opposed, but had had full liberty from birth to stretch itself in whatever way it liked. All this was admirable. But after reading a chapter or two a shadow seemed to lie across the page. It was a straight dark bar, a shadow shaped something like the letter "I." One began dodging this way and that to catch a glimpse of the landscape behind it. Whether that was indeed a tree or a woman walking I was not quite sure. Back one was always hailed to the letter "I." One began to be tired of "I." Not but what this "I" was a most respectable "I"; honest and logical; as hard as a nut, and polished for centuries by good teaching and good feeding. I respect and admire that "I" from the bottom of my heart. But—here I turned a page or two, looking for something or other—the worst of it is that in the shadow of the letter "I" all is shapeless as mist. Is that a tree? No, it is a woman. But . . . she has not a bone in her body, I thought, watching Phoebe, for that was her name, coming across the beach. Then Alan got up and the shadow of Alan at once obliterated Phoebe. For Alan had views and Phoebe was quenched in the flood of his views. And then Alan, I thought, has passions; and here I turned page after page very fast, feeling that the crisis was approaching, and so it was. It took place on the beach under the sun. It was done very openly. It was done very vigorously. Nothing could have been more indecent. But . . . I had said "but" too often. One cannot go on saying "but." One must finish the sentence somehow, I rebuked myself. Shall I finish it, "But—I am bored!" But why was I bored? Partly because of the dominance of the letter "I" and the aridity, which, like the giant beech tree, it casts within its shade. Nothing will grow there. And partly for some more obscure reason. There seemed to be some obstacle, some impediment of Mr. A's mind which blocked the fountain of creative energy and shored it within narrow limits. And remembering the lunch party at Oxbridge, and the cigarette ash and the Manx cat and Tennyson and Christina Rossetti all in a bunch, it seemed possible that the impediment lay there. As he no longer hums under his breath, "There has fallen a splendid tear from the passion-flower at the gate," when Phoebe crosses the beach, and she no longer replies, "My heart is like a singing bird whose nest is in a water'd shoot," when Alan approaches what can he do? Being honest as the day and logical as the sun, there is only one thing he can do. And that he does, to do him justice, over and over (I said, turning the pages) and over again. And that, I added, aware of the awful nature of the confession, seems somehow dull. Shakespeare's indecency uproots a thousand other things in one's mind, and is far from being dull. But

Shakespeare does it for pleasure; Mr. A, as the nurses say, does it on purpose. He does it in protest. He is protesting against the equality of the other sex by asserting his own superiority. He is therefore impeded and inhibited and self-conscious as Shakespeare might have been if he too had known Miss Clough and Miss Davies. Doubtless Elizabethan literature would have been very different from what it is if the woman's movement had begun in the sixteenth century and not in the nineteenth.

What, then, it amounts to, if this theory of the two sides of the mind holds good, is that virility has now become self-conscious—men, that is to say, are now writing only with the male side of their brains. It is a mistake for a woman to read them, for she will inevitably look for something that she will not find. It is the power of suggestion that one most misses, I thought, taking Mr. B the critic in my hand and reading, very carefully and very dutifully, his remarks upon the art of poetry. Very able they were, acute and full of learning; but the trouble was, that his feelings no longer communicated; his mind seemed separated into different chambers; not a sound carried from one to the other. Thus, when one takes a sentence of Mr. B into the mind it falls plump to the ground—dead; but when one takes a sentence of Coleridge into the mind, it explodes and gives birth to all kinds of other ideas, and that is the only sort of writing of which one can say that it has the secret of perpetual life.

But whatever the reason may be, it is a fact that one must deplore. For it means—here I had come to rows of books by Mr. Galsworthy and Mr. Kipling—that some of the finest works of our greatest living writers fall upon deaf ears. Do what she will a woman cannot find in them that fountain of perpetual life which the critics assure her is there. It is not only that they celebrate male virtues, enforce male values and describe the world of men; it is that the emotion with which these books are permeated is to a woman incomprehensible. It is coming, it is gathering, it is about to burst on one's head, one begins saying long before the end. That picture will fall on old Jolyon's head; he will die of the shock; the old clerk will speak over him two or three obituary words; and all the swans on the Thames will simultaneously burst out singing. But one will rush away before that happens and hide in the gooseberry bushes, for the emotion which is so deep, so subtle, so symbolical to a man moves a woman to wonder. So with Mr. Kipling's officers who turn their backs; and his Sowers who sow the Seed; and his Men who are alone with their Work; and the Flag—one blushes at all these capital letters as if one had been caught eaves-dropping at some purely masculine orgy. The fact is that neither Mr. Galsworthy nor Mr. Kipling has a spark of the woman in him. Thus all their qualities seem to a woman, if one may generalise, crude and immature. They lack suggestive power. And when a book lacks suggestive power, however hard it hits the surface of the mind it cannot penetrate within.

And in that restless mood in which one takes books out and puts them back again without looking at them I began to envisage an age to come of pure, of self-assertive virility, such as the letters of professors (take Sir Walter Raleigh's letters, for instance) seem to forebode, and the rulers of Italy have already brought into being. For one can hardly fail to be impressed in Rome by the sense of unmitigated masculinity; and whatever the value of unmitigated masculinity upon the state, one may question the effect of it upon the art of poetry. At any rate, according to the newspapers, there is a certain anxiety about fiction in Italy. There has been a meeting of academicians whose object it is "to develop the Italian novel." "Men famous by birth, or in finance, industry or the Fascist corporations" came together the other day and discussed the matter, and a telegram was sent to the Duce expressing the hope "that the Fascist era would soon give birth to a poet worthy of it." We may all join in that pious hope, but it is doubtful whether poetry can come out of an incubator. Poetry ought to have a mother as well as a father. The Fascist poem, one may fear, will be a horrid little abortion such as one sees in a glass jar in the museum of some county town. Such monsters never live long, it is said; one has never seen a prodigy of that sort cropping grass in a field. Two heads on one body do not make for length of life.

However, the blame for all this, if one is anxious to lay blame, rests no more upon one sex than upon the other. All seducers and reformers are responsible, Lady Bessborough when she lied to Lord Granville; Miss Davies when she told the truth to Mr. Greg. All who have brought about a state of sex-consciousness are to blame, and it is they who drive me, when I want to stretch my faculties on a book, to seek it in that happy age, before Miss Davies and Miss Clough were born, when the writer used both sides of his mind equally. One must turn back to Shakespeare then, for Shakespeare was androgynous; and so was Keats and Sterne and Cowper and Lamb and Coleridge. Shelley perhaps was sexless. Milton and Ben Jonson had a dash too much of the male in them. So had Wordsworth and Tolstoi. In our time Proust was wholly androgynous, if not perhaps a little too much of a woman. But that failing is too rare for one to complain of it, since without some mixture of the kind the intellect seems to predominate and the other faculties of the mind harden and become barren. However, I consoled myself with the reflection that this is perhaps a passing phase; much of what I have said in obedience to my promise to give you the course of my thoughts will seem out of date; much of what flames in my eyes will seem dubious to you who have not yet come of age.

Even so, the very first sentence that I would write here, I said, crossing over to the writing-table and taking up the page headed Women and Fiction, is that it is fatal for any one who writes to think of their sex. It is fatal to be a man or woman pure and simple; one must be woman-manly or man-womanly.

It is fatal for a woman to lay the least stress on any grievance; to plead even with justice any cause; in any way to speak consciously as a woman. And fatal is no figure of speech; for anything written with that conscious bias is doomed to death. It ceases to be fertilised. Brilliant and effective, powerful and masterly, as it may appear for a day or two, it must wither at nightfall; it cannot grow in the minds of others. Some collaboration has to take place in the mind between the woman and the man before the act of creation can be accomplished. Some marriage of opposites has to be consummated. The whole of the mind must lie wide open if we are to get the sense that the writer is communicating his experience with perfect fullness. There must be freedom and there must be peace. Not a wheel must grate, not a light glimmer. The curtains must be close drawn. The writer, I thought, once his experience is over, must lie back and let his mind celebrate its nuptials in darkness. He must not look or question what is being done. Rather, he must pluck the petals from a rose or watch the swans float calmly down the river. And I saw again the current which took the boat and the undergraduate and the dead leaves; and the taxi took the man and the woman, I thought, seeing them come together across the street, and the current swept them away, I thought, hearing far off the roar of London's traffic, into that tremendous stream.

Here, then, Mary Beton ceases to speak. She has told you how she reached the conclusion—the prosaic conclusion—that it is necessary to have five hundred a year and a room with a lock on the door if you are to write fiction or poetry. She has tried to lay bare the thoughts and impressions that led her to think this. She has asked you to follow her flying into the arms of a Beadle, lunching here, dining there, drawing pictures in the British Museum, taking books from the shelf, looking out of the window. While she has been doing all these things, you no doubt have been observing her failings and foibles and deciding what effect they have had on her opinions. You have been contradicting her and making whatever additions and deductions seem good to you. That is all as it should be, for in a question like this truth is only to be had by laying together many varieties of error. And I will end now in my own person by anticipating two criticisms, so obvious that you can hardly fail to make them.

No opinion has been expressed, you may say, upon the comparative merits of the sexes even as writers. That was done purposely, because, even if the time had come for such a valuation—and it is far more important at the moment to know how much money women had and how many rooms than to theorise about their capacities—even if the time had come I do not believe that gifts, whether of mind or character, can be weighed like sugar and butter, not even in Cambridge, where they are so adept at putting people into classes and fixing caps on their heads and letters after their names. I do not believe that even the Table of Precedency which you will find in Whitaker's *Almanac* represents a final order of values, or that there is any sound reason to suppose that a Commander of the Bath will ultimately walk in to dinner behind a Master in Lunacy. All this pitting of sex against sex, of quality against quality; all this claiming of superiority and imputing of inferiority, belong to the private-school stage of human existence where there are "sides," and it is necessary for one side to beat another side, and of the utmost importance to walk up to a platform and receive from the hands of the Headmaster himself a highly ornamental pot. As people mature they cease to believe in sides or in Headmasters or in highly ornamental pots. At any rate, where books are concerned, it is notoriously difficult to fix labels of merit in such a way that they do not come off. Are not reviews of current literature a perpetual illustration of the difficulty of judgment? "This great book," "this worthless book," the same book is called by both names. Praise and blame alike mean nothing. No, delightful as the pastime of measuring may be, it is the most futile of all occupations, and to submit to the decrees of the measurers the most servile of attitudes. So long as you write what you wish to write, that is all that matters; and whether it matters for ages or only for hours, nobody can say. But to sacrifice a hair of the head of your vision, a shade of its colour, in deference to some Headmaster with a silver pot in his hand or to some professor with a measuring-rod up his sleeve, is the most abject treachery, and the sacrifice of wealth and chastity which used to be said to be the greatest of human disasters, a mere flea-bite in comparison.

Next I think that you may object that in all this I have made too much of the importance of material things. Even allowing a generous margin for symbolism, that five hundred a year stands for the power to contemplate, that a lock on the door means the power to think for oneself, still you may say that the mind should rise above such things; and that great poets have often been poor men. Let me then quote to you the words of your own Professor of Literature, who knows better than I do what goes to the making of a poet. Sir Arthur Quiller-Couch writes:[1]

"What are the great poetical names of the last hundred years or so? Coleridge, Wordsworth, Byron, Shelley, Landor, Keats, Tennyson, Browning, Arnold, Morris, Rossetti, Swinburne—we may stop there. Of these, all but Keats, Browning, Rossetti were University men; and of these three, Keats, who died young, cut off in his prime, was the only one not fairly well to do. It may seem a brutal thing to say, and it is a sad thing to say: but, as a matter of hard fact, the theory that poetical genius bloweth where it listeth, and equally in poor and rich, holds little truth. As a matter of hard fact, nine out of those twelve were University men: which means that somehow or other they procured the means to get the best education England can give. As a

[1] *The Art of Writing,* by Sir Arthur Quiller-Couch.

matter of hard fact, of the remaining three you know that Browning was well to do, and I challenge you that, if he had not been well to do, he would no more have attained to write *Saul* or *The Ring and the Book* than Ruskin would have attained to writing *Modern Painters* if his father had not dealt prosperously in business. Rossetti had a small private income; and, moreover, he painted. There remains but Keats; whom Atropos slew young, as she slew John Clare in a mad-house, and James Thomson by the laudanum he took to drug disappointment. These are dreadful facts, but let us face them. It is—however dishonouring to us as a nation—certain that, by some fault in our commonwealth, the poor poet has not in these days, nor has had for two hundred years, a dog's chance. Believe me—and I have spent a great part of ten years in watching some three hundred and twenty elementary schools—we may prate of democracy, but actually, a poor child in England has little more hope than had the son of an Athenian slave to be emancipated into that intellectual freedom of which great writings are born."

Nobody could put the point more plainly. "The poor poet has not in these days, nor has had for two hundred years, a dog's chance . . . a poor child in England has little more hope than had the son of an Athenian slave to be emancipated into that intellectual freedom of which great writings are born." That is it. Intellectual freedom depends upon material things. Poetry depends upon intellectual freedom. And women have always been poor, not for two hundred years merely, but from the beginning of time. Women have had less intellectual freedom than the sons of Athenian slaves. Women, then, have not had a dog's chance of writing poetry. That is why I have laid so much stress on money and a room of one's own. However, thanks to the toils of those obscure women in the past, of whom I wish we knew more, thanks, curiously enough, to two wars, the Crimean which let Florence Nightingale out of her drawing-room, and the European War which opened the doors to the average woman some sixty years later, these evils are in the way to be bettered. Otherwise you would not be here tonight, and your chance of earning five hundred pounds a year, precarious as I am afraid that it still is, would be minute in the extreme.

Still, you may object, why do you attach so much importance to this writing of books by women when, according to you, it requires so much effort, leads perhaps to the murder of one's aunts, will make one almost certainly late for luncheon, and may bring one into very grave disputes with certain very good fellows? My motives, let me admit, are partly selfish. Like most uneducated Englishwomen, I like reading—I like reading books in the bulk. Lately my diet has become a trifle monotonous; history is too much about wars; biography too much about great men; poetry has shown, I think, a tendency to sterility, and fiction—but I have sufficiently exposed my disabilities as a critic of modern fiction and will say no more about it. Therefore I would ask you to write all kinds of books, hesitating at no subject however trivial or however vast. By hook or by crook, I hope that you will possess yourselves of money enough to travel and to idle, to contemplate the future or the past of the world, to dream over books and loiter at street corners and let the line of thought dip deep into the stream. For I am by no means confining you to fiction. If you would please me—and there are thousands like me—you would write books of travel and adventure, and research and scholarship, and history and biography, and criticism and philosophy and science. By so doing you will certainly profit the art of fiction. For books have a way of influencing each other. Fiction will be much the better for standing cheek by jowl with poetry and philosophy. Moreover, if you consider any great figure of the past, like Sappho, like the Lady Murasaki, like Emily Brontë, you will find that she is an inheritor as well as an originator, and has come into existence because women have come to have the habit of writing naturally; so that even as a prelude to poetry such activity on your part would be invaluable.

But when I look back through these notes and criticise my own train of thought as I made them, I find that my motives were not altogether selfish. There runs through these comments and discursions the conviction—or is it the instinct?—that good books are desirable and that good writers, even if they show every variety of human depravity, are still good human beings. Thus when I ask you to write more books I am urging you to do what will be for your good and for the good of the world at large. How to justify this instinct or belief I do not know, for philosophic words, if one has not been educated at a university, are apt to play one false.

What is meant by "reality"? It would seem to be something very erratic, very undependable—now to be found in a dusty road, now in a scrap of newspaper in the street, now in a daffodil in the sun. It lights up a group in a room and stamps some casual saying. It overwhelms one walking home beneath the stars and makes the silent world more real than the world of speech—and then there it is again in an omnibus in the uproar of Piccadilly. Sometimes, too, it seems to dwell in shapes too far away for us to discern what their nature is. But whatever it touches, it fixes and makes permanent. That is what remains over when the skin of the day has been cast into the hedge; that is what is left of past time and of our loves and hates. Now the writer, as I think, has the chance to live more than other people in the presence of this reality. It is his business to find it and collect it and communicate it to the rest of us. So at least I infer from reading *Lear* or *Emma* or *La Recherche du Temps Perdu.* For the reading of these books seems to perform a curious couching operation on the senses; one sees more intensely afterwards; the world seems bared of its covering and given an intenser life. Those are the enviable people who live at enmity with unreality; and those are the pitiable who are knocked on the head by the thing done without knowing or caring. So that when I ask you to earn money and have a room of your own, I am asking you to live in the presence of reality, an invigorating life, it would appear, whether one can impart it or not.

Here I would stop, but the pressure of convention decrees that every speech must end with a peroration. And a peroration addressed to women should have something, you will agree, particularly exalting and ennobling about it. I should implore you to remember your responsibilities, to be higher, more spiritual; I should remind you how much depends upon you, and what an influence you can exert upon the future. But those exhortations can safely, I think, be left to the other sex, who will put them, and indeed have put them, with far greater eloquence than I can compass. When I rummage in my own mind I find no noble sentiments about being companions and equals and influencing the world to higher ends. I find myself saying briefly and prosaically that it is much more important to be oneself than anything else. Do not dream of influencing other people, I would say, if I knew how to make it sound exalted. Think of things in themselves.

And again I am reminded by dipping into newspapers and novels and biographies that when a woman speaks to women she should have something very unpleasant up her sleeve. Women are hard on women. Women dislike women. Women—but are you not sick to death of the word? I can assure you that I am. Let us agree, then, that a paper read by a woman to women should end with something particularly disagreeable.

But how does it go? What can I think of? The truth is, I often like women. I like their unconventionality. I like their subtlety. I like their anonymity. I like—but I must not run on in this way. That cupboard there,—you say it holds clean table-napkins only; but what if Sir Archibald Bodkin were concealed among them? Let me then adopt a sterner tone. Have I, in the preceding words, conveyed to you sufficiently the warnings and reprobation of mankind? I have told you the very low opinion in which you were held by Mr. Oscar Browning. I have indicated what Napoleon once thought of you and what Mussolini thinks now. Then, in case any of you aspire to fiction, I have copied out for your benefit the advice of the critic about courageously acknowledging the limitations of your sex. I have referred to Professor X and given prominence to his statement that women are intellectually, morally and physically inferior to men. I have handed on all that has come my way without going in search of it, and here is a final warning—from Mr. John Langdon Davies.[2] Mr. John Langdon Davies warns women "that when children cease to be altogether desirable, women cease to be altogether necessary." I hope you will make a note of it.

[2] *A Short History of Women,* by John Langdon Davies.

How can I further encourage you to go about the business of life? Young women, I would say, and please attend, for the peroration is beginning, you are, in my opinion, disgracefully ignorant. You have never made a discovery of any sort of importance. You have never shaken an empire or led an army into battle. The plays of Shakespeare are not by you, and you have never introduced a barbarous race to the blessings of civilisation. What is your excuse? It is all very well for you to say, pointing to the streets and squares and forests of the globe swarming with black and white and coffee-coloured inhabitants, all busily engaged in traffic and enterprise and love-making, we have had other work on our hands. Without our doing, those seas would be unsailed and those fertile lands a desert. We have borne and bred and washed and taught, perhaps to the age of six or seven years, the one thousand six hundred and twenty-three million human beings who are, according to statistics, at present in existence, and that, allowing that some had help, takes time.

There is truth in what you say—I will not deny it. But at the same time may I remind you that there have been at least two colleges for women in existence in England since the year 1866; that after the year 1880 a married woman was allowed by law to possess her own property; and that in 1919—which is a whole nine years ago—she was given a vote? May I also remind you that the most of the professions have been open to you for close on ten years now? When you reflect upon these immense privileges and the length of time during which they have been enjoyed, and the fact that there must be at this moment some two thousand women capable of earning over five hundred a year in one way or another, you will agree that the excuse of lack of opportunity, training, encouragement, leisure and money no longer holds good. Moreover, the economists are telling us that Mrs. Seton has had too many children. You must, of course, go on bearing children, but, so they say, in twos and threes, not in tens and twelves.

Thus, with some time on your hands and with some book learning in your brains—you have had enough of the other kind, and are sent to college partly, I suspect, to be uneducated—surely you should embark upon another stage of your very long, very laborious and highly obscure career. A thousand pens are ready to suggest what you should do and what effect you will have. My own suggestion is a little fantastic, I admit; I prefer, therefore, to put it in the form of fiction.

I told you in the course of this paper that Shakespeare had a sister; but do not look for her in Sir Sidney Lee's life of the poet. She died young—alas, she never wrote a word. She lies buried where the omnibuses now stop, opposite the Elephant and Castle. Now my belief is that this poet who never wrote a word and was buried at the crossroads still lives. She lives in you and in me, and in many other women who are not here tonight, for they are washing up the dishes and putting the children to bed. But she lives; for great poets do not die; they are continuing presences; they need only the opportunity to walk among us in the flesh. This opportunity, as I think, it is now coming within your power to give her. For my belief is that if we live another century or so—I am talking of the common life which is the real life and not of the little separate lives which we live as individuals—and have five hundred a year each of us and rooms of our own; if we have the habit of freedom and the courage to write exactly what we think; if we escape a little from the common sitting-room and see human beings not always in their relation to each other but in relation to reality; and the sky, too, and the trees or whatever it may be in themselves; if we look past Milton's bogey, for no human being should shut out the view; if we face the fact, for it is a fact, that there is no arm to cling to, but that we go alone and that our relation is to the world of reality and not only to the world of men and women, then the opportunity will come and the dead poet who was Shakespeare's sister will put on the body which she has so often laid down. Drawing her life from the lives of the unknown who were her forerunners, as her brother did before her, she will be born. As for her coming without that preparation, without that effort on our part, without that determination that when she is born again she shall find it possible to live and write her poetry, that we cannot expect, for that would be impossible. But I maintain that she would come if we worked for her, and that so to work, even in poverty and obscurity, is worth while.

Copyright Acknowledgments

Grateful acknowledgment is made to the following sources for permission to reprint material copyrighted or controlled by them:

"How to Tame a Wild Tongue," by Gloria Anzaldúa, reprinted from *Borderlands/ La Frontera: The New Mestiza* (1987), Aunt Lute Books.

"Hiroshima," by John Berger, reprinted from *The Sense of Sight* (1993), by permission of Pantheon Books, a division of Random House, Inc.

"The Uses of Doubt," by Stacey D'Erasmo, reprinted from *Ploughshares* (winter 2002-03), William Morris Agency, Inc.

"Dwelling in Possibilities," by Mark Edmundson, reprinted from *The Chronicle Review*, March 14, 2008.

"Welcome to Cancerland," by Barbara Ehrenreich, reprinted from *Harper's Magazine*, November 2001, International Creative Management.

"The Hidden Teacher," by Loren Eiseley, reprinted from *The Unexpected Universe* (1969), by permission of Houghton Mifflin Harcourt Publishing Company.

"Against Meat," by Jonathan Safran Foer, reprinted from *Eating Animals* (2009), Little, Brown and Company. Adapted for *The New York Times Magazine*, October 11, 2009.

"The Way We Age Now," by Atul Gawande, reprinted from *The New Yorker*, April 30, 2007.

"Group Think: What Does 'Saturday Night Live' Have in Common with German Philosophy?" by Malcolm Gladwell, reprinted from *The New Yorker*, December 2, 2002.

"A Story About the Body," by Robert Hass (1989), reprinted by permission of HarperCollins Publishers.

"Politics and the English Language," by George Orwell, copyright © 1946 by Sonia Brownell Orwell and renewed © 1974 by Sonia Pitt-Rivers, reprinted from *Shooting an Elephant and Other Essays*, by permission of Houghton Mifflin Harcourt Publishing Company.

"Listen to This," by Alex Ross, reprinted from *The New Yorker*, February 16, 2004, by permission of the author.

"In Praise of Self-Deception," by David Livingstone Smith, reprinted by permission from *Entelechy: Mind and Culture* (spring/summer 2006).

"The Blue of Distance," by Rebecca Solnit, reprinted from *A Field Guide to Getting Lost* (2005), Viking Press, a division of Penguin Putnam, Inc.

"Attack of the Superzeroes: Why Washington, Einstein, and Madonna Can't Compete with You," by Thomas de Zengotita, reprinted by permission from *Harper's Magazine,* December 2004. Copyright © 2004 by Harper's Magazine.

"Transgression and Transformation: *Leaving Las Vegas,*" by bell hooks, reprinted from *Reel to Real: Race, Sex, and Class at the Movies* (1996), by permission of Routledge, a division of the Taylor and Francis Group.

"The Melodramatic Moment," by Daniel Mendelsohn, reprinted by permission from *The New York Times Magazine,* March 23, 2003.

"The Pleasure of Flinching," by Nicholas Sautin, reprinted from *Guernica Magazine,* February 2010.

"On Reading a Video Text," by Robert Scholes, reprinted from *Protocols of Reading* (1986), by permission of Yale University Press.

"The Track of a Teardrop, A Filmmaker's Path," by A.O. Scott, reprinted by permission from *The New York Times,* November 17, 2002.

"The Uncommon Reader," by George Steiner (1978), reprinted from *No Passion Spent,* by permission of Georges Borchardt Literary Agency.

"Argument as Emergence, Rhetoric as Love," by Jim W. Corder, reprinted from *Rhetoric Review* 4 (September 1985), by permission of Lawrence Erlbaum Associates, Inc. and Roberta Corder.

"Sentimental Journeys," by Joan Didion, reprinted from *After Henry* (1992), by permission of Simon & Schuster, Inc.

"Troublemakers," by Malcolm Gladwell, reprinted from *The New Yorker,* February 6, 2006, by permission of Pushkin Enterprises.

"On the Rights of Molotov Man: Appropriation and the Art of Context," by Joy Garnett and Susan Meiselas, reprinted from *Harper's Magazine,* February 2007, by permission of Joy Garnett.

"Letter from Birmingham Jail," by Martin Luther King, Jr. (1963), reprinted by arrangement with The Heirs to the Estate of Martin Luther King Jr., c/o Writers House, LLC. Copyright © 1963 Dr. Martin Luther King Jr; copyright © renewed 1991 Coretta Scott King.

"A Fist in the Eye of God," by Barbara Kingsolver, reprinted from *Small Wonder* (2002), HarperCollins Publishers.

"The Moral Instinct," by Steven Pinker, reprinted from *The New York Times Magazine*, January 13, 2008, by permission of The New York Times Company. Copyright © 2008 Stephen Pinker.

"Locked Horns," by Rebecca Solnit, reprinted from *Storming the Gates of Paradise* (2007), by permission of University of California Press.

"Consider the Lobster," by David Foster Wallace, reprinted from *Consider the Lobster and Other Essays* (2005), Little, Brown and Company.

Excerpt from *A Room of One's Own*, by Virginia Woolf (1929), by permission of Houghton Mifflin Harcourt Publishing Company.